A Treati
Exi.

Vol. 3

Wayfinding:
Journey to Become a Temple of God

By: *J. K. Ward*

Edited by Kevin Evangelista

Rediscovering the Triune I AM

First Series: Preparing to Set Sail under the Banner of Trinitarian Orthodoxy

Scripture quoted by permission. All scripture quotations, unless otherwise indicated, are taken from the New English Translation (NET Bible®) copyright ©1996-2006 by Biblical Studies Press, L.L.C. All rights reserved. All emphasis added to the text through italics is solely the author's intent, used to highlight specific words the author wants to draw the reader's attention to. The use of brackets indicates any formal edits made by the author and is not meant to alter the underlying meaning of the text. The use of parentheses provides additional clarifications based on the original language.

All Greek translations, unless otherwise indicated, are taken from the "Interlinear Scripture Analyzer 3" or "ISA3" © 2002-2015 Scripture4All Publishing. All rights reserved.

All Greek lexical information, unless otherwise indicated, is taken from BDAG - Greek-English Lexicon of the New Testament and Other Early Christian Literature, Third Edition, Copyright © 2000 by The University of Chicago Press. All rights reserved.

Copyright © 2025 J. K. Ward

All rights reserved.

ISBN: 9798285202714

Dedication

I dedicate this book to the forgotten, dehumanized, undervalued, marginalized, and neglected. In the environment where I grew up, such individuals earnestly practiced their religion as "resident pew-warmers" – dutifully adhering to their "part" in a weekly worship service.

A spiritual revolution begins not when the masses rise up. Such a revolution transpires when many individuals awaken to their true potential and break free from the shackles of oppression that deny their inherent worth. Jesus came to ignite such a revolution. Contrary to various voices in religious academia, He did not intend to initiate it within the political arena for a merely temporal effect. If this had been His goal, He would have raised an army to overthrow governments and replaced them with His own. Instead, He claimed His kingdom was not of this world: an alien kingdom (John 18:36).

Jesus came to initiate a spiritual revolution. This revolution challenges any sexist, racist, and class system that asserts, some claiming divine merit, that God calls only a few to be His chosen people. Jesus came to shatter any theology claiming only a few can become one of His sacred priests, possessing a "spiritual calling or vocation," serving as His representatives in a designated sacred space.

Peter, the first evangelist, promoted this revolution by publically redeclaring the eternal truth foretold by the prophets of old who shared the following proclamation from Yahweh to all humanity: "I will pour out My Spirit on ALL people" (Acts 2:17; Joel 2:28). He would later write a letter to all such would-be "pew-warmers": "You come to Him, a living stone rejected by men but chosen and precious in God's sight. You yourselves, as living stones, are built up as a spiritual house to be a holy priesthood" (1 Pet 2:4-10). As Paul the Evangelist wrote, "God chose what the world thinks foolish to shame the wise, and God chose what the world thinks weak to shame the strong. God chose what is low and despised in the world, what is regarded as nothing, to set aside what is regarded as something" (1 Cor 2:27-28).

Eternity summons every individual to become and remain a temple of the Maker, a vessel of greater worth than the entire created universe. Yahweh created each person to become a unique habitation of the Divine Being who brought all creation into existence from nothing. All worldly forces of manipulation and suppression have sought to conceal the lost identity of God's prodigal children. They seek to enslave as many as possible in a web of lies related to false identity, social rejection, misguided callings, transient ambitions, fleeting desires, and ephemeral dreams. Jesus came to rescue us all from the fate of ambiguity and nothingness, as almost all humans and the products of their labor have been eventually forgotten by posterity. Many in their lifetimes were treated as being of less worth than an animal or a machine – or in our age: AI.

Jesus came to show us the way to discover and actualize our true selves as pillars and priests of an eternal temple. This book is dedicated to this mission of illuminating a path for humanity to rediscover who we are and the purpose for which we were destined, as lost heirs of an eternal kingdom, not of this temporary world. May each of us choose to join this rebellion against "Babylon" by forsaking fleeting "slave" ambitions to pursue the true freedom of our everlasting destiny in New Zion: the eternal home of God within creation.

Hence, I dedicate this book to you, whoever you may be or not be in the eyes of the world, regardless of how lowly you may seem to others or how little they might regard your potential and value to society, within a family, inside an organization, or even during a "sacred" service. May you awaken, find your way, and become the destined self Eternity beckons you to *be* and carry out an everlasting role in the Eternal God-Story.

Table of Contents

	Introduction	13
1.	Existentialism as Wayfinding	25
2.	In a Mirror Darkly	61
3.	Castaways in Search of Belonging	97
4.	Living in Babel	135
5.	The Fateful Choice: Babylon or Zion	173
6.	Homeward-Bound Nomads	211
7.	A Heavenly Home Built by Jesus Christ	241
8.	The Fellowship of Yahweh's House	271
9.	To Be a Temple of Yahweh	303
10.	Priesthood of the End Time Temple	341
11.	Eternal Fellowship in New Jerusalem	381
12.	Eternal Stewards of Creation	424
13.	Beyond the Veil of Temporality	477
14.	Paving the Way for Existential Theology	545
	Epilogue	597

"And in the last days it will be,' God says, 'that I will pour out My Spirit on all people, and your sons and your daughters will prophesy, and your young men will see visions, and your old men will dream dreams.

Even on my servants, both men and women, I will pour out my Spirit in those days, and they will prophesy...

So as you come to Him, a living stone rejected by men but chosen and precious in God's sight, you yourselves, as living stones, are built up as a spiritual house to be a holy priesthood and to offer spiritual sacrifices that are acceptable to God through Jesus Christ...

You are a chosen race, a royal priesthood, a holy nation, a people of His own, so that you may proclaim the virtues of the one who called you out of darkness into His marvelous light. You once were not a people, but now you are God's people."

(Acts 2:17-18; 1 Pet 2:4-10)

Introduction:
Humans as World-Dwellers & Way-Finders

Current Milestones and Future Prospects

Welcome to the third stage of our journey across the Sea of Revelation, where our faith seeks understanding. In the first volume, we answered the Call of Eternity. We set sail on a homeward voyage beyond the Shores of Temporality. In the second volume, we began our quest for truth by illustrating the biblical alignment of Monotheism and Trinitarianism. We also recognized the importance of grasping the basics of Yahweh's triune nature as we embark on this journey. After all, we strive to return to the home we will share with our Creator in Eternity.

Before we move ahead, let us take a moment to consider the primary goal of our theological journeys- the very reason we have embarked. Simply put, we are on a voyage to engage in theology and seek God. Christ has called us to follow Him so we can experience "eternal life—that [we may] know [the Father] the only true God, and Jesus Christ, whom [He] sent" (John 17:3). Our journey aims to explore and document how Yahweh has made Himself known as the Triune I AM throughout the Narrative of Finitude. By learning about God, we can apply and reaffirm the truths of His immanent, triune, self-revealing existence in our own lives. This enables us to grasp His influence on us, the world, and our faith community in the 21st century.

Our theological enterprise is not a simple matter. Engaging in proper theology demands nothing less than our pursuit of the Infinite. The Infinite fundamentally transcends all our regular experience and understanding of reality. Our previous foray into the Trinity, one of the most challenging, misunderstood, and controversial subjects in Christian doctrine, exemplifies the ideas that characterize the journey of our God-relationship. We cannot approach the concept of knowing God without a clear understanding of not only WHY we must learn about our Creator but also HOW we are able to learn about Him in the first place. We must confront the limitations of our quest even as we recognize the significance of our mission.

This current volume will explore how we must properly orient ourselves for our future theological quests. We must ponder our human situation and shared humanity. To this end, we will reflect on our experience of doing theology as temporal, social, and rational creatures pursuing the endless revelations of the transcendent and infinite Maker. We must determine the theological presuppositions that should shape our mindset as we approach theological subject matters. Ultimately, we must begin from a state of surrender to the God-relationship and reliance on the Holy Spirit. Just as seafarers throughout millennia have surrendered to the winds that carried their ships across the ocean, we have no choice but to entrust ourselves to our Maker's guiding power to navigate the Sea of Revelation.

{ *What comes to mind when you think about the word "theology"?*

How do you think theology can be practical to you? }

Let us now outline the two main objectives of our pending venture. They will help us properly orient ourselves as finite creatures pursuing the Infinite. Firstly, the crew should recognize that the "Sea of Revelation" we aim to navigate contains metaphysical knowledge. This knowledge transcends the physical, visible realm we inhabit as human beings. After all, only in the spiritual, invisible realm can we discover revelations of a spiritual, invisible Creator (Colossians 1). We must distinguish between journeys of discovery that focus solely on the *phenomenological realm* (composed of sensible, material realities) and those that explore the *noumenological realm* (composed of metaphysical, spiritual realities). Our voyage is of the second kind. In this book, we will refer to this dichotomy as the "land" and "sea," "earth" and "heaven," or the "temporal" and the "eternal" respectively.

Secondly, we need to understand the concept of "subjectivity" (or overall experience) in relation to a genuine truth-seeker. How does our human condition affect our relation to eternal, spiritual knowledge? We must recognize how our existence influences the way we learn and acquire knowledge in the first place. Additionally, we should humbly acknowledge our biases and limitations while setting realistic expectations for what we can achieve or hope to gain from all of our metaphysical investigations. Afterward, we will discuss the specific subjectivity of a believer and how it contrasts with that of a non-believer. Then we will be prepared to explore what lies ahead of us in Eternity. We can only discern the best approach to learn those theological truths that transcend our human experience by embracing these revelations. Only then can we learn how to effectively apply them to establish the Way of Life we ought to follow.

Spiritual Quest for Metaphysical Truths

Let us examine these objectives more closely, beginning with what it means to undertake a quest for metaphysical truths. Our current truth-seeking quest differs from most others pursued by students at university. The object of our study in theology is fundamentally different from anything else in the universe. We are not merely studying plants, stars, the laws of physics, the human body, our psychologies, or even the abstract ideas of arcane philosophy or pure mathematics. These are all created entities existing within the universe. Finite.

To study God, however, is to explore something uncreated and transcending the universe: the Infinite[i]. We cannot fully grasp such a concept in its entirety. Even for subjects we do not completely understand (like theoretical and quantum physics), there is an expectation that we are always progressing toward a more complete picture that will one day be unveiled to us. Regarding our understanding of our Creator, however, we can attain no level of comprehension, no matter how long we study or how hard we try. It would be akin to trying to reach the "end" of a circular path or searching for the floor of a bottomless ocean.

Theology proper should not merely be an intellectual exercise. After all, most other fields of study do not challenge us to change how we live our daily lives. For example, one does not need to fundamentally alter their worldview to be a great mathematician. Most scholars approach even non-scientific pursuits, such as literature or religious studies, with similar perspectives.[ii] They vainly try to attain a detached, "purely rational" or abstract perspective. They view the subjects of study as items to be analyzed or mentally dissected rather than as elements that they permit to change their way of life, beliefs, or perceptions of the "real" world they inhabit.

> *Why is a detached study of theology insufficient for our voyage?*
>
> *Why is obtaining a degree in theology inadequate on its own to truly know God?*

Genuine theology (the study of our Maker) compels us to internalize its truths, engaging not just our minds but also our hearts and spirits. Rather than merely enriching the intellect, eternal realities can transform our self-view, life direction, and personality. There can be no such thing as a "detached study" regarding true theology. Similarly, one cannot genuinely be an expert in parenting without actually parenting a child. Our quest resembles a "journey of enlightenment" more than a university course, an exegesis exercise, or a research project.[iii] Each new truth we discover confronts us with a challenge of practical application. Furthermore, each new finding brings us closer to the object of our study in a relational way. As we advance in our knowledge of

God, He invites us to experience Him more deeply and to be transformed forever by divine encounters. Our theology must become an act of prayer and worship. Simply put, the object of our study (nothing less than our Creator Himself) does not merely wish to be "understood"; He desires to be known through His self-disclosing presence and engaged with in the context of a God-relationship. This journey is as much about developing a relationship and self-actualization as it is about enlightenment.

The Human Situation: Being "Subjects" in the World

Regarding the second objective stated above, our recognition of the special nature of our object of study naturally leads us to another question. As limited and finite creatures, how can we possibly attain any degree of knowledge about the Infinite? Can we even know the Infinite at all? How is it even possible for us to sail on the "Sea of Divine Revelation"? This seems as impossible as expecting a boat to traverse the sky or cross over to the fourth dimension.[iv] To understand how God enables us to think, perceive, and learn about His self-revelations, we must first grasp the specifics of our human condition. In other words, we must understand what being a "subjective" creature means and how our subjectivity should shape our theological pursuits.

How do you think your identity and sense of self are shaped by the world around you?

Or do you find it difficult to believe that your environment influences how you view yourself and your life story?

What does being "subjective" mean in a philosophical sense? Simply put, it refers to being "subject" to influences outside ourselves that shape our worldview, meaning, and sense of self. As we will explore in this book, this is an unavoidable aspect of our human condition. We cannot escape our humanity, nor should we desire to. Furthermore, subjectivity is an essential characteristic of any created entity. We are material beings inhabiting a sensory world, influenced by numerous factors that affect our feelings, perspectives, and judgments. Instead of viewing ourselves as individual thinkers reliant solely on reason alone (as some might lead us to believe), we are creatures inexorably engaged with the physical world, which shapes us as much as we believe we shape ourselves (perhaps even more). This reality must always be considered when approaching any field of study, especially one deeply relevant to our human situation.

Some readers may now find this distinction between our inner identities and the outer world we inhabit to be a familiar concept. We can refer to these two aspects as our "essence/form" and our "existence/nature." Indeed, philosophers who adhere to the tenets of "existentialism" have observed the fundamental nature of our human condition. They conclude we exist as creatures self-conscious while beings aware of, concerned about, and subject to our individual presence in a wider world. We have a sense of contextualized selfhood and world-fittingness. Throughout this book, we will practice with this method of philosophical inquiry as we confront our inescapably "subjective" situation from a theological perspective. In fact, it may be one of the most fitting conceptual paradigms for reflecting on the unique way our Creator has situated us in Creation and has shaped our selfhood and destiny.

In summary, existentialism teaches us that the environments and "contexts" we are born into are essential for shaping our sense of self and guiding our search for identity, including our "proper place" in the world. While we will delve deeper into the philosophical school of existentialism in the first chapter of this book, we must acknowledge upfront that, although this perspective provides a more suitable lens for our journey, it merely serves as a point of departure for theological inquiries that transcend any such philosophical framework. After all, philosophy remains inextricably linked to the bounds of human reason and experience, alienated from both revelation and the God-relationship.

To illustrate the resourcefulness of an existential approach to learning, let us consider some common contexts we all share. First, we have the context of finitude (or the realm of created reality)[v], followed by the material universe, which includes the Milky Way and Solar System; the planet Earth; and a specific environment/biome within it. This also encompasses a particular culture – which may be international, national, or regional – a specific society or tribe, certain interpersonal societal contexts such as a workplace or school, and particular relational and familial situations like friendship or being married (or not), a parent (or not), and being someone's child. All of these factors influence how we perceive ourselves, live our lives, and make decisions, whether we realize it or not. Some aspects (such as one's nationality or job) are more malleable than others (like our race and biological relations). Even so, the fact that we are defined and influenced by contextual factors (even after we move on from some of them) is unchangeable.

> *Have your expectations for embarking on these theological quests changed since the start of this book?*
>
> *If so, how?*

Viewing our lives with an awareness of our contextuality and subjectivity provides a more genuine understanding of the human condition than mere materialistic, "objective" explanations, e.g. in a biology textbook. Some scientific perspectives either directly or indirectly deny our subjective nature and free will[1] by suggesting that who we are or choose to be can be reduced to what our reason alone concludes or decides, without considering our environments. Contrary to these and many other modern philosophies, human knowledge-seeking can never be completely absolute, mechanical, or objective. Pure reason- or experience alone- can ever lead us to a final and perfect picture of how things truly *are* or *ought to be*. Such transcendent knowledge belongs solely to our Infinite Maker. Therefore, we will learn how exactly any pursuit of purely rational objectivity is a futile attempt to emulate the Divine.

Our subjectivity will always be rooted in our existential situation as interdependent world-viewers and world-dwellers (concepts we will introduce and discuss further in this book). Our perception of created realities and the uncreated revelations of our Creator cannot be separated from the contexts of our human condition. Therefore, we must understand how our contexts and subjectivity will inevitably and significantly shape how we act, speak, believe, think, reason, imagine, and judge, so we can learn to do these things in a proper theological way. This understanding will ultimately affect how we confront our awareness of both reality and the world story in general and our Creator's self-disclosure and our life-story in particular.

We recognize that an existential lens is useful not only because it provides insight into the reality in which we dwell but also gives us insight into our destinies as humans made in the image and likeness of God. Our Creator knows who we truly are, not only because He made us but also because we can fulfill our purpose and reach our fullest potential only through Him. Though we are

---

[1] Some claim ever human thought or emotion is determined by the firing of neurons.

all subject to the world we inhabit, what we are subject to matters. God's design of fittingness is not the only one offered to us. We have a choice in which of the many purposes we devote ourselves to among all those vying for our attention. As we will discuss later in this volume, many humans live in a world of transient purposes and false self-conceptions. God, however, calls us all to our true destinies to be "meeting points or places" where the eternal (heaven) and temporal (earth) intersect. More importantly, He calls us to be temples through which He manifests His Infinite being in a finite world according to the environments, life stories, and circumstances we find ourselves placed in.

By the end of this volume, I hope we will be better prepared to recognize the significance and boundaries of our pursuit to understand our Creator, both now and into eternity. Keeping our eternal identity and world context in mind, we will grasp what it means to be creatures living within finite circumstances with a heavenly calling. More importantly, we will learn that this reality, rather than being a hindrance as it may initially appear, is divinely intended. We will understand how, through our subjectivity, our Creator shapes our priestly calling and authentic selves within the realm of Finitude. Ultimately, we will explore the many ways our Creator has disclosed Himself in our finite experiences and lives, appearing in ways we can receive, respond to, and be guided by. As we gain insights and engage in self-reflections inspired by this book, I pray each of us will persevere in resisting the temptation to claim "objective" knowledge or self-mastery, instead humbly recognizing the type of knowledge and understanding that belongs to the Creator alone, versus what He offers to enlighten us. To this end, let us dive into applied theology, refusing to

> *Will you refuse to be satisfied with mere "factoids" and instead pursue life-changing revelations?*

settle for mere decontextualized "factoids" about God, salvation, and our Christian identity.

Chapter 1
Existentialism as Wayfinding
A Handmaiden to Theology in a Postmodern Era

"The Lord God made the earth and heavens...The Lord God formed the man from the soil of the ground and breathed into his nostrils the breath of life, and the man became a living being. The Lord God planted an orchard in the east, in Eden; and *there He placed the man He had formed*... The Lord God took the man and placed him in the orchard in Eden to care for it and to maintain it... The Lord God said, 'It is not good for the man to be alone. I will make a companion for him.'"

(Gen 2:4, 5,7-8, 15, 18)

"He made every nation of the human race to *inhabit* the entire earth, determining their set times and the *fixed limits* of the places where they would live."

(Acts 17:26)

"Let all who live in the world stand in awe of Him! For He spoke, and it came into existence, He issued the decree, and it stood firm... The Lord's decisions stand forever; His plans abide throughout the ages...The Lord watches from heaven; He sees all people. From the place where He lives He looks carefully at all the earth's inhabitants."

(Ps 33:8-14)

Intro to Existentialism

In this chapter, we will explore how existentialism provides a meaningful philosophical lens for understanding our unique human existence within creation. We will examine our inherent subjectivity and the folly of attempting to be fully "objective." Additionally, we will uncover how this perspective reveals a rich theological landscape revolving around God's invitation for us to be genuine, authentic individuals within our own life contexts. We will also lay the foundation that will be further built upon throughout the book, as we aim to discover and embrace the guidance of our Creator's contextual revelations.

For God to manifest Himself to us, limited and finite beings, He must first bridge the gap that separates the finite from the Infinite. Without this, we would have no hope of knowing Him or establishing a relationship with Him. Otherwise, our situation would be comparable to attempting to convey all the intricacies of history, culture, and knowledge to an infant, whose thoughts are typically limited to eating, sleeping, and crying. To relate to us, our Infinite Creator reveals Himself through the finite realities that shape our perception of ourselves and the world. Imagine explaining something to a child using pictures and stories instead of offering an abstract lecture. While the latter may contain truth, the child can only understand it if presented in a way that is relatable and comprehensible. This method does not dilute or alter the truth; rather, it packages it in a manner tailored to the audience"s specific needs. Similarly, this is how God communicates His truths to us. Our exploration of His Infinite reality would not be feasible without this. Therefore, to truly understand what He reveals about Himself through finite realities, we must first consider *how* we perceive these realities. Only then can we grasp what He discloses about His nature, our true selves, our human common human condition, and the destiny or purpose He envisions for us within our world.

We humans comprehend the world through the limited realities around us. Any study of our nature must include our environment- our dwelling. Just as understanding a person requires insight into their life's context and background, so too must we consider the overarching context when studying people. The two aspects are interconnected. Therefore, a philosophical approach can help us understand our relationship with finite realities and how we perceive ourselves and the world through them. Given this discussion, we will consider how existentialism emerges as a fitting methodology for this task.

Existentialism closely relates to ontology, the study of being in general. Ontology explores questions like, "What does it mean to *be*?" On the other hand, existentialism focuses on the relationship between *being* and *dwelling*. It seeks to answer the question, "What does it mean to *exist* in the world in relation to human life on Earth?" It examines how we, as self-aware beings, perceive reality through the various contexts of our daily lives. Additionally, it investigates our common dependence on these contexts for achieving a sense of meaning, purpose, and value. This approach to inquiry is especially relevant to our quest, particularly when grounded in a mindset of an education well suited for the children of God. This is particularly pertinent for those enthusiastically pursuing formal spiritual education in revealed truths. Consequently, this volume

> *From the outset, why do you believe it is vital to take our subjective nature into account when examining how God communicates His truths to us?*
>
> *What risks do you think arise if we overlook this important aspect in our quest for His revelations?*

will encourage us to adopt a *theocentric* existentialist paradigm that thoughtfully considers how the subjective nature of human experience ought to shape our quest for knowledge about ourselves and God.

Many people today still cling to the belief that "objective knowledge" is a closer representation of the truth. They view such knowledge as something we can personally discover and secure. These individuals often perceive the idea of humans as fundamentally subjective, as restrictive or confining. However, this perspective could not be more misguided. We must acknowledge our subjectivity as the very means through which God reveals Himself to us. Additionally, it is the pathway leading us into the extraordinary destiny He has designed for us from the beginning. Just as God disclosed Himself to humanity through the finite aspects of language, sacred texts, parables, prophecies, hymns, prayers, and human actions, He continues to reveal Himself through the tangible realities surrounding us today.[vi] They enable us to properly use the nautical charts of Scripture to navigate toward the "islands and depths" of His revelations. This undertaking will shape our worldview, self-perception, and our very life journey. Most importantly, this journey will clarify the path we must follow to fulfill our destinies as "temples" by which His Infinite presence dwells within our finite world.

An Existential Theology

At this point, we need to pause briefly to discuss a potential concern some readers might have regarding our reference to existentialism. For some, its association with anti-Christian ideas may stir up discomfort or reservations. After all, it is closely linked to postmodernism, another intellectual framework often viewed as contrary to the biblical worldview. Acknowledging how this philosophical approach has fueled numerous worldviews and belief systems that do not resonate with our faith is prudent. Nonetheless, we should set aside certain assumptions and consider the prospect that existentialism encompasses a broad range of thought with various interpretations and schools of thought. Should we not entertain the possibility that some of these interpretations might, to some extent, align with a biblical perspective, while appropriately rejecting others that conflict with our beliefs? Notably, one of the key figures in existentialism, Soren Kierkegaard, was a committed Christian and champion of an authentic God-relationship.

Like with the writings of Soren Kierkegaard, a key objective of this book is to conceive of a distinctly Christian version of existentialism. To achieve this, we draw inspiration from prominent theological figures in Christian history who employed various philosophies to express and illustrate the magnificence of our Creator.[vii] In a similar vein, Paul's Letter to the Hebrews utilized Greek philosophical methods of education to clarify the rationale behind revealed truths. For instance, he made the inspired case of how New Covenant realities concerning Christ are anticipated in Old Covenant "types and shadows," such as animal sacrifice and the Levitical priesthood. Such an analogy harkens back to Plato's Analogy of the Cave. Shadows seem real only when we have yet to encounter the true objects that cast them; we can perceive the truer realities only by leaving the cave and stepping into the sunlight. This analogy effectively illustrates the process of understanding the truths

Why is it important not to dismiss any "worldly" or non-Christian ideas or resources outright?

How can this attitude harm your theology?

What should you consider when utilizing other schools of thought as "handmaidens" of theology?

unveiled by the light of Christ in the New Covenant. Likewise, when used appropriately, these philosophical concepts can serve us as "handmaidens" or auxiliaries to theological inquiry, as the famous theologian Thomas Aquinas surmised. Therefore, this quest seeks to demonstrate some valuable insights within existentialist and postmodern philosophy, even considering the extent of misguided human reasoning.

Our faith must inform any philosophical tools we utilize. A spiritually discerning individual views the world through the lens of revealed truth rather than relying solely on human reason. This approach allows faith to guide reason harmoniously. All valid human philosophical conjectures are subordinate to revelation, which can be considered the "philosophy of God." The Spirit of Truth can use human philosophy,[2] just as He employs human language, to lead us to spiritual truths as we embark on our theological journey within the Sea of Revelation. Believers should view philosophy not as a final goal but as a means employed by the God of all wisdom to teach us through His Spirit. When we focus on our subjective human experience, philosophical frameworks like existentialism can be effectively used in our theology to enhance our understanding of the Christian faith.

Let us ponder one such example of truth present in both existentialist and postmodernist philosophies. We have previously discussed how these perspectives challenge the misguided belief that humans can be entirely objective thinkers, capable of discovering fundamental truths solely through our independent faculties. They also highlight the obstacle of "abstract objectification," as humans foolishly strive for a perspective that views everything in isolation, detached from its context. This

---

[2] For example, one can gleen some truth from studying the works of the famous Greek Philosophers.

illustrates how postmodern thought encourages the epistemological humility essential for our journey.

Abstract objectification perceives everything as a solitary item. An entity's essence is diminished to its isolated existence, disregarding its relations with other entities or broader contexts. This perspective views all phenomena not as complex, interconnected realities, but as simplistic objects that can be compartmentalized. We observe this perspective in various intellectual professions today, particularly in science. For example, in psychology or biology, human love is often interpreted through this lens. Instead of embracing our rich experiences with love, it is frequently reduced to chemical reactions in the brain, as the outcome of an evolutionary drive to ensure survival. In this view, love and affection become mere functions of hormones and neuron activity, stripped of their more profound significance, meaning, or sacredness. This mindset overlooks the profound, holistic contexts of human existence by attempting to "de-contextualize" realities- in other words, to remove them from their lived experiences. Adherents of this viewpoint strive to distance themselves from the larger realities that exist beyond their scientifically rigorous yet materially reductionistic interpretations.

Let us consider another, more concrete example: What is a hammer? A modern perspective of abstract objectification reduces a hammer to its physical characteristics, separated and simplified. A scientist might describe it as a tool featuring a wooden handle, a metal head, a specific shape and size, and a distinct molecular makeup. They might even discuss the physics involved in its functionality and efficiency. While none of these details are incorrect, a reductionistic view strips the hammer of its broader existence or its "place" in a larger context. It disregards any idea of design, purpose, or intention. Existentialism refers to this as the hammer's "phenomenological essence."

In contrast, consider how a blacksmith or carpenter perceives a hammer. They may not know its chemical makeup or the physics behind its effectiveness, but one could argue that they comprehend and value the hammer's true essence more than the scientist does. Why? Because they understand and utilize the hammer with respect to its specific purpose and within its proper existential "context" of meaning and utility. For them, the hammer transcends being just an object; it is an essential tool for constructing or deconstructing. More specifically, it plays a crucial role in creating the items on which many depend to live in comfort, such as walls, doors, or furniture.

When we examine a hammer from a holistic perspective, we appreciate its purpose and the essential role it serves in human life. Conversely, an abstract viewpoint attempts to detach the hammer from the very context that gives it meaning and relevance apart from which it would never have come to be. However, a given object's definition or identity cannot be separated from its context; doing so only leads to a superficial and incomplete understanding of that reality. Using love as an example, it is more than just neuron firing; it is a bond that can unite two individuals in a lifelong commitment of mutual partnership and fidelity. This mutual dedication in marriage not only ensures the continuation of the species but also equips parents to nurture a family, support each other emotionally, and navigate life's challenges together. An outsider or a detached observer analyzing humans cannot fully grasp the essence of love solely

> *Consider defining various objects or concepts through the contrasting lenses of "abstract objectification" and "existentialism."*
>
> *Which perspective provides a more comprehensive understanding of what things are in our world?*

through study; it must be personally experienced to be truly comprehended.

In summary, existentialism and postmodernism expose the error in simplifying an item or phenomenon as an abstract entity by demonstrating that each object's identity and existence are intricately linked to the complex matrix of finite realities, or "contexts," that shape and define it. Understanding this context is essential for grasping how an existential perspective, such as the one we will employ on our journey. Let us now explore in detail what we should bring to mind when thinking about a "context" in relation to our human situation.

"Context" and Other Relevant Existential Terminologies

In existentialism, the term "context" refers to the surroundings, environment, background, and traits that define any specific reality or finite being. For instance, a person's context can vary from aspects as minor as their job and daily activities to grander concerns such as their role in the universe and its implications on their life, including the passage of time and the law of gravity. Throughout this book, we will come across terminology connected to this concept, including the following terms:

Contextual: Refers to something that is confined and shaped by an external, limited context, including the broader Context of Finitude, as well as specific local contexts like culture, society, or nationality. The word "contextualness" serves as an adjective describing the contextual situation and nature of something.

Supercontextual: Signifies that something is not limited or defined by any external, finite context. Completely transcendent. The term "supercontextualness" serves as an adjective to describe something's transcendent nature.

Supracontextual: Refers to something that transcends its specific context while remaining broadly contextual. For instance, universal human norms or God's vision for humanity are not limited by contexts like social bias and human subjectivity, yet they remain influenced by context, as humans are inherently contextual beings. The term "supracontextualness" serves as an adjective describing the nature of being supracontextual.

Contextualities: Defines the contextual and formal boundaries surrounding any given reality or existence, such as "time" for all people, or more specific factors like a country, ideology, historical trend, social status, job, or personality for an individual. The concepts of "supercontextuality" and "supracontextuality" denote similar boundaries (or their absence). For instance, being free from time and space exemplifies supercontextuality.[3]

Contextualization: A "contextualized" being or reality is one that has experienced different levels of contextualization, including adopting an appropriate position and role within a specific context. It can also indicate that a super-contextual being or reality has partially assumed a level of contextuality. This is exemplified during moments when God has constrained Himself for our sake, such as becoming "subject" to time and language and ultimately to humanity through Jesus, in order to connect with and save His creation.

---

[3] An entity would experience a reality in which concepts like "past, " "future, " or even "change" does not apply. All reality is perceived simultaneously, without anything transitioning from future to past. Quite a mind-boggling difference from the contextual nature of our reality, is it not?

A key takeaway from these concepts is that only a supercontextual viewpoint can yield a truly objective understanding of Finitude and its various contexts. In addition, supra-contextuality originates from only that which is super-contextual. In contrast, a contextual viewpoint offers an inevitably subjective interpretation of reality. Picture this difference as akin to observing a vast city from a helicopter versus from street level. The aerial view presents a complete overview, while the street view can easily lead to confusion. Despite common beliefs to the contrary, we can only perceive reality from the "ground," through the biased perspective of an "insider." We can also liken our position to that of actors in a grand play, each receiving only their character's lines and stage directions one page at a time. The supercontextual perspective belongs exclusively to the playwright backstage, who holds, comprehends, and manages the entire script. Similarly, only the Author of the World Story possesses a truly objective and omniscient perspective on Finitude.

What contexts do you believe define you?

Which do you share with your friends or others, and which do you not?

While this perspective may seem constraining, it is essential to reiterate that humans cannot - and should not - escape the limitations of our human circumstances. Each of us exists as a contextual being, defined by the frameworks that shape our lives. These frameworks extend from the fundamental laws of the universe to our individual biology, and from the era and society into which we are born to the careers and relationships we may choose (or not). Our understanding of reality and our interpersonal connections develop through these layers of intertwined existential contexts.

Though we humans uniquely possess self-awareness among all living beings, structured contextualities are a defining characteristic of all finite, created realities. Consider how a lion behaves according to its carnivorous role, often without conscious awareness. For animals, context equates to instinct, which often defines their world. Every finite reality originates from within a specific context. Using the theatrical analogy mentioned earlier, the broad context of Finitude resembles the stage where the performance and all the character arcs unfold. Finite realities are similar to the script, actors, dialogue, stage directions, backdrop, props, costumes, lights, and curtains that allow the play to occur. We cannot exist outside of these contexts, even if we attempt to do so. But why should we even entertain such a situation? It would mean we would cease to exist as humans, like fish without the sea or birds without the air.

The Foolishness of Chasing Objective World-Viewing

Those who blindly pursue "objectivity" ignore their nature as beings embedded in the world. Here, objectivity refers to the quest for knowledge and experiences of personal experiences, biases, or contextual factors. The pursuit of a life free from human subjectivity is ultimately misguided. This longing contradicts the reality that we can only exist as beings shaped by our environment. If a world-dwelling person could escape their contextual framework of viewing the world, they would lose their humanity altogether - something inherently impossible. Even machines classified as "AI" are developed by world-dwelling individuals who invariably allow their subjectivity to seep into their programming and the assumptions embedded within their systems.

To illustrate how much we rely on our unique worldviews, let us consider how contexts affect our thinking. No matter how objective we strive to be, we cannot escape how our surroundings shape our thought processes. To truly "think objectively," one must relinquish all assumptions, identities, memories, beliefs, experiences, and perceptions of reality. What would that even mean? It is impossible to achieve. Our subjectivity always influences our conclusions. In Western philosophy, Descartes is remembered for his quest to doubt everything and construct an objective knowledge base from the ground up. Yet, he could not entirely free himself from the influences around him, as well as his own past and circumstances. His reliance on reasoning (drawn from the Western tradition's faith in rational thinking, inherited from ancient Greece) and his mathematical approach to deduction – shaped by his background as a mathematician and geometer – demonstrate this limitation. He even argued that God gives us the ability to reason deductively, asserting we can trust our reasoning since God would not deceive us. However, history shows that his successors often rejected his conclusion as not actually passing the litmus test of objectivity.

> *Do you think any of your ideas or beliefs are genuinely "objective? Take a moment to reflect on them and consider how the contexts of your upbringing or environment influence them.*

Now consider Siddhartha Gautama, better known as the Buddha. Like Descartes, he sought to uncover the fundamental truths about reality through introspection, rather than adhering to the conclusions or frameworks of others. However, unlike Descartes, who was grounded in a more Western tradition, the Buddha was shaped by Hinduism and Indian philosophical concepts like meditation, samsara, and dharma. Consequently, his views on the nature of reality and human purpose significantly differed from Descartes', despite both striving to understand the "real" world through "objective" approaches.

The fundamental conclusions of Buddha and Descartes starkly differ. Descartes determined that one of the first certainties was his own existence as a "self," based on his ability to reason and think independently. In contrast, the Buddha asserted that a crucial truth about reality is that the "self" does not really exist at all; instead, our individual identities are mere illusions that propagate suffering and bind us in this world. Acknowledging this truth is essential in Buddhism for attaining enlightenment. While Descartes relied on reason to find answers and confirm the validity of his conclusions, the Buddha attained his "enlightenment" through a spiritual revelation, meditation, and a process of mentally emptying himself, rather than through logical or deductive reasoning. The significant differences between post-Cartesian Western philosophy and Buddhism are evident. This illustrates the folly of believing we can reach an "objective," universal understanding of our identities and purposes, as varying world-shaping contexts will lead us to vastly different outcomes, regardless of efforts to extricate ourselves from them.

Our worldview's subjective nature is evident in our understanding of morality. Actions deemed morally wrong in one culture might be accepted in another. For instance, suicide has traditionally been viewed as wrong or undesirable in much of the Western world, but in recent years this view has been confounded by the emergence of the legalized practice of medically assisted suicide in some countries. Even so, such a practice remains debated heavily in our society and viewed by many as a "last resort" under extreme circumstances. Conversely, in classical Japanese culture, samurai considered *seppuku* (ritual suicide) as an honorable and often preferred way to die. In medieval times, Christians, Muslims, and Buddhists regarded human sacrifice as abhorrent and sinful, while it was an essential and revered element of Aztec religion. Society influences values and norms, which in turn shape society itself. This raises the question of whether objective morality truly exists if concepts of right and wrong are shaped by human subjectivity. We will revisit this question later in the book.

To illustrate the subjective nature of our world, we can examine the sciences. Although they might appear entirely objective due to the data they handle, the values and roles they embody are influenced by societal contexts. For instance, a theistic individual or society would perceive science and scientific reasoning differently than an atheist counterpart. While theistic scientists throughout history have often regarded science as useful, valuable, and true, they did not view it as the ultimate authority on truth and reality, whereas an atheist would likely disagree. Furthermore, atheistic perspectives also subjectively influence the aversion to theism often exhibited by people.

Most people who identify as atheists do so as a conscious rejection of theistic beliefs. Without the societal acceptance of God or a "higher being" that many uphold, there would be little reason for atheism as a deliberate rebuttal of such views. Consider it similarly to how we define "religion" today; it exists only when alternative, less belief-focused lifestyles are present. In the Middle Ages, and even now in many less secular regions, it was or is simply a way of life or an understanding of the universe's functioning. Even today, many Hindus do not perceive themselves as followers of "Hinduism," but rather as navigating the natural order of the universe, intertwined with their society and culture rather than segregated from it. It is primarily in the West where religion is defined as something separate from other aspects of life, as a reflection of the "decontextualized" environments we live in today.

The quest for "objective knowledge" often supports the philosophical and scientific inquiries of modernity. Yet, the methods claimed to uncover objective truths still originate and conclude with subjectivity. Take the concept of "infinity" as an example. Although we can contemplate it or represent it with a symbol, its essence remains completely foreign to us as "finite beings." We can never truly comprehend the reality of an infinite quantity without a "start" or "finish." Our limitations obstruct our ability to fully grasp the infinite. How did humanity conceive such an idea before mathematicians first theorized it? While one might assert that math is "always real," the way we conceptualize mathematical ideas influences our perception of reality.

Consider calculus as another example. Isaac Newton essentially had to create this entire discipline to mathematically interpret a world that is dynamic and ever-changing, rather than one that is static. Similarly, our system of counting is not universally accepted. Think about how long humanity existed without formally recognizing the number zero. The Greeks and Romans did not utilize zero as we understand it today. The concept emerged in India and only reached Europeans through Muslim intermediaries during the Middle Ages. Some scholars even suggest that the concept of zero was influenced by Buddhist philosophy's acknowledgment of "nothingness" as significant and valid rather than just a lack of something. Thus, we learn that even our basic understanding of numbers is influenced by historical contexts.

Our internal hopes and fears shape our perspectives. Indeed, every worldview is at least somewhat influenced by emotion. How often has the irrational fear of death or rejection driven someone to make certain choices or reach certain conclusions? This emotional influence is inescapable. The contexts and assumptions surrounding us affect our feelings. These in turn shape both our existence and our perception of the world. A person's perspective on life is never entirely rational or objective; it is always colored by subjectivity.

Language and linguistics offer further examples that highlight the limitations of human objectivity. A person living in the world relies on language to express and understand their perspective as they communicate with neighbors. In simpler terms, we convey our thoughts about reality through discussion, using language as our medium. However, language remains inherently subjective. The historical contexts of those who inhabit the world influence how all languages are shaped.

For example, in English, pronouns like "I" and "you" denote the speaker and listener, respectively. In English sentences, these pronouns cannot be omitted if they function as the subject. So, for instance, saying "I went to the movie last night" is acceptable, whereas "Went to the movie last night" is not. In Japanese, pronouns can often be omitted from sentences. Similarly, in Spanish, verb conjugations frequently indicate subjects instead of using pronouns. Some scholars suggest that people in cultures where pronouns are frequently dropped may adopt more collectivistic or communal values compared to those who use pronouns actively. Explicitly stating "you" and "I" is believed to reinforce the distinction between self and others, highlighting individual differentiation. Therefore, a culture that minimizes the use of these terms emphasizes a weaker focus on the self in daily life, promoting a more communal perspective of one's role in collective society.

Take, for instance, the vocabulary variations among languages shaped by their unique contexts. English features numerous terms reflecting contemporary concepts, such as "computer." In contrast, many languages, including Tagalog, use borrowed versions of the word- like *"kompyuter"* in Tagalog and *"konpyuuta"* in Japanese- rather than a native term. This borrowing occurs because the concept of computers emerged from an English-dominated context, especially American, while other cultures lacked the historical backdrop to develop their own terminology. As a result, they adopted both the terminology and the concept of computers from the English context. On the other hand, Tagalog boasts several distinct words for rice, while English uses just one.

> Based on your previous insights, how can you maintain an objective understanding of morality despite your subjective views?
>
> Do you believe that an objective moral framework is crucial for humanity? For you personally?
>
> Why or why not?

The terms *palay*, *bigas*, and *kanin* in Tagalog refer to rice plants in the field, uncooked rice grains, and cooked rice ready to eat, respectively. In English, as previously noted, they are all categorized simply as "rice," differentiated only by qualifiers. This disparity arises because Tagalog, rooted in Southeast Asian culture, sees rice as a staple crop, integral to daily existence and culture, warranting specific terminology for its various forms. Conversely, in many English-speaking nations like Britain and America, rice holds less significance and is often regarded as a foreign substitute for staples like corn, wheat (in bread or flour), and potatoes. These illustrations exemplify how subjectivity influences even the most universal aspects of language. Even our fundamental modes of communication are intertwined with the contextual factors that shape them.

All these examples illustrate that neither what we create, nor human thought can achieve true objectivity. Only that which exists beyond the realm of Finitude holds objective insight into ultimate reality, free from subjective biases. The transcendent, unhindered by specific contexts, serves as the true foundation for morals, knowledge, and our understanding of the world and ourselves. This genuine objective insight arises from a perception that transcends all contexts and is rooted in a super-contextual frame of reference. As such, only the Infinite can fully understand the finite, while the finite cannot fully grasp the Infinite. For us Christians, God alone meets the criteria for transcendent super-contextuality, from which all foundational contexts and their proper relationships emerge.

Supercontextuality (God's Perspective) vs. Contextuality (Human Perspective)

As a supercontextual being, only God can conceive everything outside the constraints of spatial, temporal, and other contextual limits that govern Creation. Metaphorically, He is not obligated to adhere to the rules and conventions that apply to the characters in the play, just as a playwright is not bound by the script they have crafted. The categories that outline the possibilities and necessities for finite beings do not restrict His engagement. To possess Infinity, in essence, means to transcend the finite. Beyond simply being unaffected by contextual factors, God does not require them to define His essence. His existence itself does not dictate who He is or what His purpose entails; He simply defines Himself through His existence.

In contrast, humans cannot fully "be anything" without the contexts that shape our identity and lives. Unlike God, whose essence and existence are the same, we cannot simply exist on our own, detached from anything else. Even if we lived as a non-corporeal "mind" in an empty, white space of complete nothingness, we would still struggle to exist independently. This scenario is somewhat akin to living in a world devoid of contexts, though it is not entirely parallel. To establish an identity, or even to exist in such an environment, we would need a point of reference, which necessitates context. For instance, a line drawn beneath us would indicate "up" and "down." While this might appear as a "limitation," without it, we would not be able to orient ourselves in any meaningful way. Through our contextualities, finite realities become real and impactful. They might restrict us, but they also allow our life story to unfold, guide our lives, and inform how we make decisions. Most importantly, it is through these contexts that our identities and sense of self develop.

If God is indeed the Author of all contextualities, it follows that our identities are not arbitrary or solely self-fashioned; instead, they are inherently shaped by the finite context of the Creator's Story of Finitude. Only His vision can define the intended narrative and the *telos* (or "final purpose") of Finitude and everything within it. This vision serves as the blueprint that sets the appropriate (or "fitting") contextual relationships among the various intertwining realities. Imagine this: when we lift the hood of a car and observe the engine, those of us who are not mechanics might perceive a chaotic jumble of pipes, wires, nuts, bolts, and components. Yet, we instinctively understand that each part has a specific role, even if we cannot identify it. Our understanding stems from the knowledge that a designer has meticulously crafted every detail of the engine, ensuring that if even one component were misplaced, the car would not function as intended.

> *How do you see yourself?*
>
> *What contexts, whether intentional or not, influence your perception of your identity? Is it your family, your career, your hobbies and passions, or perhaps something entirely different?*

The same applies to God. If we believe He is the author of every contextuality and the connections between them, we can have faith that design and intentionality exist behind each one. Furthermore, God serves as the supercontext, granting everything its true meaning, relationships, and purpose. He is not just the designer but the very design of the engine itself; the logic and scientific processes that ensure all parts function cohesively to make the car operate. He does not simply maintain the moral order; He essentially embodies it (which can only be defined as moral through Him). What are some examples of the contextual relations that God establishes through His existence? Normative standards like morality, justice, natural law, and goodness certainly fall under this, as does human oughtness- a term referring to "what we ought to do." This last point is vital for our discussions in this book. Simply put, it denotes what we must do to be considered "truly human" in the eyes of our supercontextual Creator. We fulfill our intended purpose – similar to a hammer used to construct things.

To further illustrate this concept, let us envision finitude as a book. We can view all finite realities as the ink, pages, letters, and symbols that constitute the text of this book. By themselves, none of these elements hold coherent meaning. However, when assembled into a book, they acquire structure and significance within its context. A random assortment of letters and pages can become The Lord of the Rings or the works of Shakespeare. All that is needed is the mind and skill of an author to bring coherence to them. Unlike any ordinary book, though, the author of the "Book of Finitude," who continually turns its pages, is One who is Infinite. As the foundational Being in which all other contexts exist, it follows that only the "contextual relations" established by Yahweh are fitting for us.

> *Why are "limitations" or "boundaries" essential for creating coherence and meaning?*
>
> *What occurs when these restrictions are lifted, granting you the freedom to act without any constraints?*

Nonetheless, endowed with free will, we can choose to disregard or rebel against divinely orchestrated parameters. Our decision to do so does not alter the appropriateness of those connections for us, but we possess the freedom to live at odds with them if we so desire. Returning to our theater metaphor, one can recite whatever lines they choose onstage, but it is the playwright's dialogue and overarching narrative that define the play. Any deviation from this script leads to disorder, resulting in mere noise.

Picture staging *Romeo and Juliet* while allowing each actor to depart from the script at will, without prior notice to anyone else. At the very least, the outcome could no longer be called Romeo and Juliet; it would likely descend into a chaotic muddle. Within our framework, fallen humanity is characterized as individuals who have chosen not to pursue proper contextual relationships or adhere to the script of the play they inhabit. Their "idolatry" manifests in valuing their own "independence" or submission to an alternative "script" over that of the true playwright. In fact, some expressions of existentialist thought often promote this kind of idolatry, by which humans masquerade as providence.

Sartrean Existentialism: "Existence over Essence"

Keeping these ideas in mind, we should explore the existential thoughts of the French philosopher Jean-Paul Sartre. Sartrean existentialism asserts not only that existence precedes essence but also that existence is the only certainty we have. He aligns with the existentialist perspective that our lives and the world we create are inherently subjective. We confront the truth that everything exists within a context when we strip away our assumptions. Many of these contexts show just how distant they are from what we consider "absolute reality" when we reflect on them adquately.[viii] In this regard, he aligns with our discussion of the value of existentialist thought.

Consider money: a green piece of paper (or electronic code) that we collectively agreed holds a specific value, enabling us to purchase goods and services vital (or not) to our survival. While it makes sense to us, from a truly outside perspective, it is baffling. The idea of exchanging anything for essential goods may appear strange to another being. In prehistoric society, for example, money as an intermediary unit of exchanged value may not have existed; trade occurred solely through the bartering of actual goods or services. In other small ancient communities, trust-based exchanges and personal debt may have rendered the need for something like money unnecessary. The value of money, rather than being an absolute necessity or a universal fact of life, had to be agreed upon on a social level first. After all, green pieces of paper, or even gold, possess no intrinsic value. We do not need either to survive on a biological level.

It is interesting to observe how peculiar certain cultural practices appear from an outside perspective. In Nordic families, such as those in Finland or Sweden, it is common for children to address their parents by their first names to foster a sense of equality. However, this practice might be considered shocking or even outrageous in other cultures. For instance, in many Asian cultures, children typically use more formal titles when speaking to parents or older siblings. In Chinese culture, terms like *gege* for older brothers and *jiejie* for older sisters exemplify this formality. To outsiders, these differing customs might seem odd or amusing, while for those within the culture, they feel entirely normal, potentially even universal. A Finnish individual might perceive the use of formal family titles as unnecessarily formal and indicative of emotional distance, while a Chinese individual could view referring to parents by their first names as profoundly disrespectful and presumptuous. Many existentialists, including Sartre, noted that, although these cultural practices are crucial to the societies humans have established, they are often just contextual peculiarities. From an outside viewpoint, they can seem quite extraneous and bizarre.

What sets Sartre apart is his conclusion that objectivity or supra-contextuality does not exist at all, rather than simply claiming it is beyond our reach. He views our inability to access any objectivity as evidence that overarching objectivity or

> *"Have you ever considered embracing Sartrean existentialism? What emotions did this invoke in you?*
>
> *How might this perspective divert you from following Christ?"*

supercontextuality is nonexistent. What appears to be objectivity, in his view, is merely a human construct aimed at imposing meaning or purpose on a fundamentally meaningless universe. In Sartrean philosophy, if there is no greater "script" or "playwright" to follow, we are free to act without significant overarching consequences. Thus, individuals can craft their own narratives on the stage of life. Clinging to a purpose or action merely because someone deems it "true" or "proper" is seen as pointless from a Sartrean perspective.

These insights illustrate that Sartrean existentialism ultimately suggests that individuals should actively and self-centeredly construct their identity, destiny, and sense of obligation based on their personal beliefs, akin to playing "god." This leads to relativism. Individuals vainly seek to develop their worldviews without an overarching, objective standard. Essentially, everyone becomes their own "creator." Each person navigates the possibilities presented by the human condition, both realistically and imaginatively. In simpler terms, individuals seek to craft their personal narrative and role on the global stage. This self-centered existentialism has fueled many of the relativistic endeavors popularized in post-modernity, encouraging people to pursue truth, destiny, and self-fulfillment from within themselves. Further, they interpret any attempt to oppose universal standards as an act of ciolence against individual autonomy.

Heideggerian Existentialism: "Essence through Existence"

Ass opposed to Sartrean existentialism, we can learn much by viewing the Christian worldview through the existential lens of

German philosopher Martin Heidegger. As we will explore, "Heideggerian existentialism" can deepen our understanding of the finite human condition in a manner that aligns closer to a biblical perspective.

To understand this form of existentialism, we first need to explore Heidegger's unique use of the German term "*dasein.*" While dasein translates to "existence," its literal interpretation in English is "being-there." This concept signifies existence that is tied to a particular context, as humans do not, nor could we, exist in isolation. Consider a baby not raised by humans or even a humanoid robot, but was only "raised" by machines, ensuring the child's bodily needs were met. Within this framework, *dasein* describes a being aware of its own subjective essence while residing in a world shaped by various "contextualities." When an individual recognizes how these contexts shape their identity and acknowledges that they are as much influenced by these factors as by personal choices (perhaps even more so), they consciously embody *dasein*. In simpler terms, a person consciously exists as a "*being who-is-there.*"

Sartrean existentialism differs from Heideggerian existentialism in their views on selfhood formation. The former suggests that we create our sense of self from the "sandbox" of possibilities presented by the context's inherent meaninglessness. Conversely, the latter posits that selfhood is largely influenced by external factors, shaped by the interplay between our inner self and the environment we are "thrown" into. Our perception of our "true selves" emerges from reflecting on our interactions with the larger world, whether we consciously acknowledge it or not. Unlike a Sartrean approach that emphasizes taking initiative, a Heideggerian perspective humbly recognizes our reliance on our circumstances and society to shape our identity. This contextual influence on self-perception highlights why our existential relationships are fundamentally tied to levels of "care." Our awareness of these relations makes us aware of our personal significance beyond our individual lives. It is this "care" that drives us not only to exist but also to seek our "true place" in the world.

Everyone lives with inherent biases, yet context plays a crucial role beyond merely forming biases in shaping our identities. Everyone's awareness inevitably forms through the social, linguistic, and relational contexts in which they exist. Consequently, these contexts shape each person's worldview. Everyone holds assumptions about life and the world, filtered through their unique experiences and education, often without realizing it. Some prioritize wealth, status, pleasure, or familial responsibilities as the purpose of life. Others regard honor or loyalty to a nation as essential. Whereas others place their moral convictions at the forefront.

> *What contextual factors, values, and circumstances have profoundly shaped your identity?*
>
> *How have these experiences influenced your perception of how the world operates?*

Regardless of our individual views, our human experiences allow us to perceive and engage with the world through these habituations. In the process of forming a worldview, concepts like existence, suitability, meaning, value, and morality (defining what is "right") emerge.

Let us explore further examples. Everyone's worldview ultimately develops through language. Through language, we identify and conceptualize our surroundings based on the "contexts" we experience. For instance, what constitutes a home? What are its "contextual environments"? Is it a house, a chair, a kitchen, a table, or a study room? Or perhaps family, marriage, parents, reciprocity, childrearing, play, arguments, love, or resentment? Homes can stir different memories for different individuals. Temporal elements also shape a home, such as breakfast time, dinner time, and bedtime. One household may strictly gather for dinner at 6 pm, while another might not adhere to a specific schedule, or they not even regularly dine together. There are distinct family values too; for example, a tidy room is considered good, while a messy room is viewed negatively. Meaningful conversations at the dinner table are valued, whereas sibling fights or food throwing during meals are frowned upon. Furthermore, roles and expectations in a home, like chores or being a good neighbor, vary. Some families may enforce structure around these roles, while others prioritize different expectations. The list is extensive, with countless named objects, activities, emotions, and relationships defining what a "home" means to an individual.

Every worldview is founded on underlying assumptions. These beliefs about reality shape our understanding of various contexts and inform the language we use. For instance, consider the term "home"- one individual might view life through a nihilistic lens shaped by a chaotic and hostile upbringing, while another may hold a positive perspective due to a nurturing and stable environment during their childhood. How we perceive the world enables us to connect with our surroundings and construct our lives accordingly. Language has the power to inspire hope or diminish it, motivate or dissuade, affirm existence or condemn it. Additionally, language helps us come to terms with our sense of belonging in the world. Consequently, our experiences within different environments influence our beliefs about our actions and provide a framework for understanding how things are and should be in the contexts we engage with.

Following these reflections, we can conclude that human *dasein* is an entity that not only inhabits a world but also recognizes its unique "mode of dwelling." This self-awareness allows us to reflect

> *What are the differences between the concept of self-formation from a Sartrian or Heideggerian perspective?*
>
> *How does recognizing your own "facticity" influence your view of life?*

on, care about, evaluate, and respond to our living conditions. Furthermore, our selfhood develops through our distinctive way of interacting with the world. We cannot imagine ourselves without the opportunities provided by our environment. For instance, consider a man who identifies as a "professor." He can only claim this identity because society provides employment roles and values education culturally and economically, making a career in teaching possible. In Europe during the early Middle Ages, before the establishment of universities in the 1100s, formal education was managed by monks as part of their duties. It was primarily directed at those aiming for monastic life. In such a context, envisioning a career goal as a "professor" in our present understanding would have been unimaginable. Besides employment, society also provides various other roles through which individuals can define themselves, including civil service, military service, and interpersonal relationships.

Consider how some would identify themselves by some of the following roles: as a "loving mother," "proud American," Christian, vegan, fitness enthusiast, nationalist, or communist. Without a proper context, an individual who identifies as any of these things cannot truly become a self-defined person. For example, how can you identify as a communist if you do not exist within a world shaped by capitalism and its corresponding "injustices" and "inequalities," which communism inherently opposes? Similarly, how would you deem yourself physically fit if no one were deemed unfit, creating a standard of "fitness" and a cultural division between the "fit" and the "unfit"? Our self-perception is closely linked to our existential worldview. In essence, individuals can only unveil their identities by discovering their "place" within the contexts that confine them. Additionally, we cannot establish our identities in isolation from the people surrounding us. Thus, it follows that someone who understands this contextual responsibility is more likely to take their existence seriously. They care about how their life story impacts the world they inhabit together. Heidegger described this internal awakening as a form of existential concern or "care." This care leads to the understanding that our existence is fundamentally intertwined with the existence and history of others in the world, which he termed the "facticity" of the self.

When we acknowledge our identity and the connections we share with others, we face a choice between taking a proactive or reactive stance in society. This choice can either challenge or uphold what is considered "authentic fittingness" within our surroundings. For example, in a militaristic culture, an individual who chooses to be a soldier represents an "authentic fittingness" valued by that society, while an artist choosing the same role does not share the same worth and respect. In this scenario, the artist or poet might feel meaningless, misplaced, or even worthless, as their skills may seem undervalued. Conversely, the soldier is likely to feel pride and a sense of belonging. Essentially, *dasein* perceives personal roles as reflections of one's true purpose or position in life. Thus, the interplay between the individual and the world influences one's distinct and conscious contribution to the narrative of Finitude.

A Theological Interpretation of Heideggerian Existentialism

Having explored an overview of Heideggerian existentialism, let us now reflect on these concepts from a Christian viewpoint. Connecting these ideas to theology helps us develop a paradigm for our self-perception in relation to God and our life-story. Recalling our previous discussions, the Creator stands as the *Being* that transcends the bounds and dependencies of finitude. Furthermore, He exists as the Source of the supercontextual objectivity that underlies all reality. Consequently, if our identities are inherently influenced by the contexts we inhabit, then our identities and selves carry a purpose in the Creator's plan. Each of us occupies a unique contextual setting, which corresponds to our distinctive purpose and role within the Creator's grand narrative. In contrast to a Sartrean perspective where objectivity is denied, "objectivity" (in a way) operates through the subjective, as the Maker intricately integrates every human life into His providential design.

> *What feelings arise when you consider having a personalized, authentic dwelling?*
>
> *How could understanding that there is a specific way God wants to express Himself through you, distinct from anyone else, alter your way of living?*

As beings shaped significantly by our surroundings, our sense of "fittingness"- or our authentic mode of existence- hinges on how we engage with the intricate fabric of truth around us. If we consider *dasein* in the strictly Heideggerian sense as being self-aware of our unique forms of subjectivity, then in a theological context, it signifies a creature made in the image of God who recognizes how their distinct subjectivity serves as a conduit for divine action in the world. This conduit uniquely illustrates how God interacts with and reveals Himself, tailored specifically to everyone's subjective experience and existence, crafted with intention by God for every person. We are all "thrown" by God into the realm of Finitude, the stage where the story He authored continues to unfold each day. Recognizing these truths transforms our existential "care" into a journey of uncovering and embracing a genuinely authentic way of being *present*. This journey can be described as *becoming* truly human based on some standard of ideal humanness. Given that an intelligent and compassionate Creator designed these contextual elements, we can uncover our preordained "true selves" within the broader fabric of the universe. Furthermore, it allows us to realize our true purpose or fittingness amidst our individual contexts, especially within the family of God.

To Be or Not to Be: "Becoming" as an Existential Term

Our life path in the creation narrative is not predetermined by fate. Sartre correctly acknowledged our freedom to address our consciousness of subjectivity, but he mistakenly believed this choice lacked a clear, objective meaning of being or non-being. Genuine existence does not merely arise from crafting a personal "fitting place." The notion of supercontextuality invalidates this idea. Rather, we can choose to become authentic beings or non-beings in defiance of genuine human authenticity. We have the "power" to decide who we will be, yet external factors inevitably influence this choice. As Jesus invited folks to follow Him, He followed the example of Yahweh, setting life and death before humanity (Deut 30:15).

Understanding the term "becoming" is crucial as we embark on this exploration. Consider it a connection between "being" and "non-being." It is essential to recognize that only finite beings, even if partially so, can engage in the process of becoming. To become something requires a starting point or a point of origin. Infinite and immutable *Being* cannot undergo this process, as it is inherently timeless, existing without a beginning. Finite entities, prior to creation, had no existence, substance, or life. For finite individuals, becoming represents a form of existential "ascent"- an evolution of one's existence shaped by the relationships within their thrown context. For instance, envision a person in a capitalist society transitioning from an entry-level position with a shared apartment to becoming a high-ranking executive who can afford a spacious home and multiple cars. They have progressed in the way of achievement according to this framework of success in life.

The capacity for change is essential to the process of becoming. Philosophically speaking, only an entity that can undergo existential (modal) change in its core essence can truly become. An entity incapable of change cannot transition into anything new. For instance, becoming a child of God necessitates the modal transformation of sanctification. We are called to progress in our journey of self-actualization as holy beings of God. In biblical terms, producing spiritual fruit requires living by the Spirit; a process of "existential becoming" nurtured through Spirit-to-spirit communion (John 3:5-8; Gal 5). Instead of simply being a direct path from Point A to Point B, becoming represents a lifelong journey of ongoing transformation, marked by a sense of ascent or progression.

> *How have you experienced the process of 'becoming' in your own life?*
>
> *Who are you in the process of becoming?"*

When considering free will, it is crucial to understand how the process of becoming relates to a person's role in the Story of Creation, including choices and actions. Becoming facilitates the emergence of a finite entity's facticity, illustrating that our existence is inextricably linked to the existence of others. In simpler terms, we can only unveil our "true selves" through our interactions with the surrounding environment. The process of human becoming enables our facticity to align with the Playwright's overarching vision. Yet, this facticity may also evolve according to a contrasting, misguided interpretation of how one's individual narrative fits into the broader story of Finitude.

Our becoming can be directed either toward *non-being* or *being*.

The script that a living being performs on the stage(s) of finitude must originate from either the true Playwright or a false one; there is no middle ground. The roles, identities, and actions in a person's finite existence can resonate eternally or ultimately dissipate into nothingness. Since all contextual relationships are defined by God, a finite, created individual can only achieve true, authentic being when they fulfill the eternal purposes of the Creator's Vision. What does authentic being mean according to His Scriptures? It involves enjoying fellowship with Him in an everlasting home within creation. However, when the Divine signature is absent, a person becomes a "false self." Their identity and existence drift away from the Creator's vision. In simpler terms, a finite entity leans toward non-being when it strays from the Playwright's original vision for Eternity. This situation is not merely God issuing judgments for rejecting one potential plan among many. This situation resembles attempting to deliver a speech from Hamlet for a Shakespeare competition while improvising your own lines. Ultimately, whether you succeed or fail, you are either performing Hamlet or not, no matter how "good" your alternative might be. The measure of judgment lies in whether you are indeed performing Hamlet. Similarly, we are called by our Creator-Playwright to enact His original vision.

Nevertheless, the Playwright permits these departures to occur due to His foreknowledge. He had anticipated these choices when crafting the narrative before the world was established. Consequently, even when individuals act contrary to God's will, they inadvertently contribute to the realization of His eternal vision for finite existence. Consider the countless stories in literature and films where a character's efforts to evade a prophecy ultimately led to its fulfillment.[4]

Ultimately, all finite reality will undergo a transformation that continuously brings forth an eternal state of existence. Yet, many events unfold in the flawed realms of finitude according to a vision that diverges from that of the true Playwright. The decisions made by those straying from His vision are genuinely their own, not simply predetermined by Him. Even while God, in His sovereignty, understands the consequences of our choices, He grants us the freedom to make those decisions. However, we cannot alter those consequences. As He conveyed to the Israelites in Deuteronomy 30:19, He presents us with the option of life and death, urging us to select life. Similarly, in the Garden, He placed a choice before Adam and Eve, even though He already knew the outcome of their decision beforehand. This awareness of the outcome does not stem from "predetermination," but because turning away from the very Source of life and authentic meaning leads inevitably to death and false meaning, much like how placing your hand in fire guarantees a burn.

> *Why do you believe that God, as both the Author and Playwright, gives you the freedom to choose whether to exist truly or not?*
>
> *Have you embraced God's call to become who He intended you to be, or are you filled with uncertainty?*

We cannot decide to act against the overarching context of our reality without anticipating different outcomes. It is akin to walking away from a fire while stranded in a frozen wasteland. We are free to do so. However, we cannot hope to discover warmth or solace

---

[4] A contemporary example is Anakin Skywalker ultimately being responsible for the death of his own wife turn to the dark side- driven by the desire to save his wife- ironically causes her death in Star Wars.

unless we remain close to the fire. While God truly grants us the freedom to make choices, the repercussions of chasing a dark, alternative vision are preordained and known by His providence. This malicious vision lures people away from their true essence, originating from the god of temporality and the sovereign over fallen existence *(dasein)*. He is the Evil One, whose primary goal is to lead human development toward non-being.

In this chapter, we previewed the vision that existentialism reveals when combined with theology. More than just an exploration of human existence, existentialism - particularly Heidegger's approach - serves as a profound inquiry into the human essence of *being* itself. By beginning to grasp human existence, we can differentiate it from all other creatures, as well as God's Infinite *Being*, or *Being* in its purest form. This understanding is vital to prevent the misconceptions that arise from mistakenly equating the two or viewing God merely as the highest being among others. By exploring our unique contextual mode of being, we recognize the differences among other finite modes of existence, such as those of animals and angels. For now, we will concentrate on human existence and its subtleties. In the next chapter, we will examine how humanity distinctively dwells in and perceives the world and how our contextual realities influence our concepts of the world and ourselves.

> *How has your understanding of existentialism evolved in this chapter?*
>
> *How can it inform your understanding of yourself and God, as well as your God-relationship?*

Chapter 2

In a Mirror Darkly

The World-Viewing Befitting Human World-Dwellers

"When I was a child, I talked like a child, I thought like a child, I reasoned like a child. But when I became an adult, I set aside childish ways. For now we see in a mirror indirectly... If from a human point of view I fought with wild beasts at Ephesus, what did it benefit me? If the dead are not raised, let us eat and drink, for tomorrow we die. Do not be deceived: 'Bad company corrupts good morals.' Sober up as you should, and stop sinning! For some have no knowledge of God – I say this to your shame!"

(1 Cor 13:11-12, 15:32-34)

"So then from now on we acknowledge no one from an outward human point of view. Even though we have known Christ from such a human point of view, now we do not know Him in that way any longer."

(2 Cor 5:16)

"I have examined all this by wisdom; I said, 'I am determined to comprehend this' – but it was beyond my grasp. Whatever has happened is beyond human understanding; it is far deeper than anyone can fathom... When *I tried to gain wisdom and to observe the activity on earth*... then I discerned all that God has done: No one really comprehends what happens on earth. *Despite all human efforts to discover it*, no one can ever grasp it. Even if a wise person claimed that he understood, he would not really comprehend it."

(Eccl 7:23-24, 8:16-17)

World-Dwellers in the "Context of Finitude"

In this chapter, we will ponder how humans perceive and inhabit the world not as objective or abstract beings, but through subjective and unwritten rules shaped by our environments. As beings that dwell in the world (*dasein*). Our sense of belonging develops continuously as our environmental contexts change. Our perception and relationship with the world manifests through the ways we integrate into the environments we dwell. However, how we participate in this process hinges on what we consider "contextually appropriate." Put simply, this refers to what we deem to be a suitable fit within our current context.[5] We will refer to this framework in this chapter using the Greek term oikonomia.

Oikonomia refers to the concept of an "ordered space," applicable to both nations and households.[6] It originates from the root word *oikos*, which translates to "house." Scripture describes the Earth as an "*oikoumene*"[7] or "world-house," as a world shaped by an *oikonomia*. If we believe God to be the Author of all contexts and contextual relations, as outlined in the previous chapter, we can conclude that the Creator established an *oikonomia* or "set of

---

[5] For instance, take the ancient Greek city-state of Sparta, known for its extreme militarism. Infants deemed unfit for military service- whether due to physical deformities or perceived weakness- were killed. In such an environment, a man admired for his hypermasculinity, strength, warrior prowess, ruthlessness, and loyalty to the state would be seen as fitting. In contrast, in ancient Athens, a different set of values prevailed. This city, regarded as the "birthplace of democracy," valued artistic expression and political engagement. In this context, attributes like intelligence, diplomacy, education, and eloquence were essential traits. If these qualities were transferred to a Spartan context, that individual would likely be viewed as weak or insignificant. Accordingly, both city-states operate within a framework of contextual relationships that shapes their respective notions of fittingness.
[6] BDAG, 697-698.
[7] This word refers to the "earth as [it is an] inhabited area; the world as administrative unit" (BDAG, 699).

house rules" for the context we inhabit.[8] This *oikonomia* constitutes the *oikoumene* in which we all live our lives. According to Scripture, the Word (*Logos*) of God established these rules at the inception of Finitude.[9]

We should reflect on how God created us, as world-dwellers made in His own ontological image. More specifically, He created us to be stewards of creation. We exist partly to promote the flourishing of the inhabitable world according to the proper conditions laid out in the Maker's house rules (*oikonomia*). Adam fulfilled this purpose when he named and "ordered" the animals.[10] Like Adam, God has assigned us to be "co-managers" of the house of Finitude alongside His Word (the Son) and His Breath (the Spirit). This is a central part of our original destiny and fundamental purpose in life. Even so, the Creator does not call us to be masters who exploit, abuse, or rule based on our subjective opinions. Instead of creating our own house rules, Yahweh invites us to follow His agenda to ensure creation flourishes as He originally intended.

What do you consider to be "contextually fitting"?

What house rules do you personally follow?

What do we mean by "house rules" from an existential perspective? Essentially, they are the frameworks that define how we seek to engage with the world in an appropriate or "fitting"

---

[8] Remember the "context of Finitude" avee h so often mentioned? It is the universal context that every human being born into and lives out their lives within.
[9] We will explore this subjee will exct in detail in a future quest.
[10] Adam was not simply coming up with random names. Instead, he intentionally designated the occupants of creation according to each animal's relation to the natural world including its "proper fittingness." The Greek word for this is *oikourgeo*. It represents "fulfill[ing] one's household responsibilities" (BDAG, 700).

manner. These rules influence our behaviors based on personal beliefs regarding what is deemed "wrong" or "right," as well as what ought to be. For instance, consider the opinions people hold about appropriate actions concerning our education, health (physical, mental, and emotional), careers, or the environment. For example, we might view recycling positively due to societal perceptions of what is "proper" regarding our relationship with our natural surroundings. An individual may consciously assert that members of a virtuous society should recycle to protect the planet. Their intention to protect the environment informs their house rules, leading them to regard pollution and litter as "bad," since they "damage"[11] the environment and the living creatures within it.

We must, at this point, remember that the objective world of the Creator is not the "world" as we experience it. We humans are subjective beings, after all. Instead, the "world" for us world-dweller refers to the world as we perceive it according to our finitely contextualized perspective. Put another way, each world-dweller lives according to their own orderly arranged *oikoumene* (world-house) governed by a specific *oikonomia* (framework of house rules). Unlike the Creator's ordered *oikonomia*, however, the subjective contextualities of our world-dwelling shape these house rules. After all, our *oikoumene* is something we conceive or imagine rather than what reality *is*. Ultimately, the assumptions underlying our house rules shape our worldview.

Take our previously mentioned Spartan example. He might view the world as a brutal and unforgiving environment where only the strong and callous prevail. While this perspective aligns with

---

[11] These quotations highlight how a person may label certain things as bad and harmful, while someone with different beliefs might see them as neutral, perhaps. The quotations point to the subjective nature of these terms, given that they can be used and interpreted differently by different individuals.

societal norms and his experiences, it contrasts sharply with an Athenian's. In contrast, an Athenian may perceive the world as vibrant and full of beauty, ripe for exploration and philosophical thought. Whereas one may confront existence with somber acceptance, the other approaches it with eager curiosity. These differences lead to distinct ways of perceiving and interacting with their surroundings in an ordered and meaningful way.

Forming World-Contexts for our Wayfinding

Let us consider paintings that demonstrate how we form *oikumene* (world houses) from *oikonomia* (house rules) based on our assumptions and perceptions of the world. At its core, a painting is not real; it is merely pigment and paint on a canvas. Our worldview, however, perceives the world that the painting depicts. To achieve this, we seek the meaningful contextualities that structure our perceptions. Let us attempt this with two paintings.

Our first painting is *Liberty Leading the People* by Eugéne Delacroix. The artwork features guns, swords, fallen soldiers, and people surging forward over a barricade, with determination evident on their faces. The French flag is raised proudly. A Phrygian cap adorns the woman's head. As a backdrop, the city is wreathed in smoke. These elements evoke historical memories and contextualities, enabling us to interpret the painting. Each person, however, interprets it through their assumptions, experiences, and the "house rules" that shape their unique perspective. For some, the painting may represent the bloody chaos of revolution, the tragic loss of the "good old days," and the downfall of a sacred tradition. Sympathizers of the recently overthrown French monarchy might have thought so during its creation. For others with more liberal views, it may symbolize the triumph of new ideas over the old, representing a cause worth sacrificing much to achieve, even through bloodshed. Different house rules lead to varying perceptions and conclusions. Everyone ultimately forms their own opinion about what the painting "means." We all build our individual "worlds" from the same starting point but can arrive at widely differing conclusions.

The second artwork we will examine is Jackson Pollock's *No. 5, 1948*. This piece features bursts of color and lines that appear carelessly splashed across the canvas. It lacks recognizable images or contexts to help shape our understanding. While viewers may develop their ideas about the painting's significance and meaning, the canvas does not provide a clear starting point. Interpretations can vary widely and may even share nothing in common, reflecting the painting's seemingly chaotic nature. Absent a solid contextual framework, it is challenging to draw dependable conclusions or create a reasonable interpretation from it.

A contextualized frame of reference shapes our perspective on the world. We need one to have any perspective at all. Our existence in this world and the contextual factors that shape our existence influence the frame of reference for our worldview. Without life experience, however, how can we assign meaning to guns, dead soldiers, the French flag, or the Phrygian cap?[12] We world-viewers cannot help but live as "world-participators" who actively seek our place in the "world-house" we inhabit. Such existential seeking takes shape based on world-shaping assumptions that create a schema of house rules. Through this

---

[12] Phrygian caps are soft conical caps with the tops bent over. Though they were once associated with ancient peoples from Eastern Europe, they came to signify freedom and the pursuit of liberty in the American and French Revolutions. This is an example of the importance of "dwelling" and experiences in shaping how we interpret the world. If one does not know about Phrygian caps, we could not factor this knowledge into our opinion of the painting, perhaps subtly changing our interpretation altogether. Now imagine someone who lacks any social or cultural context for the French flag, or even gu? How might they interpret the painting differently?

schema, a person manages how they act and relate to the world(s)[13] they inhabit.

Since we perceive our world as a world-house governed by house rules, the existential nature of our dwelling in this world[14] makes us naturally view things through the lens of what we perceive to be "fitting." We naturally have a deep concern for the "proper state" of various aspects of our environment. For instance, when we feel hungry, we eat to regain the "proper state" of nourishment. We work at a job to ensure our economic stability and sustain a "fitting" standard of living. When a machine malfunctions, we repair it to restore it to its "proper state." This mindset also extends to broader aspects of our lives, prompting us to seek changes in family, work, and society. As a species, we endeavor to create "proper world-dwelling arrangements" by altering the "rooms" of our global house, whether through personal decisions or national and international policies. When we perceive something as "wrong" in our world, we inherently feel compelled to correct it. To this end, we endeavor to return things to their "proper place" to preserve a sense of "rightness."

> *Have you ever wanted to restore something to its rightful state in your life, whether it be personal or societal?*
>
> *What was it?*
>
> *Where do you think your concepts of fittingness, which shaped these desires, originated from?*

As humans, we frequently make arguments to convince others to support or revive a particular vision of "world-fittingness" (often accompanied by a set of appropriate house rules). Politicians

---

[13] Whether the larger world or smaller "worlds" like your family, your job, your nation, etc.

[14] Remember our discussion on how we "care" and the *facticity* of the self from the previous chapter.

and religious leaders are usually adept at this. For instance, the United States' Founding Fathers held a distinct perspective on what a "fitting society" would constitute for a new democratic nation.[15] They outlined their beliefs about how ideal societies and governments should operate in documents such as the Declaration of Independence, the Constitution, and the Bill of Rights. Occasionally, they contrasted their concepts with unsuitable government models that hindered true human flourishing. The ideas of "world-fittingness" expressed in these documents would inspire numerous people and nations throughout modern history to create a more collectively prosperous and just social order.

Foundations of House-Rules and World-Dwelling

Our conversation about house rules and world houses aligns with many existentialist views, irrespective of their religious beliefs. However, we will delve deeper to demonstrate how these truths are not merely a reflection of reality but represent a deliberate design by our wise, all-powerful Creator. God fashioned us to inhabit the world. After all, did He not create us in His image and likeness, albeit to dwell in a finite context?[16] We possess cognitive world-viewing abilities similar to His own. These capabilities enable us to formulate, adjust, and implement our house rules, effectively constructing individual realms within the greater world in an organized and orderly fashion. They grant us free will,

---

[15] More than a mere rebellion against widespread oppression, the American founding fathers cultivated a revolutionary vision of society and governance. Their thoughts were profoundly shaped by Enlightenment philosophy and classical liberalism, which champion individual rights, the consent of the governed, liberty, the balance of power, the tendency of human tyranny, and the rule of law, among other principles.
[16] We are made in the image of a supercontextual God (Genesis 1:26). Nevertheless, we are inescapably subjective and contextual beings whose lives depend on the context of finitude.

empowering us to act according to the house rules we believe should govern and direct our existence within the world.

Beyond simply establishing guidelines for societal living, the house rules we follow significantly shape our self-perception. Our understanding of ourselves develops as we compare our identities to the "ideal, proper version" of ourselves we believe to be attainable. Our perception of this "true self" is closely tied to how we view our rightful position in the world, aligning with the house rules we have adopted. For instance, a Spartan would invariably measure himself against the cultural ideals of "manhood" and military effectiveness. His self-image is directly influenced by how he aligns with this standard through the rules that govern his lifestyle and self-perception. Similarly, someone who regards the notion of justice as "properly fitting" will subconsciously envision their "true self" as a champion of justice. They will likely adopt house rules that reflect this belief, such as opposing injustice whenever they encounter it. As a result, this individual might perceive their rightful calling as one who works within the judicial system or law enforcement.

What is your vision of your "true self"?

How is your perception of your "proper place in the world" based on a set of house rules?

A person's existential situation is fundamentally influenced by the inherently "presuppositionalistic" nature of human world-viewing and dwelling. In simpler terms, the frameworks (*oikonomia*) that shape our perspectives and experiences are built upon assumptions or pre-existing ideas about the world and our fitting place in it. We never begin from "objective reality;" instead, we start from our subjective perspectives. We consider certain beliefs right and others wrong, even when we cannot exhaustively or objectively validate them daily.

Assumptions govern how we navigate the world. Every form

of knowledge is based on assumptive frameworks. For example, nearly all mathematics relies on fundamental axioms, many established in Euclid's *Elements*.[17] Consider another example: the very foundation of science relies on the trustworthiness of our cognition and perceptions. We operate under the assumption that replicating experiments should consistently yield the same outcomes, rather than random variations, even when every variable in the experiment is perfectly controlled.[18] Even if we claim these things are objectively true, the fact is that every scientist assumes and presupposes these axioms in their work instead of, say, trying to re-establish the fundamentals of reason and experimentation each time they experiment. They, in essence, have "faith" in the scientific method and its ability to produce consistently accurate results.

---

[17] An ancient Greek mathematical treatise which proved foundational and influential to almost all mathematics that came after it, from algebra to modern geometry to calculus, and even logic itself.

[18] To illustrate this concept, leusus consider Galileo's renowned experiment involving the simultaneous drop of two objects with different masses from the same height. This experiment demonstrates that, when air resistance is removed, two objects of varying mass will fall at the same speed and land simultaneously, contradicting the assumption that the heavier object falls faster. This principle was affirmed by astronaut David Scott in 1971 when he dropped a feather and a hammer on the Moon, which lacks air resistance, and observed that they both reached the ground at the same time. Every experiment conducted under these conditions has yielded the same outcome.

However, the premise of "conducting experiments" relies on the ability to replicate results using the same objects under identical conditions. This holds true in our reality. Now, envision a world where this is not the case- a universe ruled by chaos, wherein the laws of physics might alter unexpectedly and arbitrarily. In such a scenario, predicting or influencing the reactions of physical laws with every action would be impossible. We would find ourselves unable to depend on experiments or to establish scientific laws (like Newton's laws of motion). It would be a chaotic reality where, for instance, objects might occasionally fall upward rather than downward, leaving us no reliable way to forecast outcomes. In such a random universe, the foundations of science and our achievements would not be feasible or conceivable.

We cannot completely avoid our underlying beliefs about how the world operates. For instance, we navigate life expecting the sun to rise tomorrow or that performing good deeds will bring goodwill or fortune. Additionally, consider the beliefs that assure us life is "worth" living. Reflect on the purposes or motivations that drive us to care about our present and future existence. Without these essential existential beliefs, we could not engage with the world meaningfully and reliably. Similarly, we could not function as socially adaptive individuals. Ultimately, these convictions and expectations enable us to interact and communicate within society. Our ability to methodically inhabit the world as our "home" would be fundamentally diminished without this awareness of our fitting place and role by which we conceive of our selfhood.

The presuppositional foundations of a perceived *oikonomia* (set of house rules) shape each person's existential situation. How we establish ourselves existentially in the world enables us to engage with reality in a semi-consistent and stable manner, by which our identity takes shape. This process influences the patterns that make up our character traits and lifestyle. It is from these semi-consistent actions, emotions, and interactions that our life story emerges. Without them, we would all live like schizophrenics. Many such presuppositions may be consciously selected. For example, let us imagine an individual convinces themselves that "success" revolves solely around material possessions and sensual enjoyment. Their definition of the good life would involve fast cars, large houses, abundant wealth, gourmet food, flowing drinks, sexual gratification, and the ability to acquire anything they desire whenever they wish. They would perceive and inhabit the world materialistically, prioritizing a hedonistic lifestyle, akin to a narcissistic consumer. They would live solely to possess and consume rather than be guided by a "higher" code of ethics, or duty, especially one requiring self-sacrifice or self-denial.

Conversely, emotional and sentimental assumptions, like intellectual beliefs, can significantly influence our perception of ourselves and the world. Hopes, fears, and unease routinely shape our interactions with our surroundings. Consider a person who, due to certain reasons, fears intimacy and shuns reliance on others. They are likely to view the world as harsh and indifferent, believing that the only trustworthy individual is themselves, while everyone else poses a threat. They may regard otherwise promising relationships merely as an unacceptable risk of experiencing pain, rejection, or manipulation. As a result, their life would tend to be cautious and suspicious, likely leading to an inability to trust anyone completely or engage in a deep relationship.

Why invest so much time in exploring how our perspectives on viewing and inhabiting the world are "presuppositionalistic"? We do this to comprehend the extent to which our subjectivity influences how we establish our homes and selfhood in the environments around us. As humans, we have an inherent urge for "homemaking." We instinctively work toward becoming "appropriate residents" of a world-house that exists both literally and figuratively. This impulse aims at fostering meaningful world-dwelling, motivated by our concern for everything present in our surroundings. These entities include other living beings, objects, and our thoughts and ideas. Such a desire for homemaking is deeply embedded in our nature as beings created in the likeness of the Triune I AM. We naturally seek everything, including ourselves, to occupy their proper places and to be cared for effectively.

> *Can you think of some presuppositions that have influenced your house rules and house involvement?*
>
> *What is the value of critically understanding these presuppositions?*

Nevertheless, we must recognize that all our attempts in homemaking - something every human engages in, whether consciously or not- are shaped by various assumptions and presuppositions. This is one reason there are so many differing ideas about how humans should individually and collectively live or organize ourselves, our contexts, and our societies. Our nature, influenced by the contexts surrounding us and how they affect our worldview, contributes to this. We each adhere to different *oikonomia*, or house rules, within our unique world-houses, all situated within the larger world-house of Finitude. Even the concept of "goodness" or "oughtness" is shaped by our inclination toward "befittingness." The standards of "befittingness" we follow are all established based on a specific perspective on how the world and our participation should be ordered.

A given worldview gives rise to a corresponding perspective on what is considered "proper" concerning the world and its inhabitants. This, in turn, influences how we approach homemaking. We cannot avoid such normative tendencies; we can only adapt to them. Although we can examine our beliefs to see how well they align with "reality," such examination cannot evade presuppositions or subjective prioritization, regardless of how "rational" our methods may appear. Even the act of prioritization in all scientific endeavors is inescapably shaped by this subjectivity. This subjective prioritization applies to both what is studied and what data to include in such a study, given the seemingly infinite scope of each. Our presuppositions tint even fundamental tools like language and logic, which, as discussed in the previous chapter, are not entirely objective. Such is the nature of inescapably subjective beings.

Given this context, we should pose a crucial question: How reliable are our presuppositions? To what extent can we trust the foundational beliefs that shape our perspectives and logic as inhabitants and observers of the world? Suppose we dismiss Sartre's idea that there is no overarching context or objective truth. How can we address our challenges in perceiving objectivity while still striving for truth belonging only to super-contextual Infinite *Being*? This issue is vital because, to embark on our journey, our understanding of the world must rest on our capacity to recognize true aspects of reality, especially as they illuminate our way of life.

We should begin by recognizing ourselves as "properly equipped" by our Creator to perceive, conceive, and seek after truth. Consider scientists like Johannes Kepler[19] and many Christian philosophers from the Middle Ages and the early modern period. They believed God designed us as beings capable of grasping the scientific truths about creation. They believed a benevolent and wise Creator designed humans to perceive truth despite our subjectivity. Furthermore, we must presuppose an inherent objective order in the universe and that our minds can somehow grasp this order and align our lives accordingly, even if we cannot behold such a supercontext directly. We must trust that God, who is an active entity rather than merely an abstraction or a detached Deistic being, actively bridges the gap by becoming supracontextual and contextual, revealing His infinite truths through our finite, contextual world. Otherwise, this entire pursuit of learning and a purpose in life would be a waste of time, as

> *Why is it so important to have faith in our ability to know, see, and pursue the truth, even if we can never be entirely objective?*

---

[19] To quote Kepler directly: "Those laws [of nature] are within the grasp of the human mind; God wanted us to recognize them by creating us after his own image so that we could share in his own thoughts" *(Letter (9/10 Apr 1599) to the Bavarian chancellor Herwart von Hohenburg. Collected in Carola Baumgardt and Jamie Callan,* Johannes Kepler Life and Letters *(1953), 50).*

the author of Ecclesiastes surmised. Additionally, we must presuppose that the world we inhabit is built on "fittingness"; that there is a true orderly purpose to the contexts and house rules that surround us. This is the only way the world becomes knowable or explainable in the first place, including our conception of our fitting place in the world.

Energy Consumption: Illustration of House-Management

Earlier, we discussed how God created us to co-manage Creation's "household," similar to Adam's role in Eden. To better understand how humans engage in this "house management," we can explore an extended illustration. A significant factor influencing humanity's experience is our reliance on energy. Individually, we need food to survive. Collectively, we rely on energy sources - primarily fossil fuels- to maintain our modern civilization and standard of living. Importantly, we can not create these resources independently; we must obtain them from our surroundings. These essential realities impact the *oikonomia*, or house rules, that inform our perspective of the world, ourselves, and our relations within it. As dependent energy consumers[20], these assumptions influence our world-dwelling, affecting our interactions with the environment.

What other things are we, as humans, dependent on that we could not imagine life without?

What things are you dependent on that you could not imagine your life

Consider our universal need for food. Our way of living as consumers influences every aspect of our lives. Consider the numerous "household structures and rules" accompanying this seemingly simple act. Every day, many around the world spend

---

[20] Refer to Alasdair Macintyre's *Dependent Rational Animals*.

much of their day focused on acquiring food and shelter. We dedicate considerable effort - whether on a farm or at a job - simply to "put food on the table," particularly when supporting a family or providing for customers. Our homes feature designated spaces for food preparation, from Western kitchens to the central stove in a Mongolian *ger*. Vast infrastructures- farms, plantations, ranches, factories, supermarkets, and restaurants- exist to supply us with abundant food whenever we want. Many fields of science, including agriculture, animal husbandry, and food science, focus on food. Many build their careers around facilitating food preparation, whether for pragmatic functions (like line cooks) or creative pursuits (like gourmet chefs). Even armies "march on their stomachs."[21] Our need to eat significantly influences our perspective on the world and how we live. Imagine how different our individual and collective cultures, social structures, and economies would be if we did not need to eat to survive, or if we could photosynthesize all the energy we require from sunlight like plants.

Each of us should consciously acknowledge our individual dependence as energy consumers. After all, is it not part of the Lord's prayer: "Give us today our daily bread" (Matt 6:11). This awareness serves as a humbling reminder of our reliance on the environment and our vulnerability to it. From infancy, we depended on the milk our mothers supplied. Prior to that, we thrived on the energy transferred through the placenta. As we

---

[21] A quote famously attributed to Napoleon Bonaparte, showing that even the most powerful leaders in history were not exempt from this basic reality. A massive percentage of most war budgets go toward making sure soldiers are kept well nourished. A large part of military strategy revolves around the maintenance, distribution, and obtaining of supplies like food for the army to be able to function properly and advance efficiently to avoid malnourishment and starvation. It has even been said that while amateurs study tactics, professionals study logistics.

matured, our parents provided the nourishment that our immature digestive systems and limited chewing skills could handle. In fact, being dependent on energy consumption significantly shapes a baby's perspective more than that of an adult. During their first months, energy consumption is their focus as they develop. Although we eventually learn to feed ourselves, we remain reliant on external factors, be it our parents, our earned income, or the systems that allow us to cultivate, prepare, and buy food. Our ability to consume food is crucial for our health and longevity. If we lack the means to eat or drink, our bodies gradually fail until we pass away.

Our dependence on food means we can never perceive the world from an entirely "objective" perspective. As energy consumers, our nature and experiences affect how we view and engage with our thoughts and surroundings. Take, for instance, professional scientists. Their success is tied to their livelihoods, self-esteem, and social status, and they heavily rely on funding, frequently sourced from the commercial or government sectors. Numerous tales and lawsuits highlight biased scientific studies to validate theories or confirm breakthroughs, often driven by financial incentives rather than pure, unprejudiced inquiry. A notable example is the significant financial allocation toward chemical development for crop production over fostering plant immune systems through more natural means, like improved nutrition.[22] In essence, as humans, we cannot interact with reality as self-sufficient "independent" beings; none of us can truly grasp what it is like to exist without the need for money, food, or drink.

Our dependence as energy consumers impacts more than just our essential nourishment. Many societal contexts further influence how this fundamental truth impacts individuals

---

[22] Refer to the work of John Kempf's organization Advancing Eco Agriculture.

throughout history. For example, factors such as religion, culture, health and fitness considerations, or societal norms (like athletic and beauty standards) lead to differing perspectives on eating, ideas about appropriate foods, and how eating relates to self-identity. Let us explore a few examples. In various countries, like the Philippines and India, eating with one's hands is customary. This practice enhances the experience of the food and fosters a stronger bond with fellow diners. Conversely, in Western societies, eating with hands is often deemed impolite or disgusting. In Arab cultures, it is generally disrespectful to start eating before the elders - such as grandparents or parents - have taken their first bites, while other cultures may be indifferent in the order of eating or expect everyone to begin at the same time. In the United States, slurping soup or noodles is considered rude, whereas in Japan or China, it is seen as a gesture of appreciation toward the chef or host, indicating enjoyment of the meal.

Both Jews and Muslims typically avoid pork, along with various other prohibited foods, while Muslims, Mormons, and some Christian denominations abstain from alcohol due to religious beliefs. Conversely, some non-Jews and non-Muslims, like Catholics, may view these foods and beverages as essential for socializing with friends. For instance, consider how integral wine and dry-cured hams, like prosciutto or jamón ibérico, are at family gatherings in Spanish or Italian culture. Other religious practices, such as the Christian Eucharist and Jewish kiddush, include the use of alcohol in their sacred rites. Additionally, many religious and non-religious groups emphasize ritual fasting, which is seen as a vital spiritual practice. Today, some health experts often recommend intermittent fasting for its health benefits, independently of religious contexts, and individuals pursuing specific beauty standards may support similar practices. Vegans often associate their dietary choices with their identity, worldview, and principles. Some even follow this dietary restriction based on religious convictions, e.g. Jainism. For many, being vegetarian is inherently a moral statement. In contrast, numerous non-vegans do not share these beliefs and do not view their meat consumption through the same ethical perspective as vegans. Accordingly, we see just how much various factors influence how individuals, as well as different cultures, understand their roles as energy consumers in the world.

> *Do you define yourself in a way based on the standards of a diet?*

The concept of being dependent on energy goes beyond just food or the energy needed for our own bodies. Civilizations also rely on energy derived from fuel. While food played an indirect role in fueling premodern societies through human and animal labor, resources like wind, water, and wood (for fires) were also utilized to perform work and sustain those societies. In the 21st century, our global society relies on oil, coal, natural gas, geothermal energy, hydroelectric power, solar power, and more to operate everything from our lighting to our entertainment and transportation systems. Many capitalist nations consider the consumption of resources essential for economic growth, security, and well-being, which they view as crucial for achieving an appropriate livelihood and standard of living. The *oikonomia*[23] shaping the contextualities of our energy-dependent modern societies radically affects how we view and interact with the world. Consider the historical actions that countries have taken to secure resources for themselves and their citizens, whether through trade agreements or aggressive acts.

The impact of our global energy dependence is clearly evident

---

[23] In fact, the Greek word *oikonomia* (household management) is the origin of our English word *economy* (the management of material resources).

today in the news. For instance, geopolitical conflicts around access to oil in the Middle East highlight this issue. Recently (as of writing this book), Egypt and Sudan have also experienced tensions with Ethiopia over Nile water access for crop irrigation and hydroelectric power, especially due to the construction of the Grand Ethiopian Renaissance Dam. Critics argue that if completed, the dam could significantly benefit Ethiopia's economy but would threaten water supplies for upstream countries that rely heavily on this resource. Furthermore, it could grant Ethiopia substantial geopolitical influence over its neighbors in the Nile River basin. This tension would likely be absent if nations were not reliant on the river for food and electricity.

Beyond energy and resources, our context as energy consumers also affects how we perceive our physical world (the planet) in general. Consider, for instance, how this perspective influences our understanding of success and the "social status" of those around us. In our modern consumer society, possessions often equate to prestige. We tend to view a businessman in a suit as more successful than a humble individual preacher or janitor.[24] This perspective on human flourishing has shaped influential narratives about how the pursuit of wealth serves as a suitable and self-justifying form of world-dwelling. A well-known example of this is

---

[24] To emphasize the reliance on a modern industrial context, we should examine three examples. In Medieval Europe, being part of the clergy was among the most esteemed roles a family might aspire to for their son. Conversely, in Imperial China, merchants were regarded as the lowest social class, while scholars held the highest status. Similarly, in Ancient Rome, engaging in business and commerce was frowned upon by those of the landed aristocracy, who were seen as the true "Romans." Moreover, the idea of gaining the highest social status solely through wealth and material goods, rather than through noble lineage and family background, is a relatively recent development in many societal structures.

the "American Dream."[25] None of these life views would have existed or made sense in earlier, pre-industrial societies. Furthermore, consider how industrial, capitalist nations discuss, study, and manage the earth to promote human "flourishing." As modern energy consumers in an industrial society (as opposed to an agricultural one), we interact with the planet in ways that individuals in earlier civilizations could not have even imagined or conceived.[26]

These examples illustrate how finite contextual factors, such as our energy dependence, significantly shape our efforts to feel at home in the world and "manage" our existence. While we inhabit this world striving to express our "true selves," this aspiration must align with our roles as energy consumers, both as individuals and as a society. Regardless of our desires, our true selves cannot, for instance, embody someone who exists in complete spiritual meditation without ever consuming food or water. We need to acquire sustenance, whether through foraging, hunting, or receiving it from others. No aspect of human existence or worldview can overlook these human necessities as dependent energy consumers.

> *Has your perception of yourself as a dependent energy consumer shifted after considering this study?*
>
> *How does being aware of your current situation influence thoughts about your life?*

---

[25] Novels like *The Great Gatsby* and plays like *Death of a Salesman* immortalize this narrative and its practices, views, and nuances.
[26] Consider the recent surge of the environmental movement. This broad understanding of the world and the magnitude of the issues that ignited the movement were concepts only feasible in an industrialized society like that of the 20th century. For instance, the U.S. Constitution does not address the responsibility of businesses regarding climate impacts, as the Founding Fathers could not have envisioned the ways in which individuals and enterprises might influence the planet.

How Presuppositions Influence our World-Viewing

Our presuppositions not only underlie our house rules and our way of dwelling in the world, but they also shape our perception of reality. They serve as a lens through which we view the world, one that we cannot remove; similar to how we can only see the world through our two eyes, rather than through our "souls." The way we think is contextualized, and we inevitably map the contextualities of "our there" (where we exist as *dasein* or being-there) onto our worldview. One primary way this occurs is through language.

Every language offers a structured means for humans to interpret and express the contexts shaping our world. This makes it invaluable for fostering a coherent, rational, and meaningful understanding of reality. Moreover, we rely on language to convey this information (as well as everything else) to our fellow beings. Unlike AI, which can transmit data instantly through wires or signals, most humans are confined to talking, writing, or sign language. Thus, our interactions are inherently limited by the contexts of our chosen methods of communication.

Ponder how specific languages encapsulate cultural attitudes toward society and social dynamics. For instance, Japanese employs various suffixes to express degrees of familiarity, a feature largely absent in English. If your name were John Smith, Japanese speakers would typically address you by your last name, as first names are typically reserved for close acquaintances. Instead of just saying "Smith", they would likely add "- san", a respectful suffix used for equals regardless of age, like "Mr./Ms." If John Smith held a higher status than the speaker, such as a supervisor, they would likely say "Smith-sama". This is just one example among many. In contrast, Americans usually rely on titles like "Sir" or "Mr. Smith" for politeness. Otherwise, referring to someone as

"John" would generally be acceptable in most situations.

The Japanese language developed within a unique social and historical context emphasizing the importance of "proper" social relationships and hierarchies. In contrast, English evolved in a context that lacked such intricate social nuances, making them less central to personal identity. A Japanese individual typically alters their speech patterns when communicating with friends or colleagues compared to addressing a boss or family elder. While the language one speaks does not exclusively shape beliefs or worldviews, it frequently exerts a significant influence on them.[27] None of us can entirely escape the influence of our language schemas- and the societal contexts from which they arise- on the presuppositions that shape how we perceive and relate to the world.

How can you modify your worldview without entirely avoiding or disregarding your cultural presuppositions?

In what ways should your worldview be or not be shaped by society?

Let us take a moment to consider how we can analyze language through language itself. This introspective analysis can critique our

---

[27] For more on this, check out the Sapir-Whorf hypothesis or the movie *Arrival*. Both deal with the massive passive influence language has on our presuppositions about the world and how we perceive it.

In *Arrival*, humanity must figure out how to communicate with aliens that land on Earth. In one scene of the movie, a linguistics team from China is concerned at how aggressive the aliens seem, while teams from other countries register less aggression from the aliens.

It is later revealed that the Chinese team established communication through mahjong terminology, a highly competitive winner-takes-all game. By unknowingly using aggressive and competitive language to underlie communication, the aliens "presupposed" that competition was essential to human language or psychology. This caused them to come off more aggressively than they otherwise would have, coloring the entire relationship between the aliens and the Chinese team as a result.

underlying assumptions. These critiques are essential, given that language evolves or devolves within every society and individual. For instance, the meanings of terms like "good" or "wrong" may differ significantly from their interpretations decades ago, whether for a society or an individual. We should also consider the language of "world-systematization." People employ this type of language to systematically account for and communicate what *is* or ought to *be* in relation to inhabited contexts. We often see this employed in religion, government, and behavioral science. Consider the following phrases as examples. "Everything that exists has a cause for its existence." "We can account for all phenomena." "Creation ex nihilo." "Humans have certain inalienable rights."

To conclude, language for us world-dwellers is inherently contextual. It arises in and through the various contextualities of our world, impacting our world-viewing and, through that, our world-dwelling. We use it to effectively perceive, conceptualize, systematize, relate to, and dwell in our contextual world. Language is fundamental to how we perceive and come to terms not only with our own existence, but also the reality around us. It makes sense that whatever presuppositions and contextualities underlie our language necessarily affect how we conceive of things.

Other Contextualities that Shape our World-Viewing

In addition to broad, universal factors like language or energy reliance, countless other contextual elements shape our perspectives and experiences. These factors encompass beliefs, emotions, preferences, opinions, aspirations, cultural backgrounds, relationships, self-identity, worldviews, societal values and morals, norms, ideological norms, religious tenets, and various frameworks of perception. This illustrates how flexible and influenced our worldviews can be by subjective factors. As previously mentioned, this aspect of the human experience cannot be ignored or escaped;

it must be acknowledged, assessed, and adjusted.

Ponder how the contexts of the entertainment industry and social media impact societal norms. The recent decline of morality in worldviews and lifestyles in America has been a natural consequence of the phenomena unfolding within those contexts. They influence our perceptions of what it means to be human and how the world works. What was once considered 'wrong' is now labeled 'right', primarily because people have seen it portrayed as such in this media, e.g. shows, movies, music, and games. Many behaviors or viewpoints that were once socially unacceptable have become not just accepted but celebrated, in part due to the widespread and rapid influence of media indoctrination. The worldview of a generation evolves rapidly through these channels of mass psychosis.

Do you think that the subjective and presuppositional nature of language can be tempered or avoided?

Do you think this is a good idea?

How do you feel about the subjectivity of your language in relation to the Christian faith?

Consider how the lyrics of famous music artists have significantly shifted the cultural worldview and perspectives of the youth in society. The movies, music, and television of the 1970s promoted house rules and concepts of "human befittingness" that contributed to the idea and practice of "free love."[28] These same

---

[28] This situation gave rise to a rampant rejection of sexual taboos and the physiological and psychological aftermath of such rejection. Just consider how for most of human history, whether by evolutionary impulse or a mandate of a Creator, humans have prized the preservation of our species, such that losing a baby in the womb or in childhood was one of the worst tragedies. In many cultures today, many praise and celebrate our freedom to reject the preservation of our species given the exponential rise of abortions. Society has

house rules resulted in a surge of egocentric materialism, sensuality, and an exploding demand and production of both pornography and substance abuse. This new world-dwelling *oikonomia* of greed, materialism, hedonism, and relativism has been propagated through these worldview-shaping cultural avenues.

> *What sort of house rules of befittingness do you think the contextualities of today (pop culture, political discussions, news, social media, etc.) are promoting?*
>
> *Do you think these developments are positive or negative in how they influence our way of life and views on the world?*

World-View & Self-View: The Necessity of Contextuality

As we discuss our contextualities, we must remember how essential they are for us humans to live and thrive. Without them, we would cease to be human. More than just influencing our worldview, they enable us, as world-dwellers, to function stably. Without these, we would be completely disoriented and directionless.[29] We would not know the purpose or meaning of life, if we could not even reflect on life. Both Helen Keller and Jill Bolte Taylor (a woman who lived for years after a stroke without mobility, memory, literacy, and even language before recovering) attest to this. They both spoke of how, before they gained (or regained) the ability to think in a language (a fundamental contextuality), they could not reflect on anything, including

---

shaped our views on pregnancy as an unwanted burden instead of a miraculous privilege apart from which our species would go extinct. Just research the declining birth rate in many countries today and the social factors responsible.
[29] Recall our discussion about the two paintings. The lack of any contextualities for us to latch onto and interpret means there is no reliable way to construct meaning, purpose or direction. We would all be left with wildly different interpretations based on the flimsiest of justifications.

themselves. As Keller puts it in her 1908 book, *The World I Live In*, "Before my teacher came to me, I did not know that I am. I lived in a world that was a no-world. I cannot hope to describe adequately that unconscious, yet conscious time of nothingness. I did not know that I knew aught, or that I lived or acted or desired."

Without language, we would struggle to communicate and collaborate effectively with others. Individuals who are unaware of social contextual factors like etiquette or customs often find it challenging to build authentic social connections. For instance, people on the autism spectrum often experience difficulties in social interactions. Some individuals on the autism spectrum have likened this struggle to taking a test for which everyone else has the answer key except them. Their limited understanding of social protocols hinders the formation of most social relationships unless both individuals consciously adapt. Additionally, consider those who have trouble understanding language subtleties, such as sarcasm or metaphor.

Contextualities designed to aid human interaction encompass civil structures such as schools, extracurricular activities, and workplaces; interpersonal frameworks like family, friends, and colleagues; and diverse social etiquette, protocols, and customs that foster interpersonal relationships. These factors are vital for enabling individuals to interact effectively and discover their fitting role within their environment. In essence, they form the foundation for our adaptation to social circumstances.

Our worldview enables us to engage in orderly and structured intra-personal (with ourselves) or inter-personal (with others) relationships. These presuppositions create "world-systems" of *oikonomia*, allowing our individual identities and connections with others to endure amidst the changes and flux occurring in our lives. For instance, consider any action that derives meaning only from the moments when the contexts around us align with our actions, such as building a house, treating a patient, taking an exam, casting a vote, or going on a date. Therefore, we recognize our place in the world through the interrelations that provide us meaning within these contexts.

Consider the concept of "citizenship" or "nationality" as it relates to each of us universally. We identify people based on their nation of origin. Reflect on the significance of documents like birth certificates, driver's licenses, and passports. Despite various changes throughout our lives, most of our identities as citizens remain constant, shaping our opportunities, social norms, ambitions, and behaviors. When someone states, "I'm an American," they do so based on their environment, actions, and the contexts surrounding them, including their citizenship documents.[30]

> *How has your environment, including external factors and your interactions with others, influenced your perspective of the world?*
>
> *Do you feel content with this influence, or do you think some changes are needed?*

Subjectivity Reflected in How we Perceive the World

The subjectivity of our worldview also extends to areas such as the study of music, the arts, and the humanities in general. Neither these subjects of study nor the methods used to analyze them can escape subjectivity. They are, after all, products of human existence. In academic terms, these finite contexts typically refer to foreign "world-systems" with dormant or extinct *oikonomia*. In simpler terms, they represent radically different cultures and

---

[30] Even citizenship and "nationality" are presuppositions based on notions of what it means to be human. In the Middle Ages, people thought of themselves not as "French" or "English" but as the subjects of a specific lord or king. Nation-states and the contextualities that accompany them only became common around the 17th century and onward.

societies, many of which no longer exist. Despite this, all academic studies of these cultures inevitably reflect the subjectivity of the scholars conducting the research. For instance, consider an American English speaker studying an English translation of an ancient Greek text like the Iliad. Such a scholar cannot help but interpret these texts primarily through the lens of a modern Western worldview and its presuppositions. This worldview is, most likely, a-theistic, naturalistic, and "academic,"[31] a far cry from the mythological, supernatural, belief-driven worldview of many within ancient Greek society.

> *Have you ever thought this way about an ancient text or book you have read that is from a radically different "world-system"?*
>
> *What was it, how did you think about it then, and how have your thoughts changed after coming to terms with how your subjectivity skewed your understanding of them?*

Those examining the creations of past civilizations, whose "worlds" have vanished, must recognize their own inherent biases. Yet, numerous scholars approach ancient texts with a presumption of having a superior worldview compared to those who preceded them. This often occurs without the scholar's awareness of this bias. A prevalent instance is the tendency to regard beliefs in ancient deities or mythological narratives as mere primitive superstitions, neglecting to evaluate their significance in terms of

---

[31] It is, of course, possible for scholars to be conscious of this, and to attempt to place themselves in the mindset of the studied culture in order to better understand them. Especially in regard to the practical lessons and wisdom we should draw from such ancient texts. Despite this, that underlying academic assumption is still usually there. It is rare indeed to find a scholar of the Homeric works who truly shares the same fervent belief (or lack of belief) in the Olympian gods Homer would have had (if he actually did).

social and individual influence on the concept of "life."[32] Rather than being open-minded and humble enough to contemplate how ancient worldviews should be viewed subjectively or practically, the scientific attitude often focuses solely on the material aspects of the text. Some even fail to recognize their indoctrination by the guiding myths and rewriting of history in their past education. Many individuals neglect the lessons taught or may dismiss them as outdated or irrelevant to modern society.

Even critical literary analysis approaches information in a sterile academic manner, often viewing it merely as evidence to describe and categorize historical societies. While this method is not inherently flawed, its prevailing usage in academia has overshadowed alternative and supplementary ways of engaging with these texts and artifacts with greater sensitivity and thoughtful self-reflection.[33] Scholars aim to become "experts" about these works, rather than engaging with them to enhance their own worldview and existence. They neglect to allow these texts to "read them" or to examine their own biases and lifestyles through the judgments of ancient perspectives. For instance, how might Aristotle's *Nicomachean Ethics* or Plato's *Republic* evaluate our own

---

[32] For example, it is possible the more primitive society, albeit at many disadvantages from modern ones, might have experienced a higher degree of more personal and social fulfillment and psychological stability. After all, many in the modern "affluent" world suffer from depression, anxiety, stress, and substance abuse.

[33] For an example of a perspective that aims to push against this method, look at J.R.R. Tolkien's 1936 lecture, *Beowulf: The Monsters and the Critics.*

In this lecture, Tolkien almost singlehandedly shifted the study of *Beowulf* from seeing the poem as a source for Anglo-Saxon history (which downplayed its fantastical elements) toward seeing it as a powerful symbolic work of literature representing the anxieties and concerns of Old English worldviewing.

Even today, Tolkien's lecture is seen as the most important piece of scholarship ever made about the poem.

"modern" views on "happiness," "goodness," "virtue," and "justice"? How might St. Augustine's Confessions influence our understanding of the human condition? How might the theology of St. Francis of Assisi shape our views and management of the environment? How might Kierkegaard's *Works of Love* and *The Sickness unto Death* critique our perspectives on "love," psychology, and humanity's shortcomings (sin)?

Many scholars consider existential engagement with ancient texts not only difficult but also "non-academic" and "unbefitting," as it contradicts the "rational" mindset prevalent in most academic studies. This engagement requires one to regain a student-like perspective and acknowledge their responsibility to subjectivity and discipleship. Individuals must hold themselves accountable for how they "ought" to develop and rehabituate into a "better" or "wiser" person through such engagement, rather than merely becoming more "knowledgeable." This demands a humble recognition of how one's history, beliefs, prejudices, and assumptions influence their 'expert' worldview. No expert in these fields has a worldview completely devoid of the historical context of their own situated experience. Even if it were possible to eliminate the subjective influence of human existence, a dilemma would emerge. The very subjects encompassed by the humanities (history, philosophy, government, literature, etc.) would lose their essence; they are fundamentally grounded in human experiences. They are products of world inhabitation, existing solely for world-

> *How does a "subjective" reading of a work of art or literature differ from a scientific one?*
>
> *What mindset do you generally hold toward artifacts of the past?*
>
> *What can they teach you about being fully human or living as you "ought"?*

dwellers like us.[34]

Even the sciences cannot escape subjective influences from human world-dwelling.[35] For instance, consider how the presuppositions of atheism, materialism, naturalism, and anti-supernaturalism shape the study of the natural world, muffle its revelations about the nature, attributes, and power of the Creator revealed therein.[36] Consider how people tend to trust the limited awareness humans possess of the entire cosmos and even of human existence itself. Take the following example of

---

[34] Let us use music as an example. Music is meaningful only to a world-viewer as a world-dweller. Only as a world-dweller can we, as world-viewers, appreciate music for what it is and what it signifies regarding our humanness. Attempting to study music from the perspective of another cannot be accomplished without uss sharing their subjectivity. Nonetheless, we can never truly understand how another being might perceive and relate to music. Subjects like art, music, and literature arise from subjectivity. They cannot be separated from subjectivity and remain what they are in relation to human existence. Consequently, a world-viewer's past world-dwelling experiences inevitably shape how they perceive and interpret these subjects in other cultures. They cannot account for them in isolation but only as part of a human world. Put simply, the human world provides meaning and substance to works of art and culture in the lives of world-dwellers.

[35] To provide several specific examples: Consider how physics analyzes the structure of bridges. We cannot examine bridges without considering their purpose and significance for humans living on this planet. Geologists and botanists, too, cannot avoid studying Earth through the lens of what it represents to energy-dependent consumers in modern industrialized societies. Meteorologists who investigate natural disasters such as tornadoes or hurricanes are inevitably influenced by the needs of humanity when they evaluate the impact these phenomena can have on civilization.

[36] Reflect on the arrogant presupposition that nothing exists which cannot be empirically perceived. We can observe that this presupposition can only arise from a worldview that accepts this notion rather than from the outcomes of experimentation. Have we managed to tabulate and test everything in the universe to the extent that we know this statement is undeniably true? Or is it merely true "as far as we know"? Throughout the history of scientific discovery, what was once thought to not exist has often been found to exist after advanced instruments were developed to detect them, such as black holes, atoms, spacetime, and cells.

reductionistic materialism from our introduction: many conclude that human "love" is merely a product of evolutionary impulses aimed at preserving our species, arising solely from the firing of neurons in the brain. Despite these limitations, many "experts" still strive to view the world and human existence from an objective supra-contextual perspective. Ultimately, even "pure science"- such as the study of weather and rocks in isolation- relies on human world-dwelling, as all science is ultimately intended to benefit or enrich humanity and our world-dwelling. Thus, the goal of our discussion here is not to disparage the sciences but to promote a more responsible scientific mindset that acknowledges subjectivity while we pursue scientific truth.

Death is a pivotal factor in shaping our subjective worldview. We must confront the reality that our existence in this world is finite. Each of us grapple sometimes with the fear associated with the inevitable conclusion of life, whether it pertains to ourselves or loved ones. This fear profoundly influences many of our experiences. Think about individuals in the military, law enforcement, or any high-risk professions. In the realm of science, consider those who study animals or test experimental devices, such as those who developed nuclear weapons or research radiation. The subjective fear of potentially fatal consequences can affect their work.

> How do you personally perceive scientific explanations about reality as inadequate in providing a holistic understanding of your life and the world?

For instance, a zoologist engaging with predators in a zoo must remain conscious of the danger these animals pose. There are cases of such creatures harming humans, even in secure settings, and this awareness can "color" their research despite extensive experience. Thus, our perception of animals is deeply affected by the prospect of death. It explains why we view wolves as fearsome wild creatures while regarding dogs as companions; the former poses a greater threat to us, despite biological similarities.

Conclusion: How we will Appropriately Proceed

Our worldview can never escape the human perspective focused on temporal existence. Just consider our experience of fleeting pleasures, temporary relationships, and short-lived ambitions. As we continue our journey, we will examine the differences between the subjectivity of our temporal human experience and the subjectivity of eternal contextualities and house rules. We will first explore the contextualities of our "fallen" human existence as a tabernacle of a finite "I am who I am." Then, we will investigate the contextualities of eternity and authentic human existence as a tabernacle of the Triune, Infinite I AM THAT I AM. So far, we have discussed many contextualities, becoming, world-dwelling, and worldviewing in more neutral and humanistic terms. As we advance, we will strive to relate them to the biblical truths regarding humanity's sinful nature and how it separates us from God and our original destiny for which we were created.

This investigation will further demonstrate the existential demands placed on every crew member aboard this vessel to grapple with our identity and calling. Each of us must be willing to radically transform our world-dwelling and worldview according to the contextualities of the Kingdom of Heaven. To this end, we will investigate the distinctions between temporal and eternal existential being to understand how the enlightening grace of the supra-contextual perspective of our Creator (which bridges the gap between His Infinity and our finitude) should illuminate and guide our subjectivity and ground it in genuine objectivity. Our focus, after all, is wayfinding along life's "Narrow Way" by which we might find our true place in the cosmos.

> *Given all we have discussed, how willing are you to embrace what this quest demands of you?*
>
> *Are you prepared to let the Lord transform your perspective and way of living for the sake of the Kingdom?*

Chapter 3

Castaways in Search of Belonging

How Humanity Seeks to be at Home in Transience

"But to Adam He said, "Because you obeyed your wife and ate from the tree about which I commanded you, 'You must not eat from it,' *cursed is the ground thanks to you*; in painful toil you will eat of it all the days of your life... God *expelled* him from the orchard in Eden."

(Gen 3:17, 23)

"The whole earth had a *common language and a common vocabulary*...Then they said, 'Come, *let us build ourselves a city* and a tower with its top in the heavens so that we may make a *name for ourselves*. Otherwise, we will be scattered... And the Lord said, 'If as *one people* all *sharing a common language* they have begun to do this, then *nothing they plan to do will be beyond them*. Come, let's go down and confuse their language so they won't be able to understand each other...' That is why its name was called *Babel.*"

(Gen 11:1-9)

"*Occupy* their land as the Lord your God promised you. Carefully *obey* the *law of Moses* so you *will not swerve* from it to the right or the left, or *associate with these nations that remain near you*... If you do, they will *surely shift your allegiance to their gods*... But you must *be loyal to the Lord.*"

(Josh 23:5-8; 1 Kings 11:2)

They challenged and defied the sovereign God... You [Ezekiel] are living in the midst of a *rebellious* house... these people have *lost their identity!*"

(Ps 78:55-56; Ezek 12:2; Isa 23:13)

Intro: Impact of our Human Situation on our Future Quests

It is now time to prepare our vessel, "Faith Seeking Understanding," to explore the revealed truth about the crew's human condition. This chapter explores humanity's futile attempts to seek belonging, acceptance, and a personal home through our existence in the world-house we currently inhabit. So far, we have discovered that each of us is a world-dwelling being. We dwell, think, learn, communicate, and relate to others in a subjective manner. As discussed earlier, these contexts shape our life-view and worldview, influencing how we perceive the "fittingness" of our world-dwelling. We need to understand how these existential truths should guide the crew in fulfilling our voyage's prime directive: to know and live for God. We will accomplish our mission by striving to gain an accurately contextualized understanding of ourselves and our Maker.

Now, let us focus on our human circumstances. Each individual lives as a subjective inhabitant, searching for a "suitable place" in our shared world. This raises the question: "How do we, as human beings, ensure our fittingness in relation to our environment?" Answering this will help us to properly navigate our quest. After all, our Creator intentionally contextualizes His self-revelations to align with our search for genuine selfhood and our connection with Him and each other.

$\left[\begin{array}{c}\textit{Do you think}\\ \textit{understanding yourself}\\ \textit{and your destiny is}\\ \textit{closely linked to}\\ \textit{knowing your}\end{array}\right]$

He interacts with and shapes the created world in a manner suited to our human circumstances. Therefore, it is essential for us to thoroughly comprehend both our universal and personal human situations before embarking on other theological quests. We should ponder how individuals sometimes feel an innate compulsion to strive for self-actualization. Both consciously and unconsciously, we all aspire to dwell as "fitting" and meaningful residents of the world-house. Hence, our understanding of the world is ultimately directed toward realizing our "true selves."

Caring about Self-fittingness Impacts our World-Dwelling

Our Creator has placed us, created beings, into specific contexts He originally designed just for us, because He foreknew we would inhabit. Thus, we have an innate inclination to engage in existential inquiries.[37] We aim to uncover our true place, role, and identity within our world.[38] This inherent desire to discover and fulfill our 'true' role evokes a feeling of existential responsibility. As a result, this responsibility brings forth a demand or claim, often voiced by our conscience, regarding how we live.[39] Ultimately, discovering and embodying a suitable 'role' involves fulfilling certain responsibilities while avoiding others. Embracing these obligations necessitates reconciling our deep desire for self-actualization, or 'being who we were intended to be.'[40] People try various methods

---

[37] Ponder the book of Ecclesiastes as an ancient example.
[38] Recall the "household contexts of finitude" from our previous discussions. Humans strive to find a sense of oughtness (or what is right) among many other existential concerns.
[39] Ethics serve as essential house-rules that should guide human conduct, stemming from fundamental existential questions. These rules focus on the way individuals should coexist, such as treating others as you wish to be treated, such as refraining from harming or stealing from them, as well as promoting the common good.
[40] In this existential framework, self-actualization transcends simply reaching one's highest potential. The common approach to self-actualization inadequately addresses the essence of human existence as a being immersed in context. Genuine self-actualization is inherently linked to the idea of contextuality. This notion encompasses not only one's immediate surroundings- such as society, family, and peers- but also the broader supra-contextual perspective of the world overall both now and into Eternity.

Therefore, true self-actualization involves discovering one's rightful place in the world. This idea resembles the pursuit of destiny, where one not only

to achieve this. For example, many view their main responsibilities as just to 'be a good person,' which is shaped by societal or cultural norms of right and wrong behavior and objectives. When applied to the 'households' in which humanity operates, these norms create a framework of 'house rules' that guide human perspectives, activities, and communication.

> *How much do you believe you have attained self-actualization?*
>
> *What steps can you take to attain greater purpose, inner satisfaction, or peace?*
>
> *Do you concur that understanding yourself and your purpose is closely linked with understanding your Creator?*

Driven by our inner ethics, each of us has a form of "existential *care*" regarding our lives. This care influences our journey of becoming, creating a personal sense of purpose. This purpose arises from an understood standard of "oughtness," leading us to ponder, "Am I the person I should be?" Engaging with these existential questions allows us to explore how to dwell in the world while striving for self-actualization and self-satisfaction. Our aspiration to "be who we should be" lays the groundwork for both our individual identities and our numerous interactions within the world around us. Consequently, our lives become guided toward a final goal(s).

The intentional organization of our existence opens avenues to achieving degrees of facticity with a chapter in the World Story. Furthermore, this focus on life enables us to uncover a stable

---

"internally" becomes the authentic self intended for them but also fulfills the specific "external" roles assigned in their given context. Hence, this understanding of self-actualization is built upon the theological assumptions derived from our faith in the Creator's vision for creation, as revealed in Scripture.

contextual identity amid finitude, similar to how a puzzle piece integrates into the bigger picture. For instance, a man may derive purpose from his role and responsibilities in the military. This role aids him in recognizing his position in the world and guides his daily activities with an inner resolve. When asked about his identity, he responds, "I am a soldier." This existential pursuit of self-actualization essentially reflects the yearning to feel significant and possess intrinsic self-worth. This longing is inscribed on every human heart by our Creator (Eccl 3:11).

An Existential Thumbprint Shapes Our View of Fittingness

A natural consequence of our pursuit of purpose is the journey toward self-awareness, assurance, and peace. Imagine standing before a path marked with the age-old saying: "Knowing Thyself." Such journeys profoundly influence how we inhabit the world. Consider how an individual's worldview shapes their perception of their true self. In American society, for instance, many are driven to seek higher education, hoping to secure a lucrative career and achieve membership in the middle class or beyond. Conversely, in rural Philippine communities, attaining a college degree may be secondary to effective farm management and cultivating relationships to inherit and preserve the legacy of a family farm, thereby becoming a respected member of the local community. Given these factors, it can be said that every person possesses a unique 'existential thumbprint' that informs their perspective on existence, as it relates to their unfolding life story.

Our existential thumbprint reflects unique qualities, such as our passions, beliefs, opinions, attitudes, and character traits. It represents our perspective on the world as our home, while establishing our connection to broader social contexts. It is impossible to completely remove this existential thumbprint's internal and external elements without losing a sense of "self." Due to this existential constraint, we can never achieve supra-contextually objective world-viewing. We cannot see the world and our place in it just as God, in His transcendent sovereignty, might. If we could somehow strip away the influences of personality and character from our thoughts and concerns, we would forfeit our contextual identities and humanity. Our selfhood and human perspective as inhabitants of the world would risk dissolving into self-forgetfulness and aloofness to our responsibilities. We would be out of touch with human dwelling and viewing altogether. In short, we would lose our minds.

While we cannot completely remove our existential thumbprint, we can alter it. When individuals (either through coercion or choice) fundamentally change their understanding of the limitations and possibilities of their existence, they inevitably change part of their identity. Consider the jarring moment when someone learns that all they have ever known or believed is a falsehood. A fitting example is the aftermath of the Second World War in Japan. Following Japan's surrender, the Americans enacted the *Shinto Directive* during their occupation. This directive notably included the prohibition and censorship of the doctrine asserting the Japanese emperor's divinity. Contemplate the profound existential consequences of this shift. Many Japanese officers ultimately took their own lives, unable to reconcile the 'truths' they had dedicated themselves to with the stark reality that these beliefs were suddenly rendered false - an outcome of their crushing defeat in war. Yet, despite this potential for transformation, their entire existential imprint was not entirely obliterated. They retained many facets of their unique social identity and culture. Even so, these new insights were still filtered through deeply rooted ways of thinking and feeling that

{ *What does your existential thumbprint look like?* }

were part of their identity, as the imperial tradition persisted in a formal manner.[41]

Oughtness, identity, and destiny (or calling) emerge as significant existential concepts for those who inhabit the world. Yet, the significance of these existential ideas can only originate from the awareness of a being that is conscious of its existence. This self-awareness allows for introspection. The Apostle Paul demonstrated such introspection in the following passage: "You have heard of my former way of life in Judaism, how I was savagely persecuting the church of God and trying to destroy it. I was advancing in Judaism beyond many of my contemporaries in my nation and was extremely zealous for the traditions of my ancestors" (Gal 1:13-14). In this reflection, he considers his existential alignment with the historical traditions of a Jewish sect. He stated that he "lived as a Pharisee," which was "the strictest party of [the Jewish] religion" (Acts 26:5). This was central to his identity and perceived purpose.

Like Paul, has your way of life ever changed drastically during your life?

If so, how has that experience impacted you?

Paul's role in society influenced his perception of his "true self." He recognized his proper place in accordance with the Pharisees' traditions and their house rules of religious devotion. His purpose at the time was to strictly and religiously follow a Pharisaic understanding of Mosaic law and fervently encourage others to conform to this authentically Jewish way of life. His

---

[41] The Japanese imperial tradition held significant importance in their identity, making it unlikely to abandon entirely post-war, especially the traditions, symbolisms, and formalities. While modern Japan functions as a democracy, it remains a 'constitutional monarchy' in structure. The emperor continues to act as the ceremonial head of state, despite the Prime Minister wielding true political power.

rigorous Pharisaical education shaped his sense of personal duty and his mission to counter heresy to pursue national security (Acts 22:3). He assumed the position of a religious "purifier" for the Jewish people, mimicking the traditions of his ancestors who waged holy wars against the worship of Baal. He believed the Jewish community must collectively follow these standards to avoid divine judgment and attain national prosperity.[42]

Paul's convictions not only shaped a specific religious perspective but also dictated a disciplined, devout lifestyle. This worldview led Paul to believe he was justified in demonstrating nationalistic zeal for God by persecuting Jews who followed the Way of Christ, whom he saw as a threat to the future prosperity and security of the Jewish people (Acts 22:3, 26:9-11).[43] He viewed himself as a guardian of Israel, defending his community against false leaders and "wolves in sheep's clothing." By adhering to the path set by his religious authorities, he felt he was doing God's will and fulfilling his rightful place in the world (Acts 26:9-12). Thus, during his civil defense of his new way of life after becoming an apostle of Jesus Christ, he reflected on his mission to Damascus as an integral part of altering his life's purpose (Acts 22:4-21).

Before knowing Christ, Paul considered failing to fulfill his religious crusade as being 'untrue' to himself, his religious authorities, and God (Acts 22:4). After his conversion, he recognized that his prior identity and lifestyle as a "proper" Pharisee were inauthentic to God's true plan for him. He understood this inauthenticity was based on human traditions

---

[42] To this day such religious and convictions and house rules are very prominent, especially in the present nation state bearing the title: "Israel".

[43] For him, "Zionism," as the pursuit of advocating for the restoration of the Jewish state of Israel, was a social crusade somewhat like identity politics today. This way of life centered around not just being Jewish but being a "fitting" Jew within the context of the Jewish religious institution based on the Pharisiac traditions.

rather than the Creator's will (Acts 22:3, 6-15). Consequently, Paul's path transformed drastically, as did his perception of who he was meant to be. This transformation led to a profound shift in both his worldview and way of living (Gal 1:16-17; Acts 26:6-28). He moved away from being a fervent defender of the Pharisaical interpretation of the Mosaic Law to embracing the role of an ambassador for Christ.

As humans, we can actively reflect on the connections between ourselves, our surroundings, and a perceived standard of 'fittingness' within that context. Additionally, we can consider how well our current circumstances align with our vision of 'who we should be.' Depending on the perceived alignment, such reflections can evoke feelings of fulfillment and pride, or guilt and shame. Through this self-awareness, we can alter our way of life in various ways. We may pursue virtue, rebel against it, adapt to it, or remain indifferent. We should reflect on our intra-personal relationship between our selfhood, who we are presently, and our perception of who we should or should not be. Consequently, the existential situation revolves around our contextually determined environment, facilitating intra-personal self-examination. We depend on this contextuality to achieve existential fittingness at all.

After reflecting on your world-viewing and world-dwelling, do you believe it aligns authentically with your true self and your Maker?

Does your life currently correspond with your vision of morality?

Is your sense of obligation based on something other than the Creator's will?

At various points in our lives, many of us confront and ponder the fundamental existential questions that define human existence. "Why am I here? Who am I? Who am I meant to be? Is there a reason for my existence? How did I arrive here? Is life worth living? Am I meant for something beyond what this world can provide? Do I have a destiny and a meaningful role in the universe? Is there a God who created me for a purpose? Is my life ultimately insignificant in the grand scheme of things? Do I have a responsibility or life debt to my Creator, "Mother Nature," or to humanity? Am I the person I should be? Does my true fate lie beyond this world, or is it constrained to my current mortality? What becomes of "me" after I die? Is the person I am in this world a deception or simply a shadow of my true self? What self must I embody to achieve real rest or possibly eternal life? How can I reach self-actualization? Can I attain eternal life in an ideal world?"

[*Do you have answers to any of these questions?*

If so, spend some time journaling your answers.]

Tabernacling: Becoming Fitting Members of a Community
From a biblical perspective, in what ways can human world-dwellers be considered "tabernaclers"? To truly understand the existential significance of this term, let us examine how the Bible renders it in the original biblical Hebrew and Greek. The word translated as "tabernacling" in Greek is the word "*skenoo.*" *Skenoo* refers to the act of occupying, making habitation, and residing.[44] This word emphasizes how this act affects interpersonal communion with others in a settled environment. We can find this word in the following biblical passages: "Now the Word became flesh and *took up residence (skenoo)* among us;" "Therefore you heavens rejoice, and all who *reside (skenoo)* in them!" (John 1:14; Rev 12:12).

---

[44] ISA; BDAG, 929 (also refer to the Greek word *oikeo*).

The Hebrew word for "tabernacle" is *"shakan."* This word means to abide, settle down, dwell, establish, be present, or manifest in connection with a procedure.[45] We find this word in the following passages: "I will establish a place for my people Israel and settle them there; they will *live (shakan)* there and not be disturbed anymore;" "He drove the nations out from before them; He assigned them their tribal allotments and allowed the tribes of Israel to *settle down (shakan)* (1 Chr 17:9; Ps 78:55).

We should recognize several significant implications from this brief word study. 'Tabernacling' entails not just being present in a location but truly dwelling there. To dwell in a city goes beyond mere physical presence at a particular moment; it involves being shaped by the context of that place. For instance, you would have a permanent residence, identification with local government offices, employment in the area, adherence to local laws, a subculture affiliation, membership in community organizations, and employ a specific language and idioms. While one might vacation in a different country annually, only those residing there would be considered locals rather than foreigners.

Where are you tabernacled?

What are some of the contextual factors shaping you and those you tabernacle alongside?

Tabernacling requires a fixed position of dwelling demarcated by finite contextualities or existential parameters.[46] Moreover, this

---

[45] (ISA; Baumgartner, 1496-1499)
[46] Recall our previous discussions about the finite contextualities of our world. Finite contextualities come in many forms, whether corresponding to or negating those established by God. One that agrees is the contextuality of gravity. Several bodies of the universe, as well as the properties of things in the world, move and have their place due to gravity, making it one of the most

act of settling down also impacts the roles and relations one has with oneself, others, and the environment.[47] Consequently, the abode in which a person settles impacts the various existential aspects of how they presence, or "become present," to the world. To put things in a biblical context, God created us human beings as tabernacling creatures who seek to find our place in His Creation. As discussed previously, we have an inner drive toward living in our 'households' in a 'fitting' manner. We desire security, stability, fulfillment, and peace. Pursuing this world-authenticity means reliance on contextualized roles and subjective identifications like a fish relies on water.[48] In an existential sense, we lose a core part of ourselves when separated from the self-authenticating finite contextualities of our tabernacle(world-context). We discover our roles and identities through them, which can be referred to as the being-there that properly befits our existence. For example, to be kicked out of a synagogue in the time of Jesus was to be excommunicated from the *oikonomia* governing Jewish life at that time. In other words, one would lose core contexts, relations, and roles that largely shaped their whole way of life and identity up to that point. Hence, many of those who believed in Jesus were not willing to follow Him (John 6:66-67).

Take 'the American Dream' as an example of tabernacling. Historically, it has represented a vision of personal freedom and

---

prevalent finite contextualities for any material object. This proper position of dwelling befits these fixed finitely contextualized determinants of *oikonomia*.

A relevant example of a. localized context that aligns with this idea is the general taxation laws of our land. Jesus Himself states to give to Caesar what is due to Caesar, illustrating that adhering to the taxation rules specific to your city or country exemplifies proper living within finite contexts (Mark 12:17).

[47] Remember that the Greek word for 'tabernacling' mentioned above also takes into account interpersonal communication and relationships.
[48] Recall our previous discussions about the impossibility of subjective human life within society without these finite contextualizations.

prosperity. For many contemporary Americans, it symbolizes a spacious suburban home with two vehicles and a white picket fence; the security of homeownership, children attending excellent schools with promising futures, a family vacation at least once a year, and the ability to enjoy a wide range of consumer products and entertainment options at will (outside of work). In this scenario, a parent is likely to see their role as successfully promoting the prosperity of a family with this ideal, striving to achieve this 'fitting' image. Their responsibilities would include securing a reliable, well-paying job, putting in the requisite daily effort, networking effectively, saving vacation days, and investing resources appropriately.

In the early 19th century, the 'American Dream' had a different essence. This era lacked electronics, cars, suburbs, consumer culture, and modern corporations. Instead, the ideal was to possess your own land out West, enjoy religious freedoms without government intervention, be free from oppressive social norms and tyrants, reap productive harvests annually, and maintain control over your destiny without depending on the government. In this light, a parent's presence might still involve raising a family, but with distinctly different expectations and duties.[49] To a 19th-

---

[49] To explore a different context more deeply, reflect on how consumerism has transformed our perceptions of freedom and prosperity.

In a time when the frontier was still in play and agriculture dominated the lives of many, it was logical to view 'freedom' as self-sufficiency on unspoiled land, liberated from the old European class systems (feudalism) and political tyranny. You would 'carve your own kingdom' as a ruler and judge, striving to accumulate enough wealth to maintain independence and avoid dependence on others.

In today's industrialized, capitalist society, where the 'frontier' no longer exists, the concept of freedom has evolved. The old European class structures no longer drive people away. In our urbanized and modern world, "virgin land" is a thing of the past. Consequently, 'carving out your own kingdom' might

century farmer or the Founding Fathers, the notion of 'freedom' as 'the freedom to buy what you want' would appear absurd. In essence, the concept of freedom in 19th-century America differs significantly from that in 21st-century America.

In essence, our identifications with suitable roles and the commitments made to reach these ideals influence our behavior and interactions within our shared world. Roles such as husband, father, citizen, co-worker, employer, friend, consumer, voter, and more inform a man's perception, actions, and engagement with his surroundings. By them, he strives to inhabit his world as a fitting 'man' according to his society's contextual standard of 'manhood.'[50] Moreover, these contexts influence his relationships, decision-making, the way he juggles his various roles, and their effects on his self-image, ambitions, and life perspective.

> *What ideal of fittingness are you pursuing?*
>
> *How do you think your contextual environment impacts this image?*
>
> *Do you believe this is a worthy image of fittingness to pursue?*

Let us explore biblical examples illustrating how tabernacling influences can change yet remain present. Take, for example, the traditions and social customs of ancient Jewish society. These customs shaped community identity based on the social norms established by the Law of Moses. For instance, devout Jews

---

represent the pursuit of a comfortable suburban lifestyle instead. 'Freedom' could manifest as the ability to purchase and possess desired products, allowing you to shape your identity through your consumer choices.

At any rate, the ideal of 'freedom' morphs based on the broader sociopolitical and cultural environments that surround it. As the ideals change, the roles and expectations of 'fittingness' change alongside it.

[50] Both in the general social sense of 'what is expected of a mature adult' and even the more specific cultural sense of 'what is expected of a male human being'.

traditionally wore distinct insignia to signify their dedication to the Law and their study of the Holy Scriptures. Today, many Jews continue to avoid non-kosher foods and abstain from work on the Sabbath. Although these significant contextual influences have evolved over time, they have never been completely erased or lost.

For another example, think about the early Gentile believers. Upon embracing the faith, they needed to adjust their way of living and perception to align with Jewish spirituality and a monotheistic view. In trying to reorganize their existence, they embraced previously unfamiliar religious traditions, social customs, and historical narratives. However, they were unable to fully overlook or eliminate the contextual effects of their non-Jewish heritage. Attempts by the "Judaizers"[51] to make them first Jews instead of first believers in Christ were misguided attempts to eliminate their Gentile way of tabernacling in the pursuit of Jewish "purity."[52] The social and personal standards of Christianity are similar yet distinct from those of Judaism.

Ultimately, the limitations of a person's context and living conditions will always shape their assumptions. This influences how an individual perceives and engages with the spiritual dimensions of life. For instance, consider how a person with materialistic beliefs sees the world and themselves differently from someone who adheres to spiritual truths. The former may pray solely for material success or stress relief, while the latter might pray for the grace to live righteously and the strength to endure

---

[51] A group of early Christians who believed that Gentile converts needed to strictly follow the Law of Moses to be considered true believers. The conflict between them and other Christians who did not believe this was necessary can be found in the first half of the book of Acts, specifically in Acts 15.
[52] Please recall our discussions on how a denial or erasure of contextualities and existentialisms are fruitless attempt at purity that deny the lived and God-given experiences that make us who we are.

> *Have you ever relinquished (or reframed) your way of living before?*
>
> *Did you believe you could entirely evade the impact of your previous living habits?*

persecution or suffering for Christ's sake. This does not imply that a person's context deterministically shapes their entire identity. The Gentile believers, after all, made a conscious choice to abandon or reinterpret parts of their original way of life. Our discussion implies that the 'horizon' of our dwelling shapes how we navigate the world in a 'befitting way.' We must acknowledge and cannot disregard these existential realities. Let us dive deeper into religious beliefs as cultural contextualities. Their impact on a perceived 'befitting' role within a person's world-house can, obviously, be significant. For instance, a person's notion of self-fittingness may take the form of faithful religious adherence, like Paul. Such a person seeks to *presence* themselves (to manifest their *becoming* to others) by piously holding on to the house-rules of a particular religion. However, this *presencing* of self-hood may not necessarily equate to *true* tabernacling, especially of the sort that the Divine finds appropriate.

Reflect on a Pharisee, like Paul, seeking to present himself as a righteous and true child of Abraham in the eyes of fellow Jews (Matt 3:9, 5:20, 23:2; Luke 16:14; John 7:24). The Pharisees in Jesus' time were known for their zealous adherence to laws and rituals. They did not eat until they had performed a ritual washing.[53] They frequently fasted. They held to strict

---

[53] As we read in Scirpture, "For the Pharisees and all the Jews do not eat unless they perform a ritual washing, holding fast to the tradition of the elders. And when they come from the marketplace, they do not eat unless they wash. They hold fast to many other traditions: the washing of cups, pots, kettles, and dining

interpretations of not working (even healing) on the Sabbath (Luke 6:7). They strove not to associate with 'unfitting' company (Luke 5:33). "When the Pharisees saw this, they said to His disciples, 'Why does your teacher eat with taxcollectors and sinners?'"(Matt 9:11).

Nevertheless, Christ stated that the Pharisees "[nullified] the word of God because of [their] tradition" (Matt 5:6). This means the Pharisees created their own version of righteous tabernacling, which overlooked "what was more important in the law – justice, mercy, and faithfulness" (Matt 23:23). These virtues, emphasizing inner faith rather than mere legalistic adherence as interpreted by their leaders, define proper tabernacling before God (Matt 5:6). Ultimately, the 'tabernacling' and fervor of the Pharisees, as noted by Jesus, were at best misguided, and at worst, were what Jesus labeled as "blind guides" (Matt 23:24). Jesus accused them of fundamentally distorting the faith of Abraham and Moses, misrepresenting both the God of the Torah and His expectations for human interactions.

> *How can you avoid allowing your traditions and ways of tabernacling to interfere with the type of tabernacling acceptable before God?*

If we recall our word study of 'tabernacling' we come back to the idea of residing and assuming roles according to a set of house rules. We can add the concept of presencing to these notions. This act resembles the becoming of a world-dweller but revolves around external actions. Rather than focusing on internal development within the mind and psyche, presencing addresses the manifestation of a person's becoming to the outside world.

---

couches.) The Pharisees and the experts in the law asked Him, 'Why do your disciples not live according to the tradition of the elders, but eat with unwashed hands'" (Mark 7:3-5).

For example, the typical American is a consumer living in a materialistic society. Therefore, they will likely present themselves as prosperous, trendy, and up to date with modern possessions and experiences. We see this in how people engage with their world, such as the activities they pursue, what they post on social media, the places they visit, and how they generally spend their time and money. Much of consumer society is, after all, about image-building (manifesting something to others or yourself) as much as (or even more than) it is about buying necessities. Just consider the advent of social media platforms and how people present (manifest) their identities and livelihoods on them.

Another illustration is the Japanese concept of *wa* or "harmony." In Japan, the standard way of tabernacling emphasizes peaceful unity and social conformity rather than individualism. As a result, a typical Japanese person tends to prioritize these social values over personal desires or interests. For instance, working "overtime" is often expected, where one puts the company's needs before their own. Similarly, traditional Japanese homes usually lack locks on doors, emphasizing openness to family over individual privacy. However, these practices often reflect external expectations rather than purely internal motivations. Additionally, the significance of "saving face" common in Eastern cultures highlighting this point. The recent backlash against these social norms by Japanese youth demonstrates that *presencing* is influenced as much by the environment as it is by personal development.

> *What contextual factors or standards of appropriateness influence how you present yourself to the world?*
>
> *How does awareness of this framework affect your thoughts and feelings about yourself and your place in society?*

Contextual factors, including laws, practices, and cultures, shape our perceptions of what is considered 'fitting'. We strive to meet these standards by adhering to household rules and adopting specific roles. Within this tabernacling framework, our presence in the world takes form. Thus, the unique contextual elements of a homeland and its *oikonomia* influence our perspectives and experiences in the world.

Contextualities such as cultural norms, beliefs, and traditions influence how we perceive the world. For example, people in America may struggle to overcome their contextual biases. Many Americans hold a materialistic view of human flourishing due to consumerism and capitalism worldview.[54] If an American were to visit a third-world country,[55] they might view it as ineffective in promoting the well-being of its citizens. Conversely, someone from a culture that prioritizes life enjoyment, familial honor, or being "one" with nature over material success may reach a different conclusion about human flourishing. For instance, Costa Rica ranks higher than the United States on the 2020 World Happiness Report despite being a "third-world country."

The peculiar nature of "Christian" world-living is often viewed as foreign compared to most social contexts globally, reminiscent of the ancient practices of Judaism. This disconnect created challenges for the evangelistic efforts of Paul and Silas in Philippi, identified as a "Roman colony" (Acts 16:12). Opponents of their ministry lodged a complaint with the civil authorities, stating: "These men are throwing our city into confusion. They are Jews and are advocating customs that are not lawful for us to accept or practice, since we are Romans" (Acts 16:20-21). This complaint

---

[54] Of course, this is not a prescriptive statement but a general descriptive one.
[55] This can be defined as a mostly unindustrialized country whose lower-class is much larger than its middle-class, and where modern-day luxuries, conveniences, services, and entertainment are not affordable or available to most of its population.

followed their exorcism of what they believed to be a demon or evil spirit from a girl, who was used as a fortune teller- someone her society regarded as blessed by the gods and fulfilling a significant role (Acts 16:16-19). This illustrates a clash of tabernacling paradigms.

The variations among tabernacles can lead to perspectives or lifestyles that conflict or even clash. This poses challenges for individuals to coexist. As a result, it is easier to perceive others as foreign, abnormal, or immoral. This issue has played a role in nearly every war, atrocity, and social conflict throughout human history. Even in our day, where people groups become dehumanized because of a divergence of worldviews and ways of living. Nevertheless, we can identify certain 'universal' themes across different cultures, such as the incest taboo, gender roles, the concept of marriage, and the criminalization of theft. Additionally, most individuals are social creatures who engage in various forms of communication. They share meals, drink, sleep, reproduce, appreciate art and music, experience emotions, and ponder essential existential questions like, "What is my/ our purpose? How did we come to be? What is right and wrong? What is the divine? What does the divine expect from us and how do we attain divine favor?"

> *Have you ever encountered contextualities that felt alien to you (through friends, travel, education, etc.)?*
>
> *How did you respond to them? Did you learn anything from these interactions, or did they change your point of view or lifestyle?*

Human Need for Purposeful Belonging and Acceptance

Why did God create human beings? Why did He make us as world-dwellers? This question represents a core focus of our quest to understand revealed mysteries. Firstly, we know that Yahweh made each of us to care for creation (Gen 1-2). He intended for every one of us to take on unique roles within the community as royal priests and members of the Body of Christ: The Temple of God in Creation (1 Cor 12:12-26, 1 Pet 2:9, Rev 1:6). Thus, within each person exists a deep-seated desire to find their rightful place in a tabernacle. We all yearn to experience a sense of purposeful belonging and communal solidarity. Without this sense of purpose, many individuals may spiral into feelings of shame, despair, depression, addiction, or even contemplate suicide. Scripture teaches that true purpose can only be discovered in the presence of the Creator, who has predetermined "the good works that [He] prepared beforehand so we may do them" (Eph 2:10). Additionally, a person's authentic theological identity aligns with this purposeful endeavor. This life purpose has been "predestined according to the one purpose of Him who accomplishes all things according to the counsel of His will" (Eph 1:11). One exemplary figure who fulfilled the good works God had planned for him was David, who "served God's purpose in his own generation" (Acts 13:36).

Have you ever sought purpose or fulfillment apart from God in your quest for social acceptance?

Did you achieve self-fulfilling purpose?

If so, what contributed to your success? If not, what were the obstacles?

The idea of world-fittingness inscribed on our hearts and minds also encompasses community. Our Creator designed us to live alongside other neighbors (Gen 2:18). We are inherently social beings. This concept is central to the second greatest commandment, which states: "Love your neighbor as yourself" (Lev 19:18; Matt 22:39; Gal 5:13-14). Many believe in Jesus but were not willing to suffer the social stigma associated with anyone who became a disciple of Jesus. Yahweh's original plan for neighborly cohabitation was meant to follow His established house rules and contextual guidelines, such as the Ten Commandments and the Law of Moses. As a result, we naturally seek companionship with others. This explains the powerful impact of peer pressure or family ties in all human societies. Pharisees who believed in Jesus, like Nicodemus, often refrained from public testimony due to their fear of peer rejection and expulsion from the synagogue, which stood at the core of all Jewish life (John 9:18-23; 12:42). Their longing for acceptance within their community led them to diverge from the affirmation found in Jesus Christ, "for they loved praise from people more than praise from God" (John 12:43). "They accept praise from one another [but] do not seek the praise that comes from the only God" (John 5:44). They forfeit divine community for the sake of preserving human community.

Our true purpose aligns with a community context. Consequently, we naturally desire recognition, respect, and appreciation from fellow members for our distinctive role in the world. For instance, consider the acknowledgment, support, and respect given to a father, soldier, and civic servant upon receiving a community service award at a social gathering. By fulfilling their respective roles, individuals aspire to gain recognition and validation as valuable, wanted, and irreplaceable members of

> *Do you have a community within which you feel valued and respected?*
>
> *Why do you think this is important even in a culture that values individualism?*

their respective households. The foundation of these emotions stems from our innate need for self-worth within the context of social affirmation.

At its height, the human desire for companionship and affirmation stirs up intentionality to become co-sharers of a proper home where communion flourishes. We see this in early human civilization after the worldwide flood: "When the people moved eastward, they found a plain in Shinar and settled there...Then they said, 'Come, let us build ourselves a city and a tower with its top in the heavens so that we may make a name for ourselves. Otherwise, we will be scattered across the face of the entire earth'" (Gen 11:2-4). We, as world-dwellers, tend to dwell in a way that fosters participation in a community.[56] Keeping the importance of communal unity in perspective, reflect on the following Scripture, "I urge you, brothers and sisters, by the name of our Lord Jesus Christ, to agree together, to end your divisions, and to be united by the same mind and purpose" (1 Cor 1:10). This leads us to conclude that an ideal societal environment is one where individuals have common house rules and shared perspectives. The early Corinthian church exemplified this for better or for worse.

As beings who thrive in community, we inherently strive for mutual understanding, recognition, and respect from others. This instinct exists even among those who see themselves as 'outsiders.' In seeking to resist societal norms, such individuals unite to advocate for shared interests or to feel a sense of belonging in

---

[56] Even scientists themselves cannot escape the subjective situation of being fellow associates. The scientific community itself is an outlet for this innate human subjective propensity. Referring to the mindset and profession rather than individual scientists everywhere. As mentioned in previous chapters, the "scientist" is the pursuer of objectivity and scientific categorization of life.

being counter-cultural "rebels" and proud of their "nonconformity". For instance, even the most unconventional punk rock bands, which champion non-conformity, still align with their collective beliefs, lifestyles, and values. They likely foster strong connections with fans who resonate with their perspectives. This behavior reflects humanity's intrinsic nature as social creatures. Many who do not feel they can ever achieve the high bar of common societal standards, such as beauty, success, athletic prowess, social influence, etc., turn to adopting opposing standards and loudly celebrate being "different."

Existential inclinations fundamentally shape our subjective perceptions and interactions within our environments. The earliest humans possessed a "common language and common vocabulary" (Gen 2-4, 11:1). This situation naturally fostered co-dwelling. However, their collective intent shifted toward a misguided and rebellious purpose, as they sought to construct the city of Babel to prevent being "scattered over the face of the whole earth," which is what God commanded (Gen 11:1-4). God easily disrupted this co-dwelling scenario by "confusing their language so that they would not be able to understand each other" (Gen 11:7-9). This story illustrates the co-dwelling issue hinges on a shared lens of subjectivity that influences a collective mode of existence, perception, and self-understanding. People rely on a common language and shared perspectives on life to create a society. In the case of Babel, they collectively aimed to pridefully elevate the glory of a singular human government

> *How do you believe your longing for companionship and connection could hinder your Creator's intentions for you?*
>
> *How can you prevent the outcome that befell those who constructed the Tower of Babel or those who believed but were not willing to follow Jesus?*

over God's intention to establish diverse nations, tribes, and communities (Gen 11:4).

Human Beings as Individual Tabernacles

Our life-path is guided by the teleological[57] bent of our world-dwelling. This bent represents the 'end-goal' that the house rules of an individual's dwelling aim to uphold or encourage. Consider, for example, the existential purpose of Christ's disciples. We strive to promote God's glory, expressed through *agape*-love, within our social environments (John 13:34-35). We seek God's will to be realized and His Kingdom to be manifest. Here, the end-goal of our relationship with God influences the criteria for communal fellowship, personal self-identification, and self-actualization.

One of the most profound divine mysteries is the revelation that God did not create humans merely as tabernacling beings. Instead, our Creator designed each of us to exist as a tabernacle, a dwelling for His own immanent presence (Rom 8:8-11; 1 Cor 6:19; 1 John 3:24, 4:13). The Spirit proclaims over every believer, "Do you not know that you are God's temple and that God's Spirit lives in you?" (1 Cor 3:16). In Christ, "the whole building, being joined together, grows into a holy temple in the Lord, in whom you also are being built together into a dwelling place of God in the Spirit" (Eph 2:21-22). This understanding of human existence signifies a radical shift from the prevailing notions of modern individualistic humanism and the emerging social collectivism driven by the State. We exist not for our own individual glory or that of the State but for the glory of our Creator.

---

[57] Teleosimply refers to speaking of things in terms of the purpose they serve rather than the cause by which they arise. What are the 'ends' of something? What purpose was it made to fulfill? A hammer was made to hit nails. Nails were made to connect pieces of wood together.

Keeping our true divine destiny in focus, we must reflect on the key element of a temple: the altar (Rom 8:9-16, 26-29; Rev 11:1). Traditionally, individuals offer both living and non-living sacrifices at the altar, following a specific set of religious guidelines (Lev 9:15-24). Followers of a religion engage in these sacrifices based on house rules derived from mythological or pseudo-historical narratives. These narratives explain why such offerings are fitting for human life. Some see them as a way to atone for personal or collective sins, while others believe they seek the favor of a deity for divine assistance. Scriptures illustrate that the connection between a temple, altar, and sacrifices reflects humanity's God-given role as a dwelling for His presence. As stated, "You yourselves, as living stones, are built up as a spiritual house [a temple] to be a holy priesthood and to offer spiritual sacrifices that are acceptable to God through Jesus Christ" (1 Pet 2:5). A comparable passage enhances the context of this discussion: "I exhort you… to present your bodies as a sacrifice – alive, holy, and pleasing to God – which is your reasonable service. Do not be conformed to this present world, but be transformed by the renewing of your mind, so that you may test and approve what is the will of God – what is good and well-pleasing and perfect" (Rom 12:1-2).

What does it mean to be a living temple of God's presence in your everyday life?

Fire plays a crucial role at a temple's altar. Just as fire exists in a temple, our lives embody personal sacrifice. Most house rules entail some level of self-denial, commitment, and dedication. Any environment one becomes part of comes with social obligations and expectations. Many require a type of zeal, passion, or devotion, often shown through devotion or sacrifice. For instance, consider the pride a solo virtuoso must set aside to harmonize in an orchestra, or how a top basketball player must embrace teamwork.

A relevant example for believers is found in the passage: "So if someone cleanses himself of such behavior, he [or she] will be a vessel for honorable use, set apart, useful for the Master, prepared for every good work. But keep away from youthful passions, and pursue righteousness, faithfulness, love, and peace, in company with others who call on the Lord from a pure heart" (2 Tim 2:21-22).

The sacrifices to fulfill our obligations can symbolize an 'inner flame of the soul.' This flame drives a person's commitment to a specific set of household rules. For example, a successful marriage requires each partner to daily prioritize the family's well-being over their own desires. The ultimate purpose of these house rules is to inform a person's life choices. For instance, observe the true motivation fueling Moses's decision at his pivotal moment between fit in within the tabernacle of Egyptian society or following God: "By faith, when he grew up, Moses refused to be called the son of Pharaoh's daughter, choosing rather to be ill-treated with the people of God than to enjoy sin's fleeting pleasure. He regarded abuse suffered for Christ to be greater wealth than the treasures of Egypt, for his eyes were fixed on the reward" (Heb 11:24-26).

What house rules do you follow?

What sacrifices are necessary for you to uphold them?

Is the ultimate objective of these house rules consistent with the Creator's vision for your life?

In contrast to a sacred passion, think about the destructive flames of selfish ambition or vanity linked to the house rules of consumerism. Earn money and spend it on luxury and entertainment. Discover ways to maximize profits to acquire a new car, a boat, or a larger home. Ascend the corporate ladder, even if it means working extra hours, or pushing colleagues down to rise to the top. Choose your college major and career purely based on what promises the highest salary. Build friendships only for the sake of 'useful connections' that advance your self-interest. Forego time with family to get a promotion to win in the "rat race." Accumulate wealth, indulge in the material comforts of life, and eventually retire in ease.

The ancient 'altars' of Babel celebrated the shared glory of humanity or particular worldly leaders. In contrast, most modern 'altars' are often erected to honor an individual or a culture. Regardless, when created beings establish their own *oikonomia* in the place of the Creator, it amounts to idolatry driven by a desire for a human-centered approach to glory.[58] While idolatry is commonly seen as overt paganism, it can manifest in subtler ways. Greed, materialism, celebrity worship, nationalism, and consumerism can replace the ancient polytheistic deities (Col 3:5). Whenever someone's ultimate aim lies outside of and contradicts their God-relationship, their existence shifts from being a temple of the Creator to created realities.

The presupposed *telos* of a specific *oikonomia* influences an individual's life aspirations. These aspirations revolve around the criteria and objectives that individuals deem necessary for a fulfilling life. They offer both purpose and direction for one's existence. In essence, we are beings designed to ardently support a world-focused *oikonomia*. This alignment signifies the unique existential commitment of the occupants. These allegiances can include materialism, sensual pleasure, civic altruism, religious affiliations, human

> *The ideal you devote yourself to says a lot about where your allegiances lie.*
>
> *Is it with money? God? Yourself? America? Socialism? Science? The Earth?*

---

[58] We will dive deeper into this theme in the future.

glory, scientific enterprises, the arts, environmentalism, fame and fortune, and many others.

Existential allegiances define[59] the larger world-dwelling tabernacle that *is* human existence. They shape how one views and relates to the specific dwelling-place where they choose to tabernacle.[60] For instance, allegiance to the contemporary world-dwelling criterion of the American Dream can lead a world-dweller to worship at the altars of money, worldly advantage, comfort, self-sufficiency, consumerism, and individualism. Such co-dwelling allegiance may, at times, manifest itself through altruistic humanism. This collectivism occurs when fellow co-dwellers exist as joint heirs, promoting a self-serving lifestyle in a community setting. They do so as part of a broader home-making agenda conformed to the finite contextualities of American social institutions.[61]

---

[59] Think banners plastered or flags hanging outside a house, a common sight in many American suburbs.

[60] Recall our definitions of the word 'tabernacling' previously, and how they all related to the idea of settling down and occupying a place as a resident.

[61] To illustrate this home-making aspect of the American Dream, consider how each family member pursues their individual interests: Dad enjoys watching sports and reading the newspaper; the boy plays video games and reads comics; the girl focuses on fashion, celebrities, and music stars; while the mother watches soap operas and Oprah, paying attention to home decor and celebrity gossip.

Such household dynamics involving parental and societal influences inevitably shape the loyalties of those living and growing up in these environments. Here, the focus shifts toward an "I want" mentality, with self-centered activities consuming personal time. This results in a neglect of investing time and effort into promoting the well-being of others, prioritizing more meaningful, spiritual pursuits.

Given this typical structure of American household *oikonomia*, we should reflect on the following Scripture that will be explored in this chapter: "Do not love the world or the things in the world. If anyone loves the world, the love of the Father is not in him [or her], because all that is in the world (the desire

Let us compare this world of individualism with one that values a higher allegiance, such as civic altruism. Such an individual may find their sense of belonging rooted in what enhances their household's flourishing. For example, civic motives could prioritize the well-being and preservation of a specific community over individual success and recognition. They might view their vocation as a politician or civil servant dedicated to making society safer, more loyal, or fairer. They accomplish this by establishing and advocating for a set of house rules designed to benefit the common good.

How Historicity & Storytelling Shape Wayfinding

To summarize this chapter, the contextual environment we inhabit serves as our existential realm. Each realm encompasses a broader idea of 'fittingness' that influences our perspective. The collection of contextual teleological (or 'goal-oriented') schemas we embrace also inform this worldview and our self-perception. Our commitment to these principles and goals dictates the house rules that guide how we 'properly' occupy our contextual space. Thus far, this understanding is solid. However, we need to incorporate how the sense of historicity influences our habitation.

Consider how the evolutionary narrative shapes the concept of appropriateness for living beings in the world. One might perceive their surroundings through a teleological lens focusing on survival of the 'fittest'. Within this perspective, all organisms adapt based on environmental influences, prioritizing adaptation and survival as their ultimate objectives. The criterion for 'appropriateness' lies in a creature's ability to fulfill this goal. The historical context of

---

of the flesh and the desire of the eyes and the arrogance produced by material possessions) is not from the Father, but is from the world. And the world is passing away with all its desires, but the person who does the will of God remains forever" (1 John 2:15-17).

natural selection and its ongoing impact on life today lend this perspective a sense of historical depth. It is an unavoidable reality for all creatures residing on Earth. Followers of this view interpret the human condition in this light, particularly in their understanding of psychology, sociology, and species preservation.

Our self-view of proper homemaking bears the mark of a particular historicity. For instance, consider how the history of America's pursuit of independence and individual rights has shaped the American Dream and Americans' self-view.[62] In contrast, consider how Japan's history of Confucian influence, Buddhist values of impermanence and transience, and post-World War II history[63] have shaped Japan's more communitarian self-view and ancestral loyalty.

> What historicity of 'proper' homemaking have you adopted?
>
> Do you think it should be updated at all?

Historicity for human world-dwellers typically assumes a narrative form. For this reason, cultural traditions, biographies, history, records, and the ways we tell stories about the past are central to us as social creatures. They evoke loyalty and strengthen our existential allegiances, whether familial, national, or religious.[64]

---

[62] In addition, America's lack of a feudal history and deeply entrenched social structures meant that liberal democracy with all its assumptions on human life were the central foundation of social thought in the country. Combine this lack of a historical social structure with a broad expansion of human right, and an expansive land with seemingly unlimited resources, and you get unbridled optimism along with an extremely strong sense of individualism. This is just another example of how historical factors can greatly influence the cultural world-viewing and world-dwelling of an entire society.

[63] They perceived putting the community first as a sacrificial duty to raise the collective living standards of all Japanese during the postwar years.

[64] Think of how "shared history" is so important for a national consciousness (like how India's collective identity was built by resistance to British

This sense of historicity consistently shapes a household's concept of social acceptability. Furthermore, historicity explains how narratives influence the teleological frameworks of households. Accompanying these house rules are storylines that recount the origins of a culture, country, religion, or the world. These stories not only justify the house rules but also nurture a deeper existential and practical regard for them.

Let us once again use America as an example. The historical paradigm of the American Revolution has influenced how many Americans see and interact with the world around them. For some, living by the house rules of American exceptionalism means believing that America's origins as a nation consciously founded on the 'universal' (God-given) principles of liberty, individual freedom, and individual ownership make it unique in the history of the world.[65] Furthermore, some Americans believe that this unique status gives them a mission to preserve and promote the ideals of democracy and individual liberty throughout the world.[66]

Even scientists inevitably participate in storytelling and cultural historicity. No matter how hard some of them try, they cannot escape the subjectivity of their existential allegiance to the oikonomia of a household's presuppositions. Just ponder the

---

imperialism), or how a shared set of historical stories, and perspectives on the past is so important for a religious community (like the Fall of Man, the Exodus, or the Crucifixion of Christ).

[65] The Declaration of Independence's assertion that the truths of equality and unalienable rights are "self-evident" appeals to the universal nature of their values according to reason. They espouse that such founding principles are the objective truths of humanity. This has the implicit assumption that it is possible, and indeed preferable, for other cultures, peoples, and nations to replicate these values in their own countries.

[66] This teleological schema involves promoting domestic and foreign democracy, protecting individual freedoms and rights established in the Constitution, and remembering the sacrifices of previous Americans who died in the service of freedom and liberty.

overwhelming number of a-theistic narratives they employ to account for the existence and arrangement of the world. Science was not always this consciously opposed to theism, as significant figures like Galileo,[67] Kepler, Leibniz, Newton, and Faraday were all devout theists. At the very least, none of them saw the denial of theism (i.e., Creationism) as a prerequisite for 'proper' science. Only post-Darwinian[68] scientific thought sought to provide a reasonable explanation of the world's origins in conscious opposition to theism. Consequently, a-theistic and secular presuppositions underlie the modern scientific household's *oikonomia* and culture.

Numerous scientists and behavioral specialists interpret the meaning of human existence based on a-theism. They base their conclusions on a perceived alignment within the broader context of biological evolution. Their historical context and underlying assumptions shape their perspectives on human morality, appropriateness, and worth. Consequently, they often regard humans merely as advanced animals made up solely of physical matter. This worldview can lead to

{ *What ideas or worldviews seem 'universal' but might be based on a certain a-theistic historicity?*

How might these worldviews have influenced your world-dwelling? }

---

[67] Who, despite his entanglements with the Catholic Church, remained a devout Catholic until his death.
[68] Referring to the scientific thought that arose directly or indirectly from Darwin's *Origin of Species*, the foundational work of evolutionary science. Many consider this the point where science severed itself from notions of "creation" and started on a path towards hostility with theism and religious belief.

a society that emphasizes sensual pleasure and the physical world.[69]

This perspective, naturally, dismisses the existence of spiritual realities or higher truths. In regions where this viewpoint dominates, many individuals place excessive importance on physical gratification and fleeting successes. Food, drink, sex, material wealth, advanced technical skills, numerical value, and physical resourcefulness become the only objectives or measures of human life. People's self-perception and domestic lives are molded by house rules based on naturalistic assumptions. This is largely due to the specific historical context of this perspective.

Storytelling helps to impose order on the perceived chaos within a specific context. Our core stories offer meaning, purpose, and explanations that shape our worldview. This overarching narrative serves as a backdrop for societal sub-contexts and personal stories, imparting their thematic structure and importance.

Historicity can inspire and motivate those within world-dwelling households to do their part in their respective contexts. For example, consider how some people in America join the armed

---

[69] Conversely, consider someone who sees it as their mission to facilitate the next phase of human evolution or to usher in a higher life-form destined to succeed humanity, viewing human extinction as a prerequisite. The irony lies in the fact that the evolutionary model posits that evolution is a gradual, natural process that occurs independently- without needing human intervention. Therefore, it seems contradictory for them to wish to catalyze a process that evolution, by its nature, does not require intelligence to drive, unlike the concepts presented in theistic evolution and creationism.

On the flip side, there are scientists who deem extinction as negative and thus strive to prevent a species from becoming extinct, particularly in cases where humans are not the direct cause of the threat. One might question these scientists about their reasoning, as their stance seems at odds with their professed belief in the evolutionary theory that predicates survival of the fittest on the inevitability of extinction. Furthermore, according to the historical narrative of evolution, did not the development of more advanced species lead to the extinction of others?

forces to protect the American Dream or the 'American Way.' In fact, "safeguarding liberty" seems to be a big justification for recent military actions taken by the United States.

All that we have discussed indicates that humans cannot evade the subjective essence of our existence. This subjectivity molds our understanding of what is considered normatively 'appropriate'. Parameters of world-dwelling are based on social presuppositions[70] and shape a society's contextualities.[71] Generally, contextual factors like language and communication rules shape these presuppositions. An open-minded person should question the origins of their perceived world-dwelling house rules and their understanding of appropriateness. Furthermore, we should examine the reliability of the associated biases and narrative historicity that support these house rules. All in all, they shape our lives into a tabernacle.

Truth-seekers aboard the vessel Faith Seeking Understanding should question if the societal assumptions, worldviews, and lifestyles we inherit align with or oppose the revealed truths of our Creator. As we will explore in the next chapter, existential rebellion is prevalent in this fallen world. Here, contextualized myths about created beings, based on partial truths, often distort a person's *oikonomia*, worldview, and world-dwelling in an idolatrous way. Thus, the key existential concern about how an individual

---

[70] Examples of such presuppositions are the belief that people exist to promote the ends of state, mutual communal benefit, or personal self-fulfilling happiness.

[71] Contextualities of a given society include education, the media, the government, the entertainment industry, and many other socio-cultural institutions.

Meanwhile, examples of such social presuppositions include the belief that people exist to promote the ends of state, mutual communal benefit, or personal self-fulfilling happiness.

perceives their self-actualization or sense of belonging hinges on how they answer these questions: "Who defines the assumptions of this existential paradigm? The Creator? Or the created?" After resolving this question, we should consider, "Who should truly establish my life? Who understands how my life should unfold from a super-contextual perspective?" With our self-concept in focus, we should ultimately reflect on, "Who is the author of my true identity and the roles I should fulfill within the household of finitude?" By answering these questions, we come to terms with whether we truly have become a tabernacle of the God-relationship.

> *Will you allow these lessons regarding the subjective nature of our existence (like fittingness, house rules, and end goals) to influence your own life?*
>
> *Will you deeply reflect on whether the cultural perspectives and lifestyles you embrace show loyalty or defiance toward God?*

Chapter 4
Living in Babel
World-Systems Influenced by Spirits of Darkness

"The *earth is defiled by its inhabitants*, for they have *disregarded the regulations*... So a *curse devours the earth*... This is why the inhabitants of the earth disappear[, because] they are a *rebellious house*. They have eyes to see, *but do not see*, and ears to hear, but *do not hear*."
(Ps 78:55-56; Isa 24:5-6; Ezek 12:2)

"*Babylon the Great*, the Mother of prostitutes and of the *detestable things of the earth*... She has become a *lair for demons*... All the nations have *fallen* from the wine of her *immoral passion*... She *exalted herself* and lived in *sensual luxury*... She has *proudly defied* Me, the Holy One."
(Rev 14:8, 17:5, 18:2-7; Isa 21:9; Jer 50:29)

"*The whole world lies in the power of the Evil One*... All that is in the world (the desire of the flesh and the desire of the eyes and the arrogance produced by material possessions) is not from the Father, but is from the world. *And the world is passing away with all its desires*... Idolaters will not inherit the kingdom of God."
(1 John 2:16-17, 4:5, 5:19-21; 1 Cor 6:10)

"You formerly lived according to this *world's present path*, according to the *Ruler of the kingdom of the air*, the Ruler of the spirit that is now *energizing the [children] of disobedience*... [You were] *darkened* in [your] understanding, being *alienated* from the life of God because of the *ignorance* that [was] in [you] due to the *hardness* of [your] hearts..."
(Eph 2:1-3; 4:17-18; 5:6-8)

Intro: How Fallen Beings Try to Usurp the Creator's Vision

"All things in heaven and on earth were created in [the Son] – all things, whether visible or invisible, whether thrones or dominions, whether principalities or powers – all things were created through Him and for Him" (Col 1:16-17). In His infinite wisdom, Yahweh (the true Story-Writer of Finitude) does not share the glories of establishing the *oikoumene, oikonomia,* and *historicity*[72] of the household of Finitude with anyone (Isa 45:9-13; Job 36-42). He alone is the rightful Potter of Finitude, as we read: "Your thinking is perverse! Should the potter be regarded as clay? Should the thing made say about its maker, 'He did not make me'? Or should the pottery say about the potter, 'He does not understand?'" (Isa 29:16, 64:8). He alone occupies the unique requirements necessary to truly author and enact an eternal narrative (Acts 17:24-26). As He declares, "The heavens are My throne and the earth is My footstool" (Isa 66:1). As we have witnessed, Yahweh has chosen to collaborate with finite beings to manage the world (Gen 2:4, 15, 19-20; 1 Cor 3:9). However, our Creator wisely retains the authority to establish and uphold the household rules of Eternity (Gen 1; John 1:1-3; Heb 1:3; Rev 3:14). Finite beings cannot create world-shaping contextualities that align with those set by the Infinite Creator. Only from the Creator's omniscient, supracontextual perspective can eternal contextualities and their corresponding *oikonomia* be birthed, shaped, and established (Jer 10:12, 16; Job 37:16, 38:4;

What do you envision co-managing or co-writing with the Creator to look like in your life?

How have your recent experiences reflected this?

---

[72] Recall our previous discussions about these terms. *Oikoumene* (world-house), *oikonomia* (house-rules), and *historicity* (how house-rules are based in and shaped by historical contextualities and factors).

Rom 1:20). As we read, "The Creator of the whole earth. He does not get tired or weary; there is no limit to His wisdom" (Isa 40:28) Accordingly, this chapter will explore the consequences of fallen humanity's attempts to reject God's narrative in favor of their own idolatrous substitutes, such as humanism, egocentrism, and materialism.

Yahweh did not mean that the creative storytelling abilities of earthly beings would dictate Finitude as a whole. Instead, God grants us the privilege to collaborate in alignment with His will and Spirit. Rethinking God's thoughts as He intends is permitted and encouraged (Job 32:8, 38:36; Ps 51:6; Prov 2:6; Eccl 2:26):

> "For this reason we also, from the day we heard about you, have not ceased praying for you and asking God to fill you with the knowledge of His will in all spiritual wisdom and understanding, so that you may live worthily of the Lord and please Him in all respects—bearing fruit in every good deed, growing in the knowledge of God, being strengthened with all power according to His glorious might for the display of all patience and steadfastness, joyfully giving thanks to the Father who has qualified you to share in the saints' inheritance in the light. He delivered us from the power of darkness and transferred us to the kingdom of the Son He loves."
>
> (Col 1:9-13)

Yahweh invites us to engage in stewardship alongside Him. He designed us to be "ruling priests," representing and embodying the will of the one true Creator (1 Pet 2:9; 1 Cor 4:1-2; Col 1:25; Tit

1:7). Scripture tells us, "Just as each one has received a gift, use it to serve one another as good stewards of the varied grace of God, as a holy priesthood. Whoever speaks, let it be with God's words. Whoever serves, do so with the strength that God supplies, so that God will be glorified through Jesus Christ. To Him belong the glory and the power forever and ever" (1 Pet 2:9, 4:10-11).

For an example of co-composing creativity inspired by the Creator's Spirit, consider the following passage:

> "[Yahweh] filled [Bezalel] with the Spirit of God – with skill, with understanding, with knowledge, and in all kinds of work, to design artistic designs, to work in gold, in silver, and in bronze, and in cutting stones for their setting, and in cutting wood, to do work in every artistic craft... So, Bezalel and every skilled person in whom the Lord has put skill and ability to know how to do all the work for the service of the sanctuary are to do the work according to all that the Lord has commanded."
>
> (Exod 35:30-33, 36:1; See also Exod 35:34-36:4)

Have you ever felt tempted to create your own story separate from the Creator's narrative?

How did you attempt this, and what were the outcomes?

When we utilize our creativity and talents to promote the will, plan, and vision of the Creator, we use these God-given gifts as they were meant to be used. This divinely inspired effort is crucial to His grand narrative. However, humanity has largely turned away from our Creator's original intentions. This defiance against supercontextual governance leads to lives shaped by countless narratives created solely by the 'creativity' of beings separated from divine influence and support.

Rebellious humans seek to establish, propagate, or maintain "Babylonian" world-systems.[73] In doing so, human rulers attempt to bring providential sovereignty to earth. They firmly refuse to accept the revealed truths of the Creator's pre-written story. In the Book of Revelation, such rebellious world-systems are equated with "Babylon," for they "proudly defy [the Creator's will and providence]" (Jer 50:29; Rev 18). These world-systems promote spiritual "prostitution" and "immoral passion." Babylonian world-dwellers exalt in human-centered pleasures as the purpose of life.[74] In fact, the Bible points out that those who make themselves at home in "Babylon… have sins piled up all the way to the heavens" (Rev 17:5, 18:2-24).

People who construct external or internal "Babylons" mistakenly strive to become 'objective' (supra-contextual) judges of contextual truth and morality. They think these contextual factors should influence the world-houses where humanity resides, as well as the constructed environment. As a result, they do not

---

[73] Babylon in the Bible, e.g. the books of Isaiah, Jeremiah, and Revelation, is often used as an image or symbol of the fallen human world-system. Rich and powerful, but corrupt and decadent as well.

[74] It is essential to differentiate between those labeled as "Babylonian world-dwellers" and those merely existing in the world without being predominantly influenced by it. While we all inhabit a fallen world and navigate it for survival, "Babylonian world-dwellers" refers to individuals who embrace the immoral desires and corrupted norms of Babylon as their guiding principles, shaping their identities. These individuals align themselves with Satan's kingdom instead of Christ's Kingdom. Of those forsaking Babylonian world-dwelling, Hebrews states: "They all died in faith without receiving the things promised, but they saw them in the distance and welcomed them and acknowledged that they were strangers and foreigners on the earth. For those who speak in such a way make it clear that they are seeking a homeland. In fact, if they had been thinking of the land that they had left, they would have had opportunity to return. But as it is, they aspire to a better land, that is, a heavenly one. Therefore, God is not ashamed to be called their God, for he has prepared a city for them" (Heb 11:13-16).

seek the wisdom found in the Creator's contextualities, including the house blueprint, house rules, and house arrangement, but rather rebelliously substitute them with their own.

Existential Rebellion: Rejecting Yahweh's Providence

"Land-dwellers" have built inland academies[75] for thousands of years. In them, people pridefully seek to write new house-shaping *historicity* and *oikonomia* instead of humbly and meekly acknowledging those established by the Creator. The most explicitly humanistic academies advocate for worldviews influenced by self-centered desires and a-theistic perspectives, driven by their hardened hearts. This approach alienates them from the God-relationship (Eph 4:17-18). "Like them, you were dead in your offenses and sins, in which you formerly lived according to this world's present path, according to… the ruler of the spirit that is now energizing the [children] of disobedience… indulging the desires of the flesh and the mind" (Eph 2:2-4). These educational systems nurture citizens who embrace secular or pagan ways of living and thinking. In essence, they propose an *oikonomia* where what the Creator intended "wrong" is redefined as "right" and vise versa (Isa 5:20; Rom 1:32).

Humanity's attempt to rewrite Finitude's *oikonomia* aims to reshape our views on human life's origins, ethics, and significance. Consider the prevalent belief that humans merely exist as physical beings, similar to animals, where true happiness can only be achieved by fulfilling our material and psychological needs. We frequently see advertisements suggesting that happiness depends

---

[75] As opposed to the "Sea of Revelation". We can think of land as limited temporality, and the ocean as eternity. Like the land and ocean on earth, we might think temporality is the defining characteristic of everything, but the reality is that the land exists within the ocean, not the other way around. Temporality, in the same way, is a small and tiny thing amidst the ocean of God's eternity.

on drinking a Coke, enjoying a movie, driving a new car, resting in a better bed, taking drugs, or enhancing our romantic lives. This perspective aligns with the idea encapsulated in the saying, "Eat, drink, and be merry, for tomorrow we die" (1 Cor 15:32). While it is true that material blessings are divine gifts, prioritizing them as the ultimate goals of existence over the soulful and spiritual goods derived from relationships and divine duty, especially our connection with God, transforms them into idols – much like the wise and wealthy King Solomon discovered (1 Cor 6:9-10, 6:13; Eccl 2:24, 3:12-13; Col 3:5).

> *What are some otherwise positive goals of creation that may have turned into "idols" for you?*
>
> *What have you possibly permitted to replace the primacy of the God-Relationship?*

As human beings, our fundamental roles involve following, supporting, and engaging in the Creator's *oikonomia* - much like musicians adhering to a conductor. For Adam and Eve, this meant caring for the garden and animals while freely enjoying the garden's fruits for sustenance, except for the tree of the knowledge of good and evil (Gen 2:15-17). However, through deception and their shortcomings regarding faith, trust, and devotion to the Creator, our first parents neglected their full dedication to their designated roles. They chose to forgo an eternal destiny, opting instead to craft their own life narratives. They decided to determine good and evil on their terms and to independently become like God. They aspired to be temples of humanity instead of Divinity. Figuratively, they opted to perform their own music, separate from the composer and conductor intentions.[76] They willingly accepted a different vision for how their worldview and living environment should be shaped.

By striving to become more like God than He originally intended, we risk losing our eternal destiny. This "earthbound" perspective prevents us from perceiving the world through the lens of eternal truths. Yet, many seek 'objectivity' and 'autonomy' aspiring to be our own 'gods.' We desire to determine what is best for ourselves, for others, and for the world. Ironically, this mindset is what led to the Fall initially, as noted in Scripture concerning the Original Rebel:[77] "Look how you have fallen from the sky, O shining one, son of the dawn! You have been cut down to the ground, O conqueror of the nations! You said to yourself, 'I will climb up to the sky. Above

> *What might inspire you to craft your story instead of adhering to the Creator's narrative?*
>
> *If you have how did that work out?*

---

[76] For a masterful artistic depiction of this, read the *Ainulindale* by J.R.R. Tolkien, where he depicts the fictional creation story of Middle earth. In this short story, creation is depicted as the music of a heavenly orchestra, with "God" as the conductor. The "devil" [Melkor/Morgoth] rebels against "God" by forcefully introducing his own "melody" into the symphony (think some of the musical compositions of Wagner). His brash, loud, and "vain" music ends up clashing with the beautiful harmony that the rest of the heavenly beings are following.

As the music goes on, more and more heavenly beings choose to follow the music of the "devil" rather than of "God." In the end, these beings become "fallen angels", as they chose to play a different tune than the one God had intended for them. The discord within the music that the rebellious "angels" had introduced ends up becoming evil, sin, and suffering in creation.

As a devout Catholic, it's obvious that Tolkien drew from biblical and Christian themes and ideas to inform his own fantasy world, and this can clearly be seen in his Middle-earth creation story.

[77] This, of course, refers to Lucifer. We will discuss his role in things later in this chapter.

the stars of El (God) I will set up my throne. I will rule on the mountain of assembly on the remote slopes of Zaphon. I will climb up to the tops of the clouds; I will make myself like the Most High'" (Isa 14:12-14). All of the "towers of babel" humans erect pattern themselves off Lucifer's attempt to commandeer sovereignty.

Many individuals rigidly adhere to half-truths, fictions, and illusions in their lives. Their dependence on these worldly contextual factors leads their quest for self-knowledge and understanding of the world to be rooted in the temporary rather than the eternal. This journey toward self-enlightenment often involves an existential rebellion. For instance, consider the well-known motto "write your own story,"[78] or its alternative, "let the world around you write your story." Yet, these frameworks are misleading, since they ultimately stem from the false light propogated by spiritual forces of darkness, as they lead people down the "wide path to perdition" (Matt 7:13). They orchestrate and promote existential rebellion. There is but one true Story-Writer who can provide genuine, everlasting purpose within the Narrative of Finitude. He crafted this eternal tale even before He laid the foundation of the wolrd. Only He can grant us a lasting home free from the illusions and deceptions of temporality's mirages.

The "Babylonian" (or worldly) view of self-fittingness stems from contexts that solely prioritize the glorification of creation. This perspective inherently involves a stubborn rebellion against the sole true Providential Sovereignty of the Infinitely Existing

---

[78] I personally attended a Christian university that explicitly used this motto to inspire current and potential students.

> *What are some half-truths, illusions, or temporal contextualities that have shaped (or still tend to shape) your world-dwelling?*

One (Dan 7:13-14; Ps 97:9). Those who engage in this rebellion forfeit the eternal contexts outlined by the Creator's Vision for Finitude. Just recall how many exhibits of the wonders of Creation pay no respect to the Creator. He grants eternal existence only to those devoted to the ideals and purpose of the Kingdom of Heaven. To remain committed to the Creator, we must elevate His glory above all else. This is made explicit in Scripture: "To the only God our Savior through Jesus Christ our Lord, be glory, majesty, power, and authority, before all time, and now, and for all eternity" (Jude 1:25). As the true and proper Establisher of correct world-shaping and dwelling, He certainly merits all glory (Gen 1; Deut 32:6).

We should reflect on the following proclamation in our guide whenever the Father of Lies tempts us with existential rebellion:

> "You must acknowledge the greatness of our God. As for the Rock, His work is perfect, for all His ways are just. He is a reliable God who is never unjust, He is fair and upright. His people have been unfaithful to Him; they have not acted like His children – this is their sin. They are a perverse and deceitful generation. Is this how you repay the Lord, you foolish, unwise people? Is He not your Father, your Creator? He has made you and established you... The Most High gave the nations their inheritance, when He divided up humankind, He set the boundaries of the peoples, according to the number of the heavenly assembly. For the Lord's allotment is His people, Jacob is His special possession."
>
> (Deut 32:3-9)

Only Yahweh holds a super-contextual relation to the entire created universe. Any other attempts to construct a world lead to a fleeting illusion- an idolatrous existence built on unstable ground (Deut 30:17-18; Matt 7:13). Like the house built on sand in Jesus' parable, these efforts will ultimately collapse (Matt 7:26-27). Only the Creator can grant a finite being a proper place within an eternal universe (Deut 30:15-20; John 14:2; Heb 11:10, 16, 12:22). He alone possesses the skill to be the Architect of Eternity (Isa 65:17, 66:22; Heb 11:10). By adhering to His design, we can establish the "house" of our life on a solid foundation that will endure forever.

> *What steps will you take to abandon "Babylonian" notions of self-sufficiency and fully embrace the Creator as the Architect of Eternity, including your true destiny?*

Idolatry: The Foundation of all Existential Rebellion

At the core of existential rebellion lies a denial of the God-relationship. More precisely, rebellious individuals strive to substitute the appropriate reality of submission to God with independence and world-shaping alternatives. These alternatives manifest either through intra-personal realization (seeking purpose within us) or inter-personal realization (seeking purpose in our relations with others and society). In other words, one opts to live for oneself or for each other instead of the Creator.

Reflecting on our earlier conversations regarding the formation of world-systems and paradigms, we can comprehend how beings engage in this form of "rebellion." Essentially, it takes place through an a-theistic paradigm that shapes the world without God's grace. This world-system is constructed on a forbidden foundation of temporal contextualities.[79] People navigate their lives through contextual factors shaped by assumptions about fittingness, often influenced by the will of created entities rather than the Creator's will. These assumptions reflect a form of idolatrous allegiance. They lead individuals to worship at the altars of various created commitments, such as personal glory, sensual gratification, national pride, social loyalty, religious traditions, or other transient affiliations.

Idolatry extends beyond simply bowing down and worshiping another being or image instead of the one true God. It occurs when a self-conscious being's criterion and *telos* (final purpose) become 'possessed' by created realities. The Creator designed our existence and perspective to be fundamentally guided by communion, devotion, and faith in Him and His vision. This communion in our Relationship with God represents the original tˆelos and criterion of our participation in Finitude. This essential understanding of idolatry aligns with the biblical narrative. In the subsequent passages, God illustrates how idolatry is deeply rooted in a rebellion, marked by devotion and service to created entities:

> "When you look up to the sky and see the sun, moon, and stars – the whole heavenly creation – you must *not be seduced to worship and serve them*, for the Lord your God has assigned them to all the people of the world… *You*, however, the Lord has *selected* and brought from Egypt, that iron-smelting furnace, *to be His special people* [possession] *as* you are today… Be on guard so that you do not forget the *covenant of the Lord your God* that He has made with you… The

---

[79] Prohibited in this case meaning forbidden by God as a fitting foundation for world-systems. Examples of these forbidden foundations are a-theistic humanism, consumeristic materialism, or self-seeking narcissism.

Lord your God is a consuming fire; He is a jealous God."

(Deut 4:19-20, 23-24)

"[False prophets will say to you,] 'Let us follow other gods' – gods whom you have not previously known – *'and let us serve them.'* You must not listen to the words of that prophet or dreamer, for the Lord your God will be *testing you to see if you love Him* with all your mind and being. *You must follow the Lord your God and revere only Him; and you must observe His commandments, obey Him, serve Him, and remain loyal to Him.*"

(Deut 13:2-4)

"They exchanged the truth of God for a lie and worshiped [venerated] and *served the creation [created things/ creatures]* rather than the Creator, who is blessed forever."

(Rom 1:25)

> *What lesser loves might you be chasing in your life?*
>
> *How will you hold yourself accountable to ensure love for your Creator, rather than for the created, primarily influences your existence in the world?*

Origins of Existential Rebellion

So, who is the mastermind existential rebellion? Human beings do indeed serve as co-formers, influencers, and priestly agents within these world systems. Even so, we are not the masterminds behind the philosophies of this age despite the assumptions proferred by the human egos.[80] According to Scripture, the main mastermind behind all world-systems of temporality is "the ruler (*archon*)[81] of the kingdom (*exousia*)[82] of the air," "the ruler of the spirit now energizing the sons of disobedience," "the ruler (*archon*) of this world," "for the whole world lies in the power of the Evil One" (Eph 2:2; John 12:31, 14:30; 1 John 5:19). Many bad theologies fail to adequately take into account these revealed truths.

Of *the* Evil One we read, "This is the one who made the world like a desert, who ruined its cities, and refused to free his prisoners so they could return home" (Isa 14:16-17). "[He is] The thief [who] comes only to steal and kill and destroy (John 10:10).[83] He was the one who said to Jesus Christ, "To you I will grant this whole realm [the kingdoms of the fallen world] – and the glory that goes along with it, for it has been relinquished to me, and I can give it to anyone I wish. So then, if you will worship me, all this will be yours" (Luke 4:5-7). Satan has successfully tempted world leaders among each generation with the same temptation He offered to Jesus:

{ *How does identifying and naming the mastermind behind existential rebellion change how you view the world and your life story?* }

---

[80] The philosopher refererred to this driving force as a "Spirit of the Age(s)," but he failed to understand the sinister forces at work behind this "spirit". However, he correctly understood that forces behind the minds of philosophers were at working in crafting the ideologies of their present age, in such a way that many would convey similar "new" ideas with total ignorance of one another.

[81] The Greek word "*archon*" refers to "the first in rank or power; one who has eminence in a ruling capacity, as a ruler, lord, or prince; of transcendent figures, evil spirits whose hierarchies resembled human political institutions" (BDAG 140; ISA).

[82] Here the Greek word "*exousia*" should be understood to represent "the sphere in which power is exercised, domain, jurisdiction" (BDAG, 353).

[83] See also Matt 13:28, 38-39.

world power *if* they bowed to him, whether consciously or unconsciously.

The grand illusionist, known as the "Father of Lies," does not single-handedly control the world systems. Many others also strive to mislead humanity. Satan governs a hierarchy of world shapers who assist him. These malevolent forces aim to keep us living as prodigals, resisting repentance and seeking a way to return home. They devise, spread, and uphold the temporal world systems that deceive all people (Matt 4:8-9; John 8:44; 2 Cor 11:14; Eph 6:11-12; Rev 12:9). Our Creator highlights their actions in the following scripture: "Stand against the schemes of the devil. For our struggle is not against flesh and blood, but against the rulers [principalities], against the powers, against the world rulers [system-holders] of this darkness, against the spiritual forces of evil in the heavens" (Eph 6:11-12; ISA).

The Creator instructs those who seek to defy the world-system of darkness concerning the proper way to conduct spiritual warfare: "The weapons of your warfare are not human weapons, but are made powerful by God for tearing down strongholds (*ochuroma*).[84] Tear down arguments and every arrogant (idolatrous)[85] obstacle that is raised up against the knowledge of God, and take every thought captive to make it obey Christ" (2 Cor 10:4-5). A-theistic,

> *Could you identify some human customs or spiritual struggles influencing the fallen world systems in your life?*
>
> *How do you plan to participate in spiritual warfare against these challenges?*

---

[84] This Greek word literally represents "a strong military installation, fortress" (BDAG, 746).
[85] The literal meaning of this phrase is "high thing" which in Old Testament prophecy represented idolatry, because idolatry typically took place on hill tops and other elevated places in the ancient world.

idolatrous presuppositions underlie all creation-centered arguments against the God-centered knowledge of the Creator. At the foundations of such world-systems lie "empty, deceitful philosoph[ies] [based] on human traditions (*paradosis*) and the elemental spirits (*stoicheion*) of the world, and not according to Christ" (Col 2:8).[86]

Such language should remind us how world-shaping systems propagate and maintain themselves throughout human civilization. Consider, for example, worldly human education and the priesthood of both religious and "secular" leaders, who ascribe to humanism as their religion. They frequently pass down deceptive traditions and narratives about the world, influencing how we all think, feel, and act. For instance, reflect on the worldviews inspiring Muslim suicide bombers or to slaughter infidels or the Crusadors "cleansing" the "Holy Land." Also, contemplate the political philosophy and historical analysis propagated by the political and education systems in Nazi Germany, Communists in Mao's China, and the Bolshevic revolution and mass famine in Stalin/Lenin's Soviet Union that led to the deaths of hundreds of millions.

The Greek word translated in the previous passage as "elemental spirit" is "*stoicheion*." This word should be better understood through the following definitions: "something orderly in arrangement; element, principle"; "fundamental principles that constitute the foundation of learning"; "transcendent powers that are in control over events in the world, elemental spirits" (ISA; BDAG, 946). This Greek word denotes the spiritual influence of deceptive supernatural powers. They serve the Evil One's limited sovereignty within temporality in an effort to deceive humanity.

---

[86] The Greek word translated here as traditions, "*paradosis*", means "the content of instruction that has been handed down: tradition, teachings, commandments, [and] narratives" (BDAG, 763).

Considering these insights, both human traditions and spiritual authority shape the fallen realities of the "Land of Darkness": Planet Earth. Consequently, these temporal systems have become idolatrous shrines dedicated to created beings. Worshippers at their altars revere limited 'gods' of contextual providence, including both human and demonic entities. In this way, these systems divert humanity from embodying temples of the Living God, distancing their followers from a life grounded in eternal truths.

Prodigal inhabitants of this world have opted to live out an illegitimate narrative. They adopt the world-altering models crafted by the Evil One for his followers. In doing so, they take on roles that deviate from the Creator's intended vision. They defiantly integrate temporal aspects into their world-viewing and way of life. As Jesus warned, it is foolish to build on sand instead of the solid ground of eternal truths (Matt 7:24-27). Of these prodigals, it is written: "The earth is defiled by its inhabitants, for they have violated laws, disregarded regulations… So a curse devours the earth; its inhabitants pay for their guilt. This is why the inhabitants of the earth disappear." (Isa 24:4)

> *Reflect on your world.*
>
> *How do these revelations of the Evil One resonate with what you have witnessed in your lifetime?*

Existential rebellion has led to the rise of Babylon's temporal empire (Rev 18). Babylon symbolizes a world characterized by idolatrous living and views, ultimately controlled by non-human puppet masters. Satan rules over these worldly systems within his realm of Darkness. He presents himself to the inhabitants of his domain as "an angel (messenger) of light" and "deceives" the world with his counterfeit "truth" in an elaborate masquerade (John 3:19-20; 2 Cor 11:14). Although his dominion is concealed, he has been granted the splendor of these fallen systems, for it is written that he is "god of the [present evil] age" – having usurped humanity's mantle of stewarship (Luke 4:6; 2 Cor 4:4; Gal 1:4). The Evil One misleads created beings into sacrificing their eternity by enticing them with the "glories" of independence and self-admiration. He orchestrates the history and *oikonomia* of these temporary systems, drawing humans into "slavery to immorality" (e.g., addiction) instead of offering true freedom (2 Pet 2:19). He tempts everyone with the 'freedom' not to serve as a temple and priest of the Creator, leading them instead to become temples of the self or another created 'deity.'

Those who live and think by worldly systems ultimately become, whether knowingly or unknowingly, slaves to the master visionary of Babylon (Col 2:20). Regarding this "Dragon," we read, "So that huge dragon—the ancient serpent, the one called the devil and Satan, who deceives the whole world—was thrown down to the earth, and his angels along with him" (Rev 12:9). His pawns and servants pursue the false glories of temporal self-satisfaction within environments and by rules he dictates (Matt 4:8-9; John 8:44; Eph 2:2-3; 6:11-12). Consequently, those seeking to 'find themselves' according to the standards set by temporality often unwittingly follow the contextualities devised by Satan. Satan achieves this through his extensive manipulation of the temporal order, ruling as the "god of this age" who has "blinded the minds of those who do not believe" (2 Cor 4:4; Luke 4:6). Therefore, we are reminded, "for freedom Christ has set us free. Stand firm, then, and do not be subject again to the yoke of slavery" (Gal 5:1).

[*Have you recently felt the urge to pursue "independence" and self-reliance separate from God?*

How did you react to this temptation from Satan?]

Priests of Babylon

Let us examine the establishment, development, and preservation of Babylonian world-systems. Each human civilization and subculture features 'priests', often linked to an institution.[87] They serve as the keepers, propagators, and enforcers of narratives and structures established by finite, prodigal entities. They act as representatives of world-shaping 'sovereigns.' These figures claim to provide good news through promises of guidance, purpose, fulfillment, or even salvation independent of a genuine relationship with God. They aim to address the emptiness felt by prodigal children who are lost or isolated. Their impact hinges on how effectively they shape the *oikonomia* and *historicity* of the world system to resonate with the human need to belong and fit in.

Serving in such a 'priestly' position is not restricted to explicitly religious institutions. Extremely idealistic politicians, like Hitler, Lenin, and Mao, promoted the *oikonomia* and *historicity* of their extreme models of government and society, often at the barrel of a gun.[88] These "priests" adeptly employed specific narratives about the human experience to bolster their advocated social reforms, governmental priorities, and international policies. Today's celebrities and social "influencers" frequently endorse mindsets and ground rules pertaining to lifestyles, perspectives, social systems, humanitarian efforts, and social issues. The rise of wokism and 'influencer marketing' on social media exemplifies this trend. The term highlights celebrities' influence in shaping our perceptions of the world and how it ought to be. They believe they have "earned" the authority to instruct their followers on what to

---

[87] These include religious institutions, but also political, economic, educational, and entertainment-based ones.
[88] Nazism (a distinct form of fascism) and Maoism/ Leninism (distinct forms of Marxist communism – and not the same as Marxism-Leninism), respectively.

think, what to purchase, how to vote, and how to behave. Additionally, celebrities like musicians wield significant influence in molding worldviews and lifestyles through their music and the personas they project to their audience.

In ancient times, priests were tasked with instilling loyalty to the established rules of their system. This loyalty was believed to keep their lands fertile and safe, as well as attract divine favor and blessings for families and communities. Today, modern 'priests' offer individual or collective blessings. These figures resemble charismatic evangelical preachers who encourage people, saying, "Come join our (religion) way of life and flourish, find purpose, and be part of something greater than yourself (or be true to yourself)!" It is evident that the priests of Babylon, whether consciously or not, aim to shape world orders that promote the temporal kingdoms of created beings rather than the eternal goals of the Creator's kingdom.

> *Who are some impactful modern-day 'priests' in your community or country?*
>
> *What impact do you believe they have on you and those around you? Is it positive or negative?*

Speaking to those who live in such human-centered world-systems, our Guide warns believers of how "we live in a crooked and perverse society... [We must not be] motivated by selfish ambition or vanity [like those around us]... Others are busy with their own concerns, not those of Jesus Christ... I tell you that [some former believers have done so and become] enemies of the cross of Christ. Their end is destruction, their god is the belly, they exult in their shame, and they think about earthly things" (Phil 2:3, 15, 21; 3:18-19). Ultimately, whether motivated by selfishness or altruistic ambition,[89] all human world-systems fundamentally center upon the joint effort to be free from the existential commitment, wholehearted devotion, absolute submission, and total dependence required by the God-relationship.

Only by participating in a God-relationship grounded in divine revelation can we truly establish ourselves within an eternal world-system. However, since fallen humanity desires to be free from subservience to the one true God, most people join in the charade of existential rebellion. To achieve this, they follow the 'priests' of world-systems who (implicitly or explicitly) promise them freedom from obligations to the Divine. As figures who keep the household of human existence free from the governance and vision of the Creator, they are "idolatrous priests," leading humanity astray.[90] Their followers worship at the altars or "high places" of illegitimate 'sovereignties' who govern their *oikonomia*,

> *In what ways will this realization about the widespread presence and impact of Babylonian priests' and their broadcasts alter your lifestyle or mindset?*

---

[89] Even altruism ultimately represents a partnership in self-love, where individuals believe they can love without the presence of God. This tendency fosters a shared self-love, promoting human-centered goods that allow one to thrive in the world independent of God. Kierkegaard likens this collective "alliance in self-love," and we can compare it to the Christmas season in America's culture, characterized by self-seeking consumerism and materialism. Kierkegaard notes how this way of life, "requires that [a person] sacrifice a portion of his own self-love in order to hold together in the united self-love, and it requires that he sacrifice the God-relationship in order to hold together in a worldly way with this alliance" (*Works of Love*, 119-120).

[90] Keep in mind though, that 'priests of Babylon' do not simply refer to anyone who works in an explicitly religious position of influence. Rather, it specifically refers to those who use their position of influence to promote and propagate Babylonian world-systems at the expense of the Creator's narrative. One can be a celebrity, politician, or philosopher who uses their influence and knowledge to spread anti-God narratives and world-systems.

world-viewing, and self-conceptions in place of the Creator (2 Kings 23:5; Hos 10:5).

Babylonian temples and 'inland-academies'[91] serve to promote the prideful humanistic enterprises of fallen human civilization. They achieve this by advocating for alternative world-defining narratives instead of the Creator's original blueprint. These alternative narratives shape the temporal contexts and perspectives of individuals establishing their identities within various societal frameworks. The orientation of these temporal contexts creates a different 'creator' reflecting the act of creation in a perverse way. This is characteristic of pagan religions and secular philosophies. Historically, even the idolatrous Levitical priests and false prophets in Israel aimed to reshape the contextual elements of Judaism to align with the pagan worldviews prevalent in surrounding cultures (Hos 4:5-19; Jer 23:9-23). They, like the Romanization of "Christianity" which would come centuries later[92], fused pagan rites and narratives with Jewish *oikonomia* into the narrative of Judaism and temple worship (Jer 7:9, 17-18, 30-32; Ezek 8). This resulted in syncretism (spiritual adultery), as explained in the following passage:

> "Moreover, the Lord says, 'Both the prophets and priests are godless. I have even found them doing evil in my temple. So the paths they follow will be dark and slippery. They will stumble and fall headlong... They prophesied in the name of the god Baal and led my people Israel astray... They give

---

[91] Built upon "land-locked" or temporal knowledge, rather than the "endless ocean" of eternal revelation and God's reality.

[92] This situation of syncrenism always follows any attempt to make a country in this fallen world "Christian," e.g. Europe in the Middle Ages and even after the Reformation up to the "secularization" of Europe during the 20th century.

encouragement to people who are doing evil, with the result that they do not stop their evildoing. For the prophets of Jerusalem are the reason that ungodliness has spread throughout the land… Do not listen to what those prophets are saying to you. They are filling you with false hopes. They are reporting visions of their own imaginations.'"[93]

(Jer 9:11-16)

The philosophies of influential figures in human history aim to create dependency on created realities (Col 2:8). Likewise, religious leaders often imitate the self-righteousness exhibited by the Pharisees, who prioritized their own human "biblical" traditions over divine guidance (Matt 23). They pridefully "tell" God's Spirit how a religious service ought to be ordered.

Today, the champions of civilization disseminate their narratives and perspectives to the public through various mediums, including literature (ranging from novels and textbooks to self-help books), skewed news coverage, music, talk shows, television programs, movies, and biased historical or nature documentaries. In the digital age, these leaders also utilize computers, smartphones, and tablets to showcase curated social media feeds, blogs, podcasts, games, and forums designed to indoctrinate individuals, along with worldly advertisements that seek to influence opinions and choices. These broadcasts not only affect but are also influenced by institutions and companies that shape

---

[93] This prophecy against the spiritual decline of Judaism is as true today regarding our modern Christian institutions.

how people manage their homes and engage with society according to idolatrous ways of life.[94]

How Humanity Continues to Build New Towers of Babel

Viewed from eternity, the worship of temporal human experiences tends to lead to existential, relational, and domestic disintegration rather than authentic home creation. Idolatry further alienates humanity from the divine criterion and purpose set by God. It obstructs the sanctification of an individual's worldly existence by the spiritual contexts linked to the Holy of Holies. Up to this point, we have examined how the leaders of the temporal realm influence the idolatrous experiences of earthly inhabitants. These dark spiritual entities promote and sustain the *oikonomia* of rebellion, including materialism and hedonism. The following passages support this assertion:

> "You were dead in your transgressions and sins, in which you formerly lived according to this world's present path [of world-fittingness], according to the ruler of the kingdom [world-systems] of the air, the ruler of the spirit that is now energizing the sons of disobedience [existential rebellion], among whom all of us also formerly lived out our [world-dwelling] lives in the cravings of our flesh, indulging the desires of the flesh and the mind, and were by nature children of wrath even as the rest... So I say this, and insist in the Lord that you no longer live as the Gentiles do, in the futility of their thinking. They are darkened in their understanding, being alienated

---

[94] For instance, consider how TV commercials, product placements in movies, and influencer marketing promote the interests, outlook, and lifestyles of corporations, who put profit over everything and cater to the consumers who watch movies and follow influencers.

from the life of God because of the ignorance that is in them due to the hardness of their hearts... You were taught with reference to your former way of life to lay aside the old man who is being corrupted in accordance with deceitful desire... Let nobody deceive you with empty words, for because of these things God's wrath comes on the sons of disobedience. Therefore do not be partakers with them, for you were at one time darkness, but now you are light in the Lord. Walk as children of the light... Do not participate in the unfruitful deeds of darkness, but rather expose them."

(Eph 2:1-3, 4:17-18, 4:22, 5:6-8, 5:11-14)[95]

Given this context, to this day it is unsurprising that the world systems of the Land of Darkness resist Yahweh's world-shaping contextualities. These realities mislead inhabitants into feeling comfortable in this fallen world, as they adapt to 'fabricated' contextualities. They can rightly be labeled the idolatrous citizens of Babylon. They consciously dwell in a state of 'prodigalness' lacking spiritual insight and sanctifying grace.[96]

In Babylon, citizens seek perceived or imagined advantages for worldly success. In simple terms, they aspire to advance in life to reach their own definitions of well-being, success, or being at the

---

[95] Additions made, such as "world-fittingness" and "world-systems" are my own. Nonetheless, they do highlight how the existentialities and concepts we have talked about fit within a biblical view of reality.

[96] "Land-dwellers" refer to those who form their lives and identities around idolatrous world-systems. They glorify the created above the Creator. These dwellers are "idolatrous" because they act, consciously or not, according to house-rules that glorify something other than the Creator. Nevertheless, they *willingly* inhabit these realms even if they are not fully aware of the implications and consequences for doing so.

"top" in one way or another. As a result, those who live on land embrace a lifestyle of covenant-breaking prodigalness. They adopt a worldly mindset driven by fleshly desires instead of the spiritual aspirations appropriate for those illuminated by eternal light (Gal 5:13-26). By establishing their lives based on these temporary values, humanity attempts to create their ideal future. We can easily find numerous examples of religious, political, and social frameworks reject the Creator's intentions and vision for existence, shaping what it means to belong in this world-system. This sense of belonging is dictated by perceptions of what best serves human existence, often overlooking the presence and blessings of God. They place importance on sensual enjoyment, worldly achievements, social acclaim, the praise of human endeavors, interpersonal connections, and more. While none of these pursuits are inherently wrong, they can become idolatrous when elevated above or replacing a relationship with God. Such worldly paradigms lead individuals to believe they can achieve peace and fulfillment in the universe without committing themselves to God.

> *What are examples of idolatrous home-making or self-serving paradigms in your society?*
>
> *How about in your own life?*

Illicit visions of finitude can be seen as "degenerate blueprints." Due to limited perspectives, these blueprints may seem more appealing and beneficial than the Creator's blueprint. Individuals might think they will achieve happiness by acquiring something, reaching a goal, or having an experience; however, reality often falls short of these expectations. It is akin to someone pursuing mirages in the desert. The perceptions and imaginings of created beings are inherently limited, flawed, and vulnerable to deception. Some individuals believe they can choose their identity and seek their own truths. Just reflect on the desires of the flesh: "I will be happy when… with endless iterations." Yet, they remain unaware that the systems surrounding them manipulate these pursuits, typically enriching the wealthy and empowering the powerful (Eph 2:1-2).[97] Many fail to realize that they live as mere pawns in a scheme to vie for control and dispossession by worldly demonic powers. They live like the "freed" Israelite slaves, longing to return to the taskmasters of Egypt for the sake of preserving their perceptions of temporal advantage, familiarity, and certains over and against sacrifices and risks involved in heeding Eternity's call.

Imagine the difficulty Moses faced in resisting the urge to see himself as the son of Pharaoh's daughter. This perspective allowed him to live according to an *oikonomia* that allotted him "fleeting pleasures of sin" that came from his privileged position in Egypt (his Babylon) (Heb 11:24-26). The Egyptians presented Moses with an alternative narrative and set of house rules, replacing those prescribed by the God of his ancestor Abraham. Succumbing to this temptation would have resulted in idolatrous living and a worldview that contradicted the Creator's intentions. Additionally, recall the lifestyle Paul adopted during his time as a Pharisee Saul.[98]

The world-shaping manipulation of existential rebellion influences more than just choices and narratives. Even divinely instituted structures such as government, family, marriage, education, music, and art can drift away from the Creator's intended order. The intellect and creativity of created beings may be misused to justify calling "evil good and good evil," attempting to turn existential "darkness into light" and to redefine what is

---

[97] Recall our previous discussions about how seemingly objective or independent attempts at knowledge or identity formation are impacted, shaped, and influenced by our contexts, histories, and presuppositions. We are inescapably subjective beings.

[98] Even as a "religious leader" Saul's lifestyle was in opposition to the Creator's will. Embracing the world-dwelling of the Creator does not simply mean "embracing religion" or a "religious calling".

ultimately "bitter as sweet" (Isa 5:20). Consider a person who indulges in parties and the fleeting pleasure of gluttony and drunkenness, all while ignoring the negative repercussions of such a lifestyle (Prov 23:29-35; Isa 5:22, 28:7-8, 56:12). "Wine is a mocker and strong drink a brawler; whoever is led astray by them is not wise" (Prov 20:1). One may convince themselves of anything to excuse another binge, but one can never escape the inevitable hangover and the regrettable actions taken while inebriated, especially if they lead to a prison cell.

World systematization employs finite contextualities based on incorrect world-dwelling presuppositions.[99] For instance, reflect on their views about human obligation, meaning, and society at large. As we discussed earlier, these beliefs stem from subjective roots in language, assumptions, and stories recounted by others and ourselves. Ultimately, humanity often constructs its own towers of Babel, both in a literal and metaphorical sense, across every civilization (Gen 11:1-9).

> *How will you respond to a world filled with countless narratives, ideas of "fittingness," and defiant world-systems that mislead people from the Creator's original purpose?*

Babylonian systems present a worldview that reinforces beliefs about social or selfish, indulgent living. Babylonian "priests" create paradigms and set of house rules to influence perceptions of the past, present, future, and moral expectations based on the perspectives they advocate. Essentially, "they not only do [wickedness] but also approve of those who practice it" (Rom 1:32). Typically, those constructed *oikonomia*(s) emerge from a fabricated historicity influenced by

---

[99] Or the language that creates and sustains ideas of what is "normative" or "natural" or "fundamental" in the world. Recall our previous discussions about world systematizing language.

an imagination enabled by evil spirits.[100] This is clearly apparent to anyone who has studied the history of philosophy. Such narratives lend both legitimacy and reasoning to the world-systems or house rules they endorse. For instance, examine pagan world-systems and ideologies- both ancient and contemporary- that utilize house rules endorsing sexual perversion or human sacrifices, whether in a religious ritual or a "medical" procedure, placing greater value on so-called temporal flourishing than on procreation. Priests and oracles would advocate for these house rules by insisting they appropriately appease the gods, secure their favor, or simply prioritize the well-being and prosperity of living adults over that of babies. Additionally, consider the cultic prostitution that the Israelites practiced with Moabite women, which brought a plague upon them (Num 25:1-9). They regarded sexual immorality as one of the ultimate purposes of human existence, leading ultimately to societal decay. Furthermore, reflect on how the modern narrative of evolution has established a basis for a-theistic education and perspectives, serving to justify various social evils.

Living in a World of Egocentric Materialism

Consider contemporary capitalist societies. They have largely become materialistic and self-centered. A simple drive down the highway or a glance at the television reveals enormous billboards and advertisements promoting products or medications that claim to provide true 'happiness'. These messages imply that such happiness is found in satisfying the pleasures of sight (via movies, shows, or adult entertainment), the cravings of the body (through dining out, nightlife, and sexual services), or the desires of the mind (with drugs, entertainment, or educational programs enhancing personal enlightenment and fulfillment). This environment

---

[100] Recall our discussions about how *historicity* (or the effects of historical-social context) plays a large role in crafting *oikonomia* and presuppositions.

promotes the notion that "it is all about me and my feelings, desires, and entitlements. It is my body, my money, my stuff, and my time, so I can use them however I wish."

In today's consumer-driven society, which spans both developed and developing countries worldwide, everything has been commodified and packaged for eager consumers. Nothing seems immune from this commercialization. Sexuality and the human body are prime examples of this trend. Both have been transformed into objects of commerce rather than sacred creations of God meant for a covenant-based monogamous relationship. Through both crude advertising and direct means like prostitution or pornography, the human body has been objectified for trade and sale. For example, scantily clad women are used to promote everything from swimsuits to shoes, cars, and alcohol—even when it does not make sense to do so. How are women in bikinis inherently related to sports cars? Nevertheless, such tactics have proven effective, securing their place in society. The "consumption" of women has become worse than ever before. Pornography and casual sex are now easily accessible on every smartphone, and other media like movies, TV shows, and video games are filled with sexual content or suggestive themes. For instance, in Japan, the oversexualization of women, including underage girls, is common even in many seemingly family-friendly anime and games. In societies that have, until recently, been more sexually liberal—and yet more patriarchal—than the West, such as Japan, modern influences have allowed this sexualization to permeate and appear throughout their media.

While such callous objectification of women is by no means either a recent or solely Western phenomenon, our modern world of consumerism and technology has supercharged the possibilities of satisfying people's lusts like never before. Dating apps, pornography apps, online prostitution with cam and subscription websites like *OnlyFans*, sex games, sex forums, and so much more provide far more opportunities than those available to even the most debaucherous Roman emperors. Sex is now sold with as much variety and efficiency as any other product in our capitalist world. Now, with the prevalence of AI girlfriends, such as in Japan, Singapore, and South Korea (with interest growing around the world), one does not even need to interact with real women at all to be gratified! The real and beautiful complexity of women as human beings and creations of God is being replaced by perfectly compliant, unrealistically proportioned, totally customizable virtual puppets. Things getting in the way of "the fantasy", such as bodily imperfections, being tired or "not in the mood," or even the free will inherent to a human being, can be done away with easily. AI girlfriends, after all, never have to say no. Such technology causes many men to skip the difficulties of forming real relationships, built on maturity, responsibility, and mutual respect, or even dealing with real people. Instead, they are now the masters of their own slaves.

Even if we consider a broader perspective and acknowledge that many men driven to such actions are affected by personal hardships, depression, or deep loneliness, it does not make the problem any less serious. After all, instead of receiving genuine help or support, these men are often exploited by the selfishness of developers and companies creating harmful tools. Even without involving actual women, people can now exploit the idea of women to profit from others' suffering and loneliness. Moreover, our current culture of oversexualizing and objectifying women—reducing complex human beings and sacred creations of God to objects defined solely by what others can take from them—is alarming. This has frightening implications for how many men will treat real women. Just look at how badly many men today, influenced by this culture, behave around the world, whether through horrific acts like rape or through seemingly "harmless" actions like catcalling or lewd comments about female friends.

The *oikonomia* of womanhood in our materialistic culture has led to a society that evaluates femininity by sexual appeal, often used to exert influence and market products and experiences. Such an issue goes beyond its effects on men or how men "consume" women. A significant consequence of this perspective is the unrealistic beauty standards imposed on women, defining "beauty" and "desirability" in shallow terms. Few women can achieve such skin-deep 'beauty' without resorting to plastic surgery to alter their bodies. Think about the obsession with "feeling young," often equated with "feeling beautiful, desirable, or attractive." Most of us likely know someone who frets about aging, equating a loss of beauty "uglier".[101] The inner beauty of the soul, heart, and mind has been marginalized as factors in determining human worth, due to a materialistic and consumeristic worldview. This perspective on humanity goes beyond merely glorifying the idea of 'being yourself.' The 'self' we refer to is not formed in isolation; rather, it is always influenced by cultural contexts. Therefore, this phrase suggests: "Become the socially contextualized self that society encourages you to be." In essence, we are evolving into a society where physical attributes, whether relating to our bodies or belongings, are seen as indicators of

{ *Have you ever felt exhausted by the fleeting pleasures of today's society?*

What do you believe causes all the food, entertainment, activities, and distractions to fall short of providing you with genuine and enduring fulfillment and purpose? }

---

[101] Whether they want to feel beautiful to attract others or to simply feel secure in themselves.

human flourishing. Simultaneously, our culture elevates self-love, physical pleasures, and material wealth as the ultimate goals of fulfillment. Today's society offers limitless avenues to achieve these ideals of flourishing. However, as old trends fade, new fads emerge, continuously challenging the boundaries of what is culturally acceptable and satisfying. There is always something fresh to purchase or experience. It is hardly surprising that issues like depression, drug addiction, feelings of emptiness, suicides, and violence are increasing, even amid a society filled with prosperity and pleasure. Many resort to drugs to capture transient "highs" of what society assured them could be achieved without substances but ultimately fell short. In the end, a materialistic mindset fails to provide the soulful and spiritual satisfaction necessary for true human fulfillment and significance.

A cultural crisis emerged during ancient Babylonian, Roman, and Greek societies' moral and social decline. Did they not descend into societal indulgence as carnal pleasures, perversions, and self-centered luxuries became paramount? This made them "weak," as they become increasingly open to internal division and conquest, especially by the influx of those with starkly different house rules. Many of these societies ultimately collapsed when selfish, myopic, self-serving perspectives replaced the older values of hard work, honor, and virtue that once supported their social prosperity.[102] Even today, we observe how our culture replaces the Creator's laws governing human conduct with its own moral guidelines (e.g., "it is okay as long as it does not hurt others or

---

[102] For example, consider how the massive influx of slaves and new prisoners of war and the mass concentration of wealth and land into the hands of the rich created social crises that ended up destroying the Roman Republic in the 1st century BC. When greed and a selfish lust for power replaced the virtues and values that used to hold their society together, it could not help but collapse. Look up the "Gracchi Brothers" for more about these events.

violate another's free will"), theistic beliefs (e.g., prosperity gospel), and existential views (e.g., "the world is my playground and others are means to my ends, or human relations and society are merely expressions of the will to power"). They strive to impose their own rational structure, explanations, and suitability to what exists within the confines of Finitude. As a result, these 'gods' and 'priests' of humanity establish and maintain Babylonian world-systems that stand in opposition to the authentic created order.

The concept of materialism as a suitable perspective for human existence originates from 'Babylonian priests' who shape or reinforce narratives and rules grounded in a materialistic viewpoint (1 John 4:5). These narratives and *oikonomia* entrench individuals in social traditions and norms, utilizing religion, education, culture, and politics to promote the notion that flourishing equates to living a materially 'prosperous' life (Rom 8:5). Regarding such world-systems, the Scripture states, "All that is in the world (the desire of the flesh and the desire of the eyes and the arrogance produced by material possessions) is not from the Father, but is from the world. And the world is passing away with all its desires... [So,] Guard yourselves from idols" (1 John 2:16-17). There is nothing new under the Sun, as Solomon quoted.

> *In a world that seeks to indoctrinate you into a materialistic agenda, how will you resist and concentrate on what the Creator has in store for you?*

This indoctrination of influential narratives, *oikonomia*, and contextual factors contributes to the formation of communities that revolve around the materialistic agendas of profit-driven corporations and their shareholders. For instance, how frequently do people in contemporary societies spend time shopping with friends and consuming entertainment during their leisure hours? What percentage of recreational activities involve the consumption of goods or services? Why has the pursuit of "buying unnecessary items" transformed into a life goal instead of fostering personal growth and meaningful collaboration? If you find this notion unremarkable, reflect on how such an approach to enjoyment would have been viewed as unusual in medieval times or among non-consumeristic cultures.[103]

Co-dwelling structures can emerge from various contexts and historical backgrounds. For instance, the Indian caste system historically divided society into castes that had defined socio-economic roles and cultural customs. Similarly, in Ancient Greece, city economies often revolved around deities, compelling merchants and customers to adhere to specific religious guidelines. In Ancient China's Confucian society, leisure activities for the upper classes included "writing and reciting poetry with friends" instead of "going to the market to buy things."[104]

Castaways about to Embark

This chapter explored how the Fall led to humans adapting to transient, corrupt "Babylonian" systems. Dark powers created these systems to distract individuals by encouraging them to "find themselves" within a limited, transient, and godless environment. They aim to perpetuate a false reality, opposing the Creator's vision. With such a narrow outlook, the eternal truths of our true home may seem absurd to many (1 Cor 3:18). "God chose what the world regards as foolish to shame the wise, and God selected what the world sees as weak to shame the strong. He chose what is lowly and despised, considered as nothing, to set aside what is

---

[103] For a very 'prophetic' analysis of the storyline, progression, and teleology of a "technological society" that leads to materialistic consumerism, whe humanity merely become an efficient 'consumer,' refer to "The Technological Society" by Jacques Ellul.
[104] Confucian society valued cultural pursuits over commerce and trade.

viewed as significant... The unbeliever cannot accept the things of the Spirit of God, because they are foolishness to him. He cannot understand them, as they are spiritually discerned" (1 Cor 1:27-28, 2:14). Keeping this understanding in mind, our condition as homeless and wayward castaways becomes evident. We can genuinely see how our theological journeys relate to every individual's existential circumstances. Only by acknowledging our state as homeless castaways from the fallen "Land of Darkness" can we embark on a journey home as seekers of revelation.

With these realizations in mind, each individual should reflect on a key question: "Do I genuinely feel that I am a homeless castaway in this world?" Answering in the affirmative suggests that we accept our current tabernacle is not our real home; we may feel that we do not entirely "belong here." This belief in being homeless only makes sense from the perspective of Eternity. It is only when we feel a better, more authentic home exists beyond this one that we can truly see ourselves as wanderers in the Land of Darkness. Therefore, we recognize that our true essence, as children of God, finds its rightful place in the world to come.

Our voyage symbolizes our quest for a new way to be human. We embark on this new life through a sacred rebirth, adopting an identity influenced by the everlasting context of God's temple. Our Creator designed our true selves in accordance with the *oikonomia* of this sacred place. We are meant to serve eternally as priests of His immanent disclosures. He created us to be co-managers and co-enactors of His rules within the limits of existence. By setting out on our journey home, we aim to return to this initially intended purpose. We become sanctified individuals shaped

> *Do you feel like you belong in this world? If so, why or why not?*
>
> *Do you see yourself as a castaway, navigating toward your true home? What leads you to that feeling?*

by our new reality as living spaces for our God-relationship through the Spirit.

When humanity rebelled, we, as sacred dwellings of the Living God, were vacated temples, incapable of filling such emptiness by created, finite realities. No finite existence can replace Infinite *Being*. Thus, we emerged as outcasts. We endure in this state of existential defiance due to our continued reluctance to offer our temporal lives to God. We resist becoming His children and priests. Instead, most of us have vainly attempted to feel "at home" on the Land of Darkness. We have chosen to confine our experience of the world and our perspectives to the temporal parameters of godless systems. We engage in a rebellion against prioritizing the God-relationship. By maintaining this idolatrous mindset, we either consciously or unconsciously refuse to leave the shores of the Land of Darkness and venture out on the Sea of Revelation. As "members of a rebellious house," we lack the "ears" needed to hear and respond to the call to repent (Ezek 12:2).

In opposition to a Babylonian way of life, let us now ponder the most fateful of life choices. Yahweh, our Maker, invites everyone to become and remain exiles. He urges each of us to leave behind the world-house of Babylon. This, however, necessitates a readiness to let go of fundamental aspects of our worldly living and perceptions. Only in this way can we truly cease our rebellion against Governance and a rejection of our true First Love, as we are born into this world as lovers of *Being*. It entails repenting from sinful habits while courageously embarking on a homeward-bound voyage. In this process, our lives and worldview are transformed by the Creator's established *oikonomia* for His creation, centered on the holiness of *agape*-love (Matt 5:43-48; 1 John 3-4).

> *Have you chosen to leave Babylon behind and journey to your true home?*
>
> *If not, what holds you back?*

Chapter 5

The Fateful Choice: Babylon or Zion
To be Defined by Temporality or Eternity

"If anyone wants to become My follower, he must deny himself and take up his cross. For whoever wants to save his life will lose it... For what does it benefit a person if he gains the whole world but forfeits himself?"

(Luke 9:23-25)

"Walk while you have the light... The one who walks in the darkness does not know where he is going... Believe in the light, so that you may become sons of light... [For you] do not belong to the world... The [present shape of this] world is passing away with all its desires, but the person who does the will of God remains forever."

(John 12:34-36, 17:16-17; 1 Cor 7:31; 1 John 2:15-16)

"Live out the time of your temporary residence here in reverence. You know that from your empty way of life you were ransomed by the blood of Christ... You have been born anew, from imperishable seed."

(1 Pet 1:13-18, 23)

"God delivered us from the power of darkness... Keep seeking the things above, not things of the earth, for you have died and your life is hidden with Christ... [In] reference to your former way of life, put off the old man being corrupted according to deceitful desires... We are not looking at what can be seen... For what can be seen is temporary, but what cannot be seen is eternal."

(Col 1:13-14, 3:1-10; Eph 4:22; 2 Cor 4:16-18, 5:17)

Forsaking the Lure of Temporality[105] for Eternal Prosperity

This chapter will explore the distinction between the 'land' (the fallen temporal world) and the 'sea' (the eternal realm of revelation). We will examine how 'land-dwellers' often fall prey to the deception of seeking their identities and destinies through corrupt worldly systems. Those who respond to Eternity's Call to become 'seafarers' must abandon their illusory temporal selves in order to genuinely live as 'exiles' in accordance with eternal systems and house rules.

As discussed in previous chapters, everyone seeks to find their own 'path' in life. Many simply select a route among those deemed valuable by society or a group. However, some of us pursue a heavenly homeland transcending this world. We can envision our journey akin to those crossing the ocean searching for new lands, much like the ancient Polynesians. Today, we often overlook the immense challenges faced by early navigators who lacked engines or GPS systems to complete their voyages. The ancient Polynesians did not have compasses, sextants, or spyglasses. Instead, they employed a method known as "wayfinding." They relied on the "contextualities" of their environment, such as the wind, stars, ocean currents, cloud patterns, and bird migrations, to navigate. Furthermore, they took advantage of the "contextualities" of their own vessels, like the configurations of the crab claw sail and the steering oar, to harness the wind and steer their boats skillfully. Just as the Polynesians did in the past,

{ *Do you trust the Scriptures to serve as your "wayfinding guide" even in a world filled with many alternatives?* }

---

[105] Temporality refers to the "present evil age" of the fallen world we now live in (Gal 1:4).

we today can utilize the various "contextualities" to guide the direction of our lives and our existence in the world.

Is there an objectively correct or incorrect method of "wayfinding"? Are the criteria for "good and bad" voyaging inevitably subjective? Unlike us, Polynesian seafarers did not rely on subjective interpretations. They memorized patterns such as the positions of stars, recognized wayfinding markers, and practiced boat-handling techniques that were passed down through generations. By adhering to these teachings, they successfully navigated thousands of miles of ocean without losing their way. For believers, the Scriptures act as our "star map" or "wayfinding guide," helping us avoid misdirection. Ultimately, incorrect wayfinding or improper navigation can lead to dire consequences. Our faith in Scripture reinforces the notion of true "supercontextual" realities that exist beyond our limited contextual world (Eph 2:10). In essence, there is a real "star map" to follow.

Every individual is free to choose between following the Creator's "starmap" or the misguided paths of the temporal world. This choice creates a moment of decision akin to a "to be or not to be," involving the "life" that our Creator has designed for us and the living "death" that the world imposes through rebellion against Providence (Deut 30:15-20). "The Lord says to [us] His people: 'You are standing at the crossroads. So, consider your path. Ask where the old, reliable paths are. Ask where the path that leads to blessing and follow it. If you do, you will find rest for your souls'" (Jer 6:16). Hence, the concept of a crossroads vividly represents the fundamental human struggle between living authentically and inauthentically.

What is our core purpose from the viewpoint of Eternity? Eternity invites us to seek and embrace the true self based on our Creator's vision. However, unlike the popular societal notion of "finding yourself," we can not create or self-actualize this true self

> *Do you find seeking God's greater vision more rewarding than merely focusing on self-preservation and earthly goals?*
>
> *Why or why not?*

independently of a larger context or divine assistance. Instead, our Creator connects our identity to the broader Narrative of Finitude and our Relationship with God. This larger framework transcends personal success or individual satisfaction, encompassing the entire environment in which God has placed us. Our Creator provides us with a higher purpose. This purpose transcends the self-preservation and self-interest that often define how many live their lives. Only by considering this broader perspective can we truly understand how to fulfill our predestined role in the Narrative of Finitude (Eph 1:11).

In light of all this, we, as inhabitants of this world, should reflect on a crucial question: "What narrative is influencing my experience of living and perceiving the world?" This inquiry leads us to examine the "criterion" of the self we aspire to be. Ultimately, our lives unfold in the finite realm according to how we exist in and interpret our surroundings. So, which world-influencing contexts guide our efforts to establish ourselves in our household of finitude? Are these contextualities temporal or eternal? As navigators of life, we must consistently consider whether the contexts of our lives align with the Creator's intention. Is it the narrative crafted by our limited world, or is it our Infinite Creator's overarching narrative that shapes our life story?

It may be simpler for us to answer these questions than we assume. We should just reflect on, "What am I living for?" Many people tend to respond by emphasizing the more appealing aspects of our temporary existence. We might live for our next paycheck, to attain wealth or status, or even to find personal fulfillment. The opportunities this world presents can indeed seem beneficial for fulfilling our needs for existential development. However, according to Scripture, the transient rewards offered by worldly systems do not lead to genuine and enduring existential flourishing when viewed from an Eternal perspective. Those who prioritize the fleeting satisfactions of this life will ultimately sacrifice their flourishing in Eternity. Consider the following words of Jesus: "For whoever wants to save his [or her] life will lose it, but whoever loses his [or her] life for [Christ's] sake will find it. For what does it benefit a person if he [or she] gains the whole world but forfeits his [or her] life?" (Matt 16:24-25)?

> *Do you believe striving for a purpose beyond this transient life is liberating rather than limiting?*
>
> *What motivates you to "sacrifice your life" in the name of Christ?*

Eternal Contextualities versus Temporal Contextualities

Let us now examine the distinction between the two primary existential categories that influence an individual's perception of their true self: the temporal contexts of "Babylon" and the eternal contexts of "Zion". Temporal contexts relate to the world-systems of our fleeting, contextual existence and the notions of appropriateness within a universe marked by existential defiance against the Creator's intentions. On the other hand, eternal contexts pertain to the world-systems of the House of God. They clarify the appropriateness of those who genuinely fulfill their role as a tabernacle of the God-relationship within the limits of existence.

One notable characteristic of eternal contextualities (such as house-rules) is how they have a point of origin, but no endpoint. Imagine a line starting from a point and just continuing forever without end (⟶). These contextual factors will remain within the world-house of Finitude, the overarching context of the created realm, transcending this temporal age. They emerge as enduring, essential elements of the Creator's unending Narrative of Finitude. "Heaven and earth may pass away, but the [Creator's] words will not" (Matt. 24:35). When God crafted the cosmos and humanity, His intention was for everything to persist eternally, free from suffering, decay, death, or evil (Rev 21:4). The Maker wishes for all beings to thrive forever in joy and shalom, living harmoniously with Him and one another as co-dwelling neighbors.

Even if we see ourselves as deserters of the Babylonian temporal world systems, we must reflect on the characteristics of temporal contextualities. These encompass the set of house rules, house contents, and house arrangements that are not eternal. Referring to our earlier example, they possess both a starting point and an endpoint (•—•). From Eternity's viewpoint, they are fleeting, akin to a "vapor," a "shadow," or "chaff carried off by a desert wind" (Jer 13:24-25; Ps 144:4). A good rule of thumb to remember is that if a temporal context does not directly support the Creator's Vision for the Narrative of Finitude, it holds little significance in the bigger picture.[106] Indeed, the Scriptures reveal

---

[106] Temporal contextualities can lead to eternal ones, stemming from the Creator's narrative. This includes elements like the Law of Moses, the Abrahamic covenant, the struggle for sustenance, procreation, governance, discipline, punishment, certain wars, and even natural death.

Conversely, some temporal contextualities only sometimes and indirectly facilitate the emergence of eternal contextualities. These arise from the misuse of free will by individuals, resulting in actions of a. rogue narrative, including murder, lying, stealing, gossiping, gluttony, idolatry, greed, torture, rape, and pollution.

Had God reacted immediately to these temporal contextualities that diverge from His vision for Finitude by eliminating them, the story of redemption could not have been told, and humanity would face extinction. In

that a prodigal child who lives solely within the confines of temporal circumstances is seen from Eternity's viewpoint as someone who "can accomplish nothing" or even as "non-living" (John 5:25, 15:5; Rom 7:5; Eph 2:1-5; Col 2:13; Heb 9:14; 1 John 3:14). Their role on the stage of Finitude is merely fleeting and ultimately without significance.

Scriptures indicate that temporal contexts will eventually vanish completely: "the present shape of this world is passing away" (1 Cor 7:31). They will ultimately become "useless thistles" in the sight of the Vision of Governance, "fated to be burned," as "the world is passing away with all its desires" (Heb 6:7-8; 1 John 2:17). This looming "burning fire" will consume all contextualized aspects of the temporal chapter of Finitude, since it hinders the Creator's intended infinite narrative (Matt 13:41-42; John 15:6). Therefore, our guide advises us: "Since all these things are to melt away in this manner, what sort of people must you be, conducting your lives in holiness and godliness, while waiting for and hastening the coming of the day of God? Because of this day, the heavens will be burned up and dissolve, and the celestial bodies will melt away in a blaze! But, according to His promise, we are waiting for new heavens and a new earth, in which righteousness truly resides" (2 Pet 3:7, 10-11).

> *As you go through life, how do you believe you can distinguish between the contexts of Babylon and Zion?*

Before diving deeper into the differences between "eternal contextualities" and "temporal contextualities" within this journey, let us first examine the common usage of the terms "eternal" and

---

Jesus' parable, the enemy (Satan) plants weeds of evil among the wheat field (the world); if these weeds had been removed right away, the wheat (those destined for redemption) would have also perished alongside those obstinately remaining as children of Satan (Matt 13:24-30, 36-43).

"temporal." Afterward, we will explore how these words will be utilized differently in our upcoming discussions.

The term "temporal" typically refers to something that exists in time, restricted by the progression of time, or unfolding within it. For example, how can we determine if a car is in motion? We can see that it occupies a specific position at one moment and a different position at another. We can gauge its speed by measuring the time it takes to transition from point A to point B. Thus, the car is considered "temporally bounded" in the usual sense of "temporal." Another illustration is that we humans are temporal beings. We structure our days into segments of time, and the effectiveness of our lives depends on how we utilize the time we have allocated to our lifespan. Our calendar organizes time over the span of a year, month, week, or day. History itself reflects how human existence has evolved over time. Civilizations rise and fall, new discoveries emerge while past ideas fade, and people are born and die as time relentlessly progresses.

Unlike the common perception of "temporal," the term "eternal" typically refers to something that remains unchangeable and exists beyond time. More than just meaning "lasting forever," something considered eternal is free from time constraints. In this sense, the Creator's vision and plan for creation embody "eternal" contexts. A deeper philosophical exploration of time concerning temporality and eternity will have to wait for a future quest, but for now, we focus on the conventional use of these terms. In essence, the temporal is fleeting, while the eternal is everlasting and unchanging.

> How do you believe the spiritual and theological meanings of "temporal" and "eternal" differ from their conventional definitions?
>
> How do these meanings influence your perception of yourself and your existence?

The difference between "temporal" and "eternal" in our theological journey goes beyond whether something is or is not subject to time. Let us now consider the theological distinctions between "temporal contextualities" and "eternal contextualities." This examination will clarify why using these more abstract and philosophically significant labels is preferable to simply contrasting "earthly" contextualities with "heavenly" contextualities.

The distinction between temporal and eternal contextuality is qualitative rather than just quantitative. It resembles the contrast between infinite reality and finite reality.[107] When we describe something as "eternal," we see it as qualitatively superior to that which is "temporal." For example, eternal contexts represent a "higher" essence of time and space.[108] This superiority hinges on the resonance between eternal contextualities and the original intended order of creation, aligning with Yahweh's enduring plan for the *oikonomia* (house-rules) of the *oikoumene* (world-house) of Finitude. His intention was for creation to be holy, pure, harmonious, incorruptible, and perfectly aligned with His vision.

---

[107] This will be discussed later in our journey.
[108] Eternal contextualities represent "heavenly" realities, while temporal contextualities are seen as "earthly". Here, "heavenly" qualitatively signifies a distinction between higher and lower. This concept of "heavenly" is illustrated as "being associated with a locale for transcendent things and beings" (BDAG, 388). Conversely, the term "earthly" refers to lower realms. This aligns with biblical terminology, where Earth is described in relation to the sky, with the latter being called the heavens. Additionally, the Bible refers to the entire material universe as "earth" compared to the immaterial universe, which is identified as the "heavens" (BDAG, 196, 561-563, 737-738). The created realm of Finitude, both material and immaterial, can also be termed "earth" when contrasted with the Infinite and uncreated heavens. Therefore, the superiority of eternal contextualities as "heavenly" (higher) relative to temporal realities is not solely because of their everlasting nature in a quantitative sense; rather, it stems from the qualitatively superior nature of the reality that underpins them. This higher-lower distinction is further emphasized through its metaphoric use, contrasting the superior with the inferior.

Eternal contextualities exist beyond the transient phase of reality we currently inhabit. This temporality is what Scripture references when stating: "For the present shape of this world is passing away" (1 Cor 7:31). Eternal contextualities not only transcend temporal structures in their essence but also in their interaction with finite realities. Unlike mere "temporal contextualities that last forever," they fundamentally differ from temporal realities, as they are more akin to Infinite reality - not solely due to their everlasting nature but also because they reflect the glory of Divine imminency.

Temporal contextualities are all, to various degrees, tainted by fallenness. This is described in the following Scriptural passage: "For the creation was subjected to futility... [a] bondage of decay (corruption)[109]" (Rom 8:20-21; ISA). The word for futility here is *"mataiotes,"* and is defined as a "state of being without use or value, emptiness, futility, purposelessness, transitoriness" (BDAG 621). Like a virus, these temporal contextualities occupy a domain they were not meant to in the Creator's original plan for Finitude.[110] The "endpoint" of temporal contextualities resembles a point at which the chapter in a book concludes and is folded up, never to be opened again (Heb 1:10-12).

> *Can you explain the difference between a temporal contextuality and an eternal one in your life?*
>
> *Have these definitions changed the way you think of the idea that "God's ways are higher than our ways"?*

---

[109] The word for decay here is the Greek word *"phthora."* It should be understood here as depicting the "breakdown of organic matter, dissolution, deterioration, corruption, [passing away] in the world of nature" that ends in "total destruction" (BDAG, 1054-1055).

[110] They indirectly fulfill His will, for His will directly intends for those creatures made in His image to have free will. The existence of temporal contextualities is directly due to the bad use of this free will, which is an unintended outcome that the Creator pre-ordained to be a possibility.

Temporal contextualities are deeply intertwined with the Fall, indicating a need to correct the deviation from the Creator's Vision (Acts 3:21). This deviation was an eventuality that the Creator anticipated and indirectly permitted to exist in His creation to uphold our free will, as creatures made in His image as the God who is Spirit.[111] This fallenness taints temporal contextualized realities with a corruptibility that cancels out the possibility of harmonious shalom.[112] Think of it like a poorly built building with a hidden but major design flaw that compromises the overall stability of the whole thing. Or think of it like an imperfect computer program with flaws that will inevitably lead to it becoming buggy and crashing altogether. Once temporal contextualities are done away with, however, the eternal story of finitude can commence according to its essential state of perfection, pre-established by the Creator (Matt 13:41-42; Acts 3:21). The "new heaven" and "new earth" become permanently established with unshakeable foundations even as the fallen world with its "shakable" foundations is removed from the Theater of Finitude, such that it "will not be remembered" as "only what is unshaken remains" (Isa 65:17, 66:22; Heb 12:26-27; 2 Pet 3:7, 10-13).

This does not imply that only the negative outcomes of our misuse of 'free will' will be removed. Even the "good" temporal

---

[111] Free will is meaningless without the reality of consequences. We cannot say we were free to choose something if both the results of two choices led to the same outcome. Only with the possibility of a real difference is free will truly free, just as God told the Isrealites, "I set before you life and death…" Hence, there were opposing possibilities God allowed in terms of giving Adam and Eve the choice of whether or not to eat the forbidden fruit in the Garden of Eden. The book *God is Spirit* goes into more detail on our free will that reflects the Maker's own freedom.

[112] Referring to peace, harmony, wholeness, completeness, welfare, prosperity, etc.

contexts established by the Creator will be eliminated from finitude. They will be replaced by a realm of eternal contexts, reflecting His original vision. Our Creator will "create a new heaven and a new earth! The former ones will not be remembered; no one will think about them anymore" (Isa 65:17). Only then can the Narrative of Finitude progress without the interference of any rogue playwright "who make[s] plans without consulting [God], who form[s] alliances without consulting the Spirit, and thereby compound[s] their sin" [as] "rebellious children" (Isa 30:1). The Creator's intention for the Theatre of Finitude to serve as a perfect finitely contextualized tabernacle of His immanent self-disclosure will be forever established.[113] Its inhabitants will exist in perfect harmony, akin to an orchestra. To accomplish this, each "musician" must perform a distinct, cohesive role in the Creator's eternal narrative as He reveals Himself throughout its progression. Only then can creation become a tabernacle of the Divine that consistently reflects the perfect shalom of His uncreated tabernacle (Rom 15:33; 1 Cor 14:33, 15:20-58).[114]

> *Which temporal contexts will you give up for God's eternal story to unfold in your life?*

---

[113] Recall our previous discussion about tabernacles. We ourselves and our world were originally intended to be tabernacles for Yahweh's self-disclosing presence.

[114] A much more thorough account of the Fall and temporal contextualities will be presented in a later volume that deals with the fall and its immediate aftermath.

Post-Fall

Domain of Finitude

Comprised of Finite Realities

Domain of Eternal Reality

Comprised of Eternal Realities

Temporal-Eternal Realities

Domain of Temporal Reality

Comprised of Temporal Realities

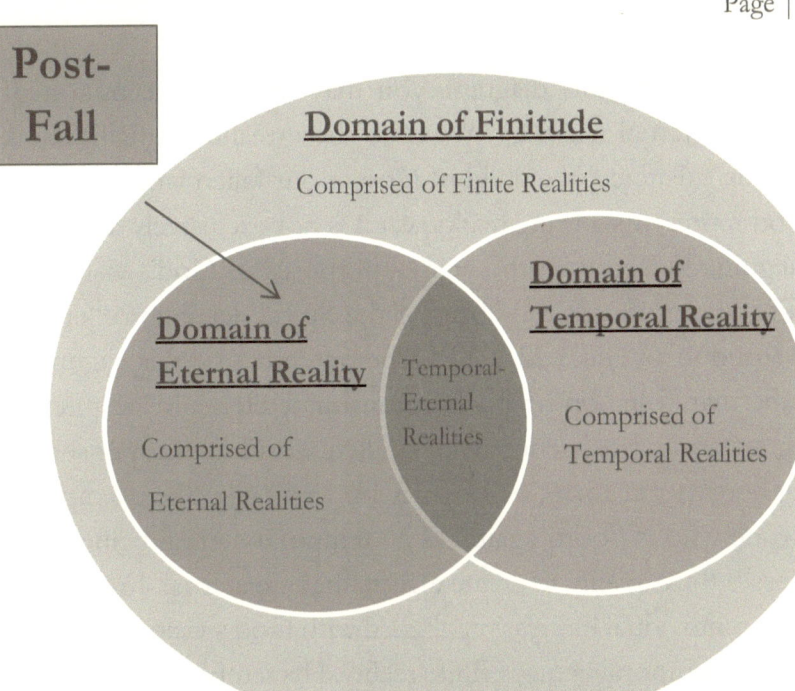

New Heavens & New

Domain of Finitude is the Domain of Eternal Reality

Solely Comprised of Eternal Realities

115

---

[115] The duality regarding the existence of temporal-eternal realities will be considered later, as for now it is important to note that during the age of temporality such a duality is temporarily present. For example, consider how

When examining this diagram, you may observe the notion of "temporal-eternal realities." What do these realities entail? Think about the existence of a child of God in our fallen world. A child of God represents a finite reality, yet it is not exclusively temporal. By aligning herself with the eternal purposes of God's vision for her life, she produces the "fruit of the Spirit" leading to "eternal life" (John 4:36; Gal 5:22-23).[116] The outcomes of this alignment and the manifestation of the Spirit resonate eternally, despite her living a transient existence in this fallen world with a perishable, dying body (John 15:16; 1 Cor 3:13-14, 15:42-44). She exemplifies someone who is "born again" as a "temporal-eternal being." She possesses the capacity to create effects that are eternal. In contrast, a secular individual has not yet aligned with God's vision. He exists solely as a temporal being, a finite reality. His temporal life can only produce temporary effects, destined to decay into nothingness (1 Cor 3:13-15). "[Such people are] like straw before the wind, and like chaff swept away by a whirlwind" (Job 21:18).

Let us explore this distinction in more depth. Both the child of God and the prodigal child represent finite realities, both being creations of God. However, only the child of God embodies the

---

human existence remains temporarily tied to a corruptible mortal body that will inevitably cease to exist. Nevertheless, the potential for human existence to bear the fruit of the Spirit endures while we inhabit these bodies until we are clothed with incorruptible immortal ones (1 Cor 15:35-58).

The new heavens and new earth diagram represent the Theatre of Finitude after all temporal realities are removed from the household of finitude. They are taken outside to Sheol, which is the metaphoric a trash heap outside the city. This allows for the eternal story of God's creation to envelope the domain of Finitude after the expiration of the age of temporality. All this will be discussed in detail throughout our journey.

[116] Jesus taught the following: "I am the vine; you are the branches. The one who remains in Me – and I in him – bears much fruit [eternal effect], because apart from Me you can accomplish nothing [only temporal effects]... You did not choose Me, but I chose you and appointed you to go and bear fruit, fruit that remains [permanently persists]" (John 15:5, 16).

"hope of eternal life" (Tit 1:2; 1 John 5:1, 11-13). When the long-awaited moment of death arrives, we will transition into a fully eternal existence, worshipping and living eternally for the God of our salvation through an incorruptible and immortal body (1 Cor 15:51-54; 2 Cor 5:1-4). As we now experience eternal life within eternal contexts, our existence as part of the Narrative of Finitude remains endless. In contrast, the individual who continues as a secular self has only a temporary existence. They resemble vapor or chaff in the wind (Job 7:16; Prov 21:6; Ps 1:4-5, 39:5-11, Ps 144:4; Hos 13:3). Their contextual existence vanishes when they permanently depart the realm of finitude at death. Those like her, who remain in rebellion will not partake in the eternal chapter of Creation's storyline (Job 8:13).[117] "The Lord says [to them], 'That is why I will scatter you people like chaff that is blown away by a desert wind. This is your fate, the destiny to which I have appointed you, because you have forgotten Me and have trusted in false gods'" (Jer 13:24-25).

---

[117] The final 'destination' of those who forfeit their opportunity to be a part of the Creator's never-ending story will be addressed later in this journey.

Page | 188

→ Eternal Effects Solely Corresponding to the Stage of Eternity
↑ Eternal Effects Corresponding to Both Stages
— Temporal Effects Corresponding to Stage of Temporality
✕ Permanently Ceases to Cause Actual Effects [Useless Twigs]

Theatre [Household] of Finitude

Stage of Eternity

Stage of Temporality

Void [Vacuum] of Finitude

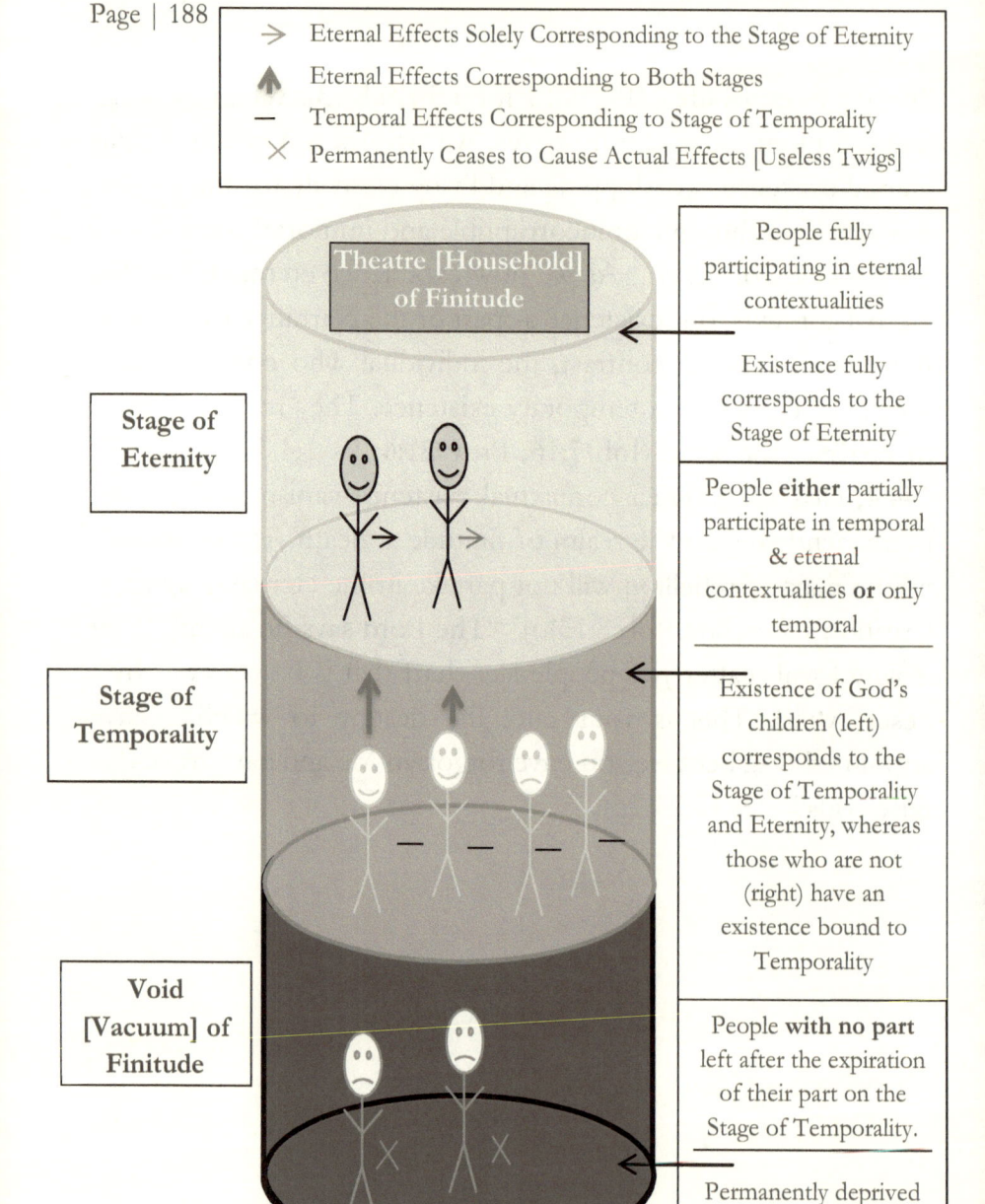

People fully participating in eternal contextualities

Existence fully corresponds to the Stage of Eternity

People **either** partially participate in temporal & eternal contextualities **or** only temporal

Existence of God's children (left) corresponds to the Stage of Temporality and Eternity, whereas those who are not (right) have an existence bound to Temporality

People **with no part** left after the expiration of their part on the Stage of Temporality. Permanently deprived of actuality upon any Stage of Finitude

118

---

[118] This illustration conveys the negative implications of a change that lacks alignment with the eternal ends of the Creator's Vision, marking a deviation from His standards of goodness. In terms of temporality, such changes bring

Being "born again" signifies a shift from a purely 'finite-temporal mode of being' to a 'finite eternal-temporal mode of being' (John 3:3; 1 Pet 1:3, 13). A finite-temporal mode of being refers to a state where human existential relations are limited to temporal contexts. Conversely, a 'finite eternal-temporal mode of being' has the capacity to engage with and yield results that align with both temporal and eternal contexts. In this state, individuals can engage with the eternal truth of God's vision for Finitude, embracing their identity as children of God. They can undergo transformation into a "new creation; what is old has passed away – behold, what is new has come" (2 Cor 5:17). This transformation is not instantaneous. Aligning with God's vision accounts for only part of the process. The actual alignment and the journey toward what we call 'eternal humanness' results from an ongoing sanctification process supported by the Spirit's indwelling presence (2 Thes 2:13; 1 Pet 1:2). We will explore this in detail later.

{ *What type of enduring influence do you think you can have as a temporal-eternal child of God?* }

Being born again and fulfilling God's vision in our limited world is just the beginning. The ultimate change of "resurrection" signifies a shift from a 'finite eternal-temporal existence' to a pure 'finite eternal existence' (1 Cor 15:23, 50-54; Phil 3:11). This occurs

---

chaos that has infiltrated and afflicted Finitude for as long as the fallen stage of temporality persists within the theatre of Finitude (that is, for as long as the temporal realm continues, and the end is yet to come). At times, particularly concerning events in human civilization during this current evil age of temporality, this chaos is not only induced but often masterminded by a figure of chaos: the Devil. The topic of the Devil will be examined later alongside the discussion of why these evil temporal realities exist, given that God created everything to be good and to participate eternally in His unending narrative. This exploration will mainly focus on the Fall, its unintended consequences, the problem of evil in light of God's absolute goodness, and the Devil's influence as a catalyst for the presence of temporal realities.

> *How can you consistently align yourself with God to exist as a finite temporal-eternal being while progressing toward becoming a finite eternal being?*

when God resurrects His children and sanctifies them through an eternal rebirth, where the old is replaced by the new (Rom 6:5; 1 Cor 15:51-58; Phil 3:10-11; 1 John 3:2). This change paves the way for a life defined fully by eternal realities. The resurrected child of God no longer sins; instead, every action, thought, desire, and movement perfectly embodies God's character and will. The trials and burdens of this world cease to affect us. We will effortlessly manifest the Spirit's outlook and desires (Gal 5:17, 22). However, this state of existence for a human remains constrained by the finite realm's temporal (time) and spatial (space) dimensions.[119]

The Deceptive World-Shaping Influence of Darkness

By exploring the differences between the terms "eternal" and "temporal," we have gained deeper insight into our quest to return home. It is important to remember that the contextualities we pursue, comprehend, and apply during this journey are eternal in nature. In contrast, they are fundamentally distinct from the contextualities found in the temporal realm, referred to as the "Land of Fallenness." Ultimately, a temporal and therefore partial perspective on human potential or purpose can only serve to promote the fleeting advantages of a perishing body and the diminishing splendors of a fading world. This notion aligns with

---

[119] The *becoming* of this eternal mode of being causes effects that solely correspond to an eternal contextualized plane of finite reality. Even in the New Heavens and New Earth, creature will not partake of Infinite reality, which is the purview of God alone.

Shakespeare's depiction of a "walking shadow" who performs a brief role on the world's stage before fading away into obscurity.[120]

Consider, for a contemporary example, the house rules of a world-system grounded in capitalist materialism- a concept with which most of us are at least somewhat familiar. Within this world-system, individuals define their identities through consumerism, an attachment to material possessions (the obsession with "keeping up with the Joneses"), seeking sensual pleasure (eating purely for enjoyment or engaging in chemical or sexual addictions), escapism through narcissistic fantasies (excessive consumption of video games and films), and living vicariously through others (whether on social media or through fanatical interest in celebrities or sport) teams).[121] The world becomes a playground of the ego. One pretends to be a king or queen over their own private kingdom by laying down the law of the land based on seeking one's own advantage above anything else.[122] This occurs when, for instance, an individual views their social media popularity and image as more important to their identity than an eternal perspective, or when moral values

Can you think of other examples of individuals chasing illusions of existential rest and attempting to construct palaces on unstable ground?

Have you ever felt the urge to engage in these behaviors, too?

---

[120] This is a line from the famous tragedy *Macbeth*.
[121] Some of these things are not in themselves sinful or evil, but they become stumbling blocks when they become more central to one's life than the God-relationship.
[122] This need not be for "selfish" reasons (wanting power over others or wealth for its own sake) but even for the purpose of finding self-fulfillment, stability, or existential satisfaction in a relationship or by living altruistically. No matter the motives, trying to flourish using these consumeristic contextualities (or any temporal contextualities) is ultimately a futile gesture.

and family connections are regarded as dispensable in the quest for glory, wealth, or status.

Those whose lives are shaped by the influence of the Evil One become his children rather than the Creator's (John 8:41-47; 1 John 3:9-12). By aligning with the Grand Deceiver, individuals effectively adopt a false identity (Rev 12:9). Jesus described these individuals, stating, "You people are from your father the devil, and you want to do what your father desires... He does not uphold the truth, because there is no truth in him... [He is] the father of lies [the falsifier]" (John 8:44; ISA). Living in this "masquerade of temporality" means forfeiting the true, divine destiny offered by the Creator. By rejecting a solely temporal legacy, we, as fellow travelers aboard our ship, admit, to our shame, that we once lived according to "the world's present path" (Eph 2:2). We now recognize our prodigal ways and seek to return home in repentance. We have chosen to abandon the pursuit of finding our fittingness solely within a finite, temporal world-system (Luke 15:11-23). We have responded to Jesus's call: "Come to Me, all you who are weary and burdened, and I will give you rest. Take My yoke on you and learn from Me because I am gentle and humble in heart, and you will find rest for your souls. For My yoke is easy to bear, and My load is not hard to carry" (Matt 11:28-30).

> *Are you ready to begin a spiritual journey, leaving behind familiar yet restricted temporal contexts?*
>
> *For those already on this path, would you say it was worthwhile?*

Through his fabricated world-systems, the Evil One aims to dominate humanity's existence and perceptions (Rom 6:6; 1 John 5:19). This domination leads to his illegitimate influence over the core aspects of those who adhere to the masquerade of temporality, striving to find themselves within his realm (John 8:41, 1 John 3:12). Consequently, people fall victim to the "devil's trap, where they are held captive to do his will" rather than God's will. God lovingly seeks to rescue us from the looming destruction of fleeting existence, yet the evil one does all he can to prevent this (John 8:41-44; 1 John 3:11-12; 2 Tim 2:26; Rom 9:22; 2 Pet 3:9).

In seeking to shape their identities and destinies within the temporal realm, short-sighted individuals arrogantly aim for the supra-contextual sovereignty that belongs solely to God. Their efforts only lead to distorted perceptions of reality, creating fleeting experiences. Their attempts to construct earthly kingdoms are foolish efforts to fashion a "home" from the shadows of temporality, striving to build an existential palace on shifting sands. Take, for instance, an adulterer who seeks fleeting pleasure or misguided "acceptance" without considering the devastating consequences for those around them, such as their family, community, and legacy. They pursue an illusion of "wholeness," ultimately leading to an emptier existence. As stated, "A man who commits adultery with a woman lacks wisdom; whoever does it destroys his own life" (Prov 6:32). By confining their pursuits to the temporal, they miss the true way of life offered by Eternity. The corruption of this temporal existence has left the world largely devoid of the Creator's abiding presence. Thus, the reality shaped by earthly dwellers lacks the illuminating light of the Creator and His originally established *oikonomia*. They are tabernacles devoid of divine relational immanence.

Removing the Veil of Transience by the Light of Eternity

The "veil" of temporality prevents those tied to a restricted view from recognizing eternal contexts, as "the god of this age has blinded the[ir] minds." (2 Cor 3:13-15, 4:4). The perception of what truly *is* (what being and reality really *are*), which validates the actual existence of all eternal realities, only comes from a supra-contextual perspective (John 8:12). This viewpoint transcends human world-viewing constraints (Eph 4:17-18). We can genuinely grasp what is true only by viewing the Story of Finitude from the Playwright's own perspective. Adopting this overarching view shifts our understanding toward a more God-centered perspective, which fully acknowledges every enduring aspect of God's eternal narrative. From the Eternity standpoint, we understand God's will and view reality through the lens of the Kingdom of Heaven.

Through the Spirit of Truth, an eternal viewpoint "transforms" our world-viewing by "renewing our mind, so that [we] may test and approve what is the will of God" (John 14:17; Rom 12:2). Anything that does not align with "God's will" will ultimately be eliminated from the Theatre of Finitude. What remains does so because its virtue is part of the Creator's original perfect design for Finitude, which represents a standard of perfection that surpasses humanity's limited grasp of perfection (1 John 2:17).

As seafarers, we must recognize that our journey home encompasses a different way of viewing the world and understanding our relationship with the divine and the rest of Creation. We should see the connection with God as our starting point for redefining reality through "the outlook of the Spirit" (Rom 8:6). By walking in the Spirit, we align ourselves with our authentic selves as shaped by this divine connection (Gal 5). The true essence of the eternal realm of Finitude, our True Home, becomes accessible through God's revelation to those who choose to "live by the Spirit" rather than "by the flesh" (Gal 5:16-17, 6:8). Only an outlook reshaped by this revelation can rise above the limits of worldly viewpoints to explore eternal possibilities (Rom 12:2).

> *Have you ever attempted to perceive eternal truths or contextualities without the Spirit of Truth reshaping your perspective?*
>
> *What did they look like? In what ways do they differ from God's eternal truths?*

Temporal perspectives can distort our understanding of what truly matters. They obscure our true calling or lead us to misinterpret it, making it easier to dismiss so-called "superstitious" concerns as trivial. Yet, we have transcended the illusions of temporality and the strategies of darkness (John 12:35-36, 1 John 2:22). The Spirit of Truth reveals the Deceiver's schemes that keep us bound to Babylonian systems (Eph 6:11; 1 Pet 5:8). We can only find authentic existential "freedom" only by choosing to "put to death" our false temporal selves, which lead to eternal death, and instead embrace our true selves, as designed by our Creator. "Instead, put on the Lord Jesus Christ, and make no provision for the flesh to arouse its desires" (Rom 13:14). Only then can we truly opt for genuine existential flourishing rather than become enslaved to the deceptive ambitions of temporality, much like the Israelites were enslaved in Egypt (2 Cor 3:17; Rom 6:6, 16-23, 8:21; John 8:34-35).

Within "Babylon," free will is merely an illusion. Humans are "free" to be and achieve "nothing" from Eternity's perspective, like a fruit branch detaching from a vine. Much like a horse led by a carrot on a string, we are manipulated by an enemy who plays with our emotions and perceptions. He suggests that authentic "life and freedom" can be achieved through existential rebellion.

> *Do you believe that only by relinquishing the hope of finding true satisfaction in this world can you genuinely realize the "true self" that God intended for you?*

While we remain land-dwellers, access to Eternity lies ever beyond our reach. The Scriptures indicate that those "alienated from the life of God" possess a "darkened" perspective caused by "ignorance" and the "futility of their thinking" (Eph 2:1-3; Eph 4:17-19). By rejecting true existential fulfillment in favor of achieving fittingess in Babylonian contexts, temporal inhabitants confine themselves to fleeting happiness (Isa 16:10, 24:7-9, 32:13; 1 Pet 4:1-6). In contrast, our faith has opened our eyes to the genuine freedom of world-dwelling and world-viewing illuminated by the light of Eternity, our true Home (John 8:31-36; Gal 5:13; 2 Cor 3:17). Thus, it is only as seafarers rather than land-dwellers that we can envision and strive to connect inwardly through spirit-to-Spirit communion, which unveils Eternity to our inner being (2 Cor 13:13(14); Phil 2:1). We understand that only the Spirit's "enlightenment" can lift the "eyes of our heart" to "know what is the hope of His calling for our lives" within eternal contexts (Eph 1:18). With this enlightenment, we gain the ability to see past the illusions of a world filled with "veiled" perspectives, spoiled dreams, and the regrets this gonewrong world (2 Cor 3:14-17, 4:6).

Unlike those on land, we seafarers, as children of light, interpret reality through faith, hope, and love (1 Cor 13:13). We perceive aspects that remain hidden from others, enabling us to witness something land-dwellers cannot: the immanent dwelling of the Creator and the *oikonomia* of Heaven on earth (Rev 21-22). Furthermore, seafarers not only perceive the world differently but also inhabit it as God intended from the beginning. Scripture tells us that, in the *oikonomia* for the forthcoming world: "death will not exist anymore – or mourning, or crying, or pain, for the former things will cease to exist" (Rev 21:4). What a stark difference from the rules and patterns governing this world!

Our aspirations for the future allow us to live differently from others. Rather than merely pursuing fame, worldly security, recognition, and achievements that will ultimately fade away, we aim for eternal treasures like God's wisdom, the fruits of the Spirit, and the joy found in saving souls. These blessings will endure forever, bringing us joy in Eternity. Our Guide teaches us: "Do not accumulate for yourselves treasures on earth, where moth and rust destroy and where thieves break in and steal. But accumulate for yourselves treasures in heaven, where moth and rust do not destroy, and thieves do not break in and steal. For where your treasure is, there your heart will be also" (Heb 6:19-21).

All seafarers must recognize the distinct nature of eternal contextualities when compared to the temporal realities of land dwelling. Being a land-dweller, rooted in created realities and worldly wisdom, creates a stark contrast with a seafaring way of life, which embodies uncreated realities and divine wisdom. Essentially, seafaring existence focuses on our role as a dwelling place for God (1 Cor 6:19). We refer to this eternal fabric of seafaring contextualities as the "Sea of Revelation." When individuals embrace the true contextualities of "inhabiting earth through heaven," it enables our identity to transcend the limitations of a land-oriented perspective (2 Cor 5:1-5; Phil 3:19-20). As previously noted, land-focused contextualities exist within a lower, earthly "mode of being" (Phil 3:19). In contrast, seafaring contextualities arise from a higher, heavenly mode of existence (Heb 3:1). The essence of Eternity is simply the ever-expanding self-revelations of the Divine. In this reality, a world-dweller pursuing an intimate relationship with God discovers a true home.

How do you believe you should live when perceiving the world as it was intended?

How would that differ from your usual way of life?

Yahweh does not just instantly implant in our minds all the eternal truths a child of God needs. Like toddlers, we must learn how to walk by the Spirit instead of the flesh (Gal 5). Jesus referred to this as being born again for a purpose. How do we learn this new way of living? We allow our God-relationship to shape our worldview and experiences, rather than relying on idolatrous external influences. Idolatry extends beyond merely worshipping pagan deities; it represents anything that diverts us from our true calling to submit to our Creator's vision. It misleads us into feeling at home in this fallen world while neglecting our role as a temple of the Divine. Such individuals will never find genuine fulfillment, as they pursue what is fleeting, akin to chasing a breeze (Prov 27:20; Eccl 1:8, 2:1-11).

Consider someone who thinks that acquiring and maintaining wealth and power are life's ultimate goals. Such a person would be oblivious to the spiritual call to love others. They would fail to utilize their resources and influence to help the homeless or to promote fairer systems that do not solely favor the privileged rich.[123] Such self-sacrifice of one's comfort and resources for the lasting benefit of others occurs only when we step into the Holy of Holies. In this sacred place, we gain insight into the true, pre-ordained narrative that the Creator has shaped for each of us. Only within His "workshop" do we uncover our destined role in a story crafted to help us embody revelation.

Only the Creator can lift the veil of temporality. He alone can reveal the eternal benefits of living for the flourishing of Creation. These veils restrict our understanding of Finitude and our role within it, leading to a feeling of existential homelessness. Think of someone who believes that climbing the corporate ladder is life's ultimate goal. Many individuals reach such heights yet still experience restlessness or a sense of "homelessness," as no amount of money or prestige can truly fulfill their souls. They may hold a position as the head of a multinational company, but behind closed doors could be facing a broken family, stress-ridden psyche, and

> *What makes allowing your relationship with God shape your reality the most effective way to learn to live by the Spirit?*

---

[123] Rather than merely a political ideology, the call to care for the poor is indeed a biblical principle and command (Deut. 15:7; Proverbs 14:31, 19:17, 22:16, Psalm 37:21; Mark 10:21; James 2:15-16)

deteriorating health (Eccl 2:18-21). They sometimes reflect on their legacy with regrets, which is marked by destruction and resentment, born from the deceit and manipulation involved in their selfish corporate climb to maintain a competitive edge.[124]

Only through our Creator's enlightening grace can our minds be renewed to re-envision the dreams of God. Without this grace, we remain trapped in illusions about what is or could be. These fantasies obscure our true destinies and suitability in the world. We wander in darkness as lost inhabitants, distracted by a superficial worldview, pursuing the mirages of fleeting ambitions. As seafarers, we must perceive reality from a fundamentally different perspective. In contrast, land-dwellers can only interpret the world within the limitations of a fallen realm. In this realm, their *being*-there lies outside the sanctuary of the Creator's revelation, leaving them blind to the mysteries of eternal truths, such as the *oikonomia* of the Kingdom of Heaven (John 12:35; 1 John 2:11). Their lack of insight keeps them from acknowledging that everything they hold onto "is passing away" (1 John 2:17).

> *Have you ever fallen for fleeting ideals of success or happiness?*
>
> *What were they, and what replaced them once you choose to live by eternal truths?*

No one walking in darkness can perceive how the world system they inhabit offers only transient happiness, purpose, or fulfillment. Seeing the true depravity of world systems can only occur through the illumination of the supra-contextual perspective

---

[124] Imagine the CEO of a company who has a net worth of millions or billions but is hated by nearly everyone who works for him. He has alienated his friends and family in his quest for power. He will be remembered after death as a terrible human being of whom many are glad to be rid. Is that really a good life and legacy? This is another example of how a selfish pursuit of temporal glory can leave one unsatisfied and full of regret.

of Eternity.[125] This viewpoint of revelation uncovers the eternal *oikonomia*: the foundational principles aligned with the Creator's vision. This is why we must "seek the things above, not things on the earth," and "spend the rest of their time on earth concerned about the will of God not human desires" (Col 3:10; 1 Pet 4:2).

The Land of Darkness signifies the world-systems of Finitude, where the Creator's world-shaping presence is missing. We can only truly live according to His vision by returning to His immanent, enduring presence. This pathway of light reveals itself to us because those of us who "walked in darkness, [have] see[n] a bright light; [for] light shines on those who live in a land of deep darkness" (Isa 9:2). As seafarers, we strive to dwell in the "light of revelation," which unveils our true destiny and eternal home (Luke 2:32). This light allows us to uncover existential possibilities that were once inaccessible. We begin to perceive the world in novel ways, unveiling our true home, narrative, and identities (Prov 6:23). Such heavenly understanding, distinct from earthly knowledge, is guided by the Creator's vision, which transcends finite boundaries.

> *Have you turned away from transient ways of living and toward the pathway of light?*
>
> *How has such a decision affected you?*

---

[125] Think of a fish that has never left the ocean. To that fish, there is no such thing as "wet or dry", since it has never experienced an existence outside of the water. Even the term "wet" would not have any real meaning without "dry" to contrast it with.

Unless one were to take the fish out of water to expose it to a world not defined by "being underwater" (and all its contextualities), it would live its entire life not realizing that, rather than its previous existence being universal, there are other ways of inhabiting the world.

Living by the Light of Eternity

Our Creator desires each of us to turn away from living as a "false self" and doing "dead works," as this inevitably leads to "perishing" by eternal separation from Him (Ezek 18:23, 32; 33:11; 2 Pet 3:9; Heb 6:1). He calls us to return home and discover our true identities as His image-bearers in this dark world (Isa 50:4-5; 1 Pet 2:9). Amid humanity's existential rebellion, He provides everyone with the chance to abandon the masquerade of temporality and embrace the responsibility of self-discovery grounded in God. This sacred duty asks us to be the world's light and salt (Isa 58:6-9; Matt 5:13-16). Eternity beckons us to "be blameless and pure, children of God without blemish," as we "shine as lights in the world" while living in a crooked and perverse society (Phil 2:15). We fulfill this calling by living according to the *oikonomia* of Eternity, following the guidance of the Wind of Eternity (John 3:8).

We seafarers distinguish ourselves from those who dwell on land. Our lives are committed to a journey home guided by revealed spiritual truths. We firmly believe that our true dwelling place has been defined by created realities for far too long. These realities have dictated our identity, lifestyle, and purpose, overshadowing the divine vision.

{ *Are you willing to relinquish some pleasures and comforts of temporality to live as a seafarer in pursuit of the knowledge of God?* }

We now choose to "trust in the Lord with all our heart," instead of "relying on our own understanding" (Prov 3:5). Only by "acknowledging Him in all our ways" can He "make our paths straight" (Prov 3:6). Transitioning from being land-dwellers, we aspire to live as nomadic rebels, resisting the homes built by temporary world-systems. We reject the temptations of impermanence, which have misled us into shaping our lives for fleeting comforts. Instead, we embark on the less-traveled path, dedicating ourselves to continually growing in understanding our Creator's self-revealing narrative (Eph 1:17).

We should not behave like those in the world who proclaim, "there is peace and security," becoming "drunk" on the abundance of worldly pleasures while overlooking the "destruction [that will] come on" those who inhabit this temporary existence, with "no escape" (1 Thess 5:3, 7). Unaware of the demands and possibilities of Eternity, they fail to embrace their eternal destinies. Of such individuals, it is remarked: "This is the fate of all who forget God; the hope of the ungodly fades away; their trust is in something meaningless, and their security resembles a spider's web. He leans against his house, but it cannot support him; he grasps it, but it cannot stand" (Job 8:13-15).

Being without God in our world equates to lacking the spiritual dignity integral to our true humanity, relegating us to the lowest ranks of the animal kingdom. This results in engaging in behaviors that clash with nature and are, in fact, contradictory to it. We pursue comfort, pleasure, power, and security – biological urges stemming from our fallen nature – often at the expense of our morals and spirituality. Consequently, we act selfishly, indulge in and even celebrate sexual perversions, sensual gratification, and inflict harm or disgrace on other beings made in God's image. In these moments, we resemble a tribe of higher-order animals instead of a royal priesthood of temporal-eternal beings. Tragically, many religious denominations and theologies not only endorse but celebrate such anti-divine behavior of living for the sake of temporality. These belief systems hinder humanity's genuine spiritual essence and destiny, striving to keep it subdued while fostering a carnal and soulish way of living among those who have entirely rejected their identity as children of the One who embodies spirit, light, and love, which are hated by those accustomed to spiritually barren contextualities (a desert).

As children of light, we should heed the Scripture's caution: "The night has advanced toward dawn; the day is near. So, then we must lay aside the works of darkness and put on the weapons of light. Let us live decently as in the daytime, not in carousing and drunkenness, sexual immorality, sensuality, discord, and jealousy. Instead, put on the Lord Jesus Christ and make no provision for the flesh to arouse its desires" (Rom 13:12-14).

Those whose world-viewing takes shape in accordance with darkness "do not know where they are going" due to the "futility of their thinking" (John 12:35; Eph 4:17). These "children" of the "night" perceive their surroundings without the guidance of God's illuminating "light," which brings clarity to all human realities, such as purpose, identity, and roles that hold eternal importance (1 Thess 5:4-5). Meanwhile, the "children of the day" discover their true "destiny" within the context of the Creator's tabernacle (1 Thess 5:5-10). Only in the Holy of Holies, through the light of our Maker's self-revelation, can our existence possibly align with our intended initial purpose of guiding people to dwell in and through the immanent Temple of God.

Why should we not live only for the sake of temporality?

Why should we distrust worldly systems that claim wealth, security, status, or the latest products will fulfill our desires?

While we remain land-dwellers, continuing our lives on earth, we choose a type of exile from the presence of Babylon. As exiles, we walk between two worlds. Inwardly, we regularly dwell in the heavenly realms of Eternity. This requires us to be a tabernacle of God's presence in the Spirit, the only way to enter the realm of eternal contextualities, the "Sea of Revelation." However, we must always remember our duty to outwardly live a life that reflects our inner faith through actions exemplifying that faith (Jas 2:14-26). As we read, "faith, if it does not have works, is dead being by itself" (Jas 2:17). Living as tabernacles with the Spirit in us opens an existential horizon that was once foreign to us. Through the Light of Eternity, we can align our lives with the eternal realities that existed long before the temporary world emerged.

> *How has your life changed since you decided to "walk between worlds"?*
>
> *Does your life reflect the inner transformations that occur when you follow Eternity's Call?*
>
> *If not, what holds you back?*

Conclusion: Self-Resignation of Temporality by Exiles

The decision is now in our hands. Which tabernacle will we choose to inhabit? Which one will influence our worldview, lifestyle, and identity? Will it be the tabernacle of Babel, constructed by humans and demons? Such places will ultimately turn into the "anti-tabernacle" of Sheol, the final death. Or will it be the eternal tabernacle of Zion, created by God? This choice is unavoidable because humans are inherently beings that dwell within tabernacles, whether we acknowledge it or not. We cannot exist without a tabernacle, as we are naturally house-dwellers. Failing to make a choice means we automatically choose Babel. Those of us navigating the Sea of Revelation must intentionally choose to dwell in this eternal realm, where only the city of Zion and its context can be discovered and practiced.

Choosing to stay and establish a home on land, compels one to dwell according to the illusions of temporal contextualities. Such attempts to discover "fittingness" and to forge an identity and life in Babylon are destined to dissolve into chaos. Those who ignore Eternity's Call inevitably succumb to the condition of "fallenness," regardless of their self-perception even if they be religious. Against this trend, the crew aboard this vessel must fully renounce the idolatrous belief in finding a true home within this disintegrating world-system. We assert that it is in the immediate presence of the Holy Spirit where we truly dwell in accordance with the realities of our genuine home. May we persevere in our journey as pilgrims until our Maker finally summons us home. Hence, we candidly recognize that we are homeless wanderers if we remain on the "coasts' of our fallen world.

All of us seafarers onboard this ship aspire to receive the Creator's "welcome" along with an everlasting "inheritance" within the finite household of the Living God (1 Cor 6:17; Eph 1:18, 2:19; Col 1:12). However, this necessitates recognizing and responding inwardly to the Creator's call to "come out from the midst [of the world-systems of Babylon], and be separate [from them]" (2 Cor 6:17; Rev 18:2-4). To distance ourselves from the transient world-systems, we must adopt a standard of "oughtness"- a pursuit of rightness and holiness that does not belong to this world-system (2 Cor 7:1; 1 Thess 3:13, 4:4-8; Eph 4:24; Rom 6:13; 2 Pet 3:11; Heb 12:14). To embark on a pilgrimage along the narrow path of holiness, we must daily enter the innermost part of our being to experience rebirth, allowing the Creator's Spirit to abide with us (John 3:3-8;

> *Are you struggling to prioritize Eternity over the fleeting moments of life?*
>
> *What could make this decision challenging, even for those who intellectually understand it is the correct one?*

1 Thess 4:7-8; 2 Thess 2:13). For believers filled with the Spirit, this is the only place where our quest to rediscover ourselves according to our Creator's vision can truly unfold.

We who choose to pursue this holiness must live as fitting inhabitants of our true, heavenly world-house. In the words of Scripture:

> "Therefore, if you have been raised with Christ, keep seeking the things above, where Christ is, seated at the right hand of God. Keep thinking about things above, not things on the earth, for you have died and your life is hidden with Christ in God. When Christ (who is your life) appears, then you too will be revealed in glory with Him. So put to death whatever in your nature belongs to the earth."
>
> (Col 3:1-5)

The world we strive for is one currently absent from the temporal realm. Nevertheless, we believe it will ultimately become the sole occupant of Finitude. To many on land, this world we hope for appears like a dream; a paradise nearly too impossible and wonderful to fully grasp or even imagine according to the logic of this present, temporal realm.

Our unwavering hope brings us joy in relinquishing the transient prosperity of this life, even for the so-called 'poverty' of being an eternity-bound pilgrim.[126] For us, this 'poverty', when

---

[126] For us, this does not necessarily mean actual poverty in a financial sense. Many may not even see it as a sacrifice to give their possessions away. What this means is that, ultimately, we are called to place everything in this world as secondary in importance to God and His will for us. There may be times when we need to give up wealth yes, but also opportunities, certain relationships, popularity, being "well-liked", influence, comforts, or alternative life plans or paths that end up conflicting with His desires or eternal contextualities.

compared to our land-dwelling neighbors, represents a worthwhile exchange compared to the rich inheritance that awaits us in the Kingdom of Heaven. The parables of Jesus illustrate this beautifully: "The kingdom of heaven is like a treasure, hidden in a field, that a person found and hid. Then because of joy he went and sold all that he had and bought that field. Again, the kingdom of heaven is like a merchant searching for fine pearls. When he found a pearl of great value, he went out and sold everything he had and bought it" (Matt 13:44-46).

Christ warns His followers saying, "Exert every effort to enter through the narrow door, because many, I tell you, will try to enter and will not be able to" (Luke 13:24). Elsewhere He says, "Be on your guard so that your hearts are not weighed down with dissipation and drunkenness and the worries of this life, and that day of eternal judgment close down upon you suddenly like a trap" (Luke 21:34). Each of us must answer for ourselves whether or not we will "follow" Christ by standing among those who "deny themselves, take up their cross daily,[127]" and put to death the false "enslaved" selfhood shaped by the "flesh with its passions and desires" (Luke 9:23; Rom 6:6; Gal 2:20, 5:24; 1 Pet 4:1). Have we freely chosen to give ourselves over to "practice[ing] the truth" by "com[ing] to the light [of eternal contextualities], so that it may be plainly evident that [our] deeds [are being] done in God [as deeds

---

Though these decisions may make us "poorer" or "more unfortunate" according to the world, we must count it all joy to sacrifice these things to follow God.

[127] This does not mean a literal cross, or even necessarily a literal sacrifice as a martyr. Many of us will likely not be in a situation where we would have to do this. Instead, this refers to the sacrifices we must make daily for the sake of Christ in laying down our allegiance to any temporal realities or contextualities that draw us away from God. However, we must be willing to lay down our life, if we face persecution for His name's sake. What might your "crosses" of sacrifice be that God is calling you to take up?

corresponding to our true identity, as His eternity-bound children]" (John 3:21)? Have we turned away from the enticing false light of the Babylonian cities in the Land of Darkness? If so, have we allowed the illumination of the Creator's vision to transform our understanding of life and reality? If not, are we prepared to humbly repent before our Maker? Are we open to letting Him reveal the new realities of our true selves to us each day? Are we ready to rely on His sanctifying presence to realize our genuine identity and guide us toward our eternal Home?

[
How do you respond to these questions?

If your answer is no, what stops you from saying yes?

If yes, what actions will you take to follow through? How
]

Chapter 6

Homeward-Bound Nomads
Forsaking Babylon to Discover our Eternal Destiny

"Come, let us go up to the Lord's mountain, to the temple of God, so we can follow His standards... O descendants of Jacob, come, let us walk in the Lord's guiding light... [Let us] Make the ascent from Babylon... to Zion [by] the good hand of our God."
(Isa 2:3-5; Ezra 7:9; Jer 50:28; Ps 27:4)

"A thoroughfare will be there – it will be called the Way of Holiness... Those delivered from bondage will travel on it, those whom the Lord has ransomed. They will enter Zion with a happy shout. Unending joy will crown them; suffering will disappear."
(Isa 14:17, 35:8-10)

"Dear friends, we are God's children now, and what we will be has not yet been revealed. We know that whenever it is revealed we will be like Him...The person who keeps His commandments resides in God, and God in him... By this we know that we reside in God and He in us: in that He has given us of His Spirit."
(1 John 3:2, 24, 4:12-13)

"You are fellow citizens with the saints and members of God's household... In [Christ] the whole building, being joined together, grows into a holy temple in the Lord, in whom you also are being built together into a dwelling place of God in the Spirit."
(Eph 2:19-22)

Embracing our Eternal Destinies as "Theological Selves"

In this chapter, we will explore how exactly we can leave Babylon behind to embrace our eternal destinies. Though a seemingly impossible task, we can undertake this profound sacrifice to live as homeward-bound seafarers, thanks to the grace, strength, and guidance of our Creator. To become such a pilgrim of Eternity, we must sincerely dedicate ourselves to allowing Him to work through us. To this end, He invites us to willingly surrender ourselves and our lives to Him.

Within the human situation established by the Creator, He created each of us as individuals meant to care about and concern ourselves with how to authentically "dwell" within our world.[128] Consider how we frequently reflect on our true selves or question our rightful position in the world. In grappling with these profound inquiries, we typically assume there is a universal framework encompassing all the who(s), what(s), why(s), how(s), and other guiding principles. However, as seafarers, we must turn to the Creator's vision to uncover the truth about our identity and purpose. "We are His workmanship, having been created [brought into existence] in Christ Jesus for good works that God prepared beforehand [preordained] so we may [walk in] them" (Eph 2:10; ISA, BDAG 572).[129] At the heart of our self-reflection lies the

> *Have you ever found yourself reflecting on the "big questions" of life?*
>
> *Where have you turned to find answers?*

---

[128] Refer to the previous chapters for the existential meanings of "selves", "care", and "dwelling" that we concern ourselves with here.

[129] The Greek word here *"peripateo"* translated as "so we may do them" or "we should walk in them" is better understood as referring to: "the sphere in which one lives or ought to live, so as to be characterized by that sphere; way of life" (BDAG, 803). It refers to more than just actions we are purposed to do, but our entire way of living and thinking.

aspiration to embody the authentic selves our Creator envisioned for us. Scripture speaks of our true self by calling us to "put on the new man [self] who has been created in God's image – in righteousness and holiness that comes from truth" (Eph 4:24).

Each day presents us with existential crossroads where the possibility of "eternal life" through the path "leading to sanctification" stands before us (Rom 6:22). The "person who does the will of God remains forever," unlike those who follow the rebellious desires of the "world," which will "pass away" along with "all [the world's] desires" (1 John 2:17; Rom 6:21). Opting for eternal possibilities requires a willingness to *become* a "new creation"; the world-dwelling self our Creator intended us to be through faith in Jesus Christ (Rom 6:4, 7:6; 2 Cor 5:17). To sincerely dedicate ourselves to being a new creation, we must adhere to the house-rules of Yahweh's ordained vision of appropriateness: righteousness and holiness (Eph 1:5-6, 4:24). For example, the world expects us to take revenge when someone has wronged us. We even have movies all about it, such as *John Wick* and *Kill Bill*. However, we show ourselves to be new and different from the world when we instead follow Jesus' seemingly foolish teaching to instead turn the other cheek when someone has wronged us (Mt 5:38-42). Ultimately, embracing a vision of "fittingness" demands embracing the purposes, responsibilities, standards, contextual roles, and modes of self-actualization that align with it.[130]

---

[130] In this existential context, self-actualization involves more than just reaching one's highest potential. This commonly accepted definition seriously neglects the essence of human existence as a being interacting with the world around them. Genuine self-actualization is deeply tied to the idea of contextuality. This concept encompasses not only one's immediate surroundings, such as society, family, and peers, but also the broader supracontextual realm of the world at large.

A personal quest for meaning can only achieve its true goal when we willingly rest before the vision of the One who creates and defines our real selves.[131] Yahweh uniquely provides a contextualized sense of "destiny" and identity (Ps 31:15). He authored every self even before He established the foundations of the world (Eph 1:4, 2:10; 2 Tim 2:21). It is through our Creator's vision that we can achieve self-actualization as a "true theological self." A noble destiny within an eternal framework awaits us. Without this, we would simply be individuals constrained by the limited opportunities of a fallen world. What is our ultimate destiny? It is to be eternal residents of Zion, the City of God (Heb 12:22-24; Eph 2:19-22). Among all the possible contexts, only this one is built on unshakable foundations, the "cornerstone" of Christ, where our "real life" is "hidden" (Rom 9:33; Eph 2:21; Col 3:3-4; 1 Pet 2:4-6).

If we become an eternally virtuous theological self, we achieve a state of truly "being-there" from the perspective of Eternity. We no longer dwell inauthentically[132] by doing nothing more than unconsciously carrying out a part in whatever narrative we find

---

Therefore, self-actualization is about discovering one's appropriate role in the world. This idea resonates with the notion of fulfilling one's destiny- not just becoming the true self one was meant to be, but also playing the specific roles and nurturing the relationships one is intended to uphold within their unique context.

Consequently, this theological perspective on self-actualization is grounded in our belief in the Creator's vision for creation, as revealed in Scripture.

[131] Reference *Sickness Unto Death* by Kierkegaard.

[132] "Inauthentically" in this usage refers to the philosophical concept of authenticity used in existentialism. In existentialism, authenticity is the degree to which a person's actions are congruent with his or her values and desires, despite external pressures to social conformity. Dwelling inauthentically, therefore, refers to how someone may live without consciously aligning their actions and lifestyle with their inner beliefs, desires, and realities. In this case, one lives without aligning oneself with eternal realities.

ourselves in. Instead, we find and fulfill our eternal purpose by becoming a self consciously aware of God's overarching narrative. We willingly embrace the role we were destined to play in alignment with the "will of God" (2 Cor 1:1; 1 Pet 4:2).

This idea of submitting to a higher will can be likened to how a musician acts in an orchestra or how a creature acts within its environment.[133] Unlike other beings, we possess the free will to operate beyond mere instincts or instinctive "programming." Birds behave as expected, singing, gathering, soaring, and nurturing their young. Humans, however, can exhibit a wide array of behaviors, ranging from altruism towards the less fortunate to committing arbitrary acts of violence. By understanding and actively fulfilling our divinely appointed roles, we can embody our true nature. This alignment allows us to become the most loving and righteous versions of ourselves, harmonizing with our Creator, our surroundings, and the

Why is pursuing and achieving eternal significance in life so important to you?

Can anything besides God provide you with this enduring purpose?

---

[133] Ecosystems are complex networks where life thrives and maintains balance within an environment. Every living organism plays a vital role in nutrient cycles, energy flow, and the upkeep of its surroundings. Plants convert sunlight into energy through photosynthesis, helping to manage soil health. Herbivores transform these plants into energy while controlling overgrowth and aiding reproduction, as seen in species like bees. Carnivores maintain herbivore populations, and scavengers, such as vultures, help prevent diseases by consuming decaying matter. Fungi and bacteria also decompose dead organic material, returning nutrients and energy to the soil.

Ecosystems are self-sustaining because each life form fulfills its role, often without awareness of the broader design by a Creator. Similarly, humans hold specific positions within a grand narrative, one far more intricate than we can grasp. By trusting the Creator and performing our roles to the best of our abilities, we align with our eternal purposes instead of selfishly pursuing individual ambitions that defy God's overarching narrative and "ecosystem."

individuals in our lives. We seek to make right what Satan has made wrong, e.g. in broken relationships. Furthermore, our lives now carry eternal significance. "The person who does the will of God remains forever" (1 John 2:17). We must regularly worship, pray, and obey. In light of eternal perspectives, anyone striving to truly understand or discover themselves must prioritize their relationship with the Creator.

Since God created us to discover our true purposes and fulfillment within the Narrative of Finitude, we naturally tend to care about and reflect on the world around us. Our thoughts about our environment intertwine with our reflections on ourselves and our relationship to the world. For us seafarers, this contemplation focuses on the roles (e.g. caregiver, helper, teacher, encourager, etc.) we are meant to assume according to our Creator's providential will (Rom 12:1; Eph 1:11-12). For example, Paul accepted God's will by embracing his calling as an apostle (1 Cor 1:1; Eph 1:1; Col 1:1; 2 Tim 1:1). Like Jesus, we should proclaim, "My food is to do the will of the One [the Father] who sent Me to complete His work" (John 4:34). We follow the Way of Jesus. His Way leads to breaking "chains," setting captives free, and sharing the Good News. Self-reflection happens as individuals connect with their perceived purpose in this world, prompting considerations of themes such as duty, moral obligation (what is "right"), and purpose within the contexts God has placed us.

In light of this self-reflection, God invites us to "live worthily of the calling with which [we] have been called" (Eph 4:1). These concerns often lead us to compare our envisioned 'ideal' (Christ-like) self with our current self-perception. As seafarers journeying home, we must recognize that we do not belong to this fallen world. In our self-reflection, we should acknowledge our ideal self. What defines our ideal self? "The new man [self] that is being renewed in knowledge according to the image of the One who created it," embodying "a mature person, attaining to the measure of Christ's full stature" (Eph 4:13; Col 3:10). We live like Christ. We speak God's words and do God's will, as we do what we "see" God doing. Thus, we should cease being "conformed to this present world" and instead be "transformed" through sanctification, which "conform[s us] to the image of [Christ]" (Rom 8:29, 12:2).

Each seafarer aspires to embody a true eternal self, created in the image of the Creator. "Do not lie to one another since you have put off the old [humanity] with its practices and have been clothed with the new [humanity] that is being renewed in knowledge according to the image of the One who created it" (Col 3:9-10). This theological self carries contextual ties to an "alien homeland" distinct from this world. Scripture tells us that in becoming a "new creation," a person dons the "new man [self]" from heaven, and just as we have borne the image of the earthly man [self], we must also reflect the image of the heavenly man [self], represented by "Jesus Christ" (1 Cor 15:45-49; 2 Cor 5:17; Rom 13:14; Eph 2:15, 4:24). Christ, the Incarnation of God, is our true standard of oughtness. With this true and eternal context (home) in mind, our journey of self-actualization reveals our "homelessness" within this transient world, as we live like a nomad just as Jesus did (Heb 11:13). This awareness should inspire each of us to embrace our eternal potential by "competing well for the faith and laying hold of that eternal life we were called [out] for" (1 Tim 6:12). "Therefore, [we must] prepare our minds for action and remain sober," as "the Holy One who [has] called [us],

> *Who do you think you should be in this world?*
>
> *If you identify as a seafarer, how will you lead a life "worthy of the calling" to become your true self: the image of Christ?*

[commands us to] become holy in all of our conduct" (1 Pet 1:13, 15-16).

As we are reminded to "address as Father the One who impartially judges according to each one's work," we must "live out the time of our temporary residence here in reverence. [For we] know that we were ransomed from the empty way of life inherited from our ancestors and have been born anew" (1 Pet 1:17-18, 23). We responsibly respond to the call of Eternity: "He will reward each one according to His works: eternal life for those who, through perseverance in good works, seek glory, honor, and immortality, but wrath and anger for those who live in selfish ambition and do not obey the truth, following unrighteousness" (Rom 2:6-8).

Set Free to Forsake Babylon & Pursue Eternity

True faith cannot be divorced from trusting in our Creator's empowering grace to transform us. This change unfolds through the process of sanctifying discipleship as we journey homeward. Therefore, we must trust Christ to lead us to a holy way of living and perceiving the world. If we choose not to rely on our Shepherd to complete the work of sanctification, we have not genuinely placed our faith in His ability to reconcile us with God and our true homestead (Eph 2:8, 2:19-22, 3:12, 4:22-24). Consequently, as we "continue working out our salvation with awe and reverence," we must humbly acknowledge that "the one bringing forth in us both the desire and the effort [to accomplish righteousness and holiness in likeness to His own] – is God" (Phil 2:12-13). We do not achieve this through our

> *What makes the grace of God and the faithfulness of Christ so crucial for you to respond to Eternity's Call?*
>
> *Why is it wrong to assume you can achieve this through your own efforts to be a "good person"?*

striving for holiness or moral improvement. Make no mistake, Christ is not a self-improvement guru or modern humanistic moralist. Did He not say, "The Spirit is the one who gives life; human nature is of no help!" (John 6:63). Rather, it is through "Christ's faithfulness" that "we have boldness and confident access to God," allowing the "eternal purpose" of God to be fulfilled in us through "Christ Jesus" (Eph 3:12-13). We can only be restored to our eternal destinies by communing with His Spirit in the Holy of Holies, not a human "lecture" even from a pulpit or "therapy session" even by a Christian counselor.

Let there be no misunderstanding. Christ's grace prevents us from staying entrenched in Babylonian ways while anticipating salvation from its impending destruction. Christ can only reach those who have consciously chosen to abandon Babylon's systems in their quest for Zion. Thus, distancing oneself from Babylonian conformity is essential for a believer in Christ. A genuine seafarer must "die" to their old worldly self and, through the sanctifying power of His Spirit, embrace a lifestyle and mindset appropriate for a child of God.

When Christ speaks of our eternal home and identity, He cautions that we will only inherit these if we "conquer" the temptations of the Land of Darkness (Rev 3:12). Therefore, we must guard against letting our hearts become hardened. We should avoid being ensnared by the "worldly cares" of transience or abandoning our mission due to the "persecutions" we encounter in Babylon (Matt 13:18-22). These temptations beckon us to seek our home and identity based on the world's temporal systems. A land-dweller who fails to, by faith empowered through grace, overcome the allure of temporality forfeits the call to holiness and the living waters of sanctification. "Remember Lot's wife. Whoever tries to keep his life will lose it (Luke 17:31-33).

The lure of "self-determination"[134] concocts an illusion that people can achieve their "true selves" apart from eternal contextualities. Regrettably, this determination means sacrificing the eternal life of Zion, following the tabernacle's rules of the Holy of Holies. To engage in this tabernacling, we must renounce our attachment to temporality and release our idolatrous ties. This endeavor does not rely solely on our strength or ability but demands sincere faith in the Spirit's transformative indwelling grace. We must dedicate ourselves to the Spirit to renew our worldview and rectify our living to become suitable for the Kingdom of Heaven. Therefore, let us "above all pursue His kingdom and righteousness" (Matt 6:33).

> *Are you prepared to give up the earthly "cares" of this life to dwell forever in the Holy of Holies?*

For too long, our world-dwelling and world-viewing have been conformed to the world-systems of temporality, such as carnality[135], materialism[136], and consumerism.[137] If we are not

---

[134] The deception of independence from God represents the oldest temptation, which Adam and Eve encountered in the Garden of Eden. Their choice to eat the fruit went beyond simple disobedience; it was a sin driven by the ambition to independently "be like God, knowing good and evil" Essentially, their wrongdoing stemmed from opting to define good and evil based on their own perspectives, rather than adhering to God's design and eternal truths. Consequently, the consequences of this sin reflect a way of life divorced from reliance on God.

[135] This refers to indulging the appetites of the physical body above all else, whether it be the disordered desire for food, sex, power, wealth, or even indulging in one's emotions such as anger, jealousy, envy, pride, or laziness over and against self-control.

[136] This refers to the view that physical concerns and realities (the material world) are either superior to spiritual concerns or the only concern.

[137] This refers to a way of world-dwelling and world-viewing that sees the acquisition of the latest goods and services in ever-increasing amounts as the most important goal or achievement in life. People living by this world-system, whether conscious of it or not, see status, being "trendy" or "up to date", and

vigilant, the Evil One aiming to undermine our eternal potential may manipulate these systems to control the who, what, why, and how of our lives (John 10:10; Eph 6:11). To resist the Enemy's temptations effectively, we need to embark on a quest for truth, establishing a more solid foundation for our core identity. This approach allows us to align our existence and perspective with the divine principles of God's Temple.

> *How must you sacrifice yourself?*
>
> *How do you entrust yourself to Christ setting you free from worldly thinking and living?*

Ultimately, our goal is to become a dwelling place for the self-revealing immanence[138] of the Creator. At the same time, we trust in Him as our benevolent shepherd, safeguarding us from the wolves and thieves aiming to take away our eternal inheritance (John 10:7-18).

We must remember that Christ's shepherding leads us to a more profound knowledge of God, serving as the transformative force in our lives and thoughts. He tenderly calls to us, declaring, "I will seek the lost and bring back the strays… I will bring them to their own land… by the streams and all the inhabited places of the land… There they will lie down in a lush pasture, and they will feed on rich grass on the mountains of Israel. I Myself will feed My sheep and I Myself will make them lie down, declares the sovereign Lord" (Ezek 34:11-16). In these verdant pastures of divine co-dwelling, where we allow Christ to guide us and wholeheartedly follow Him, we realize and embrace His revelations regarding our eternal identities, purposes, and

---

wealth as the fundamental signs of one's success and worth in life and the world.

[138] AS the God who *is phos*-light, pS the Goart of God's nature is to always reveal Himself to us in an act of continuous self-disclosure. At the same time, He is not only present with us, but with us and able to be experience and felt by us. It is this intimate presence of God, which always reveals more of Himself, that we are to be a tabernacle or temple for with our lives and selves.

experiences. These eternal truths should be the bedrock for every aspect of our earthly existence. Only then can our worldly inclinations align with the Living Word and the Life-Giving Spirit of the Creator (John 16:13; Rom 8:2; 2 Cor 10:5).

Christ is our true Shepherd, High Priest, Teacher, and King, freeing us from transient lifestyles and thinking (Matt 23:10; John 10:11; Heb 2:17; Rev 19:16). For us seafarers, He is the Captain we trust to navigate our journey across the Sea of Revelation. Beyond being just our Captain, we can also view Christ as our Navigator. In the age of sailing ships, both the captain and the navigator were essential in guiding the crew. Most other crew members typically lacked the skills to pilot or navigate their vessel.[139]

Our Divine Captain and Navigator calls us to set sail on a remarkable journey with Him. On these waters, His guiding presence will transform our lives in harmony with the eternal truths of Heaven. By willingly following His lead and allowing Him to operate within us to free us from Babylon's influence, we will fulfill His command delivered through His spokesperson Paul: "Therefore I exhort you, brothers and sisters, by the mercies of God [our Creator], to present your bodies as a sacrifice – alive, holy, and pleasing to God [i.e. living according to the house-rules of God's Temple] – which is your reasonable service[, as His redeemed creatures]. Do not be conformed to this present world [-system], but be transformed by the renewing of your mind [by

---

[139] Imagine being a crewmember in the 1700s, navigating a ship from Great Britain to the American colonies. Across the immense ocean, your only reference points are the stars, which are beyond your comprehension as a simple deckhand. Instead of questioning your destination, you must diligently follow the captain"s orders and rely on the navigator's skills to chart the correct course. Attempting to take control of the ship through mutiny is not the answer; instead, placing your trust in your leaders is the wisest choice because, while you may not fully grasp how or when it will happen, the captain and navigator are committed to ensuring the ship reaches its destination safely.

revelation], so that you may test and approve what is the will of God – what is good and well-pleasing and perfect [according to the oughtness established by His vision]" (Rom 12:1-2).

On our journey, we aim to "attain to the unity of the faith and of the knowledge of the Son of God," which helps us become "a mature person, attaining to the measure of Christ's full stature" (Eph 4:13-14). When this occurs, "we [will] no longer be children, tossed back and forth by waves and carried about by every wind of teaching… But [we will instead] practice the truth in love, [as] we will in all things grow up into Christ [our Creator], who is the [true] head [over all of Finitude]" (Eph 4:14-15). We must desire and strive for spiritual maturity. As seafarers, we refuse to view reality only through the limited perspective of the fleeting philosophies of current world-systems. We should not live solely on human traditions and deceptive ideologies. These obscure our eternal destiny as those meant to be children, co-workers, and tabernacles of the Living God (1 Pet 1:4; Col 1:12-13; Heb 9:15).

{ *What do you envision lies ahead as you heeed the Call of Eternity?* }

Those of us departing the Shores of Temporality recognize that we have been deceived and have lived under this deception for far too long. It is time to awaken from our slumber: "Awake, O sleeper! Rise from the dead, and Christ will shine on you" (Eph 5:14)! We proclaim, "I no longer wish to think and live by the idolatrous circumstances of Finitude. God, help me prioritize my relationship with You over the distractions of the created world in my daily thoughts, feelings, and actions. Moving forward, may my understanding of the world and my role within it align with the eternal truths flowing from my relationship with You. Amen."

Becoming "Homeward-Bound Seafarers" Led by the Spirit

When we pass through the "Doors of Justification" leading to eternal life, it is as if we depart from the shores of Babylon. As we unfurl our sails, we set our course for the "Seaway of Sanctification." This venture delivers us from our old selves and from ways of thinking devoid of eternal potential (2 Thess 2:13; Rom 6:19-23). Our mission on this voyage is to find and actualize our self-fittingness as a "citizen" of the everlasting "Kingdom of Heaven" (Eph 2:19; Phil 3:20; Matt 5:3). Such a voyage is possible in the first place because our "[Creator] delivers us from the power of darkness and transfers us to the kingdom of the Son, in whom we have redemption, the forgiveness of sins" (Col 1:13-14). Therefore, we travel along "a thoroughfare... called the Way of Holiness," as "those delivered from bondage... whom the Lord has ransomed" to return to "Zion," the "City of the Living God" (Isa 35:8-10; Heb 12:22-24).

Only by leaving the "Shores of Temporality" can we genuinely discover our identity as a child of God with a purpose that endures eternally. This self-discovery involves recognizing our eternal purpose in the presence of the Creator's self-revealing nature (2 Cor 5:3-6; Eph 2:19-22). When we embrace this truth, we become "homeward-bound seafarers" on a journey to fulfill our destiny as authentic children of God born of the Spirit (John 3:3-8). We are "homeward-bound" because our true home lies within God (2 Cor 5:8, 6:16; 1 John 4:13). Our true identity encompasses being bearers of *agape*-love, *phos*-light, and *pneauma*-spirit.[140] We embody

> *Have you set aside fleeting worldviews and philosophies to journey to know God?*

---

[140] Reference my book trilogy that covers each of these aspects of the divine nature in detail: God is spirit (*pneuma*), God is love (*agape*), and God is light (*phos*).

the unconditional, sacrificial love exemplified by the Cross, enduring through every circumstance. In essence, as God *is agape-love*, we live in and are filled by our Creator's omniscience (1 John 3:23-24, 4:7-8).

We have moved away from our former homes and former ways of life on the "land" of this temporary world (Eph 4:22). Now, we are "seafaring nomads" who "do not belong to the world" (John 17:16). Our allegiance lies with our Creator. He provides a way of life and thought influenced by the eternal truths of the Sea of Revelation.

{ *What does it mean for you to be a "pilgrim" on this earth while being a "resident" of another world?* }

In practice, we ask the Spirit to reveal these heavenly who(s), what(s), why(s), and how(s) to help shape our earthly views and lifestyles through the illumination of Eternity. While we continue as pilgrims in our earthly existence, we strive to embody the essence of Heaven, continually seeking the enlightening and empowering grace of the Holy Spirit. Only He can help us see the eternal truths that lie beyond the veil of our fallen state. Furthermore, His sanctifying presence within us enables us to participate as citizens of our true home: the eternal realm.

Those bound to the temporal world can only view reality through contextualities alien to the habitation of the Spirit of God. Sin. Decay. Chaos. Naturally, it follows that those who make themselves at home in these fallen world-systems forfeit the indwelling of the Spirit of God. Unlike those rejecting Eternity's call, we seafarers willfully apply the blood of the New Covenant upon the doorpost of our dwelling.[141] This blood marks our

---

[141] This refers to the First Passover story in Exodus 12, where the Israelites were commanded to mark the doorposts of their homes with the blood of a sacrificed lamb to protect their families from the Tenth Plague: the death of

affiliation with the Son of God. We now live as deserters of Babylon. We do not dwell by the flesh but by the Spirit, becoming temples of the Living God (Hebrews 9:11-15).

Those navigating the Sea of Revelation seek the ancient path that guides us to our true home (Ps 139:24; Isa 35:8-10; Jer 6:16). Our longing for everlasting rest inspires us to live as wanderers, feeling "homeless" in this fleeting world. However, we must keep the transient conditions that conflict with our eternal purpose from affecting our worldly lives as much as possible. To embark on this "other-worldly" journey, we need to adopt an outsider's view on the temporary aspects of life. We should draw on the wisdom offered by the Creator about our genuine home in Eternity (Rom 8:5-25).

As we begin our journey, we inevitably become familiar with the new realities of this true home. The Holy Spirit's sanctifying influence transforms how we dwell in and perceive the world. He assists us in "guarding our hearts and minds" by living and thinking about "things" that are "true, just, pure, lovely, commendable, excellent, and praiseworthy" (Phil 4:7-8). To truly detach ourselves from temporal world-dwelling, we must desire for our subjectivity to be re-grounded. Let us escape the "sinking sand" of worldliness. Furthermore, we should wish to discard the masks we have worn as prodigals, hiding and concealing our true selves. By doing so, we can, through the Spirit, embrace our true identities as children of God, created for a holy way of life.

As deserters of the *oikoumene* and *oikonomia* of Babylon, we see ourselves as castaways. We find ourselves on the shores of earthly kingdoms, gazing out at the sea. With clarity, we recognize that we

---

Egypt's firstborn. This event later finds a parallel in the sacrifice of Jesus, the Lamb of God, who shed His blood on the cross to grant forgiveness of sins. For believers in Christ, this New Covenant blood is now marked upon the doorposts of our hearts.

were not meant for this current world-system, but rather for a heavenly existence ordained by the Creator. Our hope lies in discovering our true identities in the realm of revelation, beyond the confines of what we perceive "on land." To achieve this, we must seek the eternal context for which God designed us. Once we uncover this context, we can begin to spiritually discern the genuine realities of our true selves. The Holy Spirit serves as our existential guide, teaching us to accurately identify the ways and oikonomia of the Kingdom of Heaven. Consequently, He leads us away from the ways of selfishness, autonomy, and godlessness. These revelations are essential as we journey as pilgrims searching for the Kingdom of Heaven, where we confidently anticipate reclaiming our lost identity.

> *Why is it essential for you to let go of your loyalty to your old home and temporal contexts in your journey to embrace your identity as a child of God?*

Thanks to God's grace, we who "were at one time darkness" have become "children of light" (Eph 5:7-10). God enables and calls us to share divine truths with the world, as evangelists. Jesus commands all His genuine followers, "Therefore go and make disciples of all nations, baptizing them in the name of the Father and the Son and the Holy Spirit, teaching them to obey everything I have commanded you" (Matt 28:19-20). "(Through the Spirit, we now recognize how we were misled by the Evil One's counterfeit light, leading us to tread the wide path of ruin that results in darkness and destruction (Matt 7:13; 1 John 2:11). We must pay attention to Jesus' warning: "Walk while you have the light, so that darkness may not overtake you. The one who walks in darkness does not know where he [or she] is going. While you have the light, believe in the light, so that you may become sons [and daughters] of light" (John 12:35-36). Consequently, we strive to live a life of repentance and truth-witnessing, moving away from our previous facade of existential rebellion.

We must always remember, though, that it is only through Christ that we can escape "the power of Satan," as He "opens our eyes so that [we can] turn from darkness to light" (Acts 26:18). Through the cross, "[our Creator] has rescued us from the power of darkness and transferred us into the Kingdom of the Son He loves, in whom we have redemption, the forgiveness of sins" (Col 1:13-14). Therefore, because this deliverance comes from God and not from our own efforts, we should continually "give thanks to the Father who has qualified [us] to share in the saints' inheritance in the light" (Col 1:12).

How can we live for the sake of Eternity? Precisely by striving daily to leave behind the illusions of being at home in temporality and showing God's love, grace, and freedom to the world. Instead, we must seek our identity and home corresponding to the Son's eternal "kingdom not of this world" (John 18:36). In doing so, we will have willfully chosen to "crucify" the false a-theistic[142] selfhood we embraced as lovers of the temporal world (John 3:19; Rom 6:5-6; Gal 5:24; 1 John 2:15-17).

> *In what ways will you embody your divine mission to be transformed into a "theological self"?*

At that time, our perceptions of the world were influenced by human traditions and dark forces. Now, we must strive to abandon this false identity and be reborn, "washed," and "sanctified" into our authentic selves, a "saint [holy one]" of God (Col 3:5; 1 Cor 1:2, 6:11; 2 Cor 5:14-17). We should surrender daily to the holy-making Spirit for undergoing renewal into a theological

---

[142] Meaning something "not oriented toward or ignorant of God and heavenly contextualities" rather than referring to atheism alone. Even agnosticism and other ways of world-dwelling and viewing that do not center on God and heavenly realities fall under these categories.

self that exists as an alien sojourner in this fallen world (John 3:5-8). Therefore, we remain resolutely defiant against the world-influencing power of the fallen Babylonian realm, and we become arrayed as spiritual warriors of light and truth (Eph 6:10-20).

Born Again by the Sanctification of the Holy Spirit

Paradoxically, finding our real selves can only happen as we give "our-selves" away by submission to Providence.[143] Only He can transform us from disobedient children into the world-dwelling likeness of Christ (Col 3:1-6). He empowers us to "live worthily of the Lord and please Him in all respects – bearing fruit in every good deed, growing in the knowledge of God, being strengthened with all power according to His glorious might for the display of all patience and steadfastness, joyfully giving thanks to the Father who has qualified [us] to share in the saints' inheritance in the light" (Col 1:10-13). Our choices in our various situations and contexts should reflect our Creator's vision for our lives. Hence, our lives should exemplify how our Creator has chosen to reveal Himself, His thoughts, and His ways through humanity.

---

[143] It follows that since we have a Creator, only He understands the purpose and contexts where we can achieve complete fulfillment. By prioritizing His design for us, we allow ourselves to be positioned where we truly belong within His larger narrative. Letting go of our "selves" here means relinquishing our illusions of independence. Despite our efforts, we can only realize our true potential by sacrificing our individual attempts to discover our purpose.

Consider the analogy of an orchestra playing Beethoven's 5th Symphony. Regardless of talent, any musician cannot contribute to the symphony's beauty if they choose to play as they wish, ignoring the composer's "plan." While adhering to the sheet music may feel like "sacrificing" the chance to play independently and seek personal glory, the musician discovers that by participating 1) within a "higher plan" and 2) alongside others who make the same choice, they can create music that is far more beautiful and powerful than they could alone.

It is only by "giving our selves" to the authority of the Creator that He can elevate us to experiences more glorious and fulfilling than anything we could achieve by ourselves.

Since we have entrusted our existential fulfillment to Christ, we owe Him our allegiance (Gal 3:26). As such, we must trust and follow our master, Christ, by submitting to Him and His will for us, even when it seems nonsensical or self-defeating.[144] As Scripture says, "He died for all so that those who live should no longer live for themselves but for Him who died for them and was raised" (2 Cor 5:15). Therefore, those who truly believe in Christ should "spend the rest of our time on earth concerned about the will of God and not human desires," as those "armed with the same attitude of Christ" (1 Pet 4:1-2). In addition, we should take heed to Scripture's caution: "If the righteous are barely saved, what will become of the ungodly and sinners? So then let those who suffer according to the will of God entrust their souls to a faithful Creator as they do good" (1 Pet 4:18-19).

> *This week, in what ways have you focused on living for Christ rather than just for yourself or others?*

To live as "children of light," our standards, principles, and lifestyle must be deeply anchored in our Creator's sanctifying influence (Eph 5:7-10; 1 John 1:7). Through communion with our Maker. We gain access to the light that enlightens and reveals our true self (John 12:35-36). When this connection is established, we begin to realize the destiny prepared for us by our Creator: "I will live in them and will walk among them, and I will be their God, and they will be My people" (2 Cor 6:16). Instead of merely receiving and following guidance by our capabilities, we can genuinely fulfill God's instructions only through His life and light

---

[144] Think of it like those martial arts movies where someone must entrust themselves to the guidance and training of a wise master, such as is in the film *Karate Kid*. By submitting to Mr. Miyagi's instructions even when they don't make sense, Daniel LaRusso becomes a far greater fighter than he would have if he tried to teach himself.

within us. Thus, He both commissions us and equips us to carry out that commission. By daily entering the "spiritual birthing chamber" of our true self within the inner Holy of Holies, we become His sanctified people (John 3:3-8; 1 Pet 1:2, 23). Through spirit-to-Spirit communion, the Holy Spirit transforms us into children of God. This is the essence of being reborn each day.

Although, we cannot stop living in this world, we can stop being "of" this world. We follow the example of the planets revolving around (and getting their light and heat from) a star. Our world-dwelling and world-viewing must be re-oriented toward not only God, but we must reside in God and He in us. This "theo-centric"[145] self-actualization centers on being born of the Spirit in likeness to the Son. This mutual "homemaking" fulfills the eternal covenant of sanctification.

Christ clarifies in the following passage how we can inherit the Kingdom of God: "I tell you the solemn truth, unless a person is born from above, he [or she] cannot see the kingdom of God… I tell you the solemn truth, unless a person is born of water and spirit, he [or she] cannot enter the kingdom of God. What is born of the flesh is flesh, and what is born of the Spirit is spirit… The wind blows wherever it will, and you hear the sound it makes, but do not know where it comes from and where it is going. So, it is with everyone who is born of the Spirit" (John 3:3-8). We all need to embrace our true identities in our current circumstances if we ever hope to find our genuine home.

Do you struggle to completely surrender and trust in your Creator?

What factors could increase your willingness to do so, considering its importance?

---

[145] "Theo" is a prefix referring to God or deities (as in theology, theocracy, theism, mono-theism, etc.)

We must be guided by the nurturing Spirit of Eternity, who recreates our inner life to reflect God's image.

Again, sanctification does not come solely from our own self-effort or personal holiness, as if only the "able" and "proven" can enter the Kingdom. Only the Holy Spirit enables our life-walk to mirror Christ's own godlike life-walk (Gal 5:16, 25). He does this by renewing our world-dwelling and world-viewing according to the same eternal contextualities that shaped Christ's world-dwelling. (Eph 4:25; Col 3:10). These who(s), what(s), why(s), and how(s) shape the *there*[146] our selfhood was meant to inhabit.

> *Will you invite Christ to enter your heart and transform you into His image today?*

Because of these truths, we should acknowledge that remaining a temporal-self shaped by "this world's present path" leaves us with an existential void (Eph 2:1). Like how "cold" and "darkness" are technically just the absence of heat and light respectively,[147] so is existing as a "temporal-self" essentially the absence of an eternal-self. Just as a house cannot be a home without a family, we cannot be our true selves without being a temple of our Maker. A temporal self is "dead in transgressions and sins" and can be compared to "thorns and thistles," which are "useless" with a "fate to be

---

[146] Refer to earlier chapters' discussions of *there* and *being-there*.
[147] While it may appear otherwise to many, physicists assert that cold is fundamentally just the absence of heat and energy in a system, leading to lower temperatures. Although we commonly perceive cold as a cause of phenomena like freezing, hypothermia, frostbite, and snow, these outcomes are a result of the lack of heat in the system. For instance, removing heat from liquid water will turn it into ice.

Air conditioners operate on this principle. Although it seems as though the unit is producing and blowing cold air, it is taking in the room's hot air, extracting the heat, and then blowing that same air, now devoid of heat, back into the room. The excess heat is transferred outside via the external radiators of the air conditioner.

burned" (Eph 2:1; Heb 6:8). Such a self has been shaped by Babylonian contexts to become something it was not created to be; rather, Satan has rendered them an "object of wrath prepared for destruction" (Rom 9:22).

As we seek to be transformed into a new self authored by the Creator's revelations, we must implore His sanctifying Spirit to make us holy as He is holy. We should earnestly pray for Him to daily clothe us with the sanctified image of the "heavenly man" (Christ), so we become a home for the One who dwells in Heaven[148] (1 Cor 15:49). Only then can we confidently say, "it is no longer I who live, but Christ lives in me" (Gal 2:19). To this end we give ourselves over to the Spirit's transforming influence as we commune with Him day by day. Therefore, we should daily pray, "Examine me, and probe my thoughts! Test me, and know my concerns! See if there is any idolatrous tendency in me and lead me in the reliable ancient path" (Ps 139:24)!

Today, will you allow your Maker to examine and explore your thoughts?

Will He discover that your concern for Eternity is being overshadowed by worries focused only on the temporary?

"When we were slaves of sin, we were free with regard to righteousness […] For when we were in the flesh, the sinful desires, aroused by the law, were active in the members of our body to bear fruit for death. We have been released from the law, because we have died to what controlled us, so that we may serve in the new life of the Spirit and not under the old written code… For the law of the life-giving Spirit in Christ Jesus has set you free from the law of sin and death." (Rom 6:20, 7:5-6, 8:2). The law of

---

[148] Recall our discussion on how we are made to be "tabernacles" for Him and His self-disclosing presence. We are to be vessels of Christ and everything He is unto the world.

the life-giving Spirit in Christ liberates us from limiting earthly perspectives- our thoughts, desires, and views shaped solely by created realities. As discussed in the previous chapter, these worldly forces can trap us within Babylonian influences that hinder our true destiny. Discovering our authentic selves is inherently tied to our relationship with the Creator. As we progress on this journey, we will increasingly recognize our complete dependence on God for true eternal self-actualization. Without communion with, being filled by, and living in Yahweh, we merely exist as shadows of the glorious eternal beings we were meant to become.

We seek the Spirit's grace to help us incorporate these revelations of our Creator's vision for human existence into our lives. By "growing in the knowledge of God," we gain insight into "His will in all spiritual wisdom and understanding," allowing us to "bear fruit in every good work" as we are "strengthened with all power in accordance with His glorious might for the manifestation of patience and steadfastness [with] you" (Col 1:9-11). Advancing in our understanding of our Creator enhances our sanctification. Revelation guides us to live under Yahweh's sovereignty and governance. It is the essence of wisdom for a created being to humbly seek guidance from the One who defined the parameters of creation to influence their world-dwelling and world viewing (Job 28:28; Prov 1:7, 9:10). In this way, we willingly position ourselves to accept His providence. He lays out (much like navigational charts) the authentic contents, arrangements, and regulations of existence according to His plan as the Creator (Ps 111:10; Eccl 12:13-14). Thus, our God-relationship should be the cornerstone of our existential and contextual realities.

> *Do you believe that increasing your recognition of your reliance on God is intertwined with you becoming your true self?*

Conclusion: Commitment to Heed Eternity's Call

Before any of us can embark on a homeward-bound journey, we should look in the mirror while asking ourselves the following:

> Why was I granted the breath of life?
> Where have I decided to call home?
> What principles have shaped my identity?
> What purpose drives my existence?
> Who do I aspire to be?
> How will I become who I am truly meant to be?

For seafarers who have genuinely set foot on a ship navigating the "Sea of Revelation," responses like the following should align with our ambitions:

> I have been granted the gift of life to foster an everlasting connection with the Living God.
> My dwelling is the House of God.
> I seek the Holy Spirit to guide my life according to the principles suited for God's Temple.
> I aim to explore the Holy of Holies, deepening my relationship with God through this journey.
> I aspire to be a steadfast pillar in God's temple.
> I desire to share eternal communion with my Creator as a cherished household member.

As seafarers, we should embrace these answers as a guiding principle, one we commit to fully as we embark on our journey home. Such declarations should encapsulate our beliefs and aspirations. Let us make the following statements as a challenge to ourselves. I commit to live as a priest, discipled by the High

> *Do these responses resonate?*
>
> *If not, what makes you reluctant to become a pilgrim in search of an everlasting kingdom?*

Priest[149], who promotes the self-disclosing glory of His temple of *agape*-love[150], the only trait that makes a world of true *shalom*[151] possible. I believe I am being set apart for my eternal destiny by being reborn through the Holy Spirit's indwelling. I have willingly surrendered to His work, seeking to purify my life from the influences of a fallen world. Daily, I turn to Him to transform my existence into a sacred space where God's Spirit dwells and interacts, uniting with us and becoming our everything. I understand that I can only stop living for myself and devote my

---

[149] Throughout history, priests in various religions and civilizations have shared the role of being "mediators" between the divine and the earthly realms, serving as the "bridge" that connects both worlds. Since we are all called to be part of a "royal priesthood" (1 Peter 2:9), we function as conduits and advocates for God's presence and work in the world.

[150] This word refers to a deep, profound, sacrificial love that transcends and persists regardless of circumstance, as opposed to the other types of love in the Ancient Greek language, such as *philia* (friendship/brotherly love), *storge* (familial love), and *eros* (romantic and sensual love). The true depth of *agape*, is far more profound than even this description, as it represents the love of God Himself, perpetually self-emptying. For an even fuller exploration of *agape*-love, check out "God is Love", the second volume in J.K. Ward's "Before the Beginning" trilogy.

[151] Shalom is a word without an exact translation in the English language. Though usually translated merely as "peace" the word has a far deeper and richer meaning.

In the book *Not the Way It's Supposed to Be: A Breviary of Sin*, Christian author Cornelius Plantinga described the biblical concept of shalom: "The webbing together of God, humans, and all creation in justice, fulfillment, and delight is what the Hebrew prophets call shalom. We call it peace, but it means far more than mere peace of mind or a cease-fire between enemies. In the Bible, shalom means universal flourishing, wholeness and delight – a rich state of affairs in which natural needs are satisfied and natural gifts fruitfully employed, a situation that inspires joyful wonder as its Creator and Savior opens doors and welcomes the creatures in whom he delights. Shalom, in other words, is the way things ought to be."

life to Him through complete trust and surrender to my Creator and His work within me.

If these proclamations do not resonate with you, you may be among those still lingering at the dock. In other words, you could still be uncertain about embarking on a journey back home. If that is the case, consider whether you prefer to be a citizen of an everlasting kingdom filled with shalom and love, or to rule as a "king/queen" or vassal in a fleeting realm defined by self-serving glory, comparison, and division. Only by wholeheartedly committing to live as citizens of God's kingdom can we let the truths of Scripture guide us. This guidance takes us toward our beautiful, rightful destiny. Moreover, these truths can only flourish within us through a deep Spirit-to-spirit connection[152], as we become priests of the One who *is* Spirit, rather than of anything created. Our devotion represents our commitment to being a fruitful vine that produces the everlasting fruit of sanctification, aligning with the appropriate contexts of God's Kingdom, which is not of this world (John 15:1-7, 18:36; Col 1:10-13; Phil 1:11).

Agreeing to an eternal destiny involves multiple choices; it requires a persevering commitment to the greatest commandment: loving God wholly and enduringly (Deut 6:4; Matt 22:37-38). Consider it akin to a marriage. It is not just about the vows exchanged during the ceremony or the legal documents that formalize the relationship. A marriage demands regular renewal of commitment, expressed through sacrifices, compromises, communication, reconciliation, duties, and choices. Being married means you choose to live for yourself and focus on putting your partner's needs above your wants. Those who marry with an understanding of these responsibilities truly make a heartfelt commitment. Without consistent actions of love, understanding,

---

[152] The Holy Spirit communing with our individual spirits.

and sacrifice following the decision and ceremony, the relationship cannot sustain itself as a genuine partnership.

Like marriage, the commitment to embark on our spiritual seafaring journey requires our complete dedication, a promise we must renew throughout our lives. Consider Jesus's parable of the ten wise virgins (Matt 25:1-13). We should reach a point where we willingly surrender our 'right' to our own home in exchange for a life that is not solely ours but is rather guided by our Captain. This means trading our home on land for a spot on His "ship." In this act, we genuinely choose to move away from being a temple for ourselves and instead become His temple; filled with His presence and led by His purpose (2 Cor 5:14-15).

> *What are your thoughts on giving up your right to "create your home" in this world for a place on a ship heading to your eternal home?*
>
> *Have you made this choice? How does your life reflect this commitment?*

Only those who renounce citizenship in this fleeting, fallen world will inherit the future Kingdom of Heaven (Zion). We are all to be "foreigners and exiles [in this fallen world of Babylon, meant to] keep away from fleshly desires [for temporal 'happiness'] that wage war against the soul" (1 Pet 2:11). We should persevere like the Patriarchs of Israel: Abraham, Isaac, and Jacob. They viewed their transient existence in this world as "foreigners... seeking a homeland" that is not part of this present world. Instead of considering this world their home, they steadfastly "looked forward to the city with firm foundations whose architect and builder is God" (Hmmitmeneb 11:9-10, 13-14). Similarly, we are called to "aspire to a better land, that is, a heavenly one" because, for willingly to become "His people," "He has [graciously] prepared a city" (Heb 11:16, 12:22).

The Scriptures compare the temporary world to a veil we must pass through to reach our true home: "Mount Zion, the city of the Living God, the heavenly Jerusalem," the only "unshakable kingdom" (Heb 12:28). Our only refuge as "heirs of the promise" is found behind this veil, for "we have this hope as an anchor for the soul, sure and steadfast, which reaches inside behind the curtain, where Jesus our forerunner entered on our behalf" (Heb 6:17-20). "According to His promise, we are waiting for new heavens and a new earth, in which righteousness truly resides" (2 Pet 3:13). However, as we wait, we must remain vigilant: "if [we] think [fix our gaze on our longing memoirs] of the land that [we have] left, [then we will] have the opportunity to return" (Heb 11:15). Instead of wistfully looking back at what we leave behind, let us boldly anticipate the everlasting destiny that lies ahead!

Only those who resist the pull of temporal distractions will hear the Captain of our ship say: "I will make [you] a pillar in the temple of my God, and [you] will never depart from it [never go outside of it]. I will write on [you] the name of my God and the name of the city of my God (the new Jerusalem – descending out of heaven from God, made ready like a bride adorned for her husband" (Rev 3:12, 21:2). When the world of temporality comes to an end, we, who have remained steadfast in our journey homeward, will finally reach our true destination: the eternal realm of New Jerusalem (Rev 21-22). As this final dawn breaks after the long night of temporality, the beloved priests of Yahweh will no longer be separated from the Sabbath rest in Zion. We will no longer face the temptation to live inauthentically as wayward children of God. The existential darkness of Babylon's world system will haunt us no longer.

How will you make sure not to be lured by the enticements of temporality and instead live as a "foreigner" here as you await your everlasting residence in the new heaven and a new earth?

Chapter 7

A Heavenly Home Built by Jesus Christ

Old Covenant Shadows & New Covenant Realities

"Let them make for Me a sanctuary, so that I may live among them. According to the pattern of the tabernacle… You must make it exactly so."
(Exod 25:8-9)

"God does not really live on the earth! Look, if the sky and the highest heaven cannot contain [Him], how much less this temple I have built! Who can really build a temple for Him? … [Lord, I pray that] night and day may You watch over this temple… Hear from inside Your heavenly dwelling place and respond favorably."
(1 Kings 8:27-30; 2 Chr 2:5-6)

"The Lord who rules over all says, 'Look – here is the man whose name is Branch, who will sprout up from His place and build the temple of the Lord. Indeed, He will build the temple of the Lord, and He will be clothed in splendor, sitting as king on His throne.'"
(Zech 6:12-13)

"Through the [Son] we both have access in one Spirit to the Father. You are… members of God's household, because you have been built on the foundation… with Christ Jesus himself as the cornerstone. In Him the whole building, being joined together, grows into a holy temple in the Lord, in whom you also are being built together into a dwelling place of God in the Spirit.'"
(Eph 2:18-22)

Yahweh's Delling-Place: Our True Home

All of us seafaring nomads must aspire and strive for our lives to take on the eternal who(s), what(s), why(s), and how(s) that relate to our homeward-bound journey (Heb 11:14). We recognize these eternal contextualities through revelation, as they align with the "Kingdom of Heaven," our genuine homeland (Matt 8:11; Heb 11:16). However, these concepts are mostly foreign to the temporal world we currently inhabit. To grasp their meaning, we must delve into the depths of the Sea of Revelation, which extends far beyond the shores of our transient existence. As we read, "Therefore, if you have been raised with Christ, keep seeking the things above, where Christ is, seated at the right hand of God. Keep thinking about things above, not things on the earth, or you have died and your life is hidden with Christ in God" (Col 3:1-3).

Our journey symbolizes our "exodus" from the Babylonian systems that dominate the "land" we have left behind (Rev 18:4). We aim to reinvent our world-dwelling and world-viewing within the "temple" of our Creator. We are determined to make "the ascent from [the land of Babylon]" to the heavenly "Jerusalem" and Mount "Zion," guided by "the good hand of [our] God" (Ezra 7:9; Jer 50:28; Ps 27:4; Rev 21:2). To embrace this other-worldly destiny, we must accept the existential role of an explorer of revelation. By doing so, we become knowers, lovers, and stewards of the Divine Personhood's revelation (Luke 10:27; John 17:3; 1 John 3:24).

{ *Why must you comprehend and pursue God's immanent dwelling place to partake of your eternal destiny?* }

To fulfill our theological destiny, one fundamental requirement exists: the Creator's personhood must reside within a finite context—us, His creation. God established these bounded contexts with a specific intent long before He created the cosmos.

Through them, He maintains an intimate governance over His relationship with the finite realm, particularly via a finite tabernacle. Hence, like the Israelites regarding the tabernacle, we should actively pursue the conditions suitable for God's presence to dwell among us. Grasping these vital truths is essential for nurturing a close relationship with Him and realizing our true destiny.

In general, a temple refers to any space filled with the indwelling presence or glory of a divine being.[153] When discussing Yahweh's immanent dwelling, we should concentrate on His Temple as depicted in Scripture. It is a location where one can learn about and experience the revelations of the deity that either resides there or is represented by intermediaries serving at this location. Thus, the Holy of Holies is a place filled with manifestations of Yahweh's boundless self-disclosure.[154] This exemplifies Bethel in Genesis, where Jacob proclaimed, "Surely the Lord is in this place… what an awesome place this is! This is nothing else than the house of God! This is the gate of heaven!" (Gen 28:16-17). We can also draw a parallel to the "holy ground" Moses fell prostrate on during his encounter with God at the burning bush (Exod 3:4-6). These sacred locations illustrate the finite, contextually defined environments where divine encounters in the relationship with God transpired. Within these places, a dialogue unfolds between the finite and the Infinite, revealing God's glorious personhood in a contextually relatable and practical way.

---

[153] While a temple often refers to a physical structure as noted in the Old Testament, it does not always have to take that form. In the Japanese Shinto faith, *jinja* (shrines) may be represented by certain natural environments such as forests, trees, mountains, and rocks, which Shintoists regard as sacred, as the dwelling places of *k, as mi* (gods or spirits). Considering this broader definition, we can define a "temple" as any location where a divine being resides, whether that be a building, an area, a natural element, or even a person.
[154] Referring to the innermost, most holy space of the Temple in Jerusalem (distinct from the Holy Place/Inner Court and the Outer Court).

Let us revisit the imagery of the Jerusalem Temple. The inner and outer courts encircling the Holy of Holies symbolize the earthly context. Here, where the divine intersects with the natural, priests conducted sacrifices and offerings to the Lord. In this sacred space, God revealed aspects of His personhood, power, and authority through both transcendent (noumenal) and physical (phenomenal) events within creation. For us seafarers, entering this realm can be seen as metaphorically 'stepping into' the Sea of Revelation. We proudly recognize that our purpose as humans is not merely to enter but also to inhabit and be inhabited by this divine context; it is our true homeland.

> *When last did you consciously enter a sacred space where the divine intersects with the earthly, as a transitional domain between this world and our homeland?*

Old Covenant Temple: Foreshadow of the New Covenant

Our Creator designed our eternal home to reside within His immanent presence in creation: the Temple of the Living God. David's steadfast belief in this revelation is fully displayed as he earnestly prayed, "I have asked the Lord for one thing – this is what I desire! I want to live in the Lord's house all the days of my life, so I can gaze at the splendor (beauty) of the Lord and contemplate in His temple… He will surely give me shelter… He will hide me in His home" (Ps 27:4-5). Any genuine pilgrim of Eternity, like David, yearns to dwell in the Holy of Holies within God's temple. It is very important to point out David, as a member of the tribe of Judah, was not a member of the Levitical priesthood. Even so, he saw himself as a priest. It is in this sacred space that the spiritual person experiences true existential awakening.

Just as Christ taught, our true self emerges only from within the Holy of Holies where the Spirit of God resides (John 3:3-8). The psalmist repeatedly emphasized how the temple of Yahweh serves as a "habitation" and a "place of tabernacling" for "His glory," and He responds to this revelation with a desire to approach God's altar (Ps 26:6-8). Accordingly, the psalmist frequently sang praises to God and testified to His revealed greatness displayed at the Temple in Jerusalem, which Yahweh commanded the Israelites to construct as a physical dwelling for Him. Like the psalmist, we should regularly pray, "O Lord, I love the temple where You live, the place where Your splendor is revealed" (Ps 26:8).

Now, let us examine the historical background of the house of God built as the temple in Jerusalem, which served as the temporary physical place of worship established under the Old Covenant. According to Scripture, King David wished to replace the mobile tabernacle (tent) of Moses with a permanent temple dedicated to Yahweh on Mount Moriah in Jerusalem. He proclaimed, "I will not let my eyes sleep, or my eyelids to slumber, until I find a place [context] for the Lord, a dwelling place (tabernacle) for the powerful ruler of Jacob" (Ps 132:4-5).

How does the understanding that the temple of God is not a physical structure but an internal state of being impact your understanding of religion?

Does this perspective shift your thoughts on being in "the house of the Lord"?

Clearly, David "really wanted to build a temple (*bayith*) [house][155] to honor the Lord [for His namesake]" (1 Chr 22:7).

The Scriptures recount how Solomon realized his father's vision: "King David rose to his feet and said: 'Listen to me, my

---

[155] It is important to note that although the Greek has separate words for tabernacle, house, and temple, the Hebrew uses the same word for house and temple (*bayith*), and a separate word for tabernacle (*mishkan*). English translations often distinguish them in view of the context, yet it is important to realize that the same Hebrew word "*bayith*" is used.

brothers and my people. I wanted to build a temple where the ark of the Lord's covenant as a footstool for our God. I have made the preparations for building it'... [However], [the Lord] said to me, 'Solomon your son is the one who will build My temple and My courts, for I have chosen him to become My son and I will become his Father'" (1 Chr 28:2-7). In Stephen's final sermon before his martyrdom in the Book of Acts, he stated, "[Solomon] found favor with God and asked that he could find a dwelling place (*skenoma*) [tabernacle] for the God of Jacob," and God instructed Solomon to "build (*oikodomeo*) a house (*oikos*) for Him" (Acts 7:46-47). Moving forward, we will explore the biblical insights regarding our true dwelling (contextual abode) by examining how the physical temple under the Old Covenant symbolizes the authentic nature of our heavenly home.

The Jerusalem Temple, along with its predecessor, the wilderness tabernacle, symbolized the earthly abode of Yahweh's close presence, through which He honored His promise to reside with His people (2 Chr 2-5)[156]. In commanding the tabernacle to be built, Yahweh said to Moses, "Let them make for Me a sanctuary [a holy place], so that I may live [tabernacle] among them." (Exod 25:8). He told His symbolic chosen people, "I will put My tabernacle in your midst, and I will not abhor you. I will walk among you, and I will be your God, and you will be My people" (Lev 26:11-12). God said of this temple, "this is the place of My throne and the place for the soles of My feet, where I will live [tabernacle/dwell] among the people of Israel forever" (Ezek 43:7). Under the Old Covenant, the temple signified the place where "God's name made itself perpetually present" (1 Kings 8:29, 9:3). He promised *if* the Israelites were faithful to the covenant,

---

[156] In both the division and purpose of its different spaces, as well as its orientation towards the east and its design motifs, the Temple purposefully was built like the Tabernacle.

"His eyes and heart would be there always." Some translators and scholars have taken this phrase to indicate that God was saying He would "live" there as "[His] permanent home" (1 Kings 8:29, 9:3, 9:6-8; 2 Kings 21:4, 7; NET).

Throughout the Scriptures, we see how Yahweh remained faithful to His promise based on the Israelites' faithfulness in serving Him. From the Temple in Jerusalem, He powerfully revealed Himself to both the Israelites and their neighboring nations. For centuries, the first and second Temple[157] symbolically facilitated Infinite-finite communion between Heaven and Earth. They became genuine "meeting places" for the Creator and the created. Yahweh's immanent presence manifested in these structures, while He simultaneously occupied His transcendent heavenly abode (Lam 2:6). Solomon underscored this revelation: "God does not really live on the earth! Look, if the sky and the highest heaven cannot contain You, how much less this temple I have built!" (1 Kings 8:27). Since God transcends all finite concepts of space and location, He is both truly present within the Temple and in Heaven at once. He is both fully omnipresent in Finitude and simultaneously exists in complete transcendence beyond the context of Finitude. In essence, Yahweh's temple symbolized a connection between creation and the supernatural engagement of the Creator. It can be likened to a computer serving as the bridge between our physical world and cyberspace. The latter exists "all around us" but is only accessible through a computer, whether in the form of a desktop, laptop, or smartphone. However, none of these things *contain* cyberspace. In

---

[157] The First Temple refers to the one built by Solomon and destroyed by the Babylonians in 586 BC, while the Second Temple refers to that which was built after the return from exile. This Second Temple was the one standing during the period of the New Testament and was later destroyed by the Romans in AD 70, just as Jesus predicted (Matt 24:2).

the same way, though the Israelites accessed the presence of God through the tabernacle and temple, He was not contained in or by either.

In the Scriptures, Solomon's dedication of the temple is a prominent symbol of the link between the divine and earthly realms. We read, "When Solomon finished praying, fire came down from heaven and consumed the burnt offering" and "the Lord's Splendor filled the temple" (2 Chr 7:1). This fire illustrated to the gathered crowd the Creator's supernatural power—referred to as a "consuming fire" (Deut 4:24)—that rested upon the temple. This manifestation of divine immanency assured them that within its confines, they could experience Yahweh's immanent presence, which brings sanctification, power, and revealed splendor (Ezek 20:12). The regular sacrifices conducted in the temple served as significant reminders to the Israelites of God's promises. For instance, Yahweh's assurance that He would "cleanse their heart and the hearts of their descendants so that they could love Him with all their mind and being and so that they could (truly) live" (Deut 30:6). Thus, "when all the Israelites saw the fire come down and the Lord's splendor over the temple, they got on their knees with their faces downward toward the pavement. They worshiped and gave thanks to the Lord, saying, 'Certainly He is good; certainly His loyal love endures'" (2 Chr 7:3)!

> *What is your perspective on why God chose a particular contextual dwelling in the Old Covenant, instead of dwelling directly within His people as He does in the New Covenant Period?*

The Temple (*bayith*) was called the house of Yahweh. Thus, when the Patriarch Jacob (Israel) had a divine encounter involving the ladder to heaven, he named the location "Bethel" (*Beyth-'El*)[158] (Gen 28:16-19; 1 Kings 8:27-30, 9:3). He shouted, "surely the Lord is in this place… This is nothing else than the house (*bayith*) of God! This is the gate of heaven" (Gen 28:16-19). Similarly, the Israelites regarded their temple as the official place for humanity to communicate with and engage with their Creator. For thousands of years from the time of King Solomon and onwards – and even still to this day at the Western Wall in Jerusalem – people have come the "house of Yahweh" to "pray", "worship", and "cry out," to God (1 Kings 8:33-39, 9:25; Ezra 3:8-13; Luke 18:10).[ix]

The Israelites regarded the Temple not merely as a location where they believed Yahweh "watched over" and "listened" to them, but as the sacred place from which He communicated—either as a voice from Heaven or through a prophetic messenger (1 Kings 8:27-39; 1 Sam 3:3-4; Jer 19:14). Recall how God's angelic messenger imparted divine revelation to Zechariah foretelling of the ministries of John the Baptist and Jesus Christ (Luke 1:8-23). Yahweh instructed priests and prophets to relay both His previous messages and new revelations to the people within the Temple (Jer 36:5-8; Mal 2:5-7; 2 Chr 15:3; 2 Kings 12:2). For instance, Yahweh repeatedly commanded Jeremiah: "Go stand in the courtyard of the Lord's temple. Speak out to all the people who are coming from the towns of Judah to worship in the Lord's temple. Tell them everything I command you to tell them" (Jer 26:2; See also Jer 7:2, 19:14, 26:2, 26:7, 36:5-8).

Additionally, Yahweh foretold through His prophet Micah that "in the future," His "Temple Mount" would become a place where "all" people from "many nations" would "come" to learn His commands and hear His "instructions" and "teachings" (Mic 4:1-

---

[158] The Hebrew word "Bethel," "*Beyth-El*", is a compound of "bayith" (house) and "*El*" (God), and literally means "house of God" (ISA).

2). Even during Jesus' time and in the early church, the "temple courts" were viewed as the main location for religious instruction. Jesus and the apostles often "daily [taught]" there throughout their ministries (Luke 19:47, 21:37-38; John 7:28, 8:2; Acts 5:20-21, 42).

We can rightly say that the temple served as a site of divine decree. In its context, the Creator established a realm of communion between Heaven and earth, where the Infinite interacts with the finite. David recognized this truth about the temple when he stated, "I [want to] gaze at the splendor of the Lord and contemplate in His temple... [For here,] we [can] reflect on [His] loyal love within [His] temple" (Ps 27:4, 48:9). Reflect on the worship that occurred during the temple's dedication ceremony, a response to the Creator's manifest splendor (2 Chr 7:1-3). "They worshipped and gave thanks to the Lord, saying, 'His loyal love endures'" (2 Chr 7:2-3)!

> *Do you wish to be in the Lord's temple as David did?*
>
> *Do these revelations inspire you to worship there?*

Nevertheless, Yahweh did not envision the temple as solely a space for communion between the Creator and the Israelites, His "chosen" people. Instead, it was meant to be a "temple where all nations may pray" (Isa 56:7-8). From this location, Yahweh sought His engagements with humanity to resonate globally, manifesting as significant events that stem from Him, demonstrating "His power" from "[His] temple" (Ps 68:28-29). Therefore, Solomon foretold, "Foreigners, who do not belong to Your people Israel, will come from a distant land because of Your reputation. When they hear about Your great reputation and Your ability to accomplish mighty deeds, they will come and direct their prayers toward this temple" (1 Kings 8:41-42). These passages remain very controversial even to this day, especially in the "Holy Land."

Types & Shadows: Yahweh's Heavenly Dwelling Place

Solomon recognized that no physical structure could ever encapsulate the totality of Infinite *Being*. David also affirmed that the Lord "lives" (*mishkan*) [tabernacles] in His "holy temple," yet His "throne" remains "in heaven," where He observes the realm of Finitude as its sole supercontextual witness (Ps 11:4, 26:8). Accordingly, the Temple of Jerusalem was distinctive among ancient cultures for its absence of any image or statue representing Yahweh. While cherubim statues were present in the Holy of Holies, they were not intended to depict Yahweh Himself, nor were they an object of worship. In contrast, we can look at the Temple of Zeus at Olympia or the Statue of Athena in the Parthenon as examples that did include such representations.

The New Testament echoes this concept of the physical temple serving merely as a symbolic representation of God's heavenly tabernacle. We read: "The Most High does not reside (*katoikeo*) [to house permanently, dwell] in temples (*naois*) [temples] made by human hands, as the prophet states, 'Heaven is My throne, and earth is the footstool for My feet. What kind of house (*oikos*) will you build (*oikodomeo*) for Me, says the Lord, or what is My resting place? Did My hand not make all these things?'" (Acts 7:48-50; Isa 66:1-2; ISA; BDAG, 534).

> *In what ways does God's infinite nature set Him apart from the gods revered by almost every civilization?*
>
> *What are the implications of the fact that God cannot be confined to any space, including His own Temple?*

Reason supports the idea that God cannot fully manifest in the limited physical world. How can the Infinite, which is uncreated and unbounded, fit into the finite, which is created? It is not merely that God is "too large or powerful" to dwell within a temple, akin to trying to fit an ocean into a bottle. If you had a sufficiently large container, it might seem feasible to hold the ocean. The truth is, attempting to limit the Infinite within the finite is a logical impossibility. This is like the challenge of writing out every digit of *pi*; no matter how much paper you amass, you will never completely document a seemingly infinitely long number. Just as *pi* cannot be confined to any amount of paper, God also cannot be restricted to any finite space, regardless of its size.

The Holy Spirit "made clear" that the temple symbolized the Old Covenant. We read: "the way into the [true] holy place [immanent dwelling place of God] had not yet appeared as long as the old tabernacle was standing" (Heb 9:8, 12). The Old Testament also expressed the inaccessibility of God's true immanent presence. When the majesty of God's visibly revealed presence filled the temple, no one could enter, not even Moses or the priests (Exod 40:34-38; 1 Kings 8:10-11; 2 Chr 7:1-3). The dwelling place of God within the finite Creation was beyond anyone's reach.[159] On one occasion, the people cried out, "Anyone who even comes close to the tabernacle of the Lord will die" (Num 17:12-13)! Similarly, when God concretely revealed His immanent presence to Moses, He said, "You cannot see My face, for no one can see Me and live" (Exod 33:18-23; Heb 1:3).

The sole way Moses witnessed the true glory of God's presence within finite Creation was through "the rock," which signifies Jesus Christ (1 Cor 10:4). The Scriptures state that "no one has seen" the transcendent nature of "God the Father" "at any time," since only through the Son can the Father be revealed (John 1:18, 6:46; 1 Tim

---

[159] This is not because God's presence is evil or harmful in and of itself. Instead, our corruption as fallen beings keeps us from approaching divinity. It is similar to drawing near to the sun; while its heat and energy are essential for life, any life form that gets too close or lacks the protection of the atmosphere is incinerated by that overwhelming intensity.

6:16; 1 John 4:12). With these verses in mind, it is evident how God's immanent presence in the temple was symbolic. His true presence could not be confined to a building, even if the whole planet were a building. Even if it were possible, it would still be unreachable for anyone wishing to approach Him. While the Old Testament indicates that God dwelt among His people through the physical tabernacle and temple, He did not fully inhabit or dwell within them.

How should we interpret this seeming contradiction? We can resolve this issue similar to how we address the contradiction of atonement through sacrifice found in the Scriptures. The Old Testament describes how the blood of sacrificial animals within the tabernacle or temple atoned for the sins of God's people. Conversely, the New Testament reveals that only the blood of the Son of Man can atone for these sins (Lev 4, 16; 1 Cor 11:25; Heb 9:12-22, 10:1-12). We can harmonize these concepts by recognizing that the rituals and practices of the Old Covenant acted as significant symbols.[160] We can refer to them as "types and shadows" of realities belonging to the New Covenant. Just as we read in Scripture, "the law possesses a shadow of the good things to come but not the reality itself" (Heb 10:1).

Both the Old and New Testaments clearly indicate that the design of the physical tabernacle and temple was based on "a sketch and shadow of the heavenly sanctuary," reflecting and foreshadowing "the true tabernacle that the Lord, not man, set up" (Exod 25:8-9; Heb 8:2, 5, 9:23-24; Acts 7:44). In simpler terms,

---

[160] Instead of viewing a symbol solely as an intellectual concept, rituals connect transcendent truths to time and space through actions that individuals and communities can recognize and engage in together. Therefore, we should see these as more than just "intellectual symbols,"" yet still not equating them with the realities unveiled in the New Covenant (since the ritual's power arises not from the bloodshed itself, but what it signifies).

they serve as "representations of the true sanctuary" in "heaven" (Heb 9:23-24). Concerning heavenly tabernacle of God, we read, "But now Christ has come as the high priest of the good things to come. He passed through the greater and more perfect tent not made with hands, that is, not of this creation" (Heb 9:11). The Book of Revelation describes this temple: "Then the temple (*naos*) of God in heaven was opened and the ark of His covenant was visible within His temple (*naos*)" (Rev 11:19; Also see Rev 15:7-8).

God has made it abundantly clear that He resides only in a heavenly temple, not any physical building constructed by human hands no matter how majestic. As the creator of all physical matter, He Himself is not fundamentally a material being (1 Kings 8:27-30; Ps 11:4, 18:6-10, 20:6; Isa 66:1-2). The Spirit of God imparted truths to David, Solomon, and Isaiah that hinted at the existence of the Heavenly Temple, God's genuine dwelling within Finitude. Nonetheless, a question persists: how is the actual, non-symbolic reality of God's dwelling place within Finitude fulfilled under the New Covenant?

> *Can you think of other examples of types and shadows in the Scriptures?*
>
> *What do you believe is the reason God employs so many of these teaching tools throughout the Bible?*

The physical Temple reflects God's true sanctuary within Creation (Exod 25:8-9; Heb 8:2, 5, 9:23-24; Acts 7:44). As with all types and shadows in the Old Covenant, Jesus Christ, the "mediator" of the "New Covenant," fulfills the Temple's symbolic meanings (Heb 9:15, 12:24). "When God speaks of a new covenant, He makes the first [which includes the physical temple and its sacrificial and cleansing rituals] obsolete. Now what is growing obsolete and aging is about to disappear," for all physical structures in this fallen world will ultimately decay (Heb 8:13).

When considering the essence of this "true sanctuary", we

must remember an important point. Only God can create a genuine immanent dwelling place (*oikos*) of the Divine within the "house" of Finitude (Heb 8:2). As God Himself, only Jesus Christ can construct a legitimate immanent dwelling for God in the created world (John 1:1, 1:18; Col 1:19, 2:9; Heb 1:3). His existence as both fully man (finite) and fully God (Infinite) simultaneously demonstrates the possibility of bridging Heaven and Earth. Moreover, only Jesus Christ, as the eternal High Priest, can "build" this immanent house (*oikos*) of God within the realm of Finitude and make it inhabitable by humanity.

Messianic Symbolism of the Physical Temple of Zion

In the physical temple, a curtain concealed the Holy of Holies, the innermost chamber believed to be filled with God's presence. This curtain symbolized the separation between unholy humanity and the holy, uncreated God (Exod 26:33; Lev 16:1-2). When Jesus died on the cross, this curtain was torn, illustrating that His death eliminated the barrier permanently (Luke 23:45). Consequently, the children of God now confidently "enter the true heavenly sanctuary [of Yahweh's immanent presence]," thanks to the "blood of Jesus," which established the New Covenant (Heb 8:2, 8:5, 9:24, 10:19).

We can now confidently enter Yahweh's presence through "the fresh and living way [Jesus] inaugurated for us through the curtain," as He became the "high priest over the [true] house (*oikos*) of God" for all humanity (Heb 10:20-21). He eternally fulfilled the Israelite priests' symbolic role in the physical temple. Today, our "hope" as "priests" in the heavenly temple "reaches inside behind the curtain," since "Jesus" is "our [pioneering] forerunner who [first] entered on our behalf" (Heb 6:19-20). His completed work during His first coming opened up a path for us to connect and commune with the presence of Yahweh, who continuously reveals

> *What makes Jesus Christ the sole individual qualified to establish God's authentic house within the limitations of our existence?*
>
> *How does this highlight His importance for us to reside in God's house alongside Him?*

Himself through the omnipresence of His Spirit. As the "high priest" of God's "heavenly" temple, Jesus "now appears in God's presence for us," uniquely able to "purify" and sanctify this "true sanctuary" and all who enter it, through His "blood" (Heb 9:23-24, 10:19, 12:24). The reconciliation achieved by Jesus at the cross allows us to serve as priests or "ambassadors of God" in His heavenly temple, with Him as our High Priest (Heb 10:19-20; 2 Cor 5:18-21). This sacred role is available to all who respond to the Call of Eternity. He promises to restore to us an inheritance as citizens of Yahweh's eternal house. This was made possible by removing our uncircumcised (un-set-apart) inwardness and replacing our lack of holiness [uncleanness] with His holiness (Rom 3:24; 1 Cor 6:11; Heb 2:17, 7:24-26; Eph 2:14-16).

Only Christ's blood can genuinely purify the priests of the heavenly temple from their worldly impurities. In contrast, priests of the earthly temple relied on animal blood for symbolic cleansing (Lev 16:34; Heb 9:7, 25). Through Christ, we are cleansed and "set free" into our authentic heavenly identity as a "royal priesthood." "At the cost of His own blood, [Christ] has appointed us kings and priests serving His God and Father" (Rev 1:5-6).

The anointing of the Holy Spirit dedicates us to our new divine roles through the rebirth of baptism, facilitated by Christ (John 1:33, 3:3-8; Rom 6:3-4, 15:16; 1 Pet 1:2; 2 Thes 2:13). This spiritual anointing represents the fulfillment of Old Testament sanctification, similar to how the priests of the earthly temple were anointed with oil (Num 19:7, 13; Exod 30:30). In Christ, we embrace our true identities as holy priests, serving Him as our high priest (2 Pet 2:4, 9). "Through Him we have access in one Spirit to the Father," allowing us to freely "offer spiritual sacrifices that are acceptable to God through Christ Jesus" (Eph 3:11-12; Heb 6:20; 2 Pet 2:4-11).

The biblical account of "Phinehas son of Eleazar, the son of Aaron the priest" prefigures the groundbreaking mission of the heavenly priesthood. Phinehas notably "made atonement for the Israelites" through his "zealous[ness] for His God" (Num 25:10-13; Heb 2:17). As a representation of Christ, Yahweh pledged to establish a "covenant of peace" through him, ensuring that "his descendants after him [would serve as a] covenant of a permanent priesthood" (Num 25:10-13; Heb 10:19-21; Eph 2:14-16; 2 Pet 2:4-11). Likewise, in creating the eternal dynasty and priesthood through the New Covenant, Jesus affirmed all the types and shadows from the Old Covenant. His mission was more than just establishing priests or temples; it marked the fulfillment of the eternal covenant of reconciliation between God and humanity (Jer 33:21-22; Rom 5:10; 2 Cor 5:18-21; Col 1:20).

> *What makes it essential for Jesus' blood to be shed for you to enter God's true temple and serve Him as a priest?*
>
> *Do these insights inspire a longing in you to reside within God's temple?*

Christ as the Builder and Foundation of the True Temple

To this point, we have explored how the Holy Spirit sanctifies priests of the heavenly temple through the redemptive grace of the New Covenant, which is activated and mediated by Christ. This sanctifying grace allows us to enter the true heavenly temple of God, as we are purified and dedicated to His service. It resembles the anointing of the British monarch with holy oil before receiving the crown; ruling was regarded as a divine responsibility bestowed by God. Hence, the monarch must first be "set apart" and made holy before embracing their roles and duties. This concept has a spiritual parallel. As illustrated in Scripture, Christ has cleared the path for us to serve as His holy priests in God's true house (*oikos*) to be anointed and baptized in the Spirit (Mark 1:8; Acts 1:5).

However, we have yet to clarify *what* this divine house of God truly is and *how* Jesus Christ facilitates its establishment within the created world. First, we need to explore how Christ makes the construction of this house (*oikos*) of God possible within the finite realm (Ps 110:4). The New Testament, through divine inspiration, illustrates how Jesus accomplished the prophecies found in 1 Chronicles 17:11-14 and 2 Samuel 7:13-14 (Heb 1:5). These prophecies indicate that the one who becomes a son to God "will build a temple for [Yahweh's] name." Additionally, His reign will be everlasting, as He inherits "permanent charge over [Yahweh's] house and [His] kingdom." Ancient Jews interpreted these prophecies similarly to how modern fantasy characters view a promised chosen one or heir. Remarkably, Jesus Himself asserted that His Father's work involved the temple ministry, shocking His listeners by proclaiming He would reconstruct God's temple in just three days after its destruction (Luke 2:49; John 2:19).

In Abraham's era, Melchizedek served as both a "king" and "priest of the Most High God" in what would eventually become Jerusalem. Through him, Old Testament prophecies again hint at the ultimate realization of earthly symbols, as he represents a type of Christ (Heb 7:1-17; Gen 14:18-20; Heb 6:20, 7:1-17; Rev 19:16). Another Christ-like figure is found in "Joshua son of Jehozadak, the high priest," who symbolizes the awaited "branch"

> *Based on the clues provided up to this point, what do you believe is the genuine heavenly house of God established by the New Covenant?*

from the everlasting Davidic line (Jer 23:5, 33:15-16; Isa 11:1-5; Zech 3:8, 6:11-13). He foreshadows Christ's eternal inheritance of the Kingdom of God and His reign as King of Kings over David's everlasting dynasty (Jer 30:9; Hos 3:5; 1 Chr 7:12-15, 22:10; Isa 9:6-7).

> *What other types and shadows of Christ and His work can you find within the Old Testament?*

God declared that Joshua would not just be "crowned king" but also "would build the temple of the Lord" while being "clothed in splendor" (Zech 6:11-13). Just like Joshua, Jesus Christ is the ultimate fulfillment of the prophecy in Scripture: "I will raise up for myself a faithful priest. He will do what is in My heart and soul. I will build for him a secure dynasty and he will serve My chosen one for all time" (1 Sam 2:35).

In Isaiah, another prophecy indicates how the Messiah would "proclaim the release of the captives" and liberate the "prisoners" through God's Spirit. These liberated individuals would then serve Yahweh permanently as "[His] priests," the genuine "servants of God" (Isa 61:1-6). Additionally, it is stated that through this Messiah and the priests He liberates, Jerusalem and the Temple would be restored (Isa 61:4). This Messiah refers to Jesus; the Son of God and the true eternal king descended from David. Through Him, the authentic house of God will dwell among humanity (Rev 22:16). We also learn about this same Jesus being the "high priest… who is faithful to the one who appointed Him." We read the following:

> "He has come to deserve greater glory than Moses, just as the builder (*kataskeuazo*) [structural-preparer] of a house (*oikos*) deserves greater honor than the house (*oikos*) itself! For every house (*oikos*) is built by someone, but the builder (*kataskeuazo*) of all things is God […] Christ is faithful as a Son over God's

house (*oikos*)," and through Him "we are [members] of His house (*oikos*)."

(Heb 3:1-6)

The Greek word, *kataskeuazo* translated here as "builder" in reference to Christ, is special. In contrast to the term *oikodome*, it goes beyond mere physical construction. It encompasses the concept of "making ready for some purpose, [to] prepare" or "to bring a structure into being, erect" (BDAG, 526-527). Consider the difference between applying paint strokes to a canvas and creating a painting. Painting involves more than mechanically applying paint; it requires the thoughtful preparation of a masterpiece. The artist must layer, adjust colors, and contemplate how the work will resonate with the audience who will appreciate and be inspired by it. Jesus was not just a builder; He is the one who prepared the foundation for the true house of God to come into existence.

Without Jesus, there would be neither a house nor even a plan for one. Jesus stated, "I tell you that something greater than the [physical] temple is here," for it is in and through Him that the true heavenly house of God exists within Finitude (Matt 12:6). Scripture shows that "God was pleased to have all His fullness dwell [to-house-permanently] in the Son Jesus," "for in Him all the fullness of deity lives (*katoikeo*) [dwells] in bodily form" (Col 1:19, 2:9). In the next section, we will explore how Jesus Christ establishes and builds-up the house (*oikos*) of God within finitude (Heb 1:2, 10).

[*Do these insights into Christ as the architect of God's house inspire you to seek and follow Him?*]

High Priest Who Lays the Foundation of Yahweh's Home

Scripture describes Jesus Christ as the "foundation" of "God's house (*oikodome*)" (1 Cor 3:9-11). He is also foretold to be the "cornerstone… laid in Zion," although the house of Israel rejected Him. "Look, I am laying a stone in Zion, an approved stone, set in place as a precious cornerstone for the foundation" (Isa 28:16; 1 Pet 2:6-7; Matt 7:24, 21:42-43). As, the Scriptures mention:

> "You are members of God's household (*oikeios*), because you have been built on (*epoikodomeo*) the foundation of the apostles and prophets, with Christ Jesus himself as the cornerstone. In Him the whole building (*oikodome*), being joined together (*sunarmologeo*)[12], grows into a holy temple in the Lord, in whom you also are being built together (*sunoikodomeo*) into a dwelling place (*katoiketerion*) of God in the Spirit."
>
> (Eph 2:19-22)

This passage suggests that we see Jesus Christ as much more than the foundational stone of God's true house; He is central to the entire construction process. Furthermore, it emphasizes that the genuine temple of God, established and overseen by Jesus Christ, is none other than the Body of Christ. Therefore, through Christ, God's promise to dwell among us in creation is realized within the community of His children.

The Scriptures vividly depict Christ as He builds His body into the imminent heavenly dwelling of the Creator: "We will in all things grow up into Christ, who is the head. From Him, the whole body grows, fitted and held together through every supporting ligament. As each one does its part, the body grows in love" (Eph 4:15-16). Biblical prophecy

> *In what ways will you embody your identity as a holy priest of Christ in your everyday life?*
>
> *What do you believe this calling compels you to be or do?*

further emphasizes how the living temple of the Children of God fulfills the symbolic foreshadowing of the physical Temple in Jerusalem:

> "For we are the temple of the living God, just as God said, 'I will live (*enoikeo*) in them and will walk among them, and I will be their God, and they will be My people.' Therefore 'come out from their midst, and be separate,' says the Lord, 'and touch no unclean thing, and I will welcome you, and I will be a father to you, and you will be My sons and daughters,' says the All-Powerful Lord."
>
> (2 Cor 6:16-18; Lev 26:12; Jer 32:38; Ezek 37:37; Isa 52:11; ISA; BDAG, 338)

We see here how the children of God, when completely sanctified and cleansed, become the final temple of God where His immanent presence dwells. The Greek word "*enoikeo*" drives this home. It is a verbal form of "*oikos*" and here means "to inhabit and dwell in" or more specifically "to make into one's home" (ISA; BDAG, 338).

Scripture also expresses Jesus' central role in making possible this true house (*oikos*) of God:

> "You have received Christ Jesus as Lord, continue to live your lives in Him, rooted and built up (*epoikodomeo*) in him;"
>
> "[He is] the head from whom the whole body, supported and knit together through its ligaments and sinews, grows with a growth that is from God."
>
> (Col 2:6-7, 19; See also Rom 7:4)

God expects His children to become "living stones," "built up (*oikodomeo*)" with Christ as the essential cornerstone "into a spiritual house (*oikos*)" (1 Pet 2:5-7). This perspective clarifies why the Scriptures refer to *oikos* (house) as a spiritual establishment rather than a physical entity; it is composed of "living stones." Yet, we must never forget that only God's power can truly construct His house—human effort alone is insufficient (unlike many denominations espouse). Through the Spirit, the Creator establishes a dwelling for Himself among His children via the work of His Son. Just as God stands as His own Infinite Temple, He transforms us into His true finitely contextualized temple through His indwelling presence within us (1 Cor 3:17, 6:19; Eph 2:22; 1 Tim 6:16; 1 John 1:5; Rev 21:22). This dwelling serves as the home of God within Creation, constructed by the Creator, not by created beings.

> *What does the revelation that you (along with fellow believers) are the temple of God awaken in you?*
>
> *Does it instill a sense of meaning, purpose, and destiny?*

Up to this point, we have explored various aspects of our true home in God's house and how Christ's work has opened the way to this eternal dwelling. Now, let us take a moment to reflect on some of Christ's final teachings before His crucifixion, which He shared with our true home in focus:

> "Where I am going, you cannot follow Me now, but you will follow later... Do not let your hearts be distressed. You believe in God; believe also in Me. There are many dwelling places (*mone*) in My Father's house (*oikos*). Otherwise, I would have told you, because I am going away to make ready a place for you. And if I go and make ready a place for you, I will come again and take you to be with Me, so that where I am you may be too... I am the way, and the

truth, and the life. No one comes to the Father except through Me... And I set myself apart on [your] behalf, so that [you] too may be truly set apart... I want those [of] you [who] have given Me to be with Me where I am, so that [you] can see My glory that [my Father] gave me."

(John 13:36, 14:1-6, 17:19)

In this passage, Jesus reassures His disciples by promising to prepare a place in God's house where each child of God can dwell for eternity. By the time of His resurrection, He had completed this preparation. When He returned to His disciples after rising, He bestowed upon them the Holy Spirit (John 20:22). This allowed His disciples, along with all believers in the New Covenant, to enter God's house personally within their innermost selves (John 14:16-17, 20:22). We enter the spiritual house by letting Christ build us into a dwelling place for God in the Spirit (1 Cor 6:16; Eph 2:22). We become the true house of God, both as individuals and as a community of believers. As we are built up both personally and collectively, the true house of God within our finite existence becomes built up into many dwelling places. Ultimately, through our unity with each other and with Jesus in the Body of Christ, we are formed into the true home of God (1 Cor 12:12-27).

> *What does it mean for you to exist as a living stone, being built into God's house through Christ?*
>
> *Does this provoke any challenges for you or prompt a reevaluation of your life choices?*

The true house of God is a house of the Father, not just the Son and the Spirit. We see this revealed in the following teaching:

"If anyone loves Me, he will obey My word, and My Father will love him, and We will come to him and take up residence (a dwelling place) [*mone*] with him... [Later the Son of Man prayed to the Father saying,] I pray that they will be in us... I in them and You in Me.¹³"

(John 14:23, 17:21-23; 1 John 2:24)

The previous passage about Christ preparing a dwelling for us highlights the same term, *mone*. This underscores that the dwelling Jesus mentions in both verses represents a shared cohabitional existence with the Triune I AM. To truly reside in God's house means to inhabit the divine space of the Father, Son, and Spirit (John 14:17, 15:26, 16:13-15; 1 John 3:24). The Scriptures reveal that the incarnate Son and the Father reside within the collective Body of Christ and each believer through the Holy Spirit (1 Cor 6:16; Eph 2:22). The Spirit assures us, declaring, "by this we know that we reside in God and He in us: by the Spirit He has given us" (1 John 3:24, 4:13). As we are reborn through the Spirit, we transform into God's heavenly dwelling place (John 3:3-8).

By the indwelling of the Holy Spirit, God's children "remain (abide) [*meno*] in the Son and in the Father," as well as in the Spirit, for the Divine is indivisibly unified (1 John 2:24; 2 John 1:9). It is impossible to abide in the Son, the Father, or the Holy Spirit without simultaneously abiding in the entire Trinity. Thus, these revelations affirm the biblical truth that the temple, house, and tabernacle of God are essentially God Himself. This understanding applies both to His transcendent, infinite dwelling place and to the "house" He creates within finite existence. We can compare this to an embassy being defined by the people who inhabit it, rather than just the building itself. Without their presence, the building lacks genuine purpose. The embassy exists wherever the people are, transcending any specific structure. Similarly, wherever God resides, there too is His Temple, as His triune nature is His dwelling place. This explains why, in the new heavens and new earth, there is no temple apart from God, who is Himself the temple (Rev 21:22).

Christ's Body symbolizes the temple of the Living God, who is the Temple Himself (Rev 21:22). If God is the temple in every aspect, we can only embody His temple in Creation by having Him dwell within and through us. His divine presence converts us into both His temple and its priest. Consider how a particular building and its features do not define a church, but rather, it becomes a true church when God's presence gathers there through His children. Even spaces like warehouses and basements can serve as authentic churches, not due to their physical attributes, but because of God's presence. In this way, ordinary locations are transformed into sacred spaces by those who occupy them.

Similarly, Christ, being God Himself, transforms us into the Temple of God by residing within us. More precisely, He shapes us into "a pillar in the temple," as we together form the Body of Christ. As the complete embodiment of humanity and divinity, He is the Temple we become, even as He resides within us. Additionally, He assures us that "[we] will never depart from it" (John 1:18; Col 1:19, 2:9; Heb 2:14, 17; Rev 3:12, 21:22). Due to these profound truths, we find that "our [true] life is hidden with Christ in God" (Col 3:3).

{ *How does the understanding that God Himself is sHis house alter your perspective on our intended purpose: to reside in the house of the* }

Concluding Thoughts on the Temple: Our Eternal Destiny

With this spiritual understanding, we can finally grasp the enigmatic passage of Scripture stating, "So the beast opened his mouth to blaspheme against God [the Divine] – to blaspheme both His name and His dwelling place (tabernacle), that is, those who dwell (tabernacling) in heaven" (Rev 13:6). At this present period of the Narrative of Finitude, the new heavens and new earth are yet to be created and established (Isa 65:17, 66:22; Rev 21:1; 2 Pet 3:13). Nevertheless, the genuine heavenly temple within finitude, which Christ entered in heaven, exists today, as the Scriptures reveal. In these writings, God's heavenly temple within finitude is associated with those who dwell in heaven (Rev 13:6). This heavenly tabernacle is a dwelling made up of living beings, united in God, through Christ (the "Head" of the body) and by the Spirit. "In the [Head] the whole building, being joined together, grows into a holy temple in the Lord, in whom we also are being built together into a dwelling place of God in the Spirit" (Eph 2:21-22).

At the conclusion of temporality, the divine dwelling, referred to as the "tabernacle of God," "descends from heaven" (Rev 21:1-3). Such a conclusion makes sense given all the revelations we have examined. From these scriptures, it can be inferred that God's heavenly dwelling existed prior to the new heaven and new earth, meaning it existed before "the first heaven and earth… ceased to exist" (Rev 21:1-3). In the book of Revelation, the Body of Christ transforms into the fully prepared Bride of Christ. As the New Jerusalem, now complete, she descends to Him as "a bride adorned for her husband" (Rev 21:3). The New Jerusalem represents the fully realized house of God within the bounds of creation. Upon its arrival, the proclamation is made: "the tabernacle of God is among human beings. He will live among them, and they will be His people" (Rev 21:3). Until that moment, the heavenly tabernacle remains in heaven, awaiting the incorporation and perfection of every living stone. Only then will

> *Are you willing to let God reside in you, shaping you into a foundation of His temple?*
>
> *If not, what causes your hesitation or reluctance to accept this divine calling?*

it truly occupy the recreated house of finitude (New Creation) as God's intended immanent dwelling place (2 Pet 2:4-9; Rev 3:12).

We should end this section reflecting on the following:

> "For we know that if our earthly house (*oikos*), the tent [tabernacle] we live in, is dismantled, we have a building (*oikodome*) from God, a house (*oikos*) not built by human hands, that is eternal in the heavens... the one who prepared us for this very purpose is God, who gave us the Spirit."
>
> (2 Cor 5:1-5)

Our true "heavenly" "homeland" is God's temple "that He has prepared for [us]" (Heb 11:10, 14, 16). In this homeland, we discover the "City of the Living God," the New Jerusalem, which serves as the Bride of Christ. It is a city "with firm foundations [Christ], whose architect and builder is God" (Matt 25:1-13; Luke 5:35; John 3:29; Eph 5:27-29; Heb 12:22; Rev 19:7, 21:2-3, 21:9, 22:17). Our true homeland, where we will dwell as God's royal priests, is a celestial realm rather than a physical location. Currently, only our soul and spirit, not our body, can reside there, in the spiritual New Jerusalem. Our earthly homeland will ultimately transform into the tangible New Jerusalem, the City of the Living God (Heb 12:21-22; Rev 21:9-14). We read that "flesh and blood cannot inherit the Kingdom of God" because "the Kingdom of God does not consist of food and drink, but righteousness, peace, and joy in the Holy Spirit" (Rom 14:17; 1 Cor 15:50). The Kingdom of Heaven is God's temple, "a spiritual house" made up of "living stones" and living "pillars." This is our true homeland, where we, as priests, spiritually commune and coexist with the Living God in His heavenly dwelling (2 Pet 2:4-5; Rev 3:12).

Genuine seafarers long to find our way to our true home in the eternal sanctuary of our relationship with God. We have chosen to live permanently with our Creator and share His presence for all eternity. However, as we recognize the true temple of Yahweh as our ultimate destination, we must understand that this sacred space of worship is not actually a physical place. All such locations are shwadows and symbols of a greater reality. Consider Jesus's message to the Samaritan woman at the well, where He clearly illustrated that, unlike the religious beliefs held by Jews and Samaritans, the location of worship—whether at the temple in Jerusalem or another sacred site—no longer holds final significance (John 4:19-21). Instead, in the New Covenant, worship primarily signifies an internal state evidenced by external fruit (Matt 7:20). More specifically, the temple symbolizes how God transforms our innermost selves into His temple by the Holy Spirit. Authentic worship occurs whenever we sincerely engage in the two-way God-relationship happening within us, regardless of where we are in the world (John 4:23-24).

Chapter 8

The Fellowship of Yahweh's House

How the Creator's Triune Nature Shapes our Destiny

"No one has seen God at any time. If we love one another, God resides in us, and His [*agape-*]love is perfected in us. By this we know that we reside in God and He in us: in that He has given us of His Spirit... God is love, and the one who resides in [*agape-*]love resides in God, and God resides in Him."

(1 John 4:12-13, 16-17)

"I pray that according to the wealth of [the Father's] glory He may grant you to be strengthened with power through His *Spirit*... that *Christ* may dwell in your hearts through faith, so that... you may be able to comprehend [and] know the [*agape-*]love of Christ... [and be] filled up to all the fullness of God... Practicing the truth in [*agape-*]love, we will in all things grow up into Christ... From Him the whole body grows, fitted and held together through every supporting ligament. As each one does its part, the body grows in [*agape-*]love."

(Eph 3:16-19, 4:15-16)

"[You have been] chosen according to the foreknowledge of God the *Father* by being set apart by the *Spirit* for obedience and for sprinkling with *Jesus Christ's* blood... You have been *born anew*... a *living stone* rejected by men but chosen and priceless in God's sight... *built up as a spiritual house* to be a *holy priesthood* and to offer spiritual sacrifices... *through Jesus Christ*..."

(1 Pet 1:1-2; 2:4-5, 9)

Our Destiny Reflects the Maker's Nature

As pilgrims on the Sea of Revelation, we should regularly meditate on what Scripture reveals regarding our eternal destination. To truly comprehend the essence of our true home, we must contemplate the character of our Creator. Specifically, we must grasp how He embodies His own dwelling and how His nature is *agape*-love.

Firstly, our Creator is triune. This does not imply that God is three separate Beings or distinct personalities collaborating in unity.[161] His triune nature signifies He exists as a triune yet co-equal, co-eternal, and co-substantial personhood. We see this perfectly illustrated in how the Son only says words that come from the Father and only does the deeds of the Father (John 5:31-47). Numerous images and illustrations have been employed to elucidate the essence of the Trinity, although none can completely capture Yahweh's triune nature. However, these representations can still be helpful, if only to highlight the complexity of the concept.

Sunshine has historically served as one image of the Trinity. Sunshine is composed of light, radiation, and heat. Without these elements, it would not exist as we know it. However, this analogy is inadequate, as light, heat, or radiation alone does not define the sun. Each of God's three "persons" is fully divine, but without one, God ceases to be God. Another analogy compares the Trinity to a musical chord composed of three notes, which can be viewed individually or collectively (the same chord played at a different octave). These three distinct notes coexist simultaneously, unified

---

[161] Anyone who studies the Early Church theologians responsible for the Trinitarian Creeds from Nicea to Cappodocia would find this made adamantly and repeatedly clear. In the near future, I will be releasing a published version of my master's thesis that covers this topic in detail.

in their purpose and essence while also being separate. However, such an analogy fails to demonstrate the uniqueness of the Son as "compared" to the Father, e.g., the Son alone *is* the Word of God, through Whom the Father created the world, and the Incarnation of God. While not perfect, these examples help illustrate the concept of the Trinity as one and three simultaneously. Embracing this mystery is vital for our journey, as His triune nature shapes our destination. We explored this profound mystery in the previous volume.

Secondly, Yahweh's *agape*-love signifies that He naturally creates, fills, and upholds a dwelling place for communion with us (1 John 4:8-17). His love transcends the bonds shared among friends, family, or intimate partners[162], but inspires all these. *Agape* is a sacrificial, unconditional, and self-emptying love. It is the kind of love that led the Creator to come to earth and take on flesh to be sacrificed so we could be saved. Furthermore, God does not merely possess *agape*-love; in fact, He IS *agape*-love (1 John 4:8-16). It is in His nature and essence to operate out of this love in everything He does.[163]

How do you believe embracing the mystery of God's true essence, both as triune and agape-love, should influence your journey home?

Let us revisit what we discovered when we first "raised anchor." The Father, the Son, and the Holy Spirit exist in a shared communion of Infinite Being without a hint of disparity. Yahweh, *being agape*-love and *being* a triune personhood, is fundamental to Infinite Being. These aspects are not simply characteristics or attributes; they inherently exist within the self-actualization of the Infinite I AM (Exod 3:14). We cannot divorce God's nature or

---

[162] This refers respectively to *phileo, storge,* and *eros.*
[163] For a more in-depth discussion on the nature of God as *agape*-love, see the third volume of the *Before the Beginning* series by J.K. Ward, *God is Love.*

personality from these two critical realities. As Scripture states, since "[He] is light," "He dwells [makes-His-home] in unapproachable light" (1 Tim 6:16; 1 John 1:5).

Thus, we need to understand how His Infinite Home inherently influences the home He creates for Himself within the finite world. In other words, the essence of the Triune I AM establishes the purpose He has designed for us (to become finitely contextualized tabernacles). This foundation underlies our transformation into vibrant temples. We will explore this further throughout this chapter.

We understand how Yahweh shapes us to mirror His Infinite home through the indwelling of the Holy Spirit within each of us (Rom 8:9-11; 1 Cor 3:16, 6:19; Eph 2:22, 3:16-17; 2 Tim 1:14; 1 John 3:24). Consequently, we partake in God's Triune nature. Is it not true that the fullness of the Divine is meant to dwell within us both individually and as a community (2 Pet 1:4)? This is why Scripture informs us that the Father and Son, not just the Spirit, inhabit our innermost being (John 14:23, 16:12-15). To be the residence for the inseparable unity of the Divine means we simultaneously become the dwelling place for the Triune I AM.

Biblical Basis for Our True Home

As we progress toward our goal, we seek to experience the close presence of our Triune God, drawing us nearer to our everlasting homeland. Thus, we need to grasp what it means to embody the temple of the Triune I AM. At the heart of such a temple is communion, wherein we reside in God and He in us (1 John 3:24, 4:13). To understand our final destination, we must follow the revelations of *agape*-love, a fundamental element in transforming our eternal home. This "up-building element" is rooted in our Creator's triune nature, which is characterized by His being *agape*-love, *phos*-light, and *pneuma*-spirit (John 4:24; 1 John 1:5, 4:16).

Now, let us turn to our Guide to explore how they affirm and illuminate the communion of *agape*-love present within the Temple of the Triune I AM. In these pertinent passages, the Spirit unmistakably reveals that God designed every individual to partake in His communal dwelling of *agape*-love in the created world:

> "For we are the *temple of the living God*, just as God said, '*I will live in them* and *will walk among them*, and I will be their God, and they will be *My people*... the [*agape*-]love of God and the fellowship (*koinonia*) of the Holy Spirit be with you all."
>
> (Ezek 37:27; 2 Cor 6:14-16, 13:13)

> "Through the [*Son*] we both have *access* in one *Spirit* to the *Father*. You are fellow citizens with the saints and *members of God's household*, because you have been *built* on the foundation of the apostles and prophets, with *Christ Jesus* himself as the *cornerstone. In Him the whole building*, being joined together, *grows into a holy temple in the Lord*, in whom you also are *being built together into a dwelling place of God in the Spirit*...
>
> I pray that according to the wealth of [the *Father's*] glory He may grant you to be strengthened with power through His *Spirit* in the inner person, that *Christ* may *dwell* in your hearts through faith, so that, because you have been *rooted and grounded in* [*agape*-]*love*, you may be able to comprehend with all the saints what is the breadth and length and height and depth, and thus to know the [*agape*-]love of *Christ* that surpasses knowledge, so that you *may be filled up to all the fullness of* [the Divine]."
>
> (Eph 2:18-22, 3:16-19)

"[You have been] chosen according to the foreknowledge of God the *Father* by being set apart by the *Spirit* for obedience and for sprinkling with *Jesus Christ's* blood...

You have purified your souls by obeying the truth in order to show sincere mutual (brotherly) love. So [*agape-*]love one another earnestly from a pure heart. You have been born anew, not from perishable but from imperishable seed, through the living and enduring [abiding] Word of God...

So as you come to Him, a living stone rejected by men but chosen and priceless in God's sight[164], you yourselves, as living stones, are built up as a spiritual house to be a holy priesthood and to offer spiritual sacrifices that are acceptable to God through Jesus Christ...

But you are a chosen race, a royal priesthood, a holy nation, a people of His own, so that you may proclaim the virtues of the one who called you out of darkness into His marvelous light."

(1 Pet 1:1-2, 1:22-23, 2:4-5, 9)

{ *Reflect on your life story and contemplate how Christ has called you out of darkness and into His marvelous light.*

What darkness?

What light? }

---

[164] God established our beauty and value when He created and fashioned us as a unique member of God's household and priesthood. We can only find this eternal beauty when we individually abide in God. Our communal abiding results in a spiritual union which is distinct for each individual, because each person's "face" uniquely unveils the mysteries of God's face.

"And the person who keeps His commandments resides in God, and God in him [or her]…

No one has seen God at any time. If we [*agape-*]love one another, God resides in us, and His [*agape-*]love is perfected in us. By this we know that we reside in God and He in us: in that He has given us of His Spirit…

If anyone confesses that Jesus is the Son of God, God resides in Him and He in God. And we have come to know and to believe the [*agape-*]love that God has in us. God is [*agape-*]love, and the one who resides in [*agape-*]love resides in God, and God resides in him [or her]."

(1 John 3:24, 4:12-13, 15-16)

The scriptures illustrate the authentic bond we can have with God:

"[*Agape-*]love builds up (*oikodomeo*)… We are *coworkers*[165] with God. [We] are God's field, God's *building* (*oikodome*). According to the grace of God given to me, like a skilled master-builder I laid a foundation, but someone else builds (*epoikodomeo*) on it. And each one must be careful how he *builds* (*epoikodomeo*). For no one can lay any *foundation* other

---

[165] The word here translated as "co-labors" is the Greek word "*sunergos*". This Greek word can better be understood in English as: "companion laborers, work-fellows, fellow-workers, together-acters" (ISA; BDAG, 969). It is important to note how this word implies a type of communion or association, like an assembly, rather than simply being colleagues or working together on any single project or undertaking. Imagine a business where the same team works together on different projects, building a level of camaraderie and cooperation that is far beyond simply one undertaking.

than what is being laid, which is Christ."

(1 Cor 3:9-12, 8:1)

Seeking the "final destination" or "paradise" of the divine connection of *agape*-love is not a vain ambition. We are justified in believing that our true home resides in being a finite vessel of the Triune I AM, filled with spiritual communion grounded in *Yahweh's nature*.

We should reflect on how our true home and ultimate destination represents not merely a single "house," but rather a "family" or "household" within a heavenly homeland (Gal 6:10; Heb 3:2-6; 1 Pet 2:5). This family, rooted in *agape*-love, signifies our citizenship in a divine realm. The capital of our heavenly homeland is the New Jerusalem on Mount Zion, where a vibrant spiritual community will exist eternally (Heb 12:22-24). We can envision our homeland as a close-knit city akin to a large family, characterized by shared affections, open communion, common goals, and collective "household duties." This City of the Living God thrives on fellowship with the Triune I AM, angels, and our fellow humans – all members of the finite family of the Infinitely Existing One. Here, Yahweh's essence unites all creation in love, truth, and a shared vision. Therefore, we honor Yahweh, the Triune I AM, as the sole leader of this eternal household, the "Abraham" of a new Zion.

> *Consider how your genuine home is a "heavenly community" rooted in agape-love, rather than merely a solitary "household."*
>
> *How does this shift influence your perspective and quest for your ultimate destination?*

How the Homemaking of Christ's Body Mirrors the Trinity

Scripture tells us how, given that "[God] dwells[166] (*oikeo*) in unapproachable light" and "[He] *is* light", "the Eternal God is a habitation [for Himself]" (1 Tim 6:16; 1 John 1:5; Deut 33:27). However, we should remember how He wishes to dwell within us and within the world through our speech and actions. His infinite home-making nature is central to the Body of Christ (John 15; 1 Cor 3:9-12, 8:1, 14:1-4; 1 John; Jude 1:20-21). God created us in His own image and likeness, fully realizing this design through the Spirit He breathes into us, which continually transforms us into the likeness of Jesus Christ (Job 33:4; John 3:3-8, 20:22; Col 3:10). This enables Him to dwell within us, so that when we "love one another, God resides in us, and His [*agape-*]love is brought to completion in us. By this we know that we reside in God and He in us: in that He has given us of His Spirit" (1 John 4:12-13).

The co-tabernacling between God and us unfolds through a Spirit-to-spirit connection within our deepest selves. By walking closely with Him, He sanctifies our lifewalk to mirror His own. When this occurs, we live as He lives, caring for one another and creation as He does. This is like children who uphold their father's integrity and values, continuing a family business, or maintaining a monarch's authority and legacy. Importantly, this dwelling and caring align with God's nature and are expressed through our individual personalities. Not every child reflects their parents' values in the same way as their siblings. Likewise, God does not expect us to lose our unique identities. Instead, our unique fulfillment is found in Him. We can visualize this as every tool in a toolbox serving its specific and perfected purpose in the hands of a skilled craftsman, rather than being a bag just filled with hammers. Nevertheless, His indwelling presence shapes our roles,

---

[166] Greek word here is same Greek root of *oikos*.

purposes, and identities according to a predetermined plan (Rev 2:17, 3:12). Tools only achieve their potential when they contribute to creating a beautiful design or bringing a blueprint to fulfillment.

Through deep communion with the Spirit, Yahweh sanctifies us to serve Him as His temple. Embracing our true identity allows the unfolding of *agape*-love within us, empowered by the Spirit of God as He fills us with His love, light, and essence. Instead of relying on our own efforts, like offering sacrifices or merely trying to lead good lives, His transformative work within us becomes effective when we choose to abide in Him. Picture a bottle filled with dirty water. Instead of trying to remove the murkiness, we place the bottle under a faucet flowing with clear water. Gradually, through no effort on our part other than keeping it under the clean water, the dirty water will be replaced until only the clear water remains. Similarly, this is how we commune with God, allowing His *agape*-love, *phos*-light, and *pneuma*-spirit to fill us and shape us into His image.

By embodying His image, we become temples and priests of Yahweh, showcasing His self-revealing presence to the world. Like a bottle beneath a faucet, the "clean water" that fills us perpetually spills out into our surroundings, purifying and changing them just as it changes us. We also come to be known as "children of light" and "children of love," born from the One who is both *phos*-light and *agape*-love (John 12:35-36; Eph 5:7-10; Phil 2:15; 1 John 1:5, 3:9-10, 4:7-8, 16). As temples of light, we partake in "the saint's inheritance in the light," as we are those "transferred" "to the kingdom" of the One who is the "light of life" (John 1:4, 9, 8:12; Col 1:12-14). We become "a people of His own, so

> *Will you allow God to transform you into a dwelling place for Himself?*
>
> *How do you think you can facilitate this transformation, or how should it change your way of life?*

that [we] may proclaim the virtues of the one who called [us] out of darkness into His marvelous light" (1 Pet 2:9). This transformation stirs our spirit toward its genuine destiny. We experience authentic belonging founded on our creation in Yahweh's image and the life He breathes into us (Gen 1:26-27, 2:7). We resemble prisms exhibiting diverse revelations of the God who is light, reflecting the various hues of divine glory akin to a diamond (John 1:5; Rev 2:17). Consequently, Yahweh unveils His distinct character through us, His temples, as we adopt the new humanity that mirrors "the light of the glorious [revelatory] knowledge" of the one who "*is* the image of God" (2 Cor 3:18, 4:4-6).

Our Creator utilizes the spiritual practice of *agape*-love to transform us into a dwelling for Himself, abundant with fellowship, joy, and shalom. Through involvement in God's homemaking, we grow more like Yahweh and foster unity among all creation through His Breath and Word. This unity mirrors the oneness of the Triune I AM, while preserving the distinct multiplicity of humanity, which is foreign to God (who is always One, even as Three). This differs from other religious or scientific ideas of ultimate "oneness," as in God, we are united with a transcendent Divine while still upholding our unique individualities, which He created and intended.[167] Through this

---

[167] Recall the initial chapters of this book. They illustrate how God designed our contextualities to remain integral while fulfilling us within those very contexts rather than abolishing them altogether. This can be contrasted with the notions of "uniting with the divine/nothingness" found in religions such as Hinduism and Buddhism, where individuality and contextualities are erased. In Hinduism, moksha is typically understood as the enlightenment that "everything is the Self," suggesting no essential distinction between One and All. In Buddhism, nirvana represents the acceptance of the notion of "No Self" entirely.

unity, humanity coexists with our Creator's abiding presence, walking and communicating with Him (2 Cor 6:16-18). We unite with Him as His temple, functioning in and through His presence as He sanctifies us. Together, we embody a collective temple as the Body of Christ, where each unique individual adds to the whole in distinct ways (Rom 7:4; Eph 2:19-22; Col 2:19; Rom 12:3-10).

In our journey with God, we unite to dwell with Him, just as He dwells within us (1 Cor 3:9-17). As His priests, we are called to proclaim His Word, demonstrate His love, and embody His truth, shine His light, and carry out our roles as His children. This transformation happens through His Spirit, which turns us into God's holy dwelling (Rom 8:9-11; Eph 2:22; 1 John 4:12-13). By embracing and living through His triune nature, we discover our true identities and fulfill *agape*-love to completion.

We collaborate with our Maker as He creates, restores, and builds us into His home within Creation, both now and for eternity (1 John 2:5, 4:16-17). His purpose is to bring Heaven to Earth through us, His priestly ambassadors. Essentially, He aims to make each of us a "meeting place" between Heaven and Earth. Picture us as a window into another world, a new reality filled with possibilities that seem foreign to worldly ways. Visualize ourselves as silhouettes traversing a barren, dusty terrain, where others, looking at us, see through as if gazing

{ *When last did you exist as a "meeting place" between Heaven and Earth for another person?* }

Although both concepts offer deeper insights worth studying, they provide a valuable contrast for our discussion here. Conversely, in God, our individualities reach their fullest expression within His grand design, resembling a mosaic or symphony that creates a harmonious whole, yet is still composed of distinctly unique pieces. There is no requirement for us to relinquish our individualities or identities. However, this does involve a certain level of sacrificing our autonomy regarding how we envision our fulfillment compared to how God intends it to be, just like in a marriage partnership.

through a window into a radiant sunlit glade with trees, flowers, and rivers. More than just a window, Yahweh's revelations flow into our world through our lives and actions, as if the river from the glade flows through us, rejuvenating the barren earth. Through our words, actions, and lives, we help realize His vision for the world. Our eternal destiny leads to a harmonious creation that reflects the supercontextual Infinite Home of the Triune I AM, who *is agape*-love (1 John 4:8).

The Heavenly Father invites His genuine children to serve as gateways for heavenly communion to manifest on Earth. He invites us to become living, walking "Bethels,"[168] through which people encounter God's heavenly Home in this present fallen world (Gen 28:16-19). Through His priests, the Divine Creator aims to create a dwelling on earth that mirrors the divine *agape*-love found in heaven (1 Tim 6:16; 1 John 1:5; 1 John 4:8, 16; Rev 21:22). As discussed earlier, *agape*-love sets the foundational guidelines for His creation (1 John 4:7-19). Notably, just as Jesus attested, all the Old Covenant laws can be encapsulated in two commandments, both grounded in love (Matt 22:36-40). Ultimately, the Triune I AM designed us to contribute to the construction and establishment of His home and contextualized presence on Earth, serving as priests in His homemaking *oikonomia* (2 Cor 3:9-13; Eph 4:22; Rom 14:19; 1 Thess 5:11; Jude 1:20).

At this point, we should remember that Yahweh's triune existence serves as His Infinite home and Heavenly temple. He transforms us into "houses of God on earth" by modeling us after His own existence through a close communion and relationship

---

[168] Bethel refers to the place where Jacob dreamed of a ladder connecting Heaven and Earth, on which angels would ascend and descend. Upon awakening, Jacob named the area "Bethel", meaning "House of God." We today are to be vessels through which Heaven and Earth connect and through which the world can experience God's presence.

with Him as the Triune God. Instead of showcasing solely Heaven, we present God Himself. Only by genuinely surrendering our lives and selves to His eternal vision can we liken ourselves to clay willingly yielding to the potter's hands, emerging as more than we could be alone. For us, God's sculpting occurs internally as we dwell in His presence and promote His dwelling in our world. His "Spirit" commits us to this purpose by setting us apart (circumcising us) to be "sanctified," designated to serve as His "priests" forever (Rom 15:16; Rev 5:10). In the Old Covenant, the Children of Israel were distinguished by the circumcision of their males at birth or upon joining the community. Today, while no physical circumcision is required, we are still to be spiritually "set apart" from the world. As God's priests, we are charged with sharing His love and presence globally, ensuring that the magnificence of His revealed nature is reflected in all facets of Creation. To achieve this, we must mirror God's glory in ourselves, as any temple should do.[169]

Only in love can we respond to Eternity's Call, becoming the

---

[169] Temples reflect the essence of the deity that inhabits them. Many ancient temples showcased the grandeur and majesty associated with their gods and followers. Today's temples display diverse architectural styles and design elements that correspond to the cultural beliefs tied to specific deities or worship practices, but all are intentionally crafted to reflect the nature of the deity they represent or the beliefs surrounding them.

Taking Christianity as an example, we can observe the distinction between typical Catholic and Eastern Orthodox churches. Many Gothic-style Catholic churches, such as Notre-Dame, inspire feelings of power and majesty, guiding the gaze upward towards Heaven and the light filtering through high-placed windows. In contrast, Orthodox churches often feature rounded designs adorned with images of saints, fostering a sense of community where all believers, including the saints of old, unite in worship.

As temples of God, we are called to reflect His character and glory on earth, so that those who meet us may glimpse the divine presence within us and the reality He desires to manifest in the world.

Maker's "true Levites," members of a "priestly nation" serving Yahweh eternally (1 Pet 2:4-9, 1 Cor 6:19-20). It is then that we can introduce creation to the enlightening presence of the Triune I AM. We will discover how to guide each aspect of creation to reveal a distinct understanding recognized by God's people. This mission helps creation become a dwelling for the communion that befits a house of Yahweh.

By being active participants in the "divine nature," we yield the eternal fruit suitable for God's tabernacle through the "divine power" of His Spirit that resides in our "inner person" (Eph 3:16; 2 Pet 1:3-4). Yahweh grants us all we need for true life and godliness as He dwells within us, enabling us to reflect both His character and power (Gal 5:16-18, 25). Just as a window does not create the light illuminating a home but depends on the sun to shine through, we also rely on the One who *is phos*-light (1 John 1:5). As Scripture reveals,

> *Look at yourself in the mirror and say, "I am a priest." How does that change your view of yourself and your mission in life?*

"His divine power has bestowed on us everything necessary for life and godliness through the rich knowledge of the One who called us by His own glory and excellence... [So we might] become partakers of the divine nature, after escaping the worldly corruption... [and manifest] godliness, brotherly affection... [and] unselfish love... [This prevents us] from becoming ineffective and unproductive in [our] pursuit of knowing our Lord Jesus Christ more intimately."

(1 Pet 1:3-8)

As we journey through life alongside the Holy Spirit, our

connection with God produces spiritual fruit through His guiding hand. It is important to reflect on how the fruit of the Spirit reveals agape-love, highlighting the Divine's nurturing and up-building nature (Rom 5:5; Gal 5:22). It is no surprise that Jesus likened Himself to the vine, us to the branches, with *agape*-love as our abundant fruit (John 15:1-17).

Our connection to God's Spirit allows us to journey through life with our Creator as our closest partner, resembling Enoch and Noah (Gen 5:21-24, 6:9). Indeed, Yahweh designed us to reflect His own profound life-walk (Gal 5:25). As temples of God, we are filled with the Spirit to share His sanctifying presence across Creation. A prime example of this is our role in reconciling others to a relationship with God. This is the rightful way we should lead our earthly lives as priests o f the Triune I AM, who *is agape*-love (2 Cor 5:18-21; 1 John 4:8-17).

> *Have you ever thought of the religious myth that being an ambassador of Christ is a special "calling" meant only for a select few- those "hardcore" believers who choose celibacy or pursue full-time ministry?*
>
> *How does recognizing that this role is something every child of God must embrace shift your perspective?*

Communion of Agape in the Triune I AM's Finite Temple

Our Guide states that upon arriving at our ultimate destination, we will enjoy complete and eternal "rest" (shalom). As Scripture says, "a Sabbath rest remains for the people of God," "for the one who enters God's rest has also rested from His work, as God did from His,[170]" "for [His rest] remains for *some* to enter it" (Heb 4:6-10).

---

[170] On the seventh day of Creation (Genesis 2:2-3)

The Sabbath represents not only a day but also a symbol of our relationship with God. Yahweh designed it to reflect our fellowship both with Him and with each other, rooted in His triune nature (John 14-17).

> "I also gave them My Sabbaths as a reminder of our relationship, so that they would know that I, the Lord, sanctify them... Do not defile yourselves with their idols. I am the Lord your God; follow My statutes, observe My regulations, and carry them out. Treat My Sabbaths as holy and they will be a reminder of our relationship, and then you will know that I am the Lord your God."
>
> (Ezek 20:12, 18-20)

As the sabbath fellowship of *agape*-love unfolds, our body, soul, and spirit resemble the distinct elements of Yahweh's Temple in Jerusalem. Our bodies reflect the Outer Court, where Israelites had free access. Here, priests and Levites performed sacrifices and served the congregation. Our communion with God influences the physical realm and our surroundings in this space. Just as God's presence interacted with the Israelites visiting the Temple, our bodies serve as the initial way the world, especially others, encounters and experiences our God-relationship through our actions, lifestyles, and choices. When we align our lives with God's laws and commands—both by refraining from sin and actively loving and being generous—people see God's Spirit manifested in us.

What makes love, above all else, vital for you to answer God's call to serve as heavenly priests on earth?

Our souls—comprising our heart, mind, and identity—form

the Inner Court, a sacred space where only priests could enter to conduct rituals before the Lord. Similarly, we are called to be made holy in the presence of God as we engage in, pursue, and live out our relationship with Him. In this process, our minds, hearts, and entire beings undergo transformation and renewal (Rom 12:2, 2 Cor 3:18).

Ultimately, our spirits become akin to the Holy of Holies, the most revered section of the Temple that served as the focal point of God's transcendent presence on earth. In this sacred space, His presence dwells within us, radiating outward to sanctify the temple. When we express our spiritual identities this way, we don the Living Word of God, revealing the Father through our lives by the power of His Spirit (2 Cor 3:18, 4:4-6; Col 3:10; Gal 3:27).

Through the Spirit of Yahweh residing in us, we collaborate with Him to transform our lives and all of Creation into a suitable dwelling for the immediate presence of the Triune I AM in this finite reality. We become God's children, reflecting His image within our inner selves (John 20:17; Col 3:10; Gal 4:4-6; Eph 4:24; 1 John 5:1) as our thoughts, emotions, and identities become molded after Christ's example (Rom 13:13-14; 2 Cor 3:18, 4:4-6, 5:14; Col 1:15, 28; Gal 2:20; Eph 4:13). This revelation of our "true, theological selves" calls us, as the Body of Christ, to act as agents of His *agape*-love and truth in the world. By choosing to serve as vessels of His presence, this love – the very essence of Yahweh's Infinite home—flows outward to embrace the world.

A question may arise at this point: Why does God opt to use us as conduits and intermediaries for manifesting His presence in the finite world? Why not reveal Himself directly or through more "glorious" means, such as appearing in a magnificent chariot of fire soaring across the sky? One reason is that the entirety of

{ *How does this view of your tripartite existence impact your self-view?* }

finitude – the earth, the heavens, and even the highest heavens – "cannot contain" the fullness of the Infinite I AM (1 Kings 8:27-30; 2 Chr 2:5-6; Isa 66:1-2; Acts 17:24-25, 7:47-50; 1 Tim 6:16). As previously discussed, the only true house (Temple) of God in Eternity is God Himself, who is His own super-context. It is impossible for God to "fully manifest" His complete essence apart from Himself. Let us use cyberspace as an analogy once again. We can interact with this vast digital realm through our laptops and smartphones, yet we cannot experience it with our direct physical senses. It exists continuously, even when our devices are not in use. Even still, it remains perpetually beyond our reach and comprehension, except in the limited form presented to us through our electronics.[171]

Scripture tells us that "the Lord God – the All-Powerful [the one who holds all] – and the Lamb are its temple" (Rev 21:22). The only way for God to dwell immanently in the finite world is through Himself. More precisely, He resides within Creation by contextually manifesting His presence through His Word and Breath. Now, we must recognize that we have not become God simply because He has chosen to manifest through us; we are a window

Why is it crucial to dwell in Yahweh's presence in our individual lives and circumstances?

Do you allow the Holy Spirit to transform you into a vessel for the manifestation of the Triune I AM?

---

[171] This idea of meditation expands when we realize that cyberspace, in its "pure form,"" would seem completely foreign to us. It exists as a vast universe of ones and zeros, alongside various incomprehensible electrical signals. We can only engage with it when it is structured in a way that we can grasp and interact with, such as through URL addresses, graphics, websites, code, and processes. Similarly, God transcends the metaphors, contexts, symbols, and realities we use to relate to Him, as He is not confined by elements such as time, space, language, or human emotions. Still, He fully embraces these tools so that we can understand and establish a relationship with Him.

allowing His light to shine through us. We cannot influence this light or dictate how it shines. Consequently, humanity only serves as His living temple by existing through and within Him. Still, we fulfill this role according to the specific contexts in which He places us, with Him alone knowing the ultimate purpose and design. We understand that design as we commune with Him daily, nurturing our God-relationship and following His commands.

A created being can only serve as a dwelling for God when birthed out of and through His uncreated essence. We, as finite, exist solely in and through God, sharing a nature and essence akin to His own. "The Spirit of God has made me, and the breath of the Almighty gives me life… For in Him we live and move about and exist" (Job 33:4, Acts 17:28). The divine infinite life can manifest through us, finite beings, only while we are filled with the Son, who is the "radiance of God's glory and the representation of His essence," allowing us to become contextual representations of God's divine abode (Heb 1:3, John 6:56; Rom 8:9-11; Eph 1:23; Col 1:19, 2:9; Gal 2:19; 1 John 4:13). By being filled with God's nature, which empowers Him to construct and be His own Temple, we too can embody temples. Ultimately, only as members of the Body of Christ functioning within both the spiritual and physical realms can we truly house the fullness of divinity within Creation. How can we expect to exhibit this if we do not abide in, become filled with, and reflect divinity?

By communing with the Son of God, who is both Infinite and finite, within our inner selves, we become finite children of God,[172]

---

[172] By this, we do not mean that we will not eventually live forever with Him, but that we are finitely constrained beings, even after we die. Only one being is truly Infinite: God Himself. Even in our glorified states at the conclusion of the Narrative of Finitude, we will remain "finite" and "contextualized" (albeit according to eternal contextualities). We will never become as God is in His absolute fullness, though we become like Him within our finite realities as He dwells within us.

by being filled with the fullness of divinity. As a result, we act as vessels for God's presence to dwell in and interact with creation. Jesus Christ, the Lamb of God, represents the ultimate divine dwelling on Earth, and through Him, divine revelations continually flow (Eph 2:16-21; Col 2:19; 2 Cor 2:14-15; Rev 21:9, 22-23).

> *Does learning about God's boundless nature and our inability to fully comprehend it inspire you to explore His self-revealing presence?*

Thus, the Body of Christ—the embodiment of God within the created realm – is perpetually enriched by divine revelations shared among humanity (Heb 1:3). These heavenly manifestations arise from our connection with God, unfolding deep within our souls, where He resides in our spirit (Eph 2:22).

God inhabits the finite world through us, continuously revealing Himself from glory to glory forever and ever (2 Cor 3:18). However, God can never be fully exhausted by these self-disclosures. Our understanding of God in His complete fullness is inherently limited as finite beings. Yet, God genuinely resides within us and the finite realm, forever unveiling His infinite nature. Consider this as a much larger parallel to the reality that you can never completely exhaust your knowledge and experiences of your spouse, even after many years of marriage. There is always something new to learn that uncovers an aspect of them never previously known. God will forever inhabit creation through the Body of Christ, and His self-revelation in and through this Body will never end. Imagine it as an endless puzzle, becoming more complex the more pieces, we assemble, yet it always grows.

The Trinity & Our Eternal Destiny

Being temples of the divine, we embody the unity of the Trinity within our tripartite nature: body, soul, and spirit. The Father grants us life, while His Word (the Son) infuses that life into us.

The Father's Breath represents God's life within us, guiding, sanctifying, and working through us. He sends His Word into our hearts to eliminate the barrier separating us from the Holy of Holies. This is like a device allowing us to commune with someone on the other side of the planet. Similarly, the Son sends the Spirit to connect our spiritual and physical selves. The Holy Spirit facilitates the flow of Christ's indwelling presence into our actions and lives within the contexts God has placed us. The Son empowers our inner being to encounter God the Father in the "Holy of Holies," which is the core of our relationship with Him.

> How can you, after reflecting on these passages, represent the Father's will and embody Christ in your life?

The Sanctifying Spirit enables us to live righteously and actively share that holiness with the world. Through the Son's intercession, the Father's "hand" transforms our inner selves to reflect His image and likeness. The Spirit conveys the Father's divine power into our humanity and the environments we inhabit, manifesting in the lives, situations, and opportunities we experience. Each child expresses the Father's power uniquely (like how each sibling reveals a unique likeness of the parent both physically and psychologically), although we are all guided by the singular wisdom of His illuminating Word.

The Holy Spirit, often referred to as the "Breath of God" in Scripture, serves as a bridge for communication between heaven and earth, similar to how physical breath facilitates interaction among people. Through the Spirit, God establishes a link between our spiritual essence and the external world. In this unique intermediary role, we act as priests within creation. Eternity calls us to embody and convey the Father's will and authority, embracing the identity of Christ. This role can be likened to that of an ambassador for a country. Ambassadors not only follow the directives of their homeland but also represent it legally; their actions reflect their nation. The Spirit empowers us to accept and express our priestly identities. The Spirit shapes our souls in the image of Christ, filling us with spiritual vitality. He empowers us to live as the "children of light," "for the fruit of the light consists in all goodness, righteousness, and truth" (Eph 5:8-9). As it is written: "The fruit of the Spirit is love, joy, peace, patience, kindness, goodness, faithfulness, gentleness, and self-control… If we live by the Spirit, let us also behave in accordance with the Spirit" (Gal 5:22-25). God's presence flows from within us (our "Holy of Holies"), revealing eternal reflections of God's likeness.

Temple of the Triune God

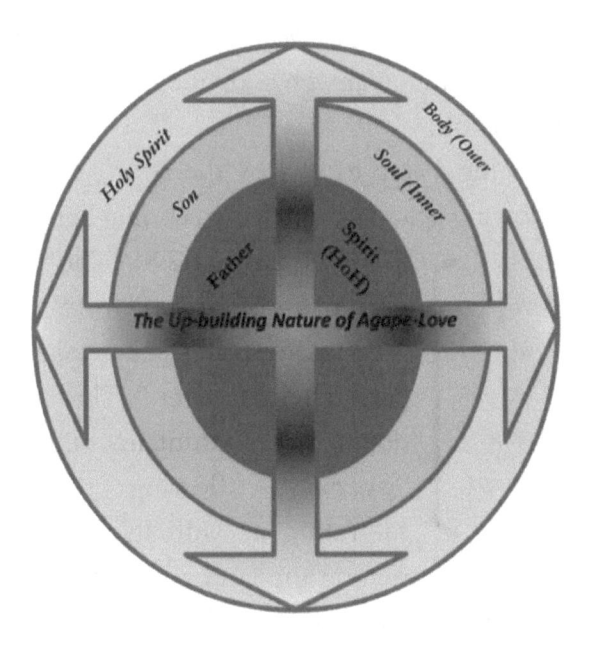

These three circles symbolize the complete realization of our identity as heavenly priests. Our relationship with God, as His finite children, originates from the Father. The Son conveys our inheritance. He shepherds us in the ways of true humanness as manifesters of the divine presence by baptizing our spirit with His own. The Spirit of God flows from this relationship and manifests our status and inheritance as God's children. Consequently, we serve as the dwelling place of the Triune God, a temple of His *agape*-love contextualized in our finite existence. The Spirit, residing within our innermost being, allows God's transformative and uplifting nature—originating from the Father—to flow into human life empowering Christ-likeness. This divine influence enters the "inner court" of our soul, sanctifying our mind, will, and identity. This regenerative change empowers us to reflect our new selves in the image of the Son. Ultimately, God's uplifting nature extends into the world through the "outer court" of our bodies via our actions, attitude, words, and choices. In this manner, we become vessels of God's *agape-phosnoumenos*[173] to the world, as true tabernacles conveying Yahweh's divine, infinite presence and nature to all creation.

Envision being a tree rooted by the river of God's presence, with nature flowing around— imagery echoing Scripture (Jer 17:7-8, Ps. 1:3, Ps. 52:8). The waters of His presence originate from the Father's "mountain spring," an everlasting source of "crystal-clear water." This water cascades down the mountains through Christ's "riverway," flowing toward us and saturating us with its current. The Spirit embodies the river, enriching the land and penetrating the fertile earth where we are planted, bringing the river's life-giving essence into our existence. As His presence nourishes us, we grow tall and robust, adorned with plentiful leaves and fruit. We provide shade

{ *How has this journey shaped your view of the God you relate to in your God-relationship?* }

---

[173] Combination of the Greek words *agape* (love), *phos* (light), *and pneuma* (spirit). See the trilogy series: *God is Spirit, God is Light, and God is Love.*

from the harshness of a gone-wrong world and soul sustenance of peace, courage, hope, and faith for those around us, sharing the river's bounty. While others might focus on the fruit, we, as trees, recognize that we could never produce it without proper nourishment. Moreover, no tree can thrive without water from a source. This illustrates how we channel God's triune presence and *agape*-love into the world.

United with Christ, His Spirit empowers us to uplift each other as part of the Body of Christ, His communal temple within Finitude. This growth is realized through spiritual communion among individuals. We come together at our deepest level to "grow into a holy temple in the Lord," "knit[ted] together through its ligaments and sinews, grow[ing] with a growth that is from God" (Eph 2:19; Col 2:19). Through both individual and shared expressions of God's temple (*koinonia*) within Finitude, the sanctifying work of His triune nature reaches into both our physical and spiritual contexts. By embodying His *agape*-love and *phos*-light in our lives, we help to elevate all creation into the Temple of God, in line with the *oikonomia* (house-rules) laid down by our Father. This calling and destiny are both individual and collective – it cannot be fully realized by ourselves. Indeed, the relationships among members of the Body of Christ are crucial to how we are meant to reveal God's presence in the world. We are called to work together as portals between Heaven and Earth. Just as we read in the first letter to the Corinthians:

> "For just as the body is one and yet has many members, and all the members of the body—though many—are one body, so too is Christ. For in one Spirit we were all baptized into one body… And if the ear says, 'Since I am not an eye, I am not part of the body,' it does not lose its membership in

the body because of that. If the whole body were an eye, what part would do the hearing?... But as a matter of fact, God has placed each of the members in the body just as he decided. If they were all the same member, where would the body be?... Those members that seem to be weaker are essential... so that there may be no division in the body, but the members may have mutual concern."

(1 Cor 12:12-26)

As children of God, made in His image, we are called to reflect the triune nature of divinity in how we view and inhabit the world. We model Christ's example in revealing God to others. The Son embodies the divine plan and the rules of God's household. Through Him, the light of the Triune God will ultimately illuminate all within His domain. His authority and power are manifested through His siblings: the children of light. Sent into the world, both individually and collectively, as agents of His power and authority, we make His will known and worship Him with heartfelt adoration. With joyful enthusiasm, we recognize that His will alone transforms the context of our reality into a reflection of God's Infinite home. We partner with the Gardener, acting as His co-gardeners, helping others grow into their heavenly identity within this world. Through us, His glory brings forth unprecedented beauty in the world.

> *What makes it essential for you to become a temple of God and assist in uplifting others?*
>
> *How does the collective Body of Christ contribute to God's intention for you to serve as His lighthouses?*

As heavenly priests, we will learn, teach, and embody the revelatory voice of creation throughout eternity. Furthermore, we will collaborate within the Body of Christ to glorify Yahweh through our united efforts as a united co-working and royal priesthood (Rev 5:10). It is a wondrous and seemingly absurd paradox that the Infinite I AM chose to create us from dust by bestowing His own essence upon us (Gen 2:7; Job 33:4). Even more marvelous is the revelation He grants us the choice to become co-sharers of the I AM's indwelling, home-making presence within Creation (Acts 17:28; 1 Cor 3:9-12; 2 Pet 1:4).

Relevance of our Quests to the Homemaking of Eternity

Our genuine home, as a spiritual household, resides in the home of the Infinite I AM, who is an invisible (non-corporeal) spirit. In our current earthly life, we do not find our physical residence in the external world, as we have not yet received our glorified bodies. We only find our true home within the deepest part of our being, where the Spirit of God abides. The authentic home of our outer selves is the New Jerusalem created by the Creator, which He will establish on the new earth in due time (Rev 21). Therefore, until that moment arrives, we can only come to inwardly dwell in our true home as we are reborn through the Spirit (John 3:3-8; Gal 5).

While we strive to fulfill our destinies as God's vessels here on earth, we must not forget the final destination of our journey home. We aspire to reach the heavenly abode of Yahweh. His triune essence defines our purpose, our dwelling, and our highest aim in life. As we navigate our ship across the Sea of Revelation, our deepest longing should be to engage closely with the Triune I AM. We understand the significance of following His self-revelation throughout the Narrative of Finitude. Our transformational path prepares us for our eternal role as His priests. Remember, God invites those willing to eternally participate in the unfolding story of His revealing presence.

Participation in the God Story begins with receiving divine revelations. This involvement encourages meditation, reflection,

> *Do you set the joy of Eternity as the ultimate prize you seek in life?*

application of revealed truth, as well as sharing them with others through words and actions empowered by His Spirit. This eternal calling leads to sanctifying communion with Yahweh, where He dwells within us and we in Him, a core teaching of Christ to His disciples (John 14-16). This message profoundly impacted the Apostle John, known as "the beloved." Through John, the Spirit unveiled God's deepest longing for closeness with His children, as expressed in his letters (1-3 John). This intimacy should be reflected in our commitment to His transformative work, dressing creation in the glory of His indwelling presence (John 6:56, 14:20, 15:4-7, 17:26; 1 John 2:28, 3:6, 5:20). God's magnificent splendor acts as the eternal contextual light, illuminating and shaping the essence of Finitude while inviting all of creation to revel in the beauty of His presence.

Upon arriving at our ultimate destination, the end of temporality, we become a finite residence of the triune home-making presence of *agape*-communion, God Himself. At this moment, the Creator's joy in His creation will achieve its fullest and eternal realization. When this occurs, the Creator's joy towards His creation will finally and eternally be fulfilled. Before the Fall, this joy filled creation, as our Creator "rejoiced in the habitable part of His earth and delighted in its people" (Prov 8:31). However, sorrow soon followed, as Yahweh became "grieved in heart" and "regretted that He had made humankind on the earth" (Gen 6:6; John 17:13). As we journey toward our eternal home, the flag of our ship boldly declares the revealed truths of the eternal joy, peace, and love that awaits us in Eternity. Our understanding of what lies ahead encourages us to continue our task, even when it feels fruitless, difficult, or hopeless. It is certainly not easy to embody light and goodness in a world that often seems to embrace evil, hatred, selfishness, and darkness. Sometimes, it feels as though goodness is merely an invitation to be trampled, exploited, or ridiculed. After all, the world murdered divine love Incarnate. Nonetheless, let us hold fast to hope as we remember our ultimate home. May we make the prayer of David in Psalm 84 our own:

> "My heart and my entire being shout for joy to the living God... How blessed are those who live in Your temple and praise You continually! How blessed are those [that] long to travel the roads that lead to Your temple!... Certainly spending just one day in Your temple courts is better than spending a thousand elsewhere."
>
> (Ps 84:2-12)

God reserves a place on His holy mountain for the faithful heirs of the Promised Land. He has pledged, "I will bring them to My holy mountain; I will make them happy in the temple where people pray to Me" (Isa 56:5-8). We must pay attention to our Guide: "Come, let us go up to the Lord's mountain, to the temple of the God of Jacob, so He can teach us His requirements, and we can follow His standards... O descendants of Jacob, come, let us walk in the Lord's guiding light" (Isa 2:3-5). Only through a world illuminated by His revelation and truths can we make genuine progress on our journey home (1 John 1:7). Such a journey occurs only within our inner self, where the genuine "temple of the Holy Spirit" "not built by human hands" resides (1 Cor 6:19; 2 Cor 5:1; Heb 11:10, 16). No physical pilgrimage or relocation on this fallen earth can direct us to our true home, not even a literal pilgrimage to Jerusalem

Do you believe that intimacy with God, as opposed to a large project or series of actions, represents the ultimate theme of your life story?

How meaningful is your relationship with God to you?

(Heb 11:10-16). The Promised Land serves as a shadow of our true Home, as it symbolizes eternal rest beyond this temporary realm (Heb 4:1-11, 11:9, 11:13-14). Nowhere in our deteriorating universe can we discover our ultimate dwelling, as even this world and all of creation have been "reserved for fire:" "The heavens will be burned up and dissolved, and the celestial bodies will melt away in a blaze!" (2 Pet 3:7, 12; Heb 1:10-12).

We aim to ascend to a sacred realm that transcends all the finite dimensions of creation. Here, we experience continuous and eternal communion with the Triune I AM. To journey toward this true Promised Land, our first step involves pursuing a life-path dedicated to knowing, connecting with, and reflecting our Creator's triune nature. Understanding His triuneness is crucial, as our eternal life will revolve around partaking in this divine nature (John 1:17; 2 Cor 2:6-16; 2 Pet 1:4). Moreover, advancing in this pursuit will naturally deepen our comprehension of self-actualization. Our identity is fundamentally anchored in the genuine existence that our Creator originally intended for us.

As we navigate the Sea of Revelation, we delve deep to uncover more truths about our true home. This journey recognizes that truly inhabiting our trans-dimensional home requires actively participating in the divine nature (2 Pet 1:3-4). Do we not trust the words of our Guide, as it encourages us to accept our eternal destiny as heirs of the Creator, standing as pillars in God's temple and members of His priesthood. Embracing this calling demands nothing less than acknowledging Him as our Lord. Yet, we are not meant to be merely His servants, for He designed us to be equally joined with the Son of God as co-heirs. Jesus Christ desires a priestly bride who will reign as kings and questions, as well as priests, with Him on His throne. He designates each of us a unique role to fulfill His intentions in creation, as we become mediators of the *oikonomia* of God's Temple (Rev 3:21, 5:10, 19:7-8, 22:5).

Will we consciously choose to become a dwelling place for the Triune I AM? Has our Creator become our First Love? Before the eternal altar, we must decide whether to commit to this divine union, where two lives intertwine and become one (Eph 5; Rev 19-22). The *agape*-love demonstrated on the cross of Christ, poured into our hearts by His Spirit, has sparked our desire to embark on this journey homeward. "By this, the love of God is revealed in us: that God has sent His one and only Son into the world so that we may live through Him" (1 John 4:9). Our Creator's sacrificial "love [for] us," through which we "have [been] set free," inspires our dedication to become a dwelling for divine revelation (Rev 1:5).

Consequently, we declare and renew our vows as a willing bride to the One who has become like us. We dedicate ourselves to serve alongside Him as our only High Priest, as we, the priests of the Living God, devote ourselves entirely to our Maker's Vision (Deut 30:6; Ezek 16:8, 36:26-27; Rom 5:5; 1 John 4:19). Christ represents the heavenly Adam, while the church symbolizes the earthly Eve, whom He has restored to a heavenly position through our union (1 Cor 15:45-49; Eph 5:24-32). We have been created anew through Christ, just as Eve was formed "out of" Adam. Moreover, as Scripture states, "a man will leave his father and mother and will be joined to his wife, and the two will become one flesh," and "this mystery is great – but [it] actually speaks in reference to Christ and the church" (Eph 5:31-32). "It is said, 'the two will become one flesh,'" and the "one united with the Lord is one spirit with Him" (1 Cor 6:16-19). Therefore, having united ourselves to Christ in an eternal covenant, "our body [has become] the temple of the Holy Spirit," and "we are not our own," but belong to "Him," within whom the fullness of the Divine I AM resides (1 Cor 6:16-19; Col 1:15-19, 2:9).

> *Will you let go of worldly ambitions to become part of the Bride of Christ?*

Chapter 9

To be a Temple of Yahweh

Becoming Sanctified Vessels of the Divine Spirit

"For God's temple is holy, which is what you are... Or do you not know that your body is the temple of the Holy Spirit who is in you... you are not your own? For you were bought at a price... 'Therefore come out from their midst, and be separate,' says the Lord, 'and touch no unclean thing, and I will welcome you, and I will be a Father to you...' Cleans yourselves... and thus accomplish holiness out of reverence for God."
(1 Cor 3:17, 6:19-20; 2 Cor 6:16-18, 7:1)

"Be clothed with the new man that is being renewed in knowledge according to the image of the One who created it... As the elect of God, holy and dearly loved, clothe yourselves with a heart of mercy, kindness, humility, gentleness, and patience... To all these virtues add [*agape*-]love, which is the perfect bond... Let the word of Christ dwell in you... Whatever you do in word or deed, do it all in the name of the Lord."
(Col 3:10-17)

"[*Agape*-]Love builds up... Do not seek [your] own benefit, but the benefit of many... To each person the manifestation of the Spirit is given for the benefit of all... Pursue love and be eager for the spiritual gifts, especially that you may prophecy... Since you are eager for manifestations of the Spirit, seek to abound in order to strengthen the church."
(Col 3:10-17)

Being a True Temple of the Divine

In this chapter, we delve deeper into what it means to be transformed into priests of Yahweh and the responsibilities of this role. As Christ adorns us with His garments, distinguishing us as His fellow priests, we are encouraged to surrender our lives to Him by His Spirit. This surrender entails embodying His vision in our everyday lives and becoming a sacrifice that is "holy and pleasing" to God (Rom 12:1). Reflecting on the truths presented in this chapter, we will discover how our journey homeward is inseparable from our pursuit of a heavenly destiny as disciples of Christ.

To truly be children of Yahweh, we must live as "pilgrims" in this transient world. This concept resembles being a long-term temporary resident in a foreign country without ever becoming a full citizen, as we are already citizens of another realm. From God's perspective, "dual citizenship" is nonexistent. While on this earth, we should resist conforming to its rebellious ways. Instead, we should prioritize God's presence in our temporary dwelling (2 Cor 7:1).

The essence of a home is shaped by its inhabitants; you learn a lot about each family member just by observing their home. Is it tidy or disorganized? Sparse or furnished? Are there religious items or preferences for certain artists or styles? Perhaps there is even a political sign or banner. Similarly, the state and character of our soul define our body as a tabernacle (2 Cor 5:1). As we commit to being a home for Yahweh, we must also reflect Him accordingly (2 Cor 6:14-18). Yet, it is crucial to understand that a house does not change to accommodate its inhabitants; rather, the inhabitant initiates the transformation. Accordingly, we must consistently rely on the Holy Spirit to sanctify our lives and world-dwelling to

What does your spiritual "house" currently reflect about you?

reflect the holy home created by Yahweh's infinite nature (Eph 2:19-22, 4:29-32, 5:1-15; Heb 3). Unlike those who choose to reside comfortably in the present world, who only live for the here and now, we seek our true belonging in Heaven through the guidance of our Creator's Spirit.

If we wish to navigate the Sea of Revelation while encouraging fellow sailors or inspiring "land-dwellers" to join us, we must first dedicate ourselves to the house rules of God's family (Matt 28:18-20). When individuals enter a temple, they seek a divine experience rather than a human one. Thus, as God's temples, we must serve as vessels for divine encounters, enabling Yahweh's presence to be felt, notably through the gifts of the Holy Spirit (Rom 12:5-8; 1 Cor 12:4-11). Consider our Guide's following instructions concerning a fellowship of believers: "But if all prophesy, and an unbeliever or uninformed person enters, he will be convicted by all, he will be called to account by all. The secrets of his heart are disclosed, and in this way he will fall down with his face to the ground and worship God, declaring, 'God is really among you.' (I Cor 14:24-25)." Failing to do this would leave visitors disappointed regarding the anticipated experience of miracles. In the following passage, our Creator underscores how our lives should foster these encounters: "Just as each one has received a gift, use it to serve one another as good stewards of the varied grace of God. Whoever speaks, let it be with God's words. Whoever serves, do so with the strength that God supplies, so that in everything God will be glorified through Jesus Christ. To Him belong the glory and the power forever and ever" (1 Pet 4:10-11).

To effectively function as God's temple, our lifestyle and identity must be molded by the responsibilities of being a steadfast pillar in His house. We must fully embrace and align ourselves with the directives of the God-relationship. If we seek nothing but belonging within temporality, then we forsake the genuine, supernatural connection to divine potential. Considering this heavenly calling, Jesus stated, "The person who believes in Me will perform the miraculous deeds that I am doing and will perform greater deeds than these" (John 14:12). Ultimately, a true temple of the Divine should serve as a space where individuals can witness divine intervention at a supernatural level. Consequently, those who interact with us should be able to observe the power of the Divine at work in our lives.

In the Likeness of Christ, the First Immanent Temple of God

Let us delve into how God transforms us into a temple that reflects His essence and power, beginning with each person as a "living stone" and "pillar." It is important to remember Christ's vital role in this transformation (1 Pet 2:4; Rev 3:12). Only through Christ's redemptive sacrifice on the cross do we have the true opportunity to be reconstructed as a distinctly contextualized temple of God, representing the Body of Christ (John 2:18-21; Eph 2:19-21). Prior to His crucifixion, the Son was the singular, authentic temple of God, uniquely situated within creation as the "God-Man" Jesus Christ.[174] He alone fulfilled the Temple's purpose flawlessly: to "make God known" and to "reveal... His

Before we proceed, what do you believe is necessary for you to become Christ's divine temple, allowing others to experience God and His presence?

---

[174] This is not to imply that the Son and Jesus Christ are two separate entities or that Christ is just an "avatar" of the Son. They are, in fact, one being, both fully divine and fully human simultaneously – 100% of each, not 50%.

Nevertheless, the existence of the Son does predate Christ's life on earth. It is only through the Incarnation that the Son becomes a finite temple of God within creation, preparing the way for our priestly life through Him.

With the Incarnation, the Son embraced human nature as Christ, and this union of human and divine natures continues even after His Resurrection and Ascension. Thus, both natures coexist fully and inseparably in Jesus.

name" (John 1:18, 17:6, 26). He alone dwelled in Finitude, among humanity, as the finitely-contextualized "radiance of [God's] glory and the representation of His essence" (Heb 1:3).

Jesus' death and resurrection paved the way for the growth of His "body" through humanity. Each person now has the potential to mirror the divine "face" of Christ. By "putting on Christ," we affirm our identity as God's temple, becoming adorned with our heavenly home (Rom 13:14; 2 Cor 5:1-8). The Scriptures proclaim, "Christ in us the hope of glory," for as Christ imparts His life as the "representation [and image] of [Yahweh's] essence" within us, we "are transformed into the same image [of the Divine] from one degree of glory to another, which is from the Lord, who is the Spirit" (Col 1:15, 1:15-19, 1:27; 2 Cor 3:18). This process can be seen as a deeper spiritual reality where we increasingly resemble those we associate with, similar to how children adopt much of their parents' character and beliefs. However, unlike our friends or family, Christ transforms us beyond surface behavior, penetrating the core of our spiritual identity. Therefore, our actions should reflect and embody that "we are [Yahweh's] workmanship, having been [re-]created in Christ Jesus for good works that God prepared beforehand so we may walk in them" (Eph 2:10). In this way, our lives become a genuine reflection of Yahweh's self-revealing presence, showcasing His providential power, just as Christ did during His time on earth.

It is crucial to understand that we are not just being called to a higher reality but rather returning to the reality we were created to inhabit. Humanity was made in the image of God; however, just as Adam and Eve chose to reject this purpose in favor of pursuing independence from God and His design, we too have followed in their footsteps. We carry the burden of Original Sin. Each day, we face temptations that lead us to stray further from our original calling, identity, and homeland, neglecting our role as His temple

> *How can your actions more effectively showcase Yahweh's craftsmanship in your life?*
>
> *Do you think there is potential for growth in this area?*

and priests (Hos 6:7). It is only through being born again by the Spirit of God that we regain our true essence: a "new self who has been created in God's image – in righteousness and holiness that comes from truth" (John 3:3-8; Eph 4:24). The Spirit's sanctifying work occurs within us, forming our unique priestly identities in the likeness of Christ's. Consequently, "the one who says he [or she] resides in God ought to walk just as Jesus walked" (1 John 2:6). Christ exemplified how to walk in harmony with our Heavenly Father, just as Adam and Eve did before the Fall. Therefore, God calls us to emulate His God-relationship.

Christ transforms us into the temple of God when we embrace our true identity. He re-forms us into new creations, being "renewed in knowledge according to the image of the One who created it" (Col 3:10). Consequently, we become a tabernacle for heavenly communion, serving as a meeting point between heaven and earth, much like Jesus did when He walked among us (1 Tim 2:5). In Him, the fullness of divinity resides in human form. He is the cornerstone, the firstborn among many brothers and sisters in His likeness (John 1:18; Col 1:18-19, 2:9; Eph 4:13; 1 Pet 2:4-9). "In Him the whole building, being joined together, grows into a holy temple in the Lord, in Whom we are being built together into a dwelling place of [the Triune Divine] in the Spirit" (Eph 2:21-22). Therefore, just as the Son serves as the transcendent-yet-imminent dwelling place of Divinity, so too do we, through Him and by the Spirit, become a sanctified and immanent dwelling place of the Triune I AM within the finite realm.

Jesus highlighted the necessity of being reborn when He stated, "I tell you the solemn truth, unless a person is born from above, he cannot see the kingdom of God… The wind blows wherever it wants, and you can hear its sound, but you do not know where it comes from or where it is going. So, it is with everyone born of the Spirit" (John 3:3-8). As seafarers, we have responded to the Creator's invitation to be reborn by the Spirit, preparing to enter our eternal home. By following this path, we distinguish ourselves as "those who practice the [existential] truth [of our destined contextualities] by [inwardly] com[ing] to the light, so that it may be plainly evident that [our] deeds have been done in God" (John 3:21). Only those who embody spiritual personhood can genuinely exist as a dwelling for the One who is Spirit, and thus we must "die" to our independent, earthly selves and be reborn as God's children. The "Spirit himself bears witness to our spirit that we are [indeed] God's children" (John 3:23-24; Rom 8:16; 1 Cor 5:3, 14:14; Gal 6:18; Col 2:5). Only then can our Creator's intended contextualities, revealed through Christ, define our identity as a genuine temple (Rom 8:4, 11, 29-30; 2 Cor 4:4-6; Heb 1:3).

As finite beings embodying and showcasing the Lord's glory, our lives reflect the heavenly temple. Remember how the tabernacle and temple from the Old Covenant anticipated this truth (1 Kgs 8:11; Ezek 43:4; Rev 15:7). God aims to fulfill His declaration made to each individual He created, "I will fill this temple with glory" (Hag 2:7). Given that our identities represent a living "temple of God," it is fitting that Scripture refers to us as such: "And we all, with unveiled faces reflecting the glory of the Lord, are being transformed into the same image from one degree of glory to another, which is from the Lord, who is the Spirit" (2 Cor 3:18, 6:16). This is our genuine and everlasting destiny.

The Spirit's sanctifying influence resides within us, empowering us to embrace our true identity as royal priests through communion with our Creator and dwelling in His presence (1 Pet 2:9). Just as the priests tended to the Lord's tabernacle in the Old Covenant, we are called to steward our bodies, which serve as the temple of the Body of Christ and the temple of creation (Num 31:47; 1 Chr 3:28; 1 Pet 2:4-9; Rev 1:6). As eternal priests, we are urged to "glorify God with our bodies," purifying "ourselves from everything that could defile the body," thereby achieving holiness out of reverence for God" (1 Chr 3:28; 2 Chr 29:5; 1 Cor 6:19-20; 2 Cor 7:1).

One thing we must understand, however, is how this calling does not involve achieving perfection by totally avoiding sin or relying on our efforts to reform. Additionally, it is not simply a path of enlightenment requiring us to detach from the world in pursuit of divine knowledge. Rather, we should accept an existential transformation facilitated by the presence of the sanctifying Spirit, who cultivates a renewed mindset and lifestyle of holiness within us. We can transcend our limitations and attain our eternal destinies through our connection with a personal divine being.

> *Why do you believe you can only discover your true self by being a vessel for Christ rather than living for yourself?*

Putting on Christ's Garments as a True Priest of Yahweh

We encounter the mirror of Divine likeness only in the Lord's House. We gaze upon our transformation into priests of the *oikonomia* (house rules) of God's temple (1 Pet 2:4-9; Eph 2:15-22, 4:24). With this in mind, we should consider the following passage concerning Aaron, the first high priest of Israel:

> "Bring the tribe of Levi near, and present them before Aaron, the priest, that they may serve him. They are responsible for his needs and the needs of the whole community before the tent of meeting by attending to the service of the tabernacle... You are

to assign the Levites to Aaron... they will be assigned exclusively to him out of all the Israelites. So you are to appoint Aaron and his sons, and they will be responsible for their priesthood."

(Num 3:6-10)

Like Aaron, Jesus has His eternal priests serving under Him, whom He has sanctified as His "royal" and "holy" priesthood (Exod 40:15; 2 Chr 29:5; Eph 5:26-29; Rev 5:10; 1 Pet 2:4-9).

As Scripture states, "Christ loved the church and gave Himself for her to sanctify her by cleansing her with the washing of water by the word, so that He may present the church to Himself as glorious – not having a stain or wrinkle, or any blemish, but holy and blameless" (Eph 5:26-27). Although this may seem unusual to us now, we should interpret these words through the lens of consecration. Prior to assuming sacred roles, priests and monarchs were symbolically anointed and set apart to carry out their responsibilities. This is akin to how becoming a monk (or a Jedi in Star Wars) necessitates leaving the ordinary world behind to dedicate one's life to a sacred purpose, distinguishing oneself from daily life. Extending our fictional example, a Jedi must undergo rigorous training to genuinely embody the Jedi way, which requires remaining free from worldly attachments and unchecked passions. Only by completing this training and (ideally) sincerely embracing the Jedi Code could an individual fulfill the role of a fully-fledged Jedi Knight, a protector of peace and justice. In a similar vein, Christ desires for us to be prepared and distinguished for the purpose He has called us to, hence the transformation, discipleship, and cleansing He brings about within us.

As priests united with Christ, we serve within the heavenly Tabernacle, ministering to each other and to all of humanity.

> *In what ways do you believe the priests of the New Covenant can fulfill their responsibilities in today's world?*
>
> *Could you provide examples of how you can?*

Although we no longer sacrifice animals, our service is demonstrated by our willingness to sacrifice our lives and obey His command to express His love to those around us, e.g. charitable giving. In contrast to the priests of the old covenant, our role in this heavenly temple is everlasting. Even when the world fades away, our identity and sanctuary in the Temple of God will endure. Our priesthood's concept of a "new humanity" reflects a theological self in the likeness of Christ, suitable for those who serve in the Temple of God. We become His priestly body, distributing sanctifying restorative and liberating grace across creation (Eph 4:12-13; Col 3:1-4; Rev 5:10). Until Christ returns, it is through us that His priestly work persists throughout the world.

The Levitical priests donned "consecrated garments" while serving "in the Holy Place" (Exod 28:3, 29:29-30; Ezek 44:17). These garments distinguished them "to minister as [Yahweh's] priests" "for glory and for beauty" (Exod 28:2-3). In a similar fashion, the Holy Spirit adorns us in garments of holiness, embodying the Creator's vision for Finitude. By the Spirit's sanctifying power, our "robes" are "washed" and "made" "white in the blood of the lamb," allowing us access to the presence of the "throne of God" to "serve Him day and night in His temple" (Rev 7:14-15). Consider the New Covenantal prophecy: "He clothes me in garments of deliverance; He puts on me a robe symbolizing vindication. I look like a bridegroom when he wears a turban as a priest would; I look like a bride when she puts on her jewelry" (Isa 61:10; Rev 19:8). Such exquisite garments are bestowed upon those of us freed from existential rebellion. Just like the robes and signet ring of the Prodigal Son, these gifts come to us when we forsake the world and return to our Father's house as His cherished children (Luke 15:21-22). We wear these new garments as we wholeheartedly accept the heavenly call to be part of the priestly "bride" (beloved life partner) of Christ.

Beyond representing our salvation, each "garment" embodies the divine purpose of Finitude, inscribed with inherent guidelines. Consider how the vestments of catholic priests, the coat of a doctor, the armor of a knight, the crown of a king, and even the robes and lightsabers of a Jedi Knight signify their sacred roles, seemingly infused with the purpose and meaning they convey. Each piece carries its associated meanings and callings, at least in people's perceptions. Wearing them may evoke the purposes they represent, inspiring those who behold them. In a sense, they imbue the worthiness of those callings upon the wearers, as not everyone can don a priest's collar or wield a lightsaber. Our heavenly garments, much like those of the Levitical priesthood, figuratively carry a "plate of pure gold inscribed as a seal: 'Holiness to the Lord'" (Exod 28:36). This inscription proclaims to everyone within Finitude to "be holy before the Lord," placing upon us, as priests, the responsibility and empowerment to uphold the sanctity and value of all Creation, starting with ourselves.

To genuinely embrace our identity as holy priests of God, we must understand that our true self, our authentic "face," exists in the shadow of His holiness. We are not intended to discover ourselves within ourselves. Indeed, we are beings becoming "[re-]created in[to] God's image – in righteousness and holiness" (Eph 4:24). Our true self can only take shape when we become a dwelling for another being, Yahweh. Our existence must resonate with His. The scripture tells us that our "[eternal] life is hidden with Christ in God," indicating that our true self is revealed through the image of Christ, "who is our real life" (Col 3:3-4). Our genuine life is found in the One who perfectly embodies the "radiance of

[Yahweh's] glory and the representation of His essence," as we can only truly become a temple of God by being "clothed with Christ," "who is the image of God" (Heb 1:3; Gal 3:27; 1 Cor 4:4). By grace we put on His likeness, as the Spirit of God comes to guide us personally according to the patterns, which are inherent to His nature (2 Cor 4:6; 1 John 4:16-17).

Only Christ can rewrite our psychological and spiritual "software." By sending His Spirit to dwell within us, Christ restores our ability to embrace Eternity. Through the Incarnation, the original union of the Divine and Human, He revealed the potential for eternal humanness and provided the path toward it (John 1). Without the divine in us, we cannot experience spiritual sanctification, which involves renewing our minds, nor can we begin our journey back home.

We should not view sanctification as becoming "enslaved" to a harsh master but rather as discovering our purpose within a larger context, a greater aim for which we were created. This is more than simply engaging in self-help endeavors or paths to self-discovery. It represents a profound spiritual transformation rooted in establishing a transformative relationship with the Divine and Eternal. Through direct personal access to His self-revealing Word and ever-present Spirit, we can transition from the shores of temporality to become eternity-bound pilgrims, fulfilling the purpose for which we were all created (Heb 1:3; Col 1:15).

> *Will you permit God to dress you in His divine robes?*
>
> *Are you prepared to make your future reflect God's influence?*
>
> *If not, what holds you back?*

This situation is similar to fictional stories where an ordinary character learns they are meant for something significant, and by embracing this calling – often at the expense of their personal autonomy – they authentically realize their potential and become who they are destined to be. Tales like Simba's in The Lion King, Luke Skywalker's in Star Wars, Moses in the Exodus, and King Arthur's in ancient English legends illustrate this point. Many of these characters first resisted their calling, opting for a peaceful, unremarkable existence. Yet, they all ultimately set aside their desires to pursue what was right, becoming the heroes they were meant to become. Similarly, we must choose to find our purpose not solely in our wishes but in our Creator's vision. By making Christ-like behavior our standard for self-fulfillment, we embrace a greater calling.

Why do you believe that a journey of self-help or even enlightenment is insufficient to restore our communion with God?

We seafarers must heed Christ's command: "Take My advice and buy gold from Me refined by fire so you can become rich! Buy from Me white clothing so you can be clothed, and your shameful nakedness will not be exposed, and buy eye salve to put on your eyes so you can see" (Rev 3:18)! Only by His Spirit can we effectively steward our bodies as "the temple of the Holy Spirit who is in [us], whom [we] have from God, and [as such we] are not our own" (1 Cor 6:19). Being "bought at a price," we should "glorify God with [our] body," treating it as His temple—a holy place, a site for prayer, and a space for Sabbath rest (1 Cor 6:20; Luke 19:46; Isa 56:7; Ezek 20:12). By the power of His Spirit, He breaks the chains of unholy and unrighteous rebellion, allowing us and those we minister to "serve [Yahweh] without fear, in holiness and righteousness before Him[, as His priests] for as long as we live" (Zech 8:2-3; Isa 52:1-2; Luke 1:74-75; Rev 1:6).

Surrendering to a Discipleship of Agape-Love

To fully embrace our Creator's call, we must engage with the Divine Nature and express *agape*-love through our innermost being, where God's Spirit dwells (Job 33:4; Eph 4:24; Jas 3:9; 2 Pet 1:4; 1 John 3:24, 4:15-17). Only by surrendering to the lifestyle of *agape*-love can our inner being become reborn by God's Breath (or Spirit) (John 3:3-8). In this manner, we become communal participants in the divine nature. We can then act as living tabernacles of the Triune I AM, manifesting the Divine Way within the bounds of Finitude (1 Cor 12:31). To live as God's temple, we must forsake the pursuit of self-sovereignty and egocentric love. We can only adopt the lifestyle of *agape*-love by sincerely submitting to Him as the divine authority and source of a truly "fitting" life, rooted in the two greatest commandments of *agape*-love: to love God and your neighbor as yourself.[175] (Matt 22:36-40). Living a life of surrender requires living out His *caring* vision in and through our world-dwelling existence (2 Cor 5:15). "Just as the Lord has assigned to each one, as God has called each person, so must [we] live," as co-workers of *agape*-love sanctified by the Spirit (1 Cor 3:9, 7:17, 8:1, 13:1-13).

While we have explored the virtues found in hoping for our future Heavenly home, we do not have to wait until death or the end of time to experience it. The eternal homeland of the children of God resides, even now, in the communal abode of *Agape* love found in our inner Holy of Holies. Only in the Holy of Holies can we discover true existential rest, an eternal Sabbath, which serves as a "reminder of our relationship [with God]" where we will genuinely "know" the "Lord our God" who "sanctifies us" for all eternity (Ezek 20:12, 20). The Holy of Holies symbolizes the inner chambers of the deepest spiritual intimacy, close to the Creator's heart. Our First Love's selfless affection for us fuels our

---

[175] Note how both commandments order a person to direct their love outward, away from themselves and onto God and others. It is in giving our love out to others, as God continuously does, that we fulfill His will and become truly Christ-like.

commitment (1 John 4:19). By stepping into the role of stewards within His domain, we find our true sense of belonging, purpose, and peace. We must enter the Holy of Holies daily to fulfill this role effectively. It is here that, through "coming to [Him] in prayer" as we "seek [Him] with all our heart and soul," "[He] will make [Himself] available to us" for an Infinite-finite communion (*koinonia*) (Jer 29:12-14).

Even as we navigate this fallen world in our mortal bodies, we can already reside in our heavenly home as God builds His temple within us! Through the sanctifying work of the Spirit, our inner connection with the Holy of Holies also shapes our souls into God's image to serve as instruments of the priesthood. Instead of being selfish, impatient, petty, angry, or lacking control, we are empowered by God to embody love, selflessness, patience, kindness, maturity, and wisdom. When we, by His grace, choose to prioritize His will over our own in any instance, such as obeying His command to respond to our 'enemies' with goodness rather than evil, we reflect Jesus' example.

{ *Do you walk the highway of holiness or the highway of idolatry?*

Toward what destination are you heading life? }

When we embrace the heavenly dwelling by engaging with the Holy of Holies, we essentially live on earth through Heaven rather than solely through ourselves (Rev 13:6). As this transpires, Heaven manifests on earth through us as His children (2 Cor 6:16-18). We can illustrate this using the metaphorical language of Scripture. The rays of the Creator's sun filter through and express themselves within the atmosphere of our spirits. In this way, the existential light of eternal truth is translated through our souls, becoming evident through actions that align with Yahweh's self-revealing temple.[176]

Let us ground these ideas in the real world. Consider a scenario where you are in a demanding, competitive workplace, where impressing the boss and securing a promotion (along with a generous salary) is everything. Many of your coworkers exhaust themselves trying to outshine each other, with some even attempting to sabotage their colleagues. Picture a situation where someone spreads false rumors about you to the boss out of envy, resulting in several coworkers believing those lies. What steps do you take? Society likely urges you to retaliate, gossip back, or confront them. In a cutthroat capitalist environment, defending yourself seems justified. Yet, the Holy Spirit encourages you to respond differently—by turning the other cheek, refraining from evil acts, exercising patience, and recognizing peacemakers as children of God (Matt 5:39; Rom 12:17; Eph 4:2; Matt 5:9). With God's grace, you choose to act with compassion, kindness, forgiveness, and self-restraint. You overlook the rumors and your coworker's actions, defending yourself only when absolutely necessary, and opting not to retaliate; instead, you let your integrity and hard work shine. You might even go further, extending

> *What makes it essential to partake of and express the divine nature to become a temple of God?*
>
> *Why can we not achieve this without submitting to His presence?*

---

[176] A modern example can be seen in how Jedi in Star Wars "surrender" to the light side of the Force. A fundamental difference between Jedi and Sith lies in the Jedi's ability to let the Force flow through them, allowing it to fulfill its will, whereas the Sith seek to control the Force, using it as a tool for their own purposes. The Jedi metaphorically surrender to the river's current, exhibiting trust and self-denial, while the Sith manipulate it for their desired outcomes. Similarly, we resemble the Jedi by placing our trust in God, allowing Him to live and act through us (Gal 2:20) instead of imposing our own will on our lives.

grace to your coworkers by assisting them in their struggles and acknowledging their strengths in conversations with your boss. By doing this, you reflect the image of God on earth, providing a glimpse into a higher reality that transcends the modern world's focus on self-advancement, individual wealth, and social recognition.

Whether the office acknowledges your response and alters its stance or overlooks it to support the other coworker, it ultimately makes no difference. Your actions will illuminate the perpetual truths of humility, kindness, and the inner peace of your worth through Christ. In the long run, you may even gain respect from others, showcasing that integrity and adherence to God's law hold greater value than fleeting achievements. Even if respect does not come your way, your deeds will echo for eternity, honored by God once your journey concludes. This is how Yahweh reaches this fallen world through us, ministering to others through our souls and bodies as we access the Holy of Holies, our eternal home. Through us, His tabernacles, the world inches closer to Heaven, revealing God's nature and beauty to those yearning for something more profound.

In the Holy of Holies, Yahweh reveals His image, which simultaneously illuminates our unique identities. The more we gaze upon Him, the better we understand our true selves – much like how our awareness of the world grows as the sun "rises" in the morning. As creations of God, we naturally find our completeness in Him. Therefore, deepening our experiential knowledge of our Creator on the Sea of Revelation inherently requires discipleship. As our Master, the Creator teaches His followers how to govern and nurture His dominion in alignment with His will and methods. Only by entering this Holy of Holies and inviting Him to work within us, rather than depending solely on our character, can we achieve this. Therefore, we must seek daily communion with the

True Light to live according to the appropriate worldview and purpose of our true Home. Only in that inner place can we truly "surrender to the flow of the river," allowing ourselves to dwell in our Creator's home-making essence, which clothes us in His glory and teaches us to echo His life-giving song of *agape*-phosnoumenos (2 Cor 3:18; Col 3:10; Gal 3:27).

Resisting the current of the world is not easy. Without His essence, it is basically impossible. Whether it was the early Christian martyrs advocating love and pacifism in a Roman society that dismissed altruism and glorified martial duty, or a modern politician standing firm on integrity instead of seeking popularity or self-enrichment, pushing back is more challenging than we realize. This difficulty intensifies when we face the possibility of losing much, such as our reputations or quality of life. Only by remaining in the presence of our Creator and that other, Heavenly realm can we truly lay down our lives in this world. As we continue to experience and reflect God's magnificent self-revelation, we embrace our true home here on earth. Yahweh desires His heartbeat for creation to resonate within us, transforming His perspective into our own. Only then can He fully share His vision and its beauty with us. He invites us to re-envision His plans within Finitude through His Spirit, similar to how He inspired the Scriptures as a contextual revelation of Himself. This invitation grants us the opportunity to embrace His *care* for Creation and participate in His vision's everlasting fulfillment.

> *Why must you "live by the Spirit" to fulfill your calling to express agape-love through your desires, character, and willpower?*

As seafarers aboard our ship, our understanding of home stems from our beliefs about the nurturing nature of our Creator, who *is* *agape*-love (1 Cor 8:1; 1 John 4:8, 16). God generously dedicates Himself to empower us in demonstrating a lifestyle inspired by His radiant virtues (John 12:35-36, 15:1-9; 1 John 1:2, 1:5, 5:12). Just like the moon reflecting sunlight, He allows us to mirror His presence within His finite household (2 Cor 3:18, 4:4-6; Gal 5:16-25; 1 John 1:5-2:11). As the stones of His finite household, humans hold the most crucial role among all created beings. Our command to "fill the earth and subdue it" emphasizes stewardship rather than dominion. We are to care for our world, transforming it through our function as vessels of His divine presence. To achieve this, we must be sanctified according to the *oikonomia* (house rules) of holiness, offering ourselves to God "as instruments to be used for righteousness" (Rom 6:13, 19, 22; Eph 1:4, 4:23-24).

What is the primary work of righteousness that our Creator calls us to undertake? He tasks us with performing tangible acts of *agape*-love through the power and fellowship of His Spirit (John 15:1-17; Rom 5:5; Gal 5:13-14, 22). As illustrated earlier, we achieve this whenever we adhere to His commands, particularly in challenging situations. When we show generosity toward those in need, even at a personal inconvenience, when we love those who hate and persecute us, or when we sacrifice earthly gains to serve the lost, we demonstrate His love to those around us. Such actions cannot succeed solely through human effort, as they are contrary to the humanistic values of Babylon (John 6:63, Eph 2:1-3, 4:22; Col 3:5-9). After all, people may appreciate generosity but will resent it if it threatens their prosperity. They may love their families but harbor hatred for their enemies. What about forgiving and loving those who persecute us? Or choosing not to retaliate? Only those who "live by the Spirit" can "act in accordance with" the "desires of the Spirit," especially when these desires clash with our own and our conventional reasoning (Gal 5).

Therefore, we should seek the Holy Spirit's communal presence to empower us to emulate Christ, who, in turn, perfectly reflects our Heavenly Father by embodying holiness as Yahweh is holy (Eph 3:17-20, 5:1-2; 1 Pet 1:13-22). He teaches us to discard our destructive tendencies through His refining fires, similar to how impurities are removed from gold by being burned away. These flames eradicate Babylon's negative influence in our lifestyle and perspective. Every seafarer must reflect: will we allow the holy fires to purge the corruption of Babylon?

Becoming Transformed into His Tabernacles

Our true home resides in the Holy of Holies, where we discover the magnificent home-making life of the Triune I AM, who "does not live in temples made by human hands" (Acts 7:48, 17:24). His temple is one He has constructed for Himself through the very Breath that resides within and animates His children (Gen 2:7; Job 33:4; 1 Cor 6:19). Hence, all humans, made in God's image—who "live, move about, and subsist [in God]" as His "kin/offspring"—were intended to act as an abode of the home-making essence of Eternity (Acts 17:28). Here alone does our eternal potential as God's children, both in essential being (subsistence) and existential form (personhood) become fully realized (Eph 4:24).

In contrast to the theology of some other religions, becoming the unique children of God, as intended by our Creator, does not mean we lose our individuality or sense of self. Instead, as diverse members of the Body of Christ, we will eternally coexist with our unique identities as neighbors within the Household of the Triune I AM (Eph 2:19-22). Consider musicians in an orchestra; they each retain their distinctiveness through their instrument's sound and their specific role within the ensemble. Although unique, each musician fulfills a complementary role in a larger composition.

How can we inherit an inheritance within the Kingdom of Heaven? How do we dwell in our true home even while navigating a fallen world? How can we bring Heaven to earth despite it conflicting with our instincts as temporal beings? We must commit to discipleship and persevere along the narrow path with repentance and endurance (Matt 7:13-14; Luke 13:24; Phil 2:12-13). By venturing onto the Sea of Revelation, we experience "sanctification" in the image of the "heavenly [humanity]" through the "power" of God's "Spirit" (1 Cor 15:47-49; Eph 3:16, 4:24; 2 Thess 2:13).

As Yahweh's eternal dwelling place in finitude, we manifest His divine works through the power of His Spirit. He promised this to us when He declared, "I will pour out My Spirit on all kinds of people. Your sons and daughters will prophesy. Your elderly will have revelatory dreams; your young men will see prophetic visions. Even on male and female servants, I will pour out My Spirit in those days" (Joel 2:28-29). To tap into these eternal possibilities, through which others can encounter the Divine in and through us, we must let eternal contextualities shape how we become established in the temporal contexts in which He has placed us (Acts; 1 Cor 12-14; Gal 5). To do so, we must give up our self-determination. When we surrender our will to Him, the grace of divine empowerment begins.

As our grace-filled lives unfold, we as fitting temples of Yahweh become filled with His agape-love, revelation, knowledge, wisdom, and character. Through us, He manifests His personhood throughout the world. We start to act like Christ to those around us, showing them the love, mercy, and light of God in imitation of Him. We shine forth His light so that all people will see it and desire what we have and, eventually, who we have. Given such supernatural potential residing in the children of God, the Son of God says to all of us, "If you have faith the size of a mustard seed, you will say to this mountain, 'Move from here to there,' and it will move; nothing will be impossible for you" (Matt 17:20).

All of us in Christ have supernatural potential. Yahweh's omnipotent Word of divine decree occupies us. With our eternal identities of divine stewardship in mind, no wonder Christ instructed us:

> "Whatever you bind on earth will have been bound in heaven, and whatever you release on earth will have been released in heaven. Again, I tell you the truth, if two of you on earth agree about whatever you ask, My Father in heaven will do it for you. For where two or three are assembled in My name, I am there among them."
>
> (Matt 18:18-20)

Christ taught that the Body of Christ can tap into divinely backed authority even as we occupy the temporal world. If we live by faith in such wonderful promises, we take up our heavenly calling as a royal priesthood of God, which is sanctioned by the authority of Christ. Unlike the Force in Star Wars or 'magic' in fairy tales, however, such divine power is not merely ours to use and utilize in whatever manner we wish. Divine power can only be exercised when we no longer live on our own but allow Him to live through us (Gal 3). When we exercise the power of His Spirit in this way, walking by spirit-to-Spirit communion, we can accomplish supernatural work. The Body of Christ exercises Yahweh's governing authority and creative power even in this fallen world. Therefore, through the abiding presence of the Divine within our inner person, we can access Eternity even from within temporality.

Returning to our consecration metaphor, we undergo the necessary "Jedi training" to fulfill our calling authentically. Discipleship, synonymous with our journey alongside Christ, unfolds through the Creator's indwelling presence and the Spirit's work within us to realize His purposes. Our human strength must diminish, while His divine power within us should amplify. Paul gives us one way to build-up (strengthen) ourselves in the Spirit:

"The one who speaks in a tongue builds himself up... I wish you all spoke in tongues [by the gift of the Spirit] ... I thank God that I speak in tongues more than all of you" (1 Cor 13:4-5, 18). This devotion to spiritual up-building by the supernatural aligns with our purpose, as being temples serves not ultimately for ourselves but God. We must become a temple for the Creator rather than a shrine to ourselves or any other earthly powers. It should no longer be we who live, but Christ, in whose "face" the unveiled "knowledge of God's glory" is imminently revealed within us (2 Cor 4:6; Gal 2:20). After all, our spiritual vitality today is solely due to the faithfulness of the Son of God, who redeems our transgressions and envelops us in His purifying divine Spirit (Gal 2:20-21).

> *What do you believe God expects from you in terms of decreasing as He increases in your life?*
>
> *How might He empower you to embrace your unique true self?*
>
> *In what way does resolving this apparent contradiction illuminate your intended relationship with your Creator?*

By baptizing us into the revelation of God 3, Christ sets us apart for "holiness." He produces in and through us the "righteousness" of "*agape*-love" that displays the image of the Creator just as a temple ought (Rom 6:13; 1 Cor 1:30; 2 Cor 3:3-5; Gal 2:20-21, 5:5-6, 5:22; Eph 2:10; Luke 1:74-75). Through His role as our High Priest, Jesus enables us to become a new creation, shaped in His likeness and inhabited by the Divine (2 Cor 5:11-21; Eph 2:19-21). This theological identity of *agape*-love requires us to dwell intimately in and through God. As His "bride," we partner with Him to work within us as we take up our heavenly destiny (1 Pet 2:4-9; 1 John 4:13).

Ultimately, the Spirit's sanctifying work guides us toward "righteousness." We can only experience eternal life on earth by growing into our purpose as God's tabernacles. Although we are not yet united with our Creator in Heaven, we can live eternally by being His vessels of agape love, which begins when our hearts are circumcised (set apart for sacred use) and filled with this love (Rom 2:29, 5:5, 21; 2 Cor 3:8-9; 1 Pet 1:2). To inhabit our heavenly home now, we must let go of primarily living for the sake of our earthly homes in Babylon and fully embrace the divine purpose to which He calls us (John 12:25; Rom 6:22). By doing so, we present our bodies (outer court) as instruments to be "used for righteousness" and ourselves (inner court) as living sacrifices, "alive, holy, and pleasing to God – which is our reasonable service" as His priests "alive from the dead" (Rom 6:13, 12:1). We commit to no longer being "conformed to this present world," but being "transformed" into "the image of His Son," the High Priest (Rom 8:29, 12:2).

As temples, we emulate Christ. We partake in the communion of the Son of God with both the Father and the Spirit, acting as instruments to extend this tabernacle communion into the surrounding world (Luke 4:1; John 14:2, 10, 17, 23). With this eternal purpose in focus, Christ prayed, stating:

> "Just as you, Father, are in Me and I am in You, I pray that they will be in Us... The glory You gave to Me I have given to them, that they may be one just as We are one – I in them and You in Me – that they may be completely one [, as the Body of Christ]... I made known Your name to them, and I will continue to make it known, so that the love (*agape*) You have loved Me with may be in them, and I may be in them."
>
> (John 17:21-26)

The presence of God, flowing through us as tabernacles, not only inspires our spiritual transformation but can also bring new life and a glimpse of heaven to others. As mentioned in the previous chapter, the Creator's agape love begins to permeate our earthly existence when it passes through us by the Holy Spirit. This love then enters the core of our soul—our heart, mind, and personality—sanctifying them like a river that nourishes the land it flows through (Rom 5:5; Tit 3:5-7). Ultimately, His love reaches fullness through our actions and Spirit-filled communication (1 John 4:15-17). Through this process, we embody His love in ways that can profoundly affect others, effectively planting spiritual "seeds." Consider how your love towards an enemy could blossom into an unexpected friendship or how your generosity might impact a needy stranger. These seeds have the potential to grow, inspiring a similar process of spiritual development in them. When this occurs, the *agape*-love of God completes a cycle within another individual's relationship.

Up-building works of love, light, and spirit allow us to glimpse our eternal destiny. When effectively integrated into our worldly existence, these acts lead to remarkable reflections of God's Infinite Being's noumenal realities (1 John 4:8-17). Emulating the world-dwelling life of Christ, we become conduits for Yahweh's invisible love to be visibly manifested in Creation, allowing humanity to see, feel, experience, and remember (John 3:16-17; Col 1:15; 1 John 3:16). Thus, true disciples of Christ must embrace His new way of living, grounded in a timeless perspective and nurtured by the sacred care of agape love (1 Cor 2:16; 1 John 2:6; Col 2:2; Eph 3:16-19). Contrary to the revised "salvation requirements" often preached from various pulpits, the Great Commission is not merely an optional requirement for entering the Kingdom of

> *What spiritual seeds of agape-love have you planted by the Spirit this week?*

Heaven. Salvation should not be viewed as a distant future possibility; rather, it is a current reality experienced through restored fellowship with the Triune I AM. Outside this fellowship, eternal life eludes a person, regardless of any religiously endorsed "promises," "vows," or "rituals" performed.

We can only thrive per the *oikonomia* (house rules) of Heaven when "the [*agape-*]love of God has been poured out in our hearts through the Holy Spirit who [has been] given to us" (Rom 5:5). Furthermore, we must co-create and co-manage our influence with that same vision, just as a faithful priest would. Our sanctification does not just purify us individually; it also teaches us to interact with and perceive the world through His abiding presence. As our Guide states: "[God] shines in our hearts to give us the light of the glorious knowledge of God in the face of Christ" (Col 3:10; 2 Cor 4:6). "For [we] were once darkness, but now [we] are light in the Lord. [So let us] walk as children of light—for the fruit of the light is all goodness, righteousness, and truth—striving to learn what pleases the Lord" (Eph 5:8-10). As children of light, we walk by His light. The Spirit's illumination transforms our inner selves so that our engagement with the world and our perspectives reflect His own (John 12:35-36). Therefore, more than just "making one holy," sanctification enables us to serve as the hands, feet, and voice of the One who brings light to creation, just as Christ did (John 1:5-7, 2:6).

> *Even if you do not always witness the "fruits" of your efforts toward others (for example, if your enemy remains your enemy), why should you persist in showing them love?*

Like a writer crafting a book, Yahweh invites us to embody the words He has written as the author of the Narrative of Finitude. By embracing and channeling the flow of Divine Consciousness within us, the rhythm of His *oikonomia*, inspired *by* Yahweh's

Triune Home, perpetually manifests in the realm of Finitude. When this happens, Finitude is illuminated by the revelations of the Triune God. Just as a virus spreads "uncleanness" through death and disease, we are called to propagate "cleanness," holiness, and *shalom* wherever we go. Thus, we consecrate (literally "to bestow holiness upon") Creation to harmonize with the eternal chapter of the Creator's Narrative of Finitude. Consequently, the Maker's finite realm mirrors how He reveals Himself from, *through*, and *by* His Infinite triune existence.

We should, therefore, not quench the Holy Spirit's work in liberating us from an idolatrous perspective and way of living (1 Thess 5:19). When we fail to seek His sanctifying presence, we "grieve the Holy Spirit," allowing "the devil an opportunity" to lead us into sinful behaviors such as "bitterness" and "anger," rather than encouraging Spirit-filled responses like "kindness" and "forgiveness" (Eph 4:27-32). When we choose to give in to our flesh—like reacting with anger to a gossiping coworker by spreading rumors or engaging in conflict—we only contribute to the harsh, competitive nature of the world for fleeting personal gain. Sadly, we forfeit the chance to illuminate the world with God's light and possibly plant seeds of lasting transformation in others' lives. The Spirit wishes to renew us, guiding our inner selves towards viewing and residing in the world in harmony with God's truth (Gal 5:15-26; Tit 3:5), not just for our benefit, but for the broader context of the world we inhabit. Through the Holy Spirit's sanctification, our inner being transforms into a sacred place, a site of worship and service to God (1 Pet 2:5). It becomes a temple, reflecting the image of our Creator and influencing our self-actualization and virtues (1 Pet 2:9, 11).

As residents of Heaven, Eternity calls us "put to death whatever in our nature belongs to the earth," reflecting on how we once lived. We must now "put off such things" of the "old

> *Is God calling you to put to death some parts of your earthly nature?*

[humanity]" (Col 3:5-9). We are to become open sanctuaries for Yahweh, adorned with the mind of Christ and the desires and perspectives of the Spirit (1 Cor 2:16; Gal 5:17; Rom 8:5-6). This transformation enables us to live the life that God designed for us. The freedom found in the God-relationship and reliance on His Spirit starkly contrasts with the bondage of transient self-centeredness and futile self-reliance, where one is driven by impulses and lesser desires instead of surrendering them for a higher purpose (Rom 6:7, 6:18, 8:21; 2 Cor 3:17-18; Gal 5:1, 13; 2 Pet 2:19).

If we cling to our self-centered way of living and refuse the uplifting influence of *agape*-love, we lose the opportunity for eternal life that Christ offers to everyone (Mark 8:35-36). To embrace eternal life, we must see the world through the eyes of its Creator.[177] "Those who live according to the Spirit have their outlook shaped by the things of the Spirit," "which is life and peace" (Rom 8:5-6). Beyond merely seeing the world from a new perspective, we must strive to emulate our Architect by living differently. As stated, "By the Spirit [we] put to death the deeds of the body," ensuring that we "will live" because "all who are led by the Spirit of God are the [children] of God" (Rom 8:13-14). Genuine discipleship in homemaking for God involves dedicating

---

[177] We inhabit a fascinating world where the reality we perceive – though it appears to be the natural order – is fundamentally a distortion of existence as defined by God. The original state of creation was intended to embody shalom, harmony, love, relationships, light, and life. It is only due to humanity's choice to redefine the world based on its own understanding of nature, morality, and purpose (affected, of course, by the devil's rebellion) that we find ourselves in the present state—fallen, fractured, marked by survival instincts and scarcity, evil, on a path to destruction, and deeply troubled. Through the illumination of God and His *agape*-love, we are not simply introducing a new perspective; we are revealing the reality that was always meant to be.

our temporal existence to creating a space suitable for His divine presence, aided by the Spirit's holy-making sanctification and miraculous gifts. We should strive to be priestly vessels, where our relationship with the Creator informs our actions in the world, facilitating others' sanctification through His guidance (Rom 12:1, 15:6).

By walking with the Holy Spirit, our essence, already existing within divine Being, mirrors that Being in a way like light passes through a diamond (Gal 5:16, 18, 25). This sanctification process ensures that "the righteous requirement of the law is fulfilled in us, who do not walk according to the flesh but according to the Spirit" (Rom 8:4, 29; 13:14). Moreover, as His temple and priests, we showcase His power and authority to the world. Ultimately, our calling is to be "[co-]heirs of the kingdom [of God]" alongside our Lord, the Son of God (Jas 2:5). Though our representation of His presence and light may seem modest, it parallels our role as ambassadors, embodying a different kind of strength and authority than that of the world expects.[178] "The Spirit Himself bears witness to our spirit that we are God's children. And if children, then heirs (namely, heirs of God and also fellow heirs with Christ) [...] Indeed, He who did not spare His own Son, but gave Him up for us all – how will He not also, along with Him, freely give us all things?" (Rom 8:16-17, 32; Gal 4:6-7; Eph 3:6).

{ *When was the last time you acted as a window into Eternity?* }

"Through the washing of the new birth and the renewing of the Holy Spirit, whom He poured out on us in full measure

---

[178] Jesus subverted the Jewish people's expectations of the Messiah, as well as those of the Romans, Vikings, and others regarding the nature of God. Instead of presenting Himself as a mighty conqueror or a domineering (Greek-like deity, He embodied humility through His love, healing acts, and a brutal death on the cross.

through Jesus Christ our Savior... we have been justified by grace, [and] become heirs with the confident expectation of eternal life" (Tit 5-7; 1 Pet 3:7). Through our inheritance in Christ, graciously given to us as co-heirs, we can serve Him as vessels for divine encounters for the world and those around us (2 Cor 3:8-9).

Our Creator designed our existence and perception to flourish within the realm of His Spirit, akin to a spiritual incubation (John 3:3-8; Rom 8:8-11). This unfolds through the communion between Spirit and spirit in our relationship with God, which refreshes our inner vision, enabling us to view others through His lens of agape love (2 Cor 4:16; Eph 4:23). As we synchronize our living with His divine essence, the fruit of the Spirit becomes apparent in our lives (Gal 5:22-25). By choosing, through His empowering grace, to embody qualities like love, peacefulness (avoiding quick anger or conflict), faithfulness (prioritizing His purposes over our ambitions), and joyfulness (praising Him through life's hardships and nurturing a grateful spirit), we demonstrate His nature in the world. Like windows in an old warehouse, we allow light and air to reinvigorate a dim and dusty space. This spiritual birth process strengthens our souls and bodies as living parts of the contextually finite House of God, revealing His present essence within Finitude (Eph 2:19-22; 1 Pet 2:4-5).

At the core of our eternal destiny, we are to serve as temples of God, acting as conduits for His self-revealing insights. We are the main avenues among all God's creatures through which He manifests Himself and His revelations to the world.[179] We must

---

[179] Certainly, the Scriptures and the church are fundamental to God's revelation. However, in today's world, they often fail to attract individuals unless those who profess to follow them embody God's nature. Reflect on the well-known (though possibly apocryphal) quote by Mahatma Gandhi: "I like Christ, but I do not like your Christians. Your Christians are so unlike your Christ."

always remain conscious of and thoughtfully reflect on this fundamental belief of our faith. Given this conviction, the purpose of our journey home becomes clear. We undertake this journey because we trust God desires to impart insights from His heart, mind, and essence. Being "born of God" happens through "His seed [that] resides in us" (1 John 3:9). We become vessels through which God plants "seeds" of His nature and life throughout creation. As our guide teaches, "the person who sows" by "the Spirit" "will reap eternal life from the Spirit" (Gal 6:8; 2 Cor 9:10). We experience tangible outcomes arising from our union with Him and His presence within us, which showcases the divine essence (John 15:1-17; Gal 5:22-23). By envisioning the seeds God plants in us and through us, we can see how He views creation as His "field" filled with abundant harvests, where His revealed presence flourishes and grows to be "all in all" (Matt 13:38; 1 Cor 3:9, 15:28).

Are you willing to trust God to renew and transform you and your lifestyle according to eternal contextualities?

As seafarers, we must strive to put on the "image of the man of heaven," who "comes from above [heaven]," representing a "new creation" that is "born of the Spirit" (1 Cor 15:49; 2 Cor 5:1-4, 17; John 3:3-8, 6:51, 6:58, 8:23, 13:36-14:6). This sanctified path is essential for reaching the true Home of our soul. Only by becoming like Christ and following the way of His disciples can we find salvation (Matt 10:21-25; Luke 9:23-25; 1 Cor 2:9-16). Throughout this journey, as we dedicate ourselves to dwelling in the Holy of Holies with our Creator, our inner perceptions, emotions, and desires align with eternal truths. We begin to think like someone from a different realm and react to situations in ways

---

In an era overwhelmed by sermons and endless Scriptural references, it is only through God being revealed in our lives that people can truly witness the power behind the truths expressed in the Bible and conveyed by the church.

that mirror Jesus. We instinctively come to know how to act correctly in various circumstances, even if our past instincts leaned countrary. For instance, we find ourselves urged to respond to gossiping colleagues with love instead of anger or disdain. These eternal truths manifest in our temporal world, unveiling our identity and homeland, allowing us to live illuminated by the Light of Eternity (Eph 1:17, 3:5). This light provides the Creator's supra-contextual understanding, offering us the promise of our future within our eternal journey (Eph 1:18). Through the guidance of the Spirit of Truth, He reveals our true selves and the nature of Finitude as they were intended, and He invites us to engage in these eternal contextual realities (John 14:16; 15:26-27).

Through His enlightening grace, we can walk in the light of the Living Word (John 1:4-8, 8:12). Only through the illumination of the Living Word does the self-revealing presence of our Creator fill us, spilling over into everything else. "In having been made alive in Christ," we, as priests, must endeavor to make Creation entirely "subjected" to the Creator (1 Cor 15:20-28). By doing this, Creation comes subject to Christ. Through the Spirit of God, we will eternally serve alongside Christ, bringing everything into submission to the Father. This process, of course, begins with us becoming "sacrifices that are alive, holy, and pleasing to God" (Rom 6:13, 12:1; 1 Cor 15:20-28; 1 Pet 2:4-5; Rev 5:10)

Conclusion: The Sanctification of our Spirit, Soul, and Body

The sanctification process of God's Holy Spirit reaches its peak when our physical bodies serve as a conduit for the light of Divine revelations to penetrate the physical world (Rom 12:1). Imagine this as a painting: light embodies all the colors that can be found in any artwork, but the painting provides the shape and context that allows viewers to appreciate and learn from it. What once was just mundane colors without significance transforms into a representation of redemption and forgiveness, much like Rembrandt's *The Return of the Prodigal Son*. Through the contextualization of art, the abstract becomes tangible and experiential. Rather than merely using paints, human beings reflect the contextualization of God's supercontextual light by engaging in divine acts of *agape*-love, phos-light, and pneuma-spirit. These actions stem from

Have you gained a deeper understanding of why cooperating with sanctification is essential preparation for Eternity?

How has this insight influenced your life?

the Spirit's power, which includes desires, perspectives, fruits, and gifts of the Spirit (Rom 8; 1 Cor 12; Gal 5). Empowered by Christ's grace within us, our lives become the divinely inspired masterpieces through which people can perceive, understand, and put on display the *phos*-light of God.

How can we maintain the faith to carry out these actions when they frequently contradict the norms and reasoning of society? We need to adopt, the viewpoint of Eternity. By acknowledging a superior reality, we acquire the resilience to withstand challenges or advocate for the principles of Heaven. We engage with Eternity when we align with His longing to mend the world by sharing our personal stories of faith. In those instances, we reveal His message to the world. Just as a painting converts light into visible colors and forms, these grace-filled deeds express the inner workings of the Spirit, impacting and transforming the external world. Thus, our physical bodies vividly reflect the Creator's essence, attributes, power, and sovereignty (2 Cor 5:1; 2 Pet 1:13-14). "We have this treasure [of the eternal weight of glory] in clay jars so that the extraordinary power [that manifests Divine glory] belongs to God and does not come from us" (2 Cor 4:7, 17). When we understand these truths about the calling of our spirit, soul, and body, our whole person will possess greater self-awareness and self-actualization (or self-transcendence[180]) throughout our homeward-bound voyage.

We should reflect on our Guide's insights regarding the process of sanctification. It states: "Now may the God of peace Himself make you completely holy and may your spirit and soul and body be kept entirely blameless at the coming of our Lord Jesus Christ" (1 Thess 5:23). While we have an important role, the true "originator and perfecter" of our being is Christ (Heb 12:2). As we yield to His transformative work, we must not "extinguish the Spirit's" sanctifying communal influence, as He aims to separate our spirit, soul, and body to showcase God's glory (1 Thess 5:19). Therefore, we need to ensure that our worldview and everyday lives reflect our Creator's *oikonomia* and further His kingdom through our earthly existence.

For example, we can explore the relationship between our thoughts, mindset, desires, passions, character, and actions in connection with our true self as the living temple of the Holy Spirit (1 Cor 6:19). Our worldview needs to be influenced by the principles of a child of God laid out in Scripture, such as differentiating between living by the Spirit and living by the flesh (Gal 5:16-24). Essentially, our true, inner selves, filled with the Holy Spirit, should be the benchmark for assessing a spirit-filled life. Furthermore, we should model our earthly walk as God's

---

[180] Maslow later edited his original hierarchy of needs (usually consisting of physiological needs, safety and security, love and belonging, esteem, and self-actualization in ascending order) to include self-transcendence as the highest level (or one transcending the pyramid of needs altogether). His revised hierarchy contained the crucial change that the pinnacle of one's needs was not simply realizing one's fullest potential but giving oneself to something beyond the self entirely.

What better way to describe how our highest calling is not merely to find our own fulfillment, but to devote ourselves to a story greater than merely our own?

temples after the image of the Creator's self-revelation in Christ (Eph 4:24). As we are "being transformed into the same image from one degree of glory to another" by "the Spirit, "we must constantly evaluate how our "faces" "reflect the glory of the Lord" (2 Cor 3:18). Thus, theocentric self-reflection acts as a measure to determine how far we have surrendered to the Spirit.

> *When was the last time you encountered God's revealing presence?*
>
> *How can this become a regular aspect of your Eternity-bound life?*

By embracing the triune sanctification of our lives, we consistently witness the communal house-building aspect of Yahweh's existence. His presence within us and in the world continuously nurtures our growth, both as individuals and as the Body of Christ, shaping us to reflect Him more profoundly in the world. In this process, we become a dwelling for Him within the finite realm. Through these insights, we acknowledge how this nurturing activity is fundamental to our Creator as infinite triune intra-communal *Being*. His transcendent home embodies His triune essence. Thus, throughout our journey, we strive to fulfill our purpose – to be a finitely-contextualized Home of the Triune I AM, existing and thriving within Infinite *Being* (Acts 17:28).

Yahweh designed us to be finitely contextualized dwellings reflecting the divine nature. Through the "precious and magnificent promises" of the New Covenant fulfilled by Jesus Christ, "we may become partakers of the divine nature, after escaping the worldly corruption produced by evil desires" (2 Pet 1:4). "His divine power has granted us everything we need for life and godliness," as we are filled with and demonstrate "the rich knowledge of the One who [has] called us by His own glory and excellence" (2 Pet 1:3). By the transformative power of the Holy Spirit, we can relinquish our old worldview shaped by the existential rebellion of Babylonian systems. As we are reformed in Christ's likeness, we are built into God's temple, fulfilling the destiny for which we were created. The Holy Breath through the Divine Word empowers us to be a temple of the Father's revealing nature, allowing us to exhibit characteristics of the divine such as supernatural power, sacred words, brotherly affection, *agape*-love, godliness, knowledge, and excellence (2 Pet 1:5-7, 1 Pet 4:11).

Let us not be misled, though. Christ is the builder of His temple, yet we, too, must play an important role. To avoid becoming "ineffective and unproductive in our pursuit of knowing our Lord Jesus more intimately," we must engage in the "increase" of our sanctification (1 Pet 1:8). The more effectively we serve the Lord as His priests and temple, the deeper our knowledge of Him becomes. As we live out our divine calling, "the God of all grace who [has] called [us] [in]to his eternal glory in Christ" "restores, confirms, strengthens, and establishes [us]" within His "dwelling place in the Spirit" (Eph 2:22; Heb 3:1; 1 Pet 5:10). Recognizing these truths, we understand that our journey is also a pilgrimage toward a richer heavenly purpose. Only by committing ourselves to a transformative process, led and empowered by the Spirit, can we truly connect with the Divine, experiencing God's self-revealing presence manifesting in and through us as living temples.

Chapter 10

Priesthood of the End Time Temple

Building Up a United Priesthood of Yahweh

"When I arrive I [hope to] not have to deal harshly with you by using my authority – the Lord gave it to me for building up, not for tearing down! Finally, brothers and sisters, rejoice, set things right, be encouraged, agree with one another, live in peace, and the God of love and peace will be with you... The grace of the Lord Jesus Christ and the love of God and the fellowship of the Holy Spirit be with you all!"

(2 Cor 13:10-13)

"Like a skilled master-builder I laid a foundation, but someone else builds on it. And each one must be careful how he builds... [Only] in [Christ does] the whole building, being joined together, grow into a holy temple in the Lord, in whom you also are being built together into a dwelling place of God in the Spirit... [So let us,] equip the saints for the work of ministry, that is, to build up the body of Christ... As each one does its part, the body grows in love."

(1 Cor 3:10; Eph 2:21-22, 4:12, 4:16)

"My brothers and sisters, you yourselves are full of goodness, filled with all knowledge, and able to *instruct one another*... Because of the *grace given to [you] by God* to *be a minister of Christ Jesus*... Serve the gospel of God *like a priest*, so that the [others] may become an *acceptable offering, sanctified by the Holy Spirit*."

(Rom 15:14-16)

Promoting Allegiance to Yahweh

This chapter explores what it truly means to rebuild Yahweh's temple. Our journey goes beyond individual sanctification; we are called to foster allegiance to Yahweh and guide others toward holiness. Eternity beckons us to fulfill our roles as heavenly priests. To ignore this calling is to deny our true selves and responsibilities as builders of the temple. With His *agape*-love within us, we are to 'construct' others as living stones for this temple. Furthermore, we strive to cleanse our fellow members of the Bride of Christ, shielding them from spiritual darkness that aims to undermine their eternal potential. In our aspiration to reach our true home, we are also called to collaborate with God in uplifting others into His house, just as we are being uplifted for this shared purpose.

The Jerusalem Temple represented the earthly focal point of Yahweh's sovereignty, serving as the source for many of His decrees and actions (1 Kings 8:48-51). From this sacred foundation, He aimed to foster a community dedicated to an eternal worldview and existence, characterized by the God-relationship (Mic 4:1-2; Amos 5:7-24). In our Guide, the Israelites proclaimed, "'Come, let us go up to the Lord's mountain, to the temple of the God of Jacob, so He can teach us His requirements, and we can follow His standards.' Zion will be the center for moral instruction; the Lord's message will issue from Jerusalem" (Isa 2:2-3). It is important to note, however, that the community envisioned by God transcends a conventional "religious" framework. Yahweh denounced the religious practices at His temple whenever they became entangled in empty traditions or ritualistic "lip-service" (Isa 58). Religion lacking in theocentric ethics or genuine engagement with the eternal is futile, even within a house of God, as Yahweh made clear in the following passage:

"Do not bring any more meaningless offerings... You observe new moon festivals, Sabbaths, and convocations, but I cannot tolerate sin-stained celebrations!... When you spread out your hands in prayer, I look the other way... Wash! Cleanse yourselves! Remove your sinful deeds from My sight... Learn to do what is right. Promote justice. Give the oppressed a reason to celebrate. Take up the cause of the orphan. Defend the rights of the widow."

(Isa 1:11-20)

If the temple symbolizes Yahweh's immediate presence and goodwill within a community, then its priests are essential in guiding the community to experience that presence and receive His favor. Essentially, God's presence and goodwill permeate communities through His priests (Ezra 8-9), who bear the duty of nurturing loyalty to Sovereignty, which encompasses "healing" and reconciling those who have strayed from their relationship with God (Mal 2:6; Matt 18:12-14). He instructed them, saying, "Feed My sheep... seek the lost and bring back the strays: I will bandage the injured and strengthen the sick" (Ezek 34:4, 16). As priests of the New Covenant, we should desire to witness our Lord's presence manifested in creation. Furthermore, we ought to guide others in experiencing this presence, fostering worship, devotion, and loyalty to His vision. As Scripture states, our light must shine in a way that enables people to see our world-dwelling and glorify God because of it (Matt 5:16). Thus, our thoughts need to be saturated, drenched, and flooded with the revelations of God's dwelling. Through spirit-to-Spirit communion, we can delve into the

> *Why is guiding others to experience Yahweh's presence as essential as demonstrating His works?*

profound mysteries of the divine within His temple and, driven by our zeal for His glory, reveal these truths to others through enlightening teachings and actions that reflect the divine nature. We serve as His devoted servants and loyal priests (1 Pet 2:4-9; Rev 1:6, 5:10).

The Priesthood of the Old Covenant as a Shadow of the New

During the Old Covenant, people encountered Yahweh, received revelations from Him, and worshiped at His Temple. However, even before the New Covenant, this access was never meant to be exclusive to the Israelites. He states regarding His Temple, "As for foreigners who become followers of the Lord and serve Him, who love the name of the Lord and want to be His servants… I will bring them to My holy mountain; I will make them happy in the temple where people pray to Me… for My temple will be known as a temple where all nations may pray" (Isa 56:6-7). Clearly, Yahweh wanted all humanity to commune with Him, not just a specific ethnic or racial group. The Israelites, as His "chosen" people, served as a temporary representation of humanity's eternal destiny, similar to how the Tabernacle and its priests symbolized something everlasting. Even prior to Christ's ministry, the God of the Israelites indicated that "foreigners" could be 'grafted' into the 'vine' of His chosen people: those who "love the name of the Lord," "want to be His servants," "observe the Sabbath," and remain "faithful to [His] covenant" (Isa 56:3-8).[181] Therefore, "no foreigner who becomes a follower of the Lord should say, 'The Lord will certainly exclude me from His people'" (Isa 56:3). This principle remains true today. Racial discrimination, which involves viewing one group as better or worse than others, should not exist

---

[181] Recall the story of Rahab, who was a non-ethnic Israelite and prostitute, became grafted into the Jewish heritage of the Messiah (Jos 2, 6; Matt 1:5; Heb 11:31; Jam 2:25).

for those destined for the shores of Eternity. In His Kingdom, there is no room for such discrimination; it welcomes everyone, regardless of their identity or origins.[182] In pursuit of this goal, Yahweh established His holy priesthood to act as His representatives, facilitating the Divine dwelling alongside humanity (Lev 26:11-13; Num 3:5-8, 18:6-7; Ps 134:1).

Yahweh addressed His first appointed priests, saying, "Does it seem too small a thing to you that the God of Israel has separated you from the community of Israel to bring you near to Himself, to perform the service of the Tabernacle of the Lord, and to stand before the community to minister to them?" (Num 16:9). Although Yahweh appointed the Old Covenant priesthood solely to the tribal descendants of Levi, He indicated He envisioned each Israelite serving as His priests in a spiritual capacity. At the onset of Israel's establishment, Yahweh expressed His desire for His chosen people to become a "kingdom of priests" (Exod 19:5-6). As a kingdom of priests, He willed for the entire nation to share in this promise, stating they would be as "numerous as the stars in the sky and the sands which are on the seashore" (Gen 22:17). Thus, all of God's chosen people, His "children," act as His "priests," a notion reinforced by the New Covenant (Gen 22:17; Jer 33:22; 1 Pet 2:4-9; Rev 5:10). The prophet Zechariah further affirmed this truth with the revelation of

Do you recognize your membership in the Kingdom of Priests?

Do you align your life with this ambition?

---

[182] While this is certainly true, we must not take this to mean that everyone will automatically be welcomed into Eternity at the end of all things. Though His kingdom is open to all, all must make the choice to accept His grace and walk according to His commands to truly experience His presence and live with eternal world-dwelling. Though the invitation is open to all regardless of identity or actions, not all will accept it or truly set aside their own lives in the temporal to live according to the eternal.

Jerusalem becoming "borderless": "Many nations will join themselves to the Lord on the day of salvation, and they will also be My people. Indeed, I will settle in the midst of you" (Zech 2).

From the outset, Yahweh intended for all humanity to serve as His eternal priesthood. This insight is vital, as certain misleading movements in Judaism and Christianity confine the "priestly caste" to an "elite" religious minority. This does not imply that we should not support an organizational hierarchy with distinct spiritual leaders or ministers, which aligns with biblical teachings. Rather, these misguided religious groups that defy the biblical mandate perceive 'priestly duties' as tasks exclusive to this minority, neglecting the broader ministries and gifts of the entire Body of Christ (Eph 4:11-12). They designate only a select few as "priests," tasked with ministering to the larger community. Adherents of these beliefs stand out against the true purpose of our High Priest by fostering a religious divide between "priests" and "non-priests" (ministers and non-ministers), opposing His mission to create a kingdom of priests. God summons us, His people, to undertake these responsibilities within our communities. As priests, our roles extend beyond merely illuminating God's presence and light to others.

Yahweh appointed His symbolic priests under the Old Covenant to guide others along the Way of Holiness. Their societal roles exemplified what all of God's people should embody, as God intended for them to evoke the calling of a kingdom of priests among all of Israel. They were tasked with "turning many people away from sin" and encouraging adherence to the Creator's instructions, while also addressing rebellion against Him (2 Chr 15:3, 26:16-17; Mal 2:5-7). In fulfilling these responsibilities, the earthly priests of Yahweh continued the legacy of Moses, caring for God's chosen people as members of "[Yahweh's] household" (Heb 3:2-7; Ps 99:6; Eph 2:12, 19). Likewise, Paul described his own "ministry of Christ Jesus to the Gentiles" as one "serving the gospel of God (under the New Covenant) by acting as a priest, so that they [might] become an acceptable offering, sanctified by the Holy Spirit" (Rom 15:15-16). The Scriptures indicate that all who faithfully adhere to His covenant will be recognized as "the Lord's priests, servants of God," through whom He "reveals His splendor" (Isa 61:1-7). Eternity calls us to "stand before the community to minister to them" as "co-workers with God," facilitating Infinite-finite communion (Num 16:9; 1 Cor 3:9). Thus, we, as heavenly priests, must also care for others by guiding them away from unholiness and toward holiness. We can invite people to fellowship and 'tabernacle' with us, discuss the Gospel with them, and attend to their holistic well-being by supporting them in alignment with God's vision.

Yahweh consecrates the devoted servants of His house to become suitable inhabitants of Zion. Scripture depicts this profound and collective transformation as follows:

> "All of your people will be godly; they will possess the land permanently. I will plant them like a shoot; they will be the product of My labor, through whom I reveal My splendor... [I will] strengthen those who mourn in Zion by giving them a turban, instead of ashes, oil symbolizing joy, instead of mourning, a garment symbolizing praise, instead of discouragement. They will be called oaks of righteousness, trees planted by the Lord to reveal His splendor. They will rebuild the perpetual ruins and restore the places that were desolate; they will reestablish the ruined cities, the places that have been desolate since ancient times."
>
> (Isa 60:21, 61:3-4)

[*How can you guide others from unholiness to holiness in your own life situations?*]

In this life, as God's household is restored in Zion, we hold the responsibility to engage in the Spirit's mission to restore people to the God-relationship and build up the Body of Christ into the Temple of the Creator (Eph 4:11-16; Rev 21:10). We act as gardeners tending to the "oaks of righteousness," builders reviving the "perpetual ruins," and cultivators of "desolate" areas.

Our Priestly Duty to Rebuild the Temple of Yahweh

Yahweh commissions all His priests to construct His temple. This edifying process starts within our inner selves. The Spirit's transformative work then reaches those around us, particularly our fellow members of the Body of Christ, who collectively embody "the dwelling place of God in the Spirit" (Eph 2:22). Our priestly handbook instructs us, stating, "just as each one has received a gift, [you should] use it to serve one another as good stewards of the varied grace of God" (1 Pet 4:10). "Now there are different gifts, but the same Spirit... To each person the manifestation of the Spirit is given for the benefit of all... wisdom... knowledge... faith... healing... miracles... prophecy... discernment of spirits... tongues... interpretation of tongues" (1 Cor 12:4-10). Every devoted follower of Christ receives this commission equally, irrespective of whether they are "called to ministry." Our guide refers to our management of these gifts with the term "*oikonomos*" [home-administrators] (Luke 24:49; Acts 2:38; 1 Cor 12; 1 Tim 4:14, 2 Tim 1:6; Heb 2:4; ISA). This word signifies "a house-distributor (i.e., manager), overseer, or governor"; "one entrusted with management concerning transcendent matters" as an "administrator of divine things" (ISA; BDAG, 698). Since this word

Are you passionate about the spiritual gifts from God that enable you to better strengthen, encourage, and comfort others?

includes the Greek term for law (*nomos*), it also suggests managing something according to proper house regulations (*oikonomia*).

Our Guide outlines how we are to manage Yahweh's temple in alignment with His standards of holiness, treating it with the same devotion as our own homes. After all, is His temple not our ultimate eternal residence? It should come as no surprise that Scripture describes our true nature as "living stones, [that] are built up (*oikodomeo*) as a spiritual house (*oikos*) to be a holy priesthood and to offer spiritual sacrifices that are acceptable to God through Jesus Christ" (1 Pet 2:5). Thus, engaging in priestly service is akin to constructing a house. This is foreshadowed by an Old Testament prophecy stating: "The man whose name is Branch (Jesus Christ)" "will build the temple of the Lord, and He will be clothed in splendor, sitting as King on His throne" (Isa 53:2; Jer 23:5; Zech 6:12-15; 1 Cor 15:28; 1 Pet 3:21-22; Heb 8:1-2).

Like the priests of the Old Covenant, who sought to present the Lord's "sanctuary" as "pure" and "sanctified," the priests of God's living temple, the Body of Christ, carry the "work of ministry," which involves strengthening the body of Christ (Exod 40:9; Ezek 45:18-19; Eph 4:12). God entrusts us with the task of presenting

What makes holiness or sanctification essential to our identity as living temples or the Bride of Christ?

Why would God accept nothing less from us?

the church as "glorious," "holy, and blameless," free from any "blemish" (Eph 5:27). Emulating Paul, who served as a heavenly priest, we should earnestly declare, "I am jealous for [those I minister to] with godly jealousy, because I promised [them] in marriage to one husband, to present [them] as a pure virgin to Christ" (Rom 15:16; 1 Cor 11:2). Just as the High Priest of the Old Covenant was allowed to marry only an undefiled virgin, we must also strive to present the Bride of Christ as cleansed from worldly impurities and rebellion (Lev 21:12-13; 2 Pet 1:4; Jas 1:27). Our ministry to the Body of Christ aims to help our brothers and sisters truly live as "a holy temple in the Lord," sanctified by the Holy Spirit (Rom 15:16; Eph 2:21).

Our priestly ministry to the Body of Christ is twofold. Firstly, it encompasses the "ministry of reconciliation," which aims to reconstruct the Temple of God by offering and preparing new living stones for His Temple (2 Cor 5:18-21; 1 Pet 2:4-5). We collaborate with the Spirit to guide those in existential rebellion back to their true heavenly purpose (1 Cor 3:10; 2 Cor 5:18-21; 1 Pet 2:4-5; Mark 16:20; Heb 6:4). Secondly, our priestly service to the Body of Christ entails acting as "priests who present acceptable offerings." Unlike Old Covenant priests who offered animal sacrifices, we are called to foster the "sanctification" of the Holy Spirit in the lives of other "living stones" (Rom 15:15; 1 Pet 2:5). In essence, these transformed lives, made holy through the Spirit's work in us, become the offerings we present to God. Everyone we extend God's love to, each colleague we support with God-inspired kindness, and every friend we forgive for their wrongs are opportunities for the Spirit to work in their lives. In this way, we become "living sacrifices" (Rom 12:1). Every time we help someone reconcile with our Creator, we contribute new living stones to the "construction site" of His temple.

Throughout Scripture, the Holy Spirit calls us to work alongside Christ in transforming living stones into God's spiritual house, "building ourselves up in our most holy faith" (Rom 14:19, 15:2; 1 Thess 5:11; 1 Pet 2:4-5; Jude 1:20-21). Likewise, the priests of the physical temple were tasked with both "repairing any damage to the temple" and managing the "[re-]building the temple of the Lord" (2 Kings 12:5; Ezra 1:5, 3:8-13, 5:11). Christ commissions every faithful priest of Yahweh to develop His Body as a living temple of God (Eph 4:12-16). To achieve this, each of us has been granted a spiritual gift to aid in "building up the Church." As "each one [priest/living stone] does its part, the body grows in love" (1 Cor 12:7, 14:26; Eph 4:16; 1 Pet 4:10). No wonder we read the following in Scripture addressed to the priests of the New Covenant:

> "We are coworkers with God. [The Body of Christ is] God's field, God's building. According to the grace of God given to [us], like a skilled master-builder [we are to] lay a foundation, [even if] someone else builds on it. And each one [of us] must be careful how [we] build. No one can lay any foundation other than what is being laid, which is Jesus Christ… Each builder's work will be plainly seen, for the Day will make it clear, because it will be revealed by fire. And the fire will test what kind of work each has done."
>
> (1 Cor 3:9-13)

Therefore, all devoted priests of the New Covenant, as members of the Body of Christ, should commit to faithfully build up God's living temple (Eph 2:19-22).

Unlike how the Christian religion is practiced in most religious contexts, the true plan of Christ, the Head of the Body, is to assign each member to engage in the "work of ministry," with everyone receiving a unique "stewardship from God" (Col 1:25; Eph 4:12). We are all fellow "servants of the church," called by God to ensure the church makes progress in "achieving the unity of faith and the knowledge of the Son of God – a mature individual, reflecting the fullness of Christ's stature" (Eph 4:12-13). Instead of just a few church members functioning as priests,

> *In what ways can you act as "priests and ministers" within the Body of Christ, even if you are not specifically "appointed" to serve in a "church"?*

God invites all of us to serve as priests and ministers within the Body of Christ (1 Pet 2:4-5; Rev 5:10). Supporting this transformative perspective, Scripture states: "It was [Christ] who gave some as apostles, some as prophets, some as evangelists, and some as pastors and teachers (but the passage does not stop there), *to equip* the saints for the work of ministry," emphasizing that "as each one does its part, the body grows in love" (Eph 4:11-12, 16; 1 Pet 2:4-12).

Every member of the Body of Christ plays a vital role in the ministry of building up a community of believers and in managing the gifts they are given (Romans 12:4-8; 1 Cor 12:1-31). "Just as each one has received a gift, use it to serve one another as good stewards (*oikonomos*) of the varied grace" (1 Pet 4:10; Eph 3:2). This responsibility is instituted by God, empowered by the Spirit, and is essential within the faith community, as our Master will require each individual to account for how they utilize their gifts (John 5:22; Rom 14:12; 1 Cor 3:13-15; Col 3:24). "For we must all appear before the judgment seat of Christ, so that each one may be paid back according to what [one] has done while in the body," thus "each one must be careful how he [or she] build" (1 Cor 3:10; 2 Cor 5:10).

"One should think about [our calling] this way – as servants of Christ and stewards (*oikonomos*) of the mysteries. Now what is sought in stewards (*oikonomos*) is that one be found faithful" (1 Cor 4:1-2). Our Guide explains that the faithful will be rewarded in His Kingdom, receiving a part in Christ's inheritance as ruling figures within the household of Finitude (Col 3:24; Eph 6:8; 1 Cor 4:5; Matt 16:27; Rev 22:12). The most outstanding individuals in the Kingdom of God will be those with child-like faith and the humility of servants, as they will have become similar to Christ: the servant of all (Matt 18:1-5, 23:11-12; Luke 9:48, 22:24-27).

Scripture recognizes the necessity of leadership in the corporate ministry of the Body of Christ, even as we are *all* called to be priests and ministers. For example, it mentions the "apostles, prophets, evangelists, pastors (shepherds), and teachers" whom Christ has appointed to "equip (all) the saints for the work of ministry" (1 Cor 12:28-30; Eph 4:11-12). These individuals are described in the Scriptures as "master builders (*architekton*)" and "overseers" (Acts 20:18; 1 Cor 3:10; 1 Tim 3:1; Phil 1:1). Paul claims, under the guidance of the Spirit, "according to the grace of God given to me, like a skilled master-builder I laid a foundation, but someone else builds on it [*epoikodomeo*]" (1 Cor 3:10). These passages make it evident that our efforts in "building-up" must rely solely on the life and work of Christ Jesus (1 Cor 3:11). While some are designated as leaders in this world, Christ remains the only true head of the Body, over against human appointed religious "heads."

To fulfill our part of the new covenant of sanctification, we must actively participate in the collective building up of *agape*-love. By responding to this call, we discover our true identities as builders within God's house. Accepting our God-given roles, influenced by the first commandment, naturally guides us in how we carry out the second greatest commandment: "to love our neighbor as ourselves" (Lev 19:18; Matt 22:39). In doing so, we recognize that this commandment requires us to create a sanctified space for our neighbors in Eternity. Just as we seek our rightful places in God's household, we should wish for them to attain their rightful positions as well. As priests of Yahweh, our primary responsibility towards creation lies with our

> *How do you personally respond to the call of home-building?*
>
> *What responsibility do you feel you have as a steward of God's household?*

fellow human beings, "for all the law and the prophets depend on these two commandments" (Matt 22:40).

In this fellowship, we coexist as supportive members of God's family. Our interactions are influenced by a common dedication to our relationship with God and our priestly responsibilities. It is no wonder that Scripture encourages God's true children to act as ministers of His revelations and to embody His presence by building His temple both internally and externally (2 Cor 5:18; Eph 4:12). Did Christ Jesus not commission all His true disciples to represent Him (2 Cor 5:20)? Does He not call each sincere disciple to carry out His great commission (Matt 28:18-20)?

The path of existential theocentricity emphasizes the importance of cultivating the City of God alongside – not in place of – the City of Man. This spiritual communion, suited for the household of Eternity, can be illustrated as a reciprocal act of "self-emptying" toward one another, typical of the fellowship rooted in agape love. It transcends ordinary brotherly love, or phileo, found in family or organizations. It calls us to genuinely sacrifice ourselves for one another, which Scripture lauds as the highest form of love (John 15:13). This orientation directs our lives and essence towards God and others, aligning with Christ's fundamental commandment (Mark 12:30-31).

While it is easy to articulate, living it out may pose challenges. Yet, this is our calling as the Body of Christ. When our communal fellowship lacks the brilliance of *agape*-love, we risk becoming atheistic and self-centered in our interactions (Jude 1:19). In such cases, human experiences of fellowship and perspective no longer reflect the revealing presence of agape love and phos-light shaped by the Creator's unveiled countenance. Instead, these communities devolve into being "earthly, natural, and demonic," as they are ultimately anchored in "selfishness" and human pride (Jas 3:14-16). This aligns with the agenda of the Evil One, who seeks to undermine God's eternal household in favor of the fleeting household of existential defiance. Therefore, we must consistently cleanse ourselves of the worldly influences of temporary human existence, devoid of the Divine essence essential for authentic spirit-to-Spirit fellowship.

We must be cautious to avoid arrogance or assumptions. Just because we can function as a house of God does not guarantee we will always be a home for Him. Our temples can become inadequate channels for the divine if we are not vigilant and mindful. In a house, a family may allow worldly distractions to weaken their mutual communion. For example, imagine a household where members are absorbed in their personal "worlds": the father watches sports, the mother gossips with friends, and the children are engrossed in video games or scrolling through TikTok all day. Such distractions prevent them from becoming a true family, as they do not partake in acts of shared communion. Spending time alone is not inherently bad, but when a family neglects to connect with one another, they risk becoming little more than roommates. The husband may conceal his fears about unemployment, the wife may suffer from emotional loneliness, and the children might not reveal their experiences with bullying or ostracism at school. Where a family could offer support and encouragement, allowing them to confront life's challenges together, the family in this scenario is forced to face these issues alone, potentially fostering resentment. Even worse, they might substitute ignorance of each other's problems with indifference or disdain. How many families do we know that unintentionally discourage or belittle one another? For a house to transform into a home, there must be fellowship, transparency, and even repentance.

To reject the call to serve one another is to reject the call of Eternity itself. It denies our eternal identity and purpose. In making this choice, we turn our backs on the "attitude" of "Christ," instead immersing ourselves in self-serving worldly pursuits (Rom 2:7-8; Phil 2:3-4). Likewise, to abandon or claim only a few should serve in this priestly ministry to humanity is to denounce the rightful decree of the Sovereign over the inhabitants of Zion. It signifies a departure from the enriching fellowship with our Heavenly Father and His family (1 John 1:2-4).

Agape-Love Enables Us to Build-Up God's Household

Scripture uses the term "up-building" (*oikodome*) to refer to the Body of Christ in the following passages: "You are God's field, God's building (*oikodome*);" "In Him the whole building (*oikodome*), being joined together, grows into a holy temple in the Lord" (1 Cor 3:9; Eph 2:21). We go on to read: "in [Christ] you also are being built together [joint home-building] (*sunoikodomeo*)[183] into a dwelling place (*katoiketerion*)[184] of God in the Spirit" (Eph 2:22). In this context, we recognize that our genuine home is the Temple of God, where His Spirit resides. This temple is established through the rightful actions of the priests of the New Covenant, the children of God. United by the Spirit's power, we *all* contribute to constructing our true home (Eph 2:21, 3:7, 3:16, 3:20, 6:10).

The "foundation" and "cornerstone" of our true home is, of course, "Christ" (1 Cor 3:11; Eph 2:20-21; Col 2:6-7; 1 Pet 2:6-7).

---

[183] This Greek word is formed by the combination of "*oikodomeo*" (home-building) and "*sun*" (with or together) (ISA). It can be understood as implying the activity of "building together with; to build up or construct of various parts, of the various parts of a stricture, from which the latter is built up (together)" (BDAG, 974).

[184] This Greek word is a noun form of the verb "katoikeo" which refers to a verb meaning "to house permanently, i.e. reside;" "to live in a locality for any length of time, live, dwell, reside, settle down; to make something a habitation or dwelling by being there, inhabit" (ISA; BDAG, 534). The noun derived from this verb is formed by a construction indicating "place where something happens," and so this noun refers to a "dwelling-place" (BDAG, 534-535).

Only through Him are we able to "access" the home-building power of the "Spirit," who "pours out" "the love of God" "in our hearts" (Rom 5:5; 1 Cor 8:1; 2 Cor 5:18-21; Eph 2:14-18, 3:11 Heb 10:19-21). Similar to how the priests of the Old Covenant required animal blood for sanctification to serve in the earthly temple, the priests of the New Covenant must be sanctified by Christ's blood (life force) to serve in the eternal temple in heaven (Exod 19:22, 40:15; Num 19:7, 13; 2 Chr 23:5-6, 29:5; Heb 9:23-24, 12:24).

> *In what ways have others supported or encouraged you in your journey of faith?*
>
> *How have you, in turn, uplifted others?*

We truly discover ourselves when we allow the Spirit of our Creator to work through us, helping to build ourselves, each other, and all of Finitude into His tabernacle. The term used for "building-up" is *"oikodomei,"* which literally means "home-building" but also carries the figurative sense of "edifying" (ISA). This term encapsulates the essential role of a "housebuilder" or "homebuilder" in serving the world (*oikodomeo*). We construct figurative buildings as places of dwelling. This spiritual act of housebuilding can be described as: "to construct in a transcendent sense; [such as] to help improve the ability to function in living responsibly and effectively, strengthen, build up, make more able" (BDAG, 696).

Scripture refers to the church as the Temple and House of God through the term: *oikodome* (Eph 2:21-22). Literally, this Greek term means "a structure resulting from a construction process, edifice" (BDAG, 696-697). However, in Scripture, it often pertains to fostering sanctification among believers through acts of *agape*-love (Rom 14:19, 15:2; 1 Cor 3:10, 14:3, 14:26; Eph 4:12, 29; 1 Thess 3:2; Jude 1:20). For instance, we are instructed to "encourage one another and build up (*oikodomeo*) each other" (1 Thess 5:11). Our mission: to build up souls into the abode of God's self-disclosing nature. Paul tells the Corinthians, "everything we do, dear friends, is to build you up" (2 Cor 12:19).

Just as a temple requires numerous columns and pillars, we too are "members who belong to one another," sharing "mutual concern for one another," as each of us acts as a pillar in the Temple of the Triune I AM (Rom 7:4, 12:5; 1 Cor 12:25). We should embrace the belief that "Your home is my home, is it not?" Consequently, we are called to "live in harmony with one another, "demonstrating devotion through mutual love and showing eagerness in honoring each other" (Rom 12:10, 16). The dedicated commitment of this community of loving individuals should be service in God's household (Gal 6:10; Heb 3:5), equipping each other with the enlightening revelation of Yahweh, serving as fellow priests in His temple (Eph 1:17, 4:12-13).

These acts of edification ideally identify God's priests. Jesus said that people would know them by their "fruits" (Matt 7:20). These individuals facilitate divine encounters. We express God's will and vision, uplift others, illuminate His ways and truths, empower each other, and share the peace and joy of our Creator with the world. From evangelists who inspire thousands to respond to God's call, to the simple, divinely inspired acts of kindness we extend to those we encounter, God invites us all to connect Heaven and earth in all the various contexts we inhabit.

God designed us for a deep God-relationship, to be collaborators (John 14:23; 2 Pet 1:4; 1 John 4:16). The Son, who expresses the full essence of Divinity, shares God's intention for this in His prayer:

> "Father, I want those You have given Me to be with Me where I am, so that they can see My glory that You gave Me because You loved Me before the creation of the world... I made known Your name

to them, and I will continue to make it known, so that the love You have loved Me with may be in them, and I may be in them."

(John 17:24-26)

Through our connection with Yahweh, the contextualities of His *oikonomia* in Infinity is fulfilled in us as beings created in His image (Col 3:10; 1 John 2:5-6, 4:12, 4:16-17). This occurs as we commune with the Father through the Son and by the Spirit.

Scripture outlines our duty to minister to one another as part of the household of God:

> "We know that we have crossed over from death to [eternal] life because we love our fellow Christians... We have come to know love by this: that Jesus laid down His life for us; thus, we ought to lay down our lives for our fellow Christians. But whoever has the world's possessions and sees his fellow Christian in need and shuts off his compassion against him [or her], how can the love of God reside in such a person? Little children, let us *not* love with word or with tongue but in deed and truth."

(1 John 3:14-18)

Manifesting the Divine likeness requires us to express His *agape*-love and triune nature within our limited contexts to enhance fellowship. For example, the greatest expressions of divinely inspired *agape*-love emerge through our stewardship of God's diverse grace in the shape of spiritual gifts (1 Pet 4:10). We each receive these spiritual gifts through God's supernatural manifestations in the Spirit, which are given for everyone's benefit (1 Cor 12:7; 1 Pet 4:10). Therefore, if we truly wish to pursue love, we should be eager for spiritual gifts, especially prophecy, as they build up, encourage, and console others (1 Cor 14:1, 3). The giving of spiritual gifts signifies a true household of Yahweh, whose greatest gift to us is Himself. As our Guide calls Him, the "Father of lights from whom every perfect gift comes" (Jas 1:17).

According to Scripture, *agape*-love is essentially characterized by the activity of *oikodomeo* (up-building/ home-building) (1 Cor 8:1).[185] Yahweh designed us to facilitate the effective functioning of creation and to support one another in living responsibly according to His set household guidelines. He intended for us to be the stones and pillars upholding Creation as His sanctuary (1 Pet 2:4-5; Rev 3:12). Therefore, a central part of cultivating *agape*-love in this life is to uplift and appropriately position other pillars within the Body of Christ (Eph 2:19-22, 4:12-16; Col 2:19).

It is essential that we lovingly and thought*fully* help one another become a "dwelling place of God in the Spirit," as we pursue our shared goal of mutual benefit, being "members who belong to one another" (Rom 12:5; 1 Cor 3:10, 14:26; Eph 2:22, 4:12; 1 Thess 5:11). The more we support each other in recognizing our collective destiny, the deeper our understanding becomes of our true Home. This perspective shifts the understanding of transcendence from merely abandoning everything for peace or enlightenment to a journey that is not meant to be solitary.

{ *Do you encourage the sanctification of others who share life with you?* }

While we are indeed called to leave certain aspects of our lives (and perhaps some individuals), we journey together, interweaving our paths with those of others on this journey. In this journey, God invites us to emulate Ezra, Nehemiah, and others who "restored the temple of our God and raised up its ruins" (Ezra 1:5, 9:9).

---

[185] Recall that *oikodomeo* can be better understood by the following definition: "to construct a building, to construct in a transcendent sense, to help improve ability to function in living responsibly and effectively, build up, make more able" (BDAG, 696).

However, unlike them, we are tasked with building the true heavenly temple of God, made possible through Christ.

As living stones, we must come together as walls to sustain the growth of God's reign. With His agape-love, we act as conduits for His providence, serving as messengers of the Divine presence. Every member is not just an heir to God's heavenly dwelling but also a living stone that contributes to this divine residence. If you remove even the smallest stones from a grand cathedral, the structure weakens. Just as each stone and pillar supports one another, so do we in our spiritual journeys. Furthermore, loving one another reflects the nature, and indeed the essence, of our Creator. If the Trinity is essentially one being made up of three persons engaged in an eternal dance of self-giving and *agape* love, then by genuinely loving and being loved, we reflect that ultimate divine reality at the heart of all existence. Thus, by encouraging and experiencing each other's sanctification, we receive glimpses of our heavenly homeland.

Our Duty as Priests to Prepare a Heavenly Bride

Our divine mission as priests of the God-relationship involves nurturing our spiritual fulfillment and supporting the foundational pillars of the Eternal Temple. We are called to wholeheartedly and singularly assist others in entering the Holy of Holies within their deepest selves. This journey begins with effectively managing our body and soul under the Spirit's sanctifying influence. The Spirit guides us in collaborating with Him to prepare ourselves and others for the "wedding day" that will arrive at the end of temporality (Rev 19:7-9). This sacred wedding symbolizes the establishment of a renewed household beyond temporal existence, based on unwavering loyalty to the eternal covenant of the God-relationship.

The "bride" of Christ prepares for the significant event of the "wedding feast" by routinely going "deeper" into the Holy of Holies each day to become a "bride made ready." This process

{ *Are you becoming a "bride made ready"?* } aligns us with the Divine's plan to designate humanity as His eternal sanctuary. To achieve this, we must "[embrace] humility" by "working out our salvation with awe and reverence, for the one bringing forth in us both the desire and the effort – for the sake of His good pleasure – is God" (Phil 2:3, 12-13). Therefore, our journey is a commitment to yield ourselves the Spirit, growing each day as priestly members of the Triune I AM's household.

As priests, we are devoted by duty and love to support each other's journey as children of God by offering "what is beneficial for building up" (Rom 14:19; Eph 4:29). Christ invites us to emulate Paul in nurturing spiritual children through discipleship. Like him, we should be able to affirm, "My children – I am again experiencing birth pains until Christ is formed in you" (Matt 28:18-20; Gal 4:19)! In line with the figurative analogy in Scripture, we should see ourselves as "spiritual midwives." Through us, the Spirit nurtures individuals into their authentic priestly identity within the eternal Narrative of Finitude. Thus, we must encourage each other to continue our pilgrimage homeward and assist one another in becoming and remaining distinct from the worldly ways of Babylon (Heb 3:13).

Additionally, we should serve as opportunities for one another to get a taste of our eternal "home." Through our acts as fellow priests and the impact of our collective actions on the world, we witness brief reflections of Heaven's realities in this fallen world. These experiences should occur whenever we gather in genuine spiritual fellowship and fully live as God intends for the Body of Christ (Phil 2:1-2).

"What should you do then, brothers and sisters? When you come together, each one has a song, has a lesson, has a revelation, has a tongue, has an interpretation. Let *all* these things be done for the strengthening of the church... You can *all* prophesy one after another, so *all* can learn and be encouraged."

(1 Cor 14:26, 31)

Unlike a humanistic model of religion rooted in only "ordaining" an "elite" few, every genuine church member holds a priestly vocation to strengthen the Temple of God. The collective unity of the Body of Christ enables us to all collaborate together through the Spirit to enhance God's Temple; "as each does its part, the Body grows" (Eph 4:12-16). Just as in Jesus' day, God's egalitarian model offends and disturbs the natural human order of comparison, partiality, and preferentialism. We prepare Christ's "Bride" for her presentation before Him beyond this earthly existence. In this anticipated wedding, we will ultimately reach our true eternal home, assured that we will fulfill our priestly duty forever and ever (2 Cor 11:2; Eph 5:26-27).

What does it feel like to be involved in such a significant calling with the Body of Christ?

Does it motivate you to explore the Holy of Holies every day, gather in genuine spiritual communion, and prophesy?

Building up involves working in selfless love together, mirroring how our King has served us with a humble, self-emptying love (Phil 2:3-8). Jesus washing the feet of His disciples exemplified this *agape* principle among believers (John 13:14-16). We cannot separate the promotion of others' eternal interests from the Spirit's sanctifying work to prepare God's Bride for the wedding feast (Rev 19:9, 22:17). "Let us rejoice and exult and give Him glory, because the wedding celebration of the Lamb has come, and His bride has made herself ready. She was permitted to be dressed in bright, clean, fine linen (for the fine linen is the righteous deeds of the saints)" (Rev 19:7-8). Our Creator desires for everyone He has made in His image to take part in this wedding feast. This feast marks the beginning of the city of God-relationship, the realm of the everlasting Sabbath, and the united home of perpetual lovers of God. In preparation for this, our Lord invites us, just as He did Peter, to love Him by helping others become faithful lovers of Him (John 21:15-17).

By answering the Call of Eternity, we embrace the Spirit's grace and become devoted friends of the Bridegroom. We should take inspiration from John the Baptist, declaring and embodying this truth: "The one who has the bride is the bridegroom. The friend of the bridegroom, who stands by and listens for Him, rejoices greatly when he hears the bridegroom's voice. This, then, is my joy, and it is complete. He must become more important while I become less important" (John 3:29-30). Like Paul, we ought to possess a "godly jealousy" to present "a pure virgin to Christ" (2 Cor 11:2). What are the consequences of refusing the universal call to prepare the bride? Doing so signifies a rejection of our existential duty as priests of God. Those who defy the Creator's household mandate in this manner operate as enemies against the covenant of God's household and as defilers of His temple. Homewreckers hold no place in the eternal abode of the God-relationship. They inadvertently act alongside the home destroyer (Satan), further distancing humanity from the principles of the God relationship.

Those of us who have embarked on this journey of revelation must firmly embrace the truth that genuine self-actualization can only occur in the Holy of Holies. Truly, as inhabitants of this world, we can only discover our true selves by "giving ourselves away" to bring joy to our Creator. Does this mindset not befit a genuine marriage-like relationship? As disciples of Jesus, we emulate His life by serving Him, following His will, and nurturing His flock; "no longer [living] for [ourselves]" but "[living or dying] for the Lord" (John 8:31-32, 12:26; Rom 14:7-9; 2 Cor 5:15; 1 Pet 4:1-2). His concerns become our own. His interests align with ours. His passions resonate within us. By imitating Christ and embodying Him, our lives reflect the manifestation of the Father's Word and Breath, as we strive to draw all humanity into a relationship with God (Rom 13:14; 1 Cor 15:49; Gal 2:20). We collaborate with the pioneer of home restoration, thus transforming the world to align with the contextual framework of the heavenly *oikonomia*.

Those who willingly engage in this sacred mission are invested in the Maker's vision for Creation. We emulate conductors striving to manifest the creative vision of a composer or a theater director, bringing to life the script of a distinguished playwright. Jesus' parables show that only vigilant and devoted stewards in the Maker's domain will receive an eternal inheritance within Finitude, as our renewed and completely restored home (Matt 24:45-47, 25:21-23; Mark 13:32-37; Luke 12:35-48). Ultimately, the Bridegroom returns solely for an equally yoked "bride" who has prepared herself by dedicating herself, through the Spirit's strength, to the *agape* work of edification (Matt 25:1-13; 2 Cor 11:2-3; Eph 5:25-27; Rev 19:7-8). All genuine acts of love committed to Christ involve this edification. Constructing the true temple of Yahweh is a matter of great importance to Jesus, as it involves restoring His Father's household. For this purpose, we

> *Are you prepared to be a bride for Christ who is equally yoked?*
>
> *Are you ready to dedicate yourself to bringing joy to your Creator, as your First Love?*

must follow His example of "zeal for [God's] house" by purifying the true "house of God" to transform it into a true "house of prayer" (John 2:14-17; Matt 21:12-13).

How do we know that the Body of Christ represents the New Jerusalem? Scripture clearly tells us: "Come, I will show you the bride, the wife of the Lamb! So, he took me away in the Spirit to a huge, majestic mountain and showed me the holy city, Jerusalem, descending out of heaven from God" (Rev 20:10). Just as a bride must prepare before her wedding day, the inauguration of Zion necessitates preparing the bride to become the eternal temple of the Creator. How is this preparation achieved? It occurs on earth through the righteous (making-right) acts of the saints, all energized by the Spirit (2 Cor 11:2; Rev 21:2). Figuratively, this process resembles putting on garments of righteousness that have been cleansed (Rev 19:8). When Israel spiritually rebelled against the Mosaic Covenant, the physical Jerusalem faced destruction, symbolizing humanity's spiritual rebellion against God through Adam, which led to the desolation of the original, heavenly Jerusalem (Hos 6:7). We strive to follow in Christ's footsteps, aiming to restore to God what was contextually lost during the Fall of Creation (Gen 3).

> *Reflect deeply on your life. Is there any effort required or something you still need to surrender to Him for God's love to be fulfilled in you?*

Christ charges all His followers to become disciple-makers in pursuit of this significant goal. Recall His final words before ascending to Heaven: "Therefore go and make disciples of all nations, baptizing them in the name of the Father and the Son and the Holy Spirit, teaching them to obey everything I have commanded you. And remember, I am with you always, to the end of the age" (Matt 28:19-20). The act of baptism cleanses others through the sanctifying power of the Spirit, gradually preparing the Bride of our Creator for Him. Therefore, those who wish to be the

Creator's Bride must separate from their worldly 'parents' of Babylon and become suitable members of House Zion. We must willingly engage in Christ's mission to restore God's wayward children to their divine calling within the family of God. Only then can the Heavenly Bride and Groom establish their new household together after the wedding feast (Eph 5:32; Rev 19:7-9, 21:2-3, 9-10).

By the Spirit, we need to sacrifice our lives to serve God willingly, focusing on His will rather than on earthly desires: "as we spend the rest of [our] time on earth concerned about the will of God and not human desires" (1 Pet 4:2-3). We can co-manage God's house through this strong commitment to Christian integrity. We should emulate Mary of Bethany, prioritizing making our dwelling pleasing to Him over what may appear more 'practical' (John 12:1-8). These individuals move away from selfish, self-serving pursuits. Rather, they foster "joy," "comfort," and "love" within His household by strengthening the "fellowship in the Spirit" (Phil 2:1-2).

Such fellowship characterizes the members of Yahweh's household as those who share "the same mind, by having the same agape-love, [being] united in spirit, and [having] one purpose" (Phil 2:1-2). To achieve this, we must be "motivated to consider one another as more significant than ourselves" so that "each of us" acts as "concerned not only about our interests but also about the interests of others" (Phil 2:3-4, 18; 1 John 4:15-17). We commit ourselves to completing the love of God in and through us, enabling others to be "glad and rejoice together" with us in our fellowship with our First Love (Phil 2:3-4, 18; 1 John 4:15-17; Rev 2:4). By doing this, we will each and collectively be "blameless and pure, children of God without blemish," shining as lights in "perverse societies" (Phil 2:15). Therefore, if we wish to be "dressed in bright, clean, fine linen," we must dedicate ourselves to performing "the righteous deeds of the saints" as faithful homemakers of Zion (Rev 19:7-8).

Defying the Home-Destroying Work of God's Enemies

The cultivation of *agape*-love and *phos*-light fosters God's presence within creation. Consequently, our conduct as His children should reflect acts of *agape*-love, driven by spiritual fellowship. This divine-like behavior aligns with the guidelines of our true home. By engaging in such acts, our finite existence mirrors the transcendent triune nature of God (1 John 4:8, 16). As we contribute to home-building, stemming from our connection with the Divine, we experience glimpses of our eternal homeland. This entails promoting His reign within creation and overcoming the anti-*agape* spiritual darkness of Babylon (Rev 18).

The Son of God became the Christ to dismantle the home-wrecking effects of existential rebellion (1 John 3:8, 14-16). When we embrace Christ, we become a place where Heaven's power counteracts Babylon's influence. Thus, similar to the builders of the second temple during Ezra's time, we must continually construct the Temple of God by gathering new living stones, positioning them, and refining them with the sanctifying tools of the Spirit's fire of *agape*-love. Simultaneously, we must wield the fiery sword of the Spirit to protect the temple from spiritual adversaries and repel the enemy's destructive spiritual influence (Neh 4:16-18; Eph 6:10-18).

> *Are you ready to wield the sword of the Spirit to fight against the world-enslaving agendas and the schemes of spiritual home-destroyers?*
>
> *How can you incorporate spiritual warfare into your life?*

Yahweh uses His people to restore His house and overcome the world-rulers of home-destruction. In this life, we engage in a battle against the "schemes of the devil [the home-destroyer]," as we "struggle" "against the rulers, against the powers, against the world-rulers of this darkness, against the spiritual forces of evil in the heavens" (Eph 6:11-12). These dark forces enact Satan's "schemes" to ignite a rebellion on earth, aiming to deprive us of our eternal identity. The Enemy understands that if we embrace this identity, we can wield the "sword of the Spirit," posing a serious threat to his enslaving agendas (Eph 6:17). Ultimately, our true selves draw strength from a divine power that surpasses all dark forces, for in Him we "have conquered [and are conquering] the Evil One" (Eph 3:16; 1 Pet 3:22; 1 John 2:13-14, 4:4).

As co-heirs with Christ, who rebuilds God's house, we face no obstacles to advancing God's heavenly kingdom that the power and authority of God cannot overcome (Rom 8:17; Eph 1:20-23). Even so, the Enemy seeks to undermine our commitment to Christ's priestly agenda. He cunningly aims to bind humanity to the pursuits of his temporary kingdom, making us worship created things. We must resist joining his rebellion. Instead, we should confront these temptations daily by declaring, "Go away, Satan! For it is written: 'You are to worship the Lord your God and serve only Him'" (Matt 4:10). "So [in proactively] submitting to God. [We] resist the devil and he flees from [us], [as we] draw near to God and He draws near to [us]," because we have consecrated ourselves to Yahweh's sanctifying influence that "cleanses [our] hands" and "makes [our] hearts pure" to build-up the household of *agape*-love (Jas 4:7-8).

Jesus advanced His kingdom during His time on earth often by casting our demons. Even now, through His Body, He continues to strengthen His Kingdom, overcoming rebellious systems that stand against the Creator's will. When He "cast[ed] out demons by the Spirit of God," Jesus demonstrated that, by the Spirit's power, the enemy can and will be vanquished (Matt 12:28). As "the kingdom of God" advances through the lives of His followers, it outpaces the spiritual adversaries that attempt to undermine the eternal purpose of humanity (Matt 12:28; Luke 1:68-75, 10:17-19). In this broken world, we exist in enemy territory, the land of those who reject the Divine because they follow false gods that challenge His will and vision. We must choose our allegiance wisely, aligning with the City of Light rather than the City of Darkness. If we choose the City of Light, we must act as representatives and advocates of the "light" of eternal truths. Therefore, let us "not participate in the unfruitful deeds of darkness, but rather expose them" (Eph 5:11).

Nevertheless, we must remember that in this conflict, our tools are spiritual rather than physical (2 Cor 10:4). As servants of God, our foremost weapon is the *agape*-love and *phos*-light of Christ, which triumphs over all adversaries threatening to deconstruct God's Temple. However, God does not wish for us to inflict harm, kill, or conquer in His name, as was often done in medieval times and continues with false religions today, which shed the blood of "unbelievers." Instead, we wield "weapons" that are "made powerful by God for tearing down [the] strongholds" of the enemy opposing the restoration of God's living temple (2 Cor 10:4). These weapons are spiritual and target the forces of darkness, not the individuals trapped by them, whom we aim to save rather than destroy.

> *When last did you proactively wield spiritual "weapons made powerful by God?*

We believe this is our Creator's world and serving as His priests should not be viewed solely as a personal religious pursuit. After all, does not Yahweh instruct all His followers to advance His will and Kingdom on earth just as it is in Heaven (Matt 6:10)? In the current state of existential rebellion, our priestly mission involves engaging in and fostering His *oikonomia* while spiritually resisting the prevailing systems that aim to tear down the home of God

(Eph 6:11-12). We must confront the spiritual forces that threaten to destroy, dismantle, and corrupt God's household with righteous indignation. In this manner, we become reflections of Christ's zeal for God's house and His wrath against all that tarnishes it (Mark 11:15-17; John 2:14-17). The enemies of God's house approach like "thieves" who come "only to steal and kill and destroy," reminiscent of the king of Babylon's actions against the Old Covenant temple (John 10:10; Jer 50:28, 51:11-13). Only those who fulfill their roles as warrior priests, dedicated to building and safeguarding God's household, will pass through Heaven's gates to dwell in the Creator's realm. Only those who are fully committed to preserving His temple will enjoy it for eternity. Ultimately, He will return to bring home those who willingly served as His royal priests and, through acts of *agape*-love, advanced the kingdom of His Temple (Rev 3:21, 5:10, 22:5).

> *Does your fellowship with believers focus on mutually building each other up in your relationship with God?*
>
> *If not, can this be considered a genuine spiritual fellowship?*

Our Unique Destinies as Members of the Body of Christ

Aligning ourselves existentially with our Creator's *koinonia* (His fellowship) allows the priests of Yahweh to engage in spiritually united gatherings. This facilitates the development of a holy temple in the Lord, as noted in the scriptures: "the whole building, being joined together, grows into a holy temple in the Lord" (1 Cor 14:26; Eph 2:21). Through authentic spiritual fellowship, we discover our identities and meaningful roles as unique components of the collective identity of the Body of Christ (1 Cor 12). In this way, we cultivate an eternally significant community and a profound sense of belonging that encompasses our entire being (body, soul, and spirit) in true and full existential authenticity. We become essential members of a community linked by the Spirit's indwelling presence, enabling each of us "as living stones, to be built up as a spiritual house" (1 Pet 2:5).

At this stage, we should remember that we envision a theocentric community. This is different from human-centric groups, even religious ones, focused on human perspectives, agendas, will, and desires. As Scripture points out, every member is a unique and vital individual, unified by their relationship with God (1 Cor 12). Therefore, we should not have to give up our identity or stories for the collective good by blending into a faceless crowd. Reducing ourselves to mere "idle pew-sitting audience members" without engaging our individual spiritual gifts contradicts Jesus Christ's mission to cultivate a nation of priests. A temple community requires each person to become a distinct living pillar within God's heavenly dwelling. Through our personal relationships with the Creator and authentic worship, the Spirit shapes us into a robust temple, allowing the world to witness and experience the Creator's presence and His vision for Finitude.

A spiritual community can only emerge through a joint yet deep, personal relationship with God. Our hearts must be united in love through our shared commitment to promoting the vision and mission of our First Love for His sacred dwelling place (Col 2:2). Ultimately, we must remember that, contrary to what often occurs in human-centered religious settings, we all can serve as priests to Yahweh, our Creator—not to a minister, evangelist, or even an apostle. His Spirit and Word empower us to act as the hands and feet of Divinity, not of humanity. Except for Jesus Christ, no human has the authority to serve as the faithful High Priest of the eternal priesthood. Anyone attempting to take on this role dishonors both Christ and the Holy Spirit. Only through His Spirit and Word does Yahweh reveal Himself to us, engage with us, inhabit us, and guide us in fulfilling His will for Finitude.

Only Yahweh can guide us to dwell in Him, the source of our true eternal existentiality. Therefore, the vision of the Head of the Body should shape how the Body's members relate to one another if we sincerely wish to be His "bride" (Eph 4:15-16; Col 2:19). Through the Holy Spirit's influence, He enlightens our understanding, worldview, and personal journey, transforming us to mirror the humanity of the Son of God. This transformation starts with a personal God-relationship as we submit our devotion and love to Yahweh. In this process, we are individually transformed into a dwelling for the Creator's ever-present tabernacling spirit. We align ourselves with Christ's calling to be the self-revealing home for the Divine within our finite context.

Priests of the Trinity

As we meditate on our eternal world-dwelling destiny, it is vital for us to remember the triune nature of the Creator. This aspect of the Creator is not just an intriguing feature, but a fundamental truth. Among all global religious traditions, Christianity uniquely upholds both monotheism and the concept of the Trinity.[186] Our ultimate destination aligns with a finite homeland that mirrors the Creator's Infinite Home, known as the Triune Dominion of *Agape-Phosnoumenos*. It is crucial to comprehend how God's triune nature influences our fate. As a royal priesthood, eternally serving the Triune I AM, we serve as a "breath" of His "Word," through

---

[186] Hinduism shares concepts akin to a tri-partite nature seen in the Trimurti, where the "supreme deity" is divided into Brahman the Creator, Vishnu the Preserver, and Shiva the Destroyer, representing three essential cosmic forces. However, this division lacks the characteristic unity found in the agape-phosnoumenos nature of Christianity, where God is completely and eternal love, spirit, and light. Furthermore, while Hinduism is mainly polytheistic- or at least not strictly monotheistic like the Abrahamic faiths- it highlights Christianity's distinctiveness in its seemingly paradoxical assertion of one God existing as three persons.

which He realizes and implements His decrees (Acts 16:4). The Breath of God within us voices the commands of Christ through us as the united Body of Christ, appointed by Him with divine authority (Acts 13:9-11; Matt 16:18-19, 18:18-20; John 16:13-15, 20:22-23).

How does the triune nature of the Creator manifest in our mission to consecrate Finitude? The Spirit of God conveys the Divine Revelation of the Son through the authority of the transcendent Revealer, the Father. We can liken this to the sun, despite its limitations. The sun's radiation (or "heat") illuminates the earth directly from the Sun itself.[187] Likewise, the children of the Triune I AM reveal the Father by the command of the Word (Son) through the power of His Breath (Spirit). By communing with the Divine Spirit in our innermost being, where He resides, the ministry of the "inner court" – the spiritual realm – emanates from the sanctification of the Holy of Holies. From this revered inner sanctuary, we embody and present our new selves in Christ's image, nourishing the souls of our brethren as if drawing water from a deep well to sustain the land and its people. Our mission then extends from the inner

> *Do you regularly take seriously your Maker's command for you to be holy as He is holy?*
>
> *What changes should you make to your daily life to comply?*

---

[187] While this analogy aims to clarify concepts in this book, it is not a precise representation of the Trinity. The heat and light emitted by the sun do not equate to the sun itself entirely. Similarly, the Son and the Holy Spirit are as fully God as the Father; they exist as one Being in Three Persons. It is important to note that God is not just one being switching between three modes or forms. Nonetheless, this analogy effectively demonstrates how the Trinity functions concerning our divinely appointed purpose: there is a Divine Revelation, the transmitter of that Revelation, and its ultimate source. Each of these is fully God, just as the others are, while also playing distinct roles that are not entirely identical.

courts to the outer courts – the realm of the physical – to fulfill the work of the Father. We aim to align the physical world with the source of the *oikonomia* of Finitude. Thus, we must heed the Scriptural call: "Always rejoice, constantly pray, in everything give thanks. For this is God's will for you in Christ Jesus. Do not extinguish the Spirit. Do not treat prophecies with contempt. But examine all things; hold fast to what is good. Stay away from every form of evil" (1 Thess 5:16-22).

As agents of Divine Will, the Spirit connects our spirits to the Father, allowing us to be fathered by Him through the coadoption that His Son and His sacrifice provide. Scripture affirms, "[We have] received the Spirit of adoption, by which we cry, 'Abba, Father.' The Spirit Himself testifies with our spirit that we are God's children. And if we are children, we are also heirs (specifically, heirs of God and co-heirs with Christ)" (Rom 8:15-17). Our shared position as heirs with the Son grants us entry into this priestly ministry, which He initiated, aimed at transforming all Creation into Yahweh's Temple. Empowered by the Spirit, we can act as stewards in the physical realm, performing actions that impact the material world, and reflecting the likeness of Christ and the nature of God, as a Temple and priest should. Let us not "grieve the Holy Spirit" by neglecting the Call of Eternity (Eph 4:30).

The Triune I AM exists intrinsically as His own Temple – His own tabernacle or dwelling place (1 Tim 6:16; 1 John 1:5; Rev 21:22). He is eternally relational, loving, and self-giving within Himself. Although He was not obligated, He chose to create each of us humans to freely become His neighbors, partners, sharers, companions, dwellers, and co-workers in the triune life of *agape* love. Yahweh "dwells (*oikeo*) [makes His home] in unapproachable

Do you wish to exist eternally as a dwelling of the Father, Son, and Holy Spirit?

> *Do you long for a relationship with the Father like the one Jesus Christ had during His time on earth?*
>
> *Do you desire to articulate the Father's words and carry out His works?*

light," so everyone can "walk in the light" that "the Lord [who] will shine on them" provides (1 Tim 6:16; Rev 21:24, 22:5). As the light of Him, who is the "light of humanity," shines upon us, we "will reign [with Him] forever and ever" as children of light, walking by, abiding in, and reflecting His light, while guiding the rest of creation into His light (John 1:4-5, 12:35-36; Eph 5:7-10; Phil 2:15; 1 Cor 3:18, 4:4-6; 1 John 2:10; Rev 22:5). Will we shine as "the light of the world" by donning the dwelling of Christ, who is "the Light of the world" (Matt 5:14; John 8:12, 9:5)? By doing so, as the Dominion of Light, this house of Finitude will transform into a dwelling place and Temple of the One who *is* light and resides only in the light of His essential existence.

The Triune I AM exists as a *supercontextual* living household, and in a similar way, He designed us as *contextual* households that reflect His Infinite realm. Will we accept divine grace to continually fill us with energy, wisdom, and passion from Heaven? If we do, we become the instruments for the realization of a painter's abstract vision on canvas. This inspired artistry also shapes creation as His priests act as His hands, feet, and voice in His dominion (1 Pet 2:4-9; Rev 1:6, 5:10). "In Him we live and move and exist, as even some of your own poets have said, 'For we too are His offspring'" (Acts 17:28). Like a skilled gardener, we nurture Creation from the endless wellspring of love and provision found in His heart and presence, which flows from within our hearts when we commune with Him. The Creator's Divine Spirit has been flowing through humanity since the world's foundation, enabling us to engage with the physical world as His hands and feet. During the initial five days of creation, He established His house (Gen 1:3-23). The sixth day marked humanity's commissioning, allowing the Creation, brought into existence through the Divine Word, to become a true home for the Divine Spirit (Gen 1:24-2:25).

His Spirit positions us as a prism of Divine Majesty. As God's priests, "[He] leads us in triumphal procession in Christ," so that "through us" "He makes known" "the fragrance consisting of the knowledge of Him in every place" (2 Cor 2:14). This scent, recognized through spiritual senses, symbolizes the vivid supernatural colors of divine revelation. Like light filtering through clouds, we transmit the "rainbow" of revelation via our active engagement with the world, showcasing our Creator, Father, and elder Brother's "invisible attributes – His eternal power and divine nature" (Rom 1:20). His Spirit places us as a prism of Divine Majesty. We are also called to help creation act as His self-revealing prism, similar to a diamond reflecting light's hidden beauty. As caretakers of God's creation, we are prompted to ensure that the world exhibits divine revelations as a true home of God. Consequently, in this life and even more fully in the next, our involvement with Creation should inspire others, particularly humanity, to reveal the hues of Divine beauty.

> *Reflect on your life this week. Did you experience moments of spiritual transformation where you reflected the glory of the Lord?*

Engaging in the divine yet immanent life of the Trinity allows us to share in His home-making presence through the finite expression of His *agape*-communion (1 John 4:12). This expression reveals itself in the created realm, emphasizing our relationship with God. *Yahweh* chose to create a finite tabernacle for sharing with beings made in His image, filled with the essence of His Breath (Job 33:4; Eph 2:19-21; Heb 3:4-6; 1 Pet 2:4-10). The Trinity, a complete being of self-giving, love, and relationship, chose to extend that love outward to include others. He designed us as willing agents, exercising His authority and guided by His Spirit to accomplish His will. Love, however, cannot coerce. Thus, in this life, He presents each of us with the choice to live as His hands and feet, making contact with the world in a way that brings His presence to earth. By creating reflections of Divine beauty through the actions and words of His children, creation serves as a palette of colors. Our will, heart, mind, and identity become brushstrokes inspired by the Father's Word and empowered by the Holy Spirit, forming a portrait filled with the order of shalom that mirrors the Creator's perfect vision.

Conclusion: Serving as His Priests Now and Into Eternity

How should we live in light of our hope to reach our true home? First, we need to align ourselves with the *koinonia* of Heaven, as befits the household of Eternity. Next, we should respond to the call to be built into, and to build others into, a sanctified dwelling for the Triune I AM. To advance the priestly mission of God's Temple, we must collaborate with Yahweh to rescue those who are overwhelmed by existential darkness. The Letter to the Ephesians emphasizes that God intends to involve all of us in fighting against the darkness of home destruction and the deconstruction of our eternal identities in this present evil age (Eph 6:10-18; Gal 1:4). Finally, we must follow the guidance of Scripture:

> "Be strengthened in the Lord and in the strength of His power. Clothe yourselves with the full armor of God, so that you will be able to stand against the schemes of the devil. For our struggle is not against flesh and blood, but against the rulers, against the powers, against the world rulers of this darkness, against the spiritual forces of evil in the heavens."

(Eph 6:10-12)

Such divine alignment with our heavenly calling in our view of the world and our living only occurs when we accept the Spirit's transformative influence. Through communion of spirit with Spirit[188], He resides in our hearts to enable us to genuinely care for and act upon the tasks He assignsss us. Our responsibilities center around promoting the house rules of Yahweh's household in and through our lives. Thus, we must always be committed to align ourselves with the Call of Eternity, remaining mindful and alert that Yahweh will come to take only His faithful priests to reside in the Temple of Eternity.

{ *Will you commit to being salt and light to your fellow believers in a dark* }

As fellow priests, we can only dwell together in harmony when:

> "We practice the [Creator's] truth in [up-building *agape-*] love, [for then] we will in all things grow up into Christ, who is the head. From Him, the whole body grows, fitted, and held together through every supporting ligament. [And so,] as each one does its part, the body grows in love."
>
> (Eph 4:15-16)

Our identities and roles uplift each other through Christ, forming a genuine Spirit-filled community (Eph 2:19-22). By fulfilling our roles within the community, we become united through our relationship with God. As we live together as the salt and light to the dark systems of the world, Christ calls us to emulate Him by bringing God-centered kingdom living into our temporal existence

---

[188] Such as by the gift of tongues that build up a believer, and for that reason the Apostle Paul mentioned just how frequently he engaged in this spiritual practice (1 Cor 14:1-18).

(Matt 5:13-16). The Kingdom of Zion stands apart from this world, and we will always be nomads and resident aliens. Therefore, as foreign citizens and ambassadors representing our true Home, we should spread the influence of our eternal homeland "behind enemy lines."

In the next chapter, we will discover how our priestly mission will continue even after we join our Creator in Eternity. In the new heavens and new earth, the entire restored created order will be under the authority and sovereignty of the Creator (1 Cor 15). Through His priests, He will establish it as a dwelling place for Himself, where He will forever reside as "all in all" (1 Cor 15:27-28). When that much-anticipated day arrives, our responsibilities as priests will involve collaborating with Him to maintain our world and our role within it as a suitable Home for His presence. Let us now contemplate our priestly mission in Eternity.

{ *How can you better live as a resident alien and an evangelistic ambassador?* }

Chapter 11

Eternal Fellowship in New Jerusalem
Resurrection into a Home Filled with Infinite-Finite Communion

"We will not all sleep, but we will all be changed – in a moment, in the blinking of an eye, at the last trumpet. For the trumpet will sound, and the dead will be raised imperishable, and we will be changed. For this perishable body must put on the imperishable, and this mortal body must put on immortality. Now when this perishable puts on the imperishable, and this mortal puts on immortality, then the saying that is written will happen, 'Death has been swallowed up in victory.'"

(1 Cor 15:42-55)

"For we know that if our earthly house (*oikos*), the tent (tabernacle) we live in, is dismantled, we have a building (*oikos*) from God, a house not built by human hands, that is eternal in the heavens…

Now the one who prepared us for this very purpose is God, who gave us the Spirit as a down payment. Therefore, we are always full of courage, and we know that as long as we are alive here on earth, we are absent from the Lord – for we live by faith, not by sight. Thus, we are full of courage and would prefer to be away from the body and at home with the Lord."

(2 Cor 4:14, 5:1-8)

"According to His promise, we are waiting for new heavens and a new earth, in which righteousness truly resides."

(2 Pet 3:13)

The New Heavens and New Earth: Our Eternal Homeland

This chapter deals with our priestly mission in Eternity and the reality of our eternal fellowship with God in our eternal home: the New Jerusalem. We will learn about its eternal nature, how we shall reside in it with resurrected, glorified bodies (not merely as spirits), and how this should inform how we live in temporality in preparation. We are to live manifesting God's power in and through a communion of *agape*-love, since we will one day be united with God in a grand marriage ceremony at the end of days. Then shall we live forever, gifting each other and the renewed creation the homemaking befitting the New Jerusalem.

When the Home-Restorer comes again in human form, He will re-create the true home of our bodies (patterned off His resurrected body) to inhabit the "new earth" for which He originally meant for us to share and care (Isa 65:17, 66:22; 2 Cor 5:1-3). Scripture speaks of this long-awaited day, saying, "According to His promise, we are waiting for new heavens and a new earth, in which righteousness truly resides" (2 Pet 3:13). Though paradise seems far off, especially when we encounter the hardship, suffering, and struggles of accomplishing our mission in this world, we should take to heart Yahweh's promises. "The Lord is not slow concerning His promise, as some regard slowness, but is being patient toward [humanity] because He does not wish for any to perish but for all to come to repentance" (2 Pet 3:9).

Let us delve into the divine promise for which we eagerly await and hope. It is foretold in Scripture that at the end of all things, the physical universe we currently occupy will be reborn into one without decay or infirmity. Imagine a world of incorruptible vitality. Imagine a world of eternal blossoming. Imagine a world of unceasing peace. Imagine a world where all-encompassing holiness is the natural order of reality. No more death. No more entropy.

No more decay. No more suffering. No longer will transience have the final say. This is the hope promised to us by our Creator.

Contrast our hope with our fate in this fallen world. The laws of thermodynamics and the biological reality of our fallen bodies and ecosystems mean our world is defined by decay. Death is a reality for all living things without discrimination. Predation and natural disasters are a fact of the present state of nature. Even in our personal lives, we expect trials, disappointments, problems, worries, and suffering as simply a "part of life" - no matter our conduct or how holy we may live. Such revelations expose the falsehoods of the "Prosperity Gospel" that mocks the legacy of the martyrs. Human nature is itself beset with evil, and many of the moral evils of this world (from corruption to discrimination, to abuse, to human trafficking, to war, to greedy and destructive industries, to wanton living – are often done to escape the pains of the world) are clear evidence of this state of affairs.

Make no mistake, there is undoubtedly still much beauty and goodness in the world, even in the midst of suffering.[189] This is, in and of itself, a picture of God's grace for everyone – righteous or not – amid the mess we have collectively made of the world. Regardless, anyone who sees the fundamental order of this world as anything but fallen and broken is fooling themselves. Therefore, imagining a world without evil and suffering is utterly alien, even

---

[189] Consider how things like predation or disasters like natural wildfires are a means for the ecosystem to replenish and maintain itself – yielding new life from death. Remember also how tragedies, though never good in and of themselves, can be a means for maturity, strength, and renewed love to come into the world (such as how a sickness can result in the patient discovering a renewed sense of love for life and their loved ones).

God may not have caused or even planned these things, but God can and often has used what was meant for evil for good (Gen 50:20). This in and of itself is a clear picture of His grace being there even in the midst of utter fallenness.

inconceivable. Consider how a criticism against depictions of such a world in fiction often claims that such a world is undesirable because change or growth (resulting from overcoming conflict) is seen as a "vital" part of life. Ponder the Eastern concept of the eternal duality of good and evil (Ying and Yang/ Hindu Trimurti). Such criticisms prove how utterly part of our world's DNA the Fall is, such that even understanding what the New Heaven and Earth would be like is impossible for us to imagine, let alone grasp. It is so alien from our temporal world, and yet this unspeakable hope is what we must look forward to in faith as a promise from our Creator.

We need not understand how such a future world can come to pass, but we should believe it can and one day will, with even our fallen bodies and minds transformed to step into it, this new reality. At the dawning of our eternal rebirth, our Home-Restorer will re-establish the original tabernacle of our soul: an incorruptible and immortal body. Through these 'resurrected bodies,' we can carry out our eternal roles in the physical world of God's creation. Nevermore will eternal ambitions be subject to the decay and limitations of a fallen world. No more dreams of paradise turn into the spoiled dreams or regrets of old age.

Scripture has much to say about this long-awaited home of eternal bliss, such as the following:

> "Be happy and rejoice forevermore over what I am about to create! For look, I am ready to create Jerusalem to be a source of joy and her people to be a source of happiness. Jerusalem will bring Me joy, and my people will bring Me happiness. The sound of weeping or cries of sorrow will never be heard in her again… They will build houses and live in them; they will plant vineyards and eat their fruit… My chosen ones will enjoy what they have produced to

the fullest. They will not work in vain... Before they even call out, I will respond; while they are still speaking, I will hear. A wolf and a lamb will graze together; a lion, like an ox, will eat straw, and a snake's food will be dirt."

(Isa 65:18-25)

Until that great day, when we holistically arrive home in our body, soul, and spirit, we should continually seek to live for the sake of Eternity. We must think about our true home like a sailor gazing out from his ship. Imagine him yearning for his homeland – stretching out with his soul toward the conclusion of his voyage. "Since all the [present] things [of temporality] are to melt away," we should "conduct our lives in holiness and godliness, while waiting for and hastening the coming of the day of God. Because of this day, the heavens will be burned up and dissolve, and the celestial bodies will melt away in a blaze" (2 Pet 3:11-12)! With these revelations in mind, we must never forget "our citizenship is in heaven – and we await a savior from there, the Lord Jesus Christ, who will transform these humble bodies of ours into the likeness of His glorious body" (Phil 3:20-21). Let us begin our journey into the wonders of our eternal destiny by speaking of the promised resurrection of the saints to inhabit glorified physical abodes made in likeness to the transfigured glory of the Son of Man.

> *How should your awareness of the promise of eternal life in a New Heaven and Earth affect your world-viewing and world-dwelling in your present mortal life?*

Resurrected into Our Eternal Homeland

We were destined to sail the Sea of Revelation into Eternity. There, we will explore the divine mysteries of Yahweh's self-disclosing face within the spiritual dimension of the Temple of God. In

Eternity, we will continuously progress in our knowledge of the Divine through revelations and experiences. On the other hand, our present corruptible bodies are not our true home. We do not occupy them like we do our internal Holy of Holies on this side of Eternity. After all, our true, everlasting home must be both physical and spiritual. For this reason, we remain "foreigners and exiles" in temporality until that wonderful day when our spirit, soul, and body come to occupy the eternal contextualities of the New Heavens and New Earth (1 Pet 2:11).

We have a few Scriptural passages to ponder about our eternal dwelling place, the 'contextual there' of our immortal body and soul. In one such passage, the Spirit tells us through Paul:

> "The One who raised up Jesus will also raise us up with Jesus and will bring us with you into His presence... For we know that if our earthly house (*oikos*), the tent (tabernacle) we live in, is dismantled, we have a building (*oikos*) from God, a house not built by human hands, that is eternal in the heavens. For in this earthly house we groan, because we desire to put on our heavenly dwelling (*oiketerion*), if indeed, after we have put on our heavenly house, we will not be found naked. For we groan while we are in this tent, since we are weighed down, because we do not want to be unclothed, but clothed, so that what is mortal may be swallowed up by life.
>
> The One who prepared us for this very purpose is God, who gave us the Spirit as a down payment... We know that as long as we are alive here on earth, we are absent from the Lord – for we live by faith, not by sight. Thus, we are full of courage and would prefer to be away from the body and at home with the Lord."
>
> (2 Cor 4:14, 5:1-8)

We cannot dwell in the heavenly house of our body, soul, and spirit in this present mortal life. It would be like interacting with and perceiving a virtual world with our physical bodies. More than merely a place we cannot access, the virtual realm entirely exists on a different "plane" of reality. We would need virtual bodies and senses even to perceive such an existence. Even the most advanced VR equipment on the market now would only give us a shadow of such a virtual body. One would need a complete translation of our bodies into another form entirely, like digitization in the *Tron* films, to experience and truly inhabit the virtual realm. The same is true for our heavenly home. After our physical resurrection, we will no longer need to walk by faith, as our faith will be like our sight now. Divine revelation will be as "present" to us as the air we breathe and the colors we see. Only then will we totally inhabit the eternal land upon which Yahweh has built the City of the Living God for us to occupy in the tabernacle of our glorified bodies.

> *Do you realize you were made for a realm so far "beyond" this present shape of things that you can only enter it with a new body?*
>
> *How does that make you feel about the reality of your eternal identity presently hidden within Christ?*

Our present earthly bodies, through which we tabernacle on a dying earth, keep us physically separated from the risen Christ. However, we can still spiritually occupy our heavenly house through the Spirit of God, who dwells within us. The intercession of our High Priest opens a portal to this divine abode. The tearing of the curtain within the Holy of Holies prefigured this revelation. Though our soul and spirit can experience our true homeland even now within the Holy of Holies that lies within us, our physical bodies remain "absent from the Lord" (2 Cor 5:6). This is why we live *in* this world even as we are not *of* this world. This state of being will mark us until the end of all things.

While we still live in this mortal body, we should long for Eternity, as a pilgrim longs to reach their destination or a soldier longs to return home from his mission or campaign. Only there will our inner existential longings be fully and perpetually realized. Only then will we finally "be away from the [mortal] body and at home with the Lord" (2 Cor 5:4, 8). However, one crucial point to understand is how our long-awaited resurrection differs from what happens after death. To pass away from tabernacling in this present mortal body is a type of "departure (exodus)" (2 Pet 1:14-15). Through this exodus of the inner person, we "[fall] asleep in Christ," entering eternal communion within the heavenly homeland of the Lord. However, this is merely an interim state of existence, not our final destiny. We must still await the trumpet of resurrection, which will sound at the end of all things – summoning us to occupy our renewed earthly homeland (2 Pet 1:14-15; 1 Cor 15:18). When this final resurrection happens, all those who have fallen asleep will finally 'cross the Jordan into the Promised Land' to inhabit the physical New Jerusalem.

Our physical occupation of the New Earth will come when "the dead become raised imperishable (incorruptible), and the mortal body puts on immortality" (1 Cor 15:52). He "will transform these humble bodies of ours into the likeness of His glorious body by means of that power by which He is able to subject all things to Himself" (Phil 3:21). "It [will be] raised" a "spiritual body" "in power" and "in glory" (1 Cor 15:43-44). At that time, we will ultimately come into our eternal identity. The angels will remove the "image of the man of dust" and clothe us with the "image of the man of heaven" for both our outer and inner person (1 Cor 15:47-49). Our new spiritual bodies will be the bodily tabernacle of our inner person into eternity. Like how a new digitized body allowed the characters in *Tron* to inhabit cyberspace, this new glorified body will allow our soul and spirit to inhabit and occupy the new earth. Only by occupying Finitude physically *and* spiritually can we dwell and reign on the planet alongside the tabernacling presence of the Incarnate Son of God. Jesus Himself will also eternally occupy finitude via His resurrected and glorified body.

Until that Day, the New Earth and the City of the Living God will remain off-limits for us. In fact, it will not even be constructed by God until this present physical universe passes away (2 Pet 3:7-13). Even still, as we inhabit our present mortal bodies, we ought to desire to regularly put on our heavenly dwelling as God's temple as citizens of this eternal domain. We do this whenever we faithfully serve as His priests. Like the Apostle Paul, however, we should keep our gaze on our eternal destination, accepting our world-dwelling situation as sojourners in a land of exile. We must not cling to the contextualities of this mortal life. Instead, let us eagerly await the day we will pass from this earthly tent to dwell in the Eternal City of our God King.

Have you come to accept this world as your home?

Or do you eagerly await your body's resurrection when you will be with your Maker forever?

If we depart our earthly tabernacle before Jesus's second coming, we will be at home with our Lord within the spiritual sanctuary of Yahweh. If we remain on this dying planet at His return, He will translate us into our eternal abode. With this future Promise Land in mind, let us reflect on what Scripture reveals concerning the immortal bodies and our occupation within the "City of the Living God".

The Truth About Our Future Glorified Bodies

Of our resurrected physical tabernacles, we read the following:

"[Our body] is sown in dishonor, it is raised in glory; it is sown in weakness, it is raised in power; it is sown a natural body, it is raised a spiritual body. If there is a natural body, there is also a spiritual body. So also, it is written, 'The first man, Adam, became a living person'; the last Adam became a life-giving spirit. However, the spiritual did not come first, but the natural and then the spiritual. The first man is from the earth, made of dust; the second man is from heaven. Like the one made of dust, so too are those made of dust, and like the one from heaven, so too those who are heavenly. And just as we have borne the image of the man of dust, let us also bear the image of the man of heaven.

Now, this is what I am saying, brothers and sisters: 'Flesh and blood cannot inherit the kingdom of God, nor does the perishable inherit the imperishable. Listen, I will tell you a mystery: We will not all sleep, but we will all be changed – in a moment, in the blinking of an eye, at the last trumpet. For the trumpet will sound, and the dead will be raised imperishable, and we will be changed. For this perishable body must put on the imperishable, and this mortal body must put on immortality. Now when this perishable puts on the imperishable, and this mortal puts on immortality, then the saying that is written will happen, 'Death has been swallowed up in victory.'"

(1 Cor 15:42-55)

As we ponder our Guide, we must reject the Gnostic misconception that our glorified bodies, as well as the New Earth, are purely spiritual. In fact, the whole notion of our bodies being nothing more than "vessels" within which our true, purely spiritual selves reside until death is not biblical at all. The idea comes to us from Greek philosophy, particularly from Platonic Philosophy. Moreover, the idea of conflating the spiritual with "good" and the material/physical with "evil" is also antithetical to the biblical worldview. Such an extreme polarization of the spiritual above the material is reminiscent of Gnosticism, a heresy that has tempted Christ's followers since early Christianity. In this worldview, matter is viewed as fundamentally corrupted, a creation of an inferior deity. On the other hand, the spiritual world is seen as the sole realm of purity and goodness. According to Gnostics, one must seek ecstasy and detachment from the physical world and become like a "ghost" on the earth to find true fulfillment. Though few label themselves Gnostics today, many still apply this pagan worldview to Christian teachings. How often do "Christian" imaginings and illustrations seem to assume this whenever we speak of Heaven vs Earth or our spirits merely using our bodies as "earth suits" to be abandoned entirely once we die?

In contrast, we must remember the biblical worldview as one where our bodies and spirits, to put it simply, both make up our God-given identities. We are a union of body and spirit, essential to who we are and who we were created to be. Why else would God have created Adam as a fleshly being in the Garden of Eden, both with the dust of the Earth and with divine breath, instead of merely as a spirit like angels? Why else would our Creator charge us to care for our bodies and honor God with our bodies as "temple[s] of the Holy Spirit" (1 Cor 6:19-20)? Finally, why else was it so vital for Christ to come as a perfect union of God *and* man? Could He not have just come as a spiritual being to accomplish His work? Our bodies (not merely as an abstract, collective idea, but individually as well) are a vital, even fundamental, part of who we are. They are fallen, e.g. corruptible and often used for evil, now because of sin, yes, but they are not to be thought of as merely something God "tolerates" for the sake of our fallen world or something He will do away with at the end of temporality. This is why we are promised "glorified" bodies at the end of days, the result of a *transformation* of our bodies from their current fallen nature to one worthy of our redeemed existence in Christ.

Furthermore, our eternal homeland consists of both a material and spiritual dimension. If our spirits alone could inhabit the "City of the Living God", what need would there be for a resurrection? In fact, why would Christ have been resurrected with a body His disciples could touch at all? Why not simply come back as a spirit or a ghost? Just as Scripture says, "Now if Christ is being preached as raised from the dead, how can some of you say there is no resurrection of the dead? But if there is no resurrection of the dead, then not even Christ has been raised... If Christ has not been [physically] raised, then our faith is empty... And if Christ has not been raised... those who have fallen asleep in Christ have also perished" (1 Cor 15:12-14, 17). Therefore, we believe that at the resurrection of the dead, when Christ returns to Planet Earth, "God [will] give [us] an [imperishable] body just as He planned" (1 Cor 15:38, 42).

> *Have you ever entertained the misconception that our glorified bodies and the New Earth will be purely spiritual?*
>
> *Have you ever believed our bodies do not ultimately matter? How does the truth about our true home being both physical and spiritual change your mindset?*

Living Now as Resident Aliens from Temporality

So, what are we to do while we remain here, occupying temporality while awaiting the fulfillment of all these promises of our eternal home and glorified bodies? We should occupy it as the temple and priests of Yahweh, who have put on our heavenly selves within the

Holy of Holies (1 Cor 15:48-49). Our heavenly self is the existence we inhabit by the Sea of Revelation, which happens as we become like Christ, in whom God's divinity is fully disclosed (John 1:18; 2 Cor 4:4-6). We read the following mystery illuminating this very subject: "Those whom [the Father] foreknew He also predestined to be conformed to the image of His Son, that His Son would be the firstborn among many brothers and sisters" (John 3:3-8; 2 Cor 5:17; Rom 8:29). Like Christ, our heavenly self exists as a dwelling place of Divinity[190]. We walk the way of this heavenly self when we put on "the new [humanity] that is being renewed in knowledge according to the image of the one who created it" (Col 1:15, 1:19, 3:10).

As we reflect on our eternal destination, we should remember how Yahweh created us not simply as beings who 'tabernacle' in the eternal household of Finitude. Yahweh made us to become beings who *are* tabernacles. Glory be to our Divine Maker, Yahweh, for He created us to be an eternal dwelling place of His physical occupation of Finitude. Every one of us *can become* the fullest representation of the sacred, holy place where the Divine chooses to establish Himself in His interaction with the finite world. In other words, no created physical reality can be a substitute for each living temple in the form of humanity. We, not great cathedrals or monuments, are the true house of God. Through us that people must truly encounter and see God. As an immanent dwelling place of the Creator, we currently can dwell in Finitude as heaven-dwellers via our spirit communing with His Spirit. All the while we occupy Finitude as heaven-dwellers, we also ought to live as earth-dwellers via the existential connection of our soul and body. After all, each of us has priestly duties to fulfill both

---

[190] Greek orthodoxy called this *theosis*.

to the Body of Christ and to all humanity in general while we remain homeless castaways.

Sadly, throughout much of religious history, physical buildings like temples and cathedrals have been considered substantially more valuable and significant than any human being. Eternity and temporality's perspectives remain forever at odds regarding what is truly valuable. Jesus recognized the widow's single coin as eternally more significant than the wealth donated by the religious elites of his day (Mark 12:41-44). May our standard of valuation be ever informed by Eternity. Make no mistake, great places of worship and works of art dedicated to God can and often do play a part in worship or how God speaks to people, and they can be a legitimate way to glorify God by our talents, like those who constructed the first tabernacle and Temple in Jerusalem, as well as a way to imitate the creativity of God. Nevertheless, they must never be substitutes for our roles as the living temples of God. All the beautiful basilicas in the world will not convince someone to believe in Christ if the Christians they see in their daily lives are selfish, haughty, or hypocritical. Christ's commission will not be fulfilled in our lives if we do not live out our roles as meeting places of Heaven and Earth.

Let us take caution. We neglect our present responsibilities upon the earth at our own peril. We run the risk of forfeiting our heavenly responsibilities, both now and into Eternity. These responsibilities come down to providential direction rather than religious protocols or rituals. We should think of them this way. Like Christ did when He walked on the earth, we must be channels by which God touches and engages earth to reconcile all things to Himself (2 Cor 15:18-19). As members of the Body of Christ, our existential residence as earth-dwellers should take shape as we put on the Incarnate Son of God by walking in accordance with His Spirit. Through this, the Holy Spirit shapes our earthly world-dwelling engagements in the likeness of Christ's world-dwelling. We act as the mouth, hands, and feet of Divinity upon the earth. For instance, communing with His Spirit should shape our feelings and thoughts such that they become translated into words and bodily actions reflecting His wisdom and character. When our lives and lifestyles reflect Christ in this way, people will come to see and know His goodness through us. "Just as each one has received a gift, use it to serve one another as good stewards of God's varied grace. Whoever speaks, let it be with God's words. Whoever serves, do so with the strength that God supplies, so that in everything God will be glorified through Jesus Christ" (1 Pet 4:10-11).

In imitation of Christ, we forgive our enemies and show love even to strangers. Our communion with the Holy Spirit causes these biblical principles of forgiveness and *agape*-love to become awakened in our spirit man, replacing the worldly norms of holding grudges or allowing hatred to fester or only looking out for oneself. The "desires of the Spirit" cause us to find ourselves desiring this holy way of life for ourselves (Gal 5:17-25). This "saintly" behavior does not come out of a sort of "spiritual puppetry" by which God controls our will and desires. In fact, we may not even notice ourselves growing in these things as they happen, only realizing how far we have come when we reflect on it later. By a natural transformation of the Spirit of Sanctification, we end up surprised by the things we find ourselves saying, doing, or wanting in accordance with His will. We may, for example, notice ourselves feeling empathy for those we once either did not care about or saw with disdain (such as the poor, or even people like an annoying or unlikeable coworker). As a tabernacle of Yahweh, our actions reflect the character and attributes of His existence. Our lives ought to unveil the *care* of Yahweh's *agape*-love, supernatural power, and providential authority. As His priests, our actions promote the God-relationships of ourselves and one another. They must also promote the worship and glorification of Him within the created realm, so that His glory as the Creator will be magnified throughout His physical domain.

While we remain exiled in this Fallen World with our mortal bodies, we must heed the Scriptures:

> "[Do] not despair, [because] even [though] our physical body is wearing away, our inner person is being renewed day by day. For our momentary, light suffering is producing an eternal weight of glory far beyond all comparison because we are not looking at what can be seen but what cannot be seen. For what can be seen is temporary, but what cannot be seen is eternal."
>
> (2 Cor 4:16-18)

If any of us "die in faith without receiving the (fullness of) things promised," we will have "seen them in the distance and welcomed them" as we "seek a (heavenly) homeland" if we do not turn back "having an opportunity to return" (Heb 11:13-16).

We must never forget that our Maker allows us the opportunity to return to world-dwelling and world-viewing shaped solely by our temporal home in this present world if we abandon our sojourn to an eternal home. He does not force us to answer the Call of Eternity. Instead, He gives us a choice. Without the possibility of apostasy, there can be no possibility of a genuine relationship. Regardless, He has always known, and now we know from our experience the consequences of our decisions. We cannot call such an

Why is it so vital for us to freely choose to follow God instead of blindly obeying as slaves would?

Does this freedom to say yes or no challenge you?

arrangement unfair any more than we can call a parent unfair for allowing their child to, for example, choose between a life of sobriety and a life addicted to drugs, e.g. locking them in the house forever. One choice has dire consequences but because of the child's actions, not of the parent's cruelty. In the same way, God allows us to choose between reaping the wages of our sin and fallen existence or following Him.

Therefore, let us continue to live as homeless castaways, "acknowledging how we are strangers and foreigners on this (present) earth" (Heb 11:13). Only then will it be said of us that "we aspired to a better land, that is, a heavenly one," so that the Creator will "not be ashamed to be called our God, for He has prepared [for us] a city" (Heb 11:16). To those who, in Christ, conquer the enticements of temporality, this promised eternal abode will be the final resting place of our body, soul, and spirit (Heb 3; Rev 2-3). In this eternal context, we will forever remain as His Temple and priests, serving in the physical realm as royal stewards in the eternal finite domain of the Son of God (Heb 3).

> *What is the importance of remembering your status as a tabernacle of Yahweh's presence?*
>
> *What duties does this entail?*

A Communion of *Agape*-Love

One of our primary purposes as world-dwellers of the physical world stands out as spiritual fellowship with our brothers and sisters in Christ. Consider the etymological root of the Greek word for communion, "*koinonia.*" The word derives from "*koinonos,*" which refers to a person "who takes part in something with someone," such as a "companion, partner, sharer" (BDAG, 553). In Scripture, this word is employed, for instance, when speaking of being a co-sharer of the Divine nature, in the suffering of Christ, and ministry endeavors (2 Cor 1:7, 8:23; Heb 10:33; 2 Pet 1:4). With this word in mind, we should consider how Scripture says that we, as the priests of Yahweh, should live as "together-acters" with God in His household and "fellow-workers" with Him in this household, which is "God's building" (1 Cor 3:9; ISA).

Because of our mutually shared duty within God's household, the interpersonal activity of "*koinonia*" stands out as one of the most fitting occupations we could engage in from an existential perspective. The word *koinonia* also implies the following: "[to possess an] attitude of good will that manifests [as] an interest in a close relationship, fellow-feeling, proof of brotherly unity, sign of fellowship" (BDAG, 552-553). Such spiritual fellowship entails "participation and sharing in something" through a "close association involving mutual interests and associations" (BDAG, 552-553). But, for such communion to take place, there must be a common, shared interest. Think of how groups form bonds over shared loves or desires, from something as small as book clubs to something as significant as national identities. Only co-sharers engaging in *koinonos* can participate in communion (*koinonia*). With this in mind, a question arises. What is the essential association of co-sharing within the Body of Christ? What allows us to participate together in spiritual unity while corporately promoting our mutually shared eternal purpose?

The Holy Spirit reveals two overlapping facets around the core of co-sharing spiritual communion. Let us examine the passages revealing them to us. On one hand, the co-sharing at the heart of our spiritual communion in the Temple of God revolves around us being "sharers (participants) [*koinonos*] in the glory that will be revealed" (1 Pet 5:1). On the other hand, mutual co-sharing happens as we individually and then corporately come into the fullness of our destiny, as God's temple, to be "partakers (participants) [*koinonos*] of the divine nature" (2 Pet 1:4).

Firstly, we have a shared interest in the awaited hope of one nday sharing in the glory of the revealed divine Nature. When we finally come Home, we will finally experience the full realization of our co-sharing destiny with each other and God, putting on the likeness of Christ in perpetual fellowship within our eternal homeland (1 John 1:3, 3:2). Secondly, the core of co-sharing communion centers on being co-heirs with both Christ and those who are called to be clothed with Christ alongside us. As Infinite-finite communion unfolds in the temple of Yahweh, finite communion transpires simultaneously. In other words, the distinctive communion of God's household happens among co-sharers of Infinite-finite communion. This is the association that forms our spiritual *koinonia*. By such a state of "co-sharing" (*koinoneo*), we become "sharers in spiritual things," "partners in a heavenly calling," and "partakers (partners) with the Holy Spirit" (Rom 15:27; Heb 3:1, 6:4). Since the divine nature *is agape*-love, we can simply state that the root of such communion is sharing in and ministering the self-emptying love of God, rooted in self-giving (Rom 12:13; Phil 4:15; 1 John 4:8, 16). Therefore, spiritual fellowship makes such spiritual communion possible by a mutual 'flowing-between' or co-sharing of self-disclosing faces in harmonious self-emptying love, drawn from and patterned after God's original self-disclosing, self-emptying nature.

The fellowship (*koinonia*) of *agape*-love distinguishes any genuine manifestation of the Body of Christ: God's authentic

> *Why can we not forsake fellowship with other members of the Body of Christ in our world-dwelling or walk with God?*
>
> *Have you made the mistake of neglecting this in your spiritual walk?*

household (tabernacle) within finitude, shaped in likeness to Yahweh's transcendent Infinite household as the Triune God. Without this fellowship of love, we would not be the Body of Christ. Scripture helps us delve deeper into the central aspects of "fellowship in the Holy Spirit" that takes place within a genuine community of the children of God (Acts 2:42; 2 Cor 8:4, 13:14; Gal 2:9; Phil 2:1). For instance, our Lord calls all the children of God "to not neglect doing good and fellow-ship" as joint sailors on the Sea of Revelation (Heb 13:16).

Corporately engaging in the symbolic communion of Christ, the Eucharist, serves as an outward sign identifying a consecrated community of believers (1 Cor 10:16). Rather than a mere ritual celebrated due to 'tradition,' true spiritual communion nourishes us, as the Spirit binds us together on a spiritual level to promote the agendas of the Kingdom of God within this world of darkness. The Eucharist (literally called *communion* in many Christian denominations) is a symbolic representation of our fellowship with God as central to our identity, destiny, and contextual home. Drinking the "blood of Christ" and eating the "bread of Christ's flesh" is a metaphor for us partaking in the very existentiality of the Son of Man's existence. Ironically, some denominations get so caught up in the physical nature of communion that they completely overlook the symbolism of being filled with the Spirit. After all, Paul's teaching on the Eucharist takes place just before his teaching on the gifts of the Holy Spirit (1 Cor 11-14). Similarly, the parable of the vine and the branches depicts this state of existence as becoming a dwelling place of God in and through the Son of God, as He fills us with the same Holy Spirit infilling Him. We become one with Him. We become one with God. We become one with the tabernacle of God within Creation. We become energized with the Divine Spirit and assimilate the revelations of Divinity. After all, Yahweh "calls [us] into fellowship (*koinonia*) with His Son, Jesus Christ our Lord," for, *through* Him, we have true spiritual "fellowship with one another" as we mutually "walk in the light" (which is Christ Himself) (1 Cor 1:9; 1 John 1:7).

The fellowship of our eternal destiny lies at the core of the true mystery of the Eucharist. Accordingly, the existentialities of Jesus Christ define "eternal life" as "knowing God" by intimately *knowing* the "Son" who reveals Him to us and through us (John 1:18, 17:3). In context, Jesus makes clear that this experiential 'knowing' only happens through the "fellowship" of united oneness we have "with the Father and with His Son Jesus Christ" (John 17:3, 11, 21-23, 26; 1 John 1:1-3). This Trinitarian fellowship typifies any truly fitting experience within the household of Yahweh. Just as we can say God exists in unity within the Trinity, so must we exist in unity with Him. As partakers in this heavenly unity of *shalom*, we can thus experience "fellowship" with one another in the Body of Christ as co-members of His finite Trinitarian household. Together, we become transformed into mutual co-sharers of God's fellowshipping and tabernacling presence as we become mutually built up into a corporate temple of Yahweh by the inward tabernacling fellowship of the Divine Breath and Divine Word incessantly flowing from the Heavenly Father (Eph 2:19-22).

Our Heavenly Father expects His children to live as a unified community of the up-building activity of *agape*-love (Eph 2:19-22, 4:11-16). However, we should not see this unity of the Body of Christ as a homogenous mass or crowd reminiscent of a concert hall. Nor should we see it as a union where we fully surrender our individuality to become a type of hive mind or even cease existing as unique individuals, as Buddhism teaches. *Agape*-love is rooted in holistic and mutually edifying communion, particularly in the internalities of the

How do you think God's Triune Nature reveals unity as a central and essential part of our Christian life?

heart. Each person in the Body will forever retain their individuality as a distinct living pillar in God's Temple (Rom 12:4-8; 1 Cor 12; 1 Pet 2:4-11; Rev 3:12). After all, why would the God who lovingly formed each of our distinctive selfhoods suddenly erase it (1 Cor 12)? He invites each of us to be one with Him and our brothers and sisters in Him. Rather than being erased, we find our personalized 'name' identifying our fittingness in the household of Finitude as an echo of our Creator's name (Rev 3:5, 12). Jesus makes this clear when He says, "To the one who conquers, I will give him [or her] some of the hidden manna, and I will give him [or her] a white stone, and on that stone will be written a new name that no one can understand except the one who receives it" (Rev 2:17). Like the First Adam, the Second Adam fulfills the eternal destiny of humanity as a Name-Giver.

It is in Christ, the light of true humanness, that we find not an entirely new version of ourselves with no relation to what came before but a transformed, redeemed, and fulfilled version of ourselves – fully aligned to how we were lovingly formed and woven together in our mothers' wombs (John 1:4; Ps 139:13). We will discover more and more revelations of our Creator's name by becoming more acquainted with our eternal name and the names of one another, as God "makes known" "through [each of] us the knowledge of Him" (2 Cor 2:14). We learn why our Maker values each of our identities. After all, our Creator "knits" each of our eternal names together into the tapestry of the *agape*-love communion of the Heavenly Father and His created children (Col 2:2). He intimately knows each eternal thread He has woven, with more *caring* attentiveness than His knowledge of every hair on our head (Matt 10:26-31). Each of our 'names' can be likened to a unique color in an infinite "rainbow" of Divine "promises" undergirding God's household in the covenant of *agape*-love, shalom, and personal commitment (Gen 9:14-16). Thus, the "brilliant light" of the children of light, as God's Temple, becomes eternally manifested like a "rainbow" of Divine glory (Gen 9:14-16; Ezek 1:27-28; Phil 2:14; Eph 5:9-10; John 12:36).

Though it may be hard for us to conceive of how or why every single thread in a giant tapestry is vital and cared for by its Creator, this is a fundamental truth of the nature of the Bride of Christ. Every one of us is as essential in this tapestry as any other, even if it may not seem or feel that way when we look at others. Let us not make the mistake of confusing worldy prosperity or striving toward faithfulness and divine importance. A Christian who remains faithful to their calling to be a blessing in their small-town workplace and a good father and husband to their family, for example, will be rewarded in Heaven, not just someone like Moses, Paul, Augustine, or Mother Teresa. Calling only certain believers "saints" goes against the very Scriptures, such religious groups claim to follow, which calls all believers saints "holy-ones" (Rom 12:13, 15:25; 1 Cor 14:33; 2 Cor 9:1; Ph 4:21; Eph 4:22; Rev 14:12).

Let us focus on the Scriptural passage about the engraved white stone each child of God receives in eternity. Each stone has the distinctive marking of a particular child of God's purpose and part in promoting the plans for finitude pre-established by the Creator (Eph 2:10). Just as Christ has told us: "To the one who conquers, I will give him [or her] a [bright][191] stone [smooth pebble], and on that stone will be written a new name that no one can understand except the one who receives it" (Rev 2:17; ISA; NET). Each of these unique "living stones," which are "priceless in [God's] sight," are "chosen" by Him to be "built up" into the "New Jerusalem" (1 Pet 2:4-5). Each one displays the glorious likeness of Christ, the

---

[191] The Greek word "*leukos*" here is typically interpreted white, but rather than depicting an attribute of whiteness it can also characterize "an object that is bright or shining, either from itself or from an outside source of illumination" (NET).

image of Divinity, in a unique pattern set by our individual identity and special role in the Narrative of Finitude (2 Cor 3:18, 4:4-6; Col 1:15, 19, 27, 2:9, 3:10). Do we not read Scripture describe the "city" of "New Jerusalem" as a "bride adorned for her husband [Christ]" (Rev 21:2)? This bridal depiction in Scripture is otherwise only used to refer to the Body of Christ. Of this bride-like city, we read that she "possesses the glory of God; [her] brilliance is like a precious jewel, like a stone of crystal-clear jasper" (Rev 21:11). The passage later goes on to describe how "the foundations of the city's wall are decorated with every kind of precious stone," which all brilliantly showcase the glorious disclosures of the One who inhabits us (1 Pet 2:4-5; Rev 21:19).

Through these passages, the Holy Spirit conveys how the physical New Jerusalem eternally exists as a concrete physical manifestation of the spiritual New Jerusalem. As we have already discussed, the finite manifestation of the Infinite City of the Living God is the Body of Christ, the heavenly dwelling place of God within creation. The Spirit, through Daniel, prophesied: "The wise will shine like the brightness of the heavenly expanse. And those bringing many to righteousness will be like the stars forever and ever" (Dan 12:3).

Each saint exists as a meaningful part of the heavenly tabernacle of Yahweh. We all manifest the glorious revelations of the Creator uniquely. This distinctiveness comes from the Creator's decision to assign everyone unique roles to support the Temple of God dwelling within creation. Do we not read in Scripture: "Just as in one body we have many members, and not all the members serve the same function, so we who are many are one body in Christ, and individually we are members who belong to one another. And we have different gifts according to the grace given to us" (Rom 12:4-6). These roles may look different depending on the finite contextualities he assigns to each of us, such as our personalities, abilities, talents, interests, resources, influence, connections, etc. Some may be appointed as great teachers and evangelists, influencing thousands or even millions worldwide for the Kingdom. Others may be appointed to live faithful to God by loving those within the 'sphere' of their lives, though they may not be 'preachers' or 'ministers' in the traditional sense, yet Christ commissions all to make disciples. Though we are to be inspired by one another, it would be a mistake to assume we have to mimic another person's "saintly" gifts or calling or even the precise way they live out the commands of God in their lives.

For example, consider 'Sarah Smith' from C.S. Lewis' novel *The Great Divorce*. In the novel, she is a woman who once lived in England, not a person of fame or fortune. Despite this, the book's narrator sees her being honored and praised in a grand procession in Heaven. Upon questioning what she did to deserve such a reception, the narrator is told that she merely loved all who came to her (adults, children, and even animals) so that they were strengthened by her love, which "made them more into themselves." Lewis writes that "the abundance of life she has in Christ from the Father flowed over into them," so she is honored, though she did no great deeds or mighty works in her life to be recognized or even prayed to as a "saint." Though history will not remember her name, she is given the highest honor in Eternity. Such an illustration shows us how, if we faithfully devote ourselves to living out the ways of God on the earth, no matter how "small" our part may seem, we will have done great work echoing into Eternity. As the guide says in the novel:

> "It is like when you throw a stone into a pool, and the concentric waves spread out further and further. Who knows where it will end? Redeemed humanity is still young; it has hardly come to its full strength. But already there is joy enough in the little finger of

a great saint such as yonder lady to waken all the dead things of the universe into life."

(C.S. Lewis, The Great Divorce)

Regardless of how small our calling or abilities might seem, every one of us has a great purpose and power, through Christ, to wake Finitude into life by being a bridge between Heaven and Earth.

> *Does the knowledge that you are irreplaceable and priceless in God's sight move you to gratitude, praise, and surrender?*

Our Great Purpose and Destiny in the Communion of Love

Our eternal destiny *is* what it *is* because Yahweh created us for a marriage-like covenantal partnership (Eph 5; Rev 19). This is why Yahweh marks the dawning of the new heavens and earth with a wedding celebration. Such a revelation should not be lightly noted. After all, of all the possible ways His Eternal Kingdom could be inaugurated, why a wedding? Why not a coronation or knighting ceremony? Only the wedding symbol communicates the centrality of the Infinite-finite communion of the God-relationship to His plans for Finitude. Rather than a 'coronation,' which would focus on swearing fealty to the monarch, or a knighting ceremony, where the one knighted receives all the honor, a wedding would share the honor between the groom and bride. Though all glory rightly belongs to Him, God wishes to share this honor with His everlasting bride. When He opens the door into Eternity with His mighty arm, He symbolically does so in the attire of a bridegroom, not of a conquering king.

Yahweh literally and figuratively adorns His bride with beautiful garments and jewels. Our part, in turn, is to dedicate the glory He clothes us with (His glory) back to Him. In doing so, our beauty becomes His beauty, as it is all His to begin with. Ezekiel 16 paints a poetic picture of this revelation:

> I passed by you and saw you kicking around helplessly in your blood. I said to you as you lay there in your blood, 'Live!' I said to you as you lay there in your blood, 'Live!'
>
> ...Then I passed by you and watched you, noticing that you had reached the age of love. I spread my cloak over you and covered your nakedness. I swore a solemn oath to you and entered into a marriage covenant with you, declares the Sovereign Lord, and you became Mine...
>
> Then I bathed you in water, washed the blood off you, and anointed you with fragrant oil. I dressed you in embroidered clothing and put fine leather sandals on your feet... You were adorned with gold and silver... You became extremely beautiful and attained the position of royalty. Your fame spread among the nations because of your beauty; your beauty was perfect because of the splendor that I bestowed on you, declares the Sovereign Lord."
>
> (Ezek 16:6-14)

Just like the moon reflecting the sun's light, the beauty we are adorned with comes from Yahweh alone. This partnership can be compared to the divinely inspired artists of the earthly tabernacle, who used their artistic talents to build the physical tabernacle to reflect the Creator's beauty and splendor (Exodus 36). Just as the Holy Spirit enabled them to fulfill this temporal duty within His symbolic tabernacle, He allows and directs us into a similar, albeit eternal, duty within His everlasting tabernacle.

In this temporal contextual landscape, the communion of the Body of Christ unfolds in its initially intended way according to the marriage household motif. This work unfolds out of the

sanctification as His Spirit transforms us into His most holy place of residence (1 Pet 1:2; 2 Thess 2:13). In Eternity, the bride's physical actions of sanctification flowing from this Holy of Holies will directly manifest within and impact the physical domain. In so doing, the prophecy of the New Covenant will be fulfilled. Yahweh will eternally reveal His splendor through His chosen priestly and Spirit-filled bride (Isa 61:1-6).

The actual home of humanity lies in the finite habitation of the Triune I AM. He, through us, makes the created world subsist through His triune home-making activity, which unfolds by His Spirit and through His Word (Rom 5:1-5; Eph 2:18, 3:16-17). In the sanctifying realm of the God-relationship, we come into an inward state of *shalom*, consisting of *being* the House of God by *dwelling in and through* His tabernacling presence. We can only find this complete joy within our true Home of fellowship with Yahweh and one another in Him. Furthermore, it is only within this co-dwelling community, united in glorifying the Creator, that we can find ourselves. As our Good Shepherd, He eternally leads us in fitting into and promoting the harmony of the created order He pre-established. His immanent presence in and alongside us fuels our life of worship. Our devotion inspires us to promote worship worldwide (Zeph 3:9).

> *Will you devote yourself to rebuilding your Maker's tabernacle upon the earth via His supernatural power?*
>
> *What do you think is your unique calling by which you will fulfill this great purpose?*

As Yahweh's children, we glorify Him through thoughts, desires, and actions centered on fulfilling His vision for creation. Promoting the fulfillment of His vision, just like Jesus did, promotes the Creator's glory. By achieving His vision, He reveals His attributes, character, and personhood to the world. Like Jesus, we "glorify [God] upon the earth by completing the work [He] has given [us] to do," for such glorification of God reveals the splendor of God's self-disclosing face (Isa 61:3; John 17:4). The vision Yahweh has authored for such work results in creation becoming an immanent self-disclosing tabernacle. By revealing Him to the world, we prepare it to be His dwelling place. To this end, we desire all those dwelling in our Creator's contextual domain to know His self-disclosing face and participate in glorifying Him by doing deeds that cause His name to be echoed throughout creation.

Membership in Yahweh's household calls for us to eternally promote the Infinite-finite home-making communion of *agape*-love, order of *phos*-light, and providence of *pneuma*-Spirit. We can call this combined home-making communion by the name *agape-phosnoumenos*.[192] With this home-making destiny in mind, let us consider what lies ahead of us on our homeward-bound journey. Our way of life ought to revolve around a spiritual communion mirroring the Divine 'intra-personal' life of the Trinity. If God determines the divine order and proper form of world-dwelling for Finitude, then so does His nature determine and inform how our spiritual communion should unfold. It flows from mutually abiding in and tabernacling through the wellspring of Infinite *Being*: *out-of* the Divine Father, *through* the Divine Word, and *by* the Divine Breath. We can truly fellowship with others when we abide in Him and fellowship with Him, as the Trinity does within the Triune I AM. This forms a beautiful mutually reinforcing 'tapestry of *agape*-love. When we speak of how fundamental this *agape*-love lifestyle is to Divine *Being*, we must remember how Yahweh's Infinite dwelling place transcends all the limitations of finitude. The Transcendent Palace of the Trinity is boundlessly filled – a

---

[192] This nature of God is detailed more in the trilogy *Before the Beginning*, which deals with His character as *agape*-love, *phos*-light, and *pneuma*-spirit.

bottomless storehouse of the blessings of Yahweh's triune existence.

Existentialities shaped by the finitely contextualized indwelling of Infinite *Being* lie deeply rooted in mutual self-giving, whereby we exist for the sake of others (1 John 3:16, 4:8-17). These self-giving disclosures unfold between the Creator and His most beloved creation on an individual and corporate level. One of the main ways they unfold is through giving "home goods" originating from Yahweh's infinite household. These goods include the fruit of the Spirit, like love, joy, peace, patience, kindness, goodness, faithfulness, gentleness, and self-control (Gal 5:22-23). The disposition of 'gift giving' is fundamental to the home-making element of *agape-phosnoumenos*. After all, the highest gift of all is the self-disclosing splendor of Yahweh. As the children of "the Father of lights," from whom "all generous giving and every perfect gift [comes] from," we must live as a reflection of His self-disclosing face by living a gift-giving lifestyle (Jms 1:17-18).

Yahweh freely bestows blessed treasures of the Sea of Revelation on His children in finitely contextualized ways. First of all, He bestows them on us so we might be adequately adorned to live as the bride of God Incarnate. Secondly, He bestows them so we can partner with Him in filling our shared finite household with the finitely contextualized belongings of His Infinite household. As co-workers with the Son of God and Spirit of God, He gives us the spiritual means of participating in the gift-giving of Himself. Our wedding dowry, so to speak, is the purifying blood of the Lamb and the baptizing sanctification of the Holy Spirit. Through us, as the Body of the Lamb, Yahweh dwells within the household of finitude to make Himself concretely known, glorified, and worshipped (2 Cor 9:12-13).

Such home-making activity allows for all those dwelling in our Creator's house to be part of the project to make Finitude their shared home with Him. The indwelling presence of the Spirit of God personally takes us into our home and causes us to overflow with Divinity's home-making influence, enabling us to 'overflow' into finitude. As we inhabit our shared divine home, the Holy Spirit intertwines our hearts and minds with one another in agreement with the very heart and mind of Yahweh, our Maker. This harmony of self-disclosing faces takes place as we truly live out our identities as co-partakers in the Divine Nature through the Spirit's activity of house-managing *shalom*. Hence, we eternally abide in the Spirit's up-building element, will forever partake in the Infinite-finite hospitable gift-giving of *agape*-love, *phos*-light, and *pneuma*-spirit (1 John 1:5-10, 3:24, 4:8-17; John 4:23-24, 14-16).

Why do you think a lifestyle of 'gift-giving' is fundamental to the nature of God and a lifestyle of partaking in this Divine nature?

How do you see this revelation play out in your own life?

The New Jerusalem, Our Eternal Household

The Sea of Revelation represents the Holy of Holies. This sea inhabits our innermost being through God's Spirit dwelling within our soul. Spirit-to-spirit communion with our Maker opens up existential possibilities to explore and be shaped by the ocean of His presence. His self-disclosing face reflects off our soul and body as we walk out our identities as priests of God, reflecting His glory (2 Cor 3:18, 4:4-6). The more we grow into the knowledge of God's revelation, the more we can mature as those built into the Body of Christ, the New Jerusalem, our true Home. If we remain faithful to the Way, we will one day step ashore onto the banks of the "City of the Living God" at the end of our earthly journey. Upon the shores of the Land of the New Earth lies a river of living water flowing into and through each of us into the new Earth, transforming it into a reflection of God's Infinite Abode.

Through the habitation of the children of God, the City of New Jerusalem exists as a reflection of the Sea of Revelation. At the end of time, the Son of Yahweh will establish the City of the Living God within the recreated and perfected physical universe, which shall remain forever. Through us, His brothers and sisters, Jesus will permanently establish it as the concrete manifestation of the Sea of Revelation within the physical dimension of finitude. With the incarnate Son of God as our Eternal King and High Priest and our exemplar, we will rule with Him throughout His domain as His ruling governors and priests. In the New Jerusalem, we will ensure that the Son's domain in the created world serves Him as a physical temple reflecting His glorious self-disclosing splendor and fulfilling His plans.

In the book of Revelation, Christ speaks of the "one who conquers" (referring to those who have overcome the testing and trials of this life for Christ's sake) when He says, "I will make [them] a pillar in the temple of My God" (Rev 3:12). According to the revelatory witness of the same book, however, there is "no temple in the city, because the Lord God and the Lamb are its temple" (Rev 3:12, 21:22). How then, is there a temple in the New Jerusalem? The answer to this seemingly contradictory paradox lies in the fact that the Spirit depicts the city as the "bride of the Lamb" "descending" from "heaven from God" (Rev 21:2). When the Bride, which is the Body of Christ, comes down from heaven having been made perfect, "the residence of God" comes to be "among human beings" (Rev 21:3, 9). If we are indeed all temples and

> *Does this prospect of serving as a governor and priest of the New Jerusalem fill you with hope and inspire you to remain faithful to growing in your knowledge of God?*

dwelling places for His presence, we make up a great city of His presence together! Since "[God's] dwelling place [tabernacle]" is the Body of Christ, it makes sense why Scripture says the Lamb alone (who is Christ) would be the temple of God (Rev 13:6).

Do we not read the following revelation: "In [the Lamb] the whole building [tabernacle of God], (the various members of the Body) becomes joined together, [and] grows into a holy temple in the [Lamb], in whom [we] are also being built together into a dwelling place of God in the Spirit" (Eph 2:21-22)? Scripture also points out to us how the true identity of the members of the Body of the Lamb is to be "a mature person, attaining to the measure of Christ's [the Lamb's] full stature," so that we become "built up into the Body of Christ [the Lamb]" (Eph 4:12-13). Moreover, we are called "to continue to live our lives in Him [the Lamb], rooted and built up (*epoikodomeo*)[193] in Him." Therefore, let us be able to honestly say "it is no longer I who live, but Christ lives in me" (Col 2:6-7; Gal 2:20). In addition, Scripture teaches that "the church is His body, the fullness of Him [the Lamb] who fills all in all" (Eph 1:23). In putting on the Lamb, we put on the Temple of God. Moreover, when we rebecome created in God's image, we become recreated in the image of God's Temple, which is God Himself. With all this evidence from Scripture, it is no wonder that there is no 'temple' in the "City of the Living God." Instead, the Body of the Lamb and those reformed into God's image are its temple.

When that long-awaited day happens, the Temple of God within creation, which is none other than the Body of Christ, will become inaugurated by the harmony and prosperity rooted in the mutual up-building fellowship of God's completed household. When the entire family of God joins in perfected *shalom*, we will

---

[193] This form of the world for home-building here comes from a combination with the word for "upon", and so it refers to building upon something that has already been built, which refers to Christ (BDAG, 387).

partake of eternal fellowship with the Holy Spirit and the High Priest, Jesus Christ. At that time, our priestly unity becomes complete through sanctified fellow-thinking, fellow-feeling, and fellow-acting among the royal priesthood of Yahweh (Rom 8; Gal 5). We live together as brothers and sisters in a community where our hearts, minds, and spirits are in harmony as the unified family of God (1 Cor 1:10; Col 2:2; Phil 1:27-28, 2:1-2; Eph 4:3). We will then walk the streets of gold with our bodies. We will hear the angelic choruses with our ears. We will taste the fruit of the Tree of Life with our lips. At last, we will behold the radiating glory of the City of Living God and the majesty of the living stones like jewels reflecting the brilliance of the Divine (2 Cor 3:18; Col 1:27).

Rather than the end of our story, the conclusion of temporality will be an event that will mark a new beginning, the prologue to a new and far better story that never ends. As a family, we will co-compose and co-conduct a musical composition of everlasting thanksgiving to the Creator. As we do so, we will experience true existential freedom that shall never be taken away from us again. In Eternity, we will, moment by moment within endless moments, find ourselves willingly emptying ourselves toward one another in *agape*-love and heavenly *care*. These works of love act like brushstrokes of a painting, as they comprise the ever-expanding portrait of Divine Beauty on the canvas of Finitude. Our mutually shared communion of *agape*-love in Eternity stands out as a tabernacle for the familial fellowship revolving around the God-relationship. We shall reflect the perfect relational unity of *agape*-love and *phos*-light. This unity lies at the very center of the Trinity and defines the essence of God Himself.

> *Do revelations about the nature of your eternal destiny fill you with a desire to heed the Call of Eternity?*
>
> *Has it challenged your conception of how you should live your present life?*

In this new, redeemed reality, our Creator decrees that the old things of temporality will finally pass away. Transience will be replaced forever by the eternal uninterrupted fellowship of the family of God dwelling in the *rest* of their Heavenly Father (Gal 6:10; Heb 4:9-11; 1 Pet 2:17; Rev 21:4). "Thus, we must make every effort to enter that rest, so that no one may fall by following the same pattern of disobedience" (Heb 4:11).

Through the priesthood of saints, our heavenly High Priest shall convey the Word of God throughout redeemed creation. We will assist Him in bestowing and managing eternal life throughout the household of God. We will continuously shape creation into the fitting home and temple of the Triune I AM, ensuring that it succinctly and cohesively displays the glorious wonders of the Creator. In this respect, we can imagine our work *now* as preparing the grand concert hall wherein the music of our eternal habitation will reveal the grand eternal symphony of divine revelation at the end of all things. When the concert finally commences, our unfolding destinies will carry within them the never-ending notes and unceasing harmonies played by the children of God. Our music shall fill the Theatre of Divine Glory.

Given our eternal destiny, Yahweh situates Himself within fallen creation, not just by the immanency of the Spirit of God and the Son of God, but also through His children. We will proclaim and extend His legacy with pride and joy, inviting more and more people to prepare the hall for the grand concert to come. As seafarers, the banner of our ship should proudly bear witness to what we believe about our trustworthy Home and eternal destiny. We, therefore, must embrace the sanctifying call to become our true selves: to become a Sea of Revelation for the Maker in this life and the next. We must take up the task of supporting and furthering creation's destiny to be a reflection of the Living Sea of Revelation tabernacling in and through Yahweh's hands and feet.

The prophet Ezekiel received a glimpse into this great destiny. He beheld a divine vision portraying living creatures manifesting the self-disclosing glory of the Triune I AM, which then tabernacled in creation through them (Ezek 1:4-28). These angelic creatures manifested the self-disclosing glory of the Triune I AM, which then tabernacled in creation through them. They were a type of tabernacle of God's immanence, from whence He spoke and through whom He occupied Finitude. In the same way, the Living Word wills to abide in us by the Spirit, so that we might reveal both God's splendor and His work within Finitude in a way foreshadowed by the Jewish Temple (Exod 40:34; Ps 26:8; Ezek 43:4; Hag 2:7). This is why the Spirit provides instructions for an assembly of the Body of Christ to be a temple of God where the Spirit of Prophecy abounds. As we pondered, previously, we assemble for such a purpose and "all prophecy," "others who enter [our] gathering will be convicted by all" (1 Cor 14:24). In such a gathering, Scripture tells us, "the secrets of [the human] heart [will be] disclosed, and in this way [they] will fall down with [their] face to the ground and worship God, declaring, 'God is really among you'" (1 Cor 14:24-25, 31). Like the creatures in Ezekiel, the Body of Christ should be a site of divine encounters when we actualize our heavenly calling in Christ.

> *Could you honestly describe your community as a site of divine encounters transpiring through each priest present?*
>
> *How can you facilitate such an experience?*

For this reason, prophetic encounters ought to happen in any genuine religious assembly. When they transpire, those gathered will (like Ezekiel in His encounter with the Living Word) fall face down, worship God, and listen to God speak afresh through His living tabernacle, the Body of Christ (Ezek 1:28). For this reason, the Spirit calls every living stone to "pursue [*agape*-]love and be eager for the spiritual gifts, especially that you may prophesy... I wish you all spoke in tongues, but even more that you would prophesy... For you can all prophesy one after another, so all can learn and be encouraged" (1 Cor 14:1, 5, 31, 39). How often do many so-called "churches" give room for these divine commands to be realized within their four walls? Such a distinction separates tabernacles of human religion from a tabernacle of revelation. The Spirit of Revelation explicitly enforces this call, given to any genuine Body of Christ: "If anyone considers [themselves] a prophet or spiritual person, [they] should acknowledge that what I write to you is the Lord's command" (1 Cor 14:37).

One crucial reality about these prophetic encounters is that they are meant for *all* believers and members of the Body of Christ, not just one of us or "the best of us". We are not meant to emulate a representative democracy, where people have power in name but rely on elected leaders to do most of the work. Rather, the Body of Christ is more akin to a direct democracy, where everyone has a genuine and involved part in ruling without delegating anything to a class of leaders. *All* must seek to live in complete harmony with the supernatural manifestations of God's Spirit instead of simply relying on the spirit of a human leader. Leaders attempting to horde or possess a "monopoly" on the spiritual gift of "prophecy" expose themselves as fraudsters seeking to "steal" the glory of God's entire household for themselves. They proudly assert themselves as the only legitimate "priesthood." In doing so, they set up their temporal priesthood in opposition to Christ's eternal priesthood, just as the religious leaders of Jesus's day had done. We must not forget how the counterfeit priesthood of Jesus' day facilitated the very execution of the legitimate High Priest of Eternity! Many "priesthoods" dressed in religious "garb" since then have followed the example of persecuting legitimate priests of Yahweh's genuine tabernacle even making them martyrs. They masquerade as divine representatives following the patterns of many pagan religions throughout human history as they manifest human will and vision to the exclusion of Yahweh's will and vision.

All of us should also be wary of how the culture of the few leading the many can also breed "wolves" in sheep's clothing who seek to monetarily benefit from their assigned spiritual gifts while letting the masses languish with their spiritual gifts idle. They can promote a charade in which the "few" purportedly enjoy the benefits of Jesus' priesthood while expecting the congregation of the "many" to sit back and reap the grace overflowing from the spiritual roles of the "few" in God's household. Just imagine many so-called religious venues in which the masses remain, for the most part, passive and inactive, or simply a soundboard for the podium, as if they exist as second-class citizens or mere participants without a specific role to serve. A circle of priests, all taking turns prophesying together, stands out starkly against the multitude of humanistic religious venues. These venues are typically set up as auditoriums with a platform or stage upon which the "actors play their role," the audience watches and participates by following along in the performance.

In allowing the Holy Spirit to work through us, Yahweh's sanctifying omnipotent "hand" stretches out to touch the present fallen world we live in. Each of us who will be part of this work must partake of the home-making existentiality of God's indwelling presence. In being a co-worker with the Creator's self-emptying love, we promote the world-dwelling flourishing defined by His household and shaped by theocentric *oikonomia*. Our gift-giving imitating "the Father of Lights" happens as we administer His greatest gift, *phos*-light. Since He "is light," this gift is nothing less than the gift of Himself and His very home (1 Tim 6:16; Jms 1:17; 1 John 1:5). We can only reflect such a gift-giving disposition as we each participate in the same eternal fabric of world-dwelling befitting the Holy of Holies (2 Pet 1:4).

Our Maker invites us to live as those belonging to not merely another home but another age. Unlike those at home in the "ways of Babylon," we are oriented toward Eternity's "ways." We eagerly await our glorious future: the eternal chapter of Finitude, authored and initiated by the one true Sovereign. Until that Great Day, when "we will have put on our heavenly house," "a[n eternal] house not built by human hands," and "we walk by faith, not by sight" (2 Cor 5:1-7). We walk by the Spirit, whom God gave us as a "down payment" on His commitment to restore our rightful place. Accordingly, walking by faith should remain a central part of our world-dwelling and world-viewing until the long-awaited day when our faith becomes vindicated by what our physical eyes perceive.

> *What would happen if gatherings of the Body of Christ neglected the prophetic powers and encounters mentioned in Corinthians?*
>
> *Why is it vital for us as the Body of Christ to not ignore or downplay the spirit of prophecy as one of the central egalitarian principles of the Body of Christ as co-equal priests?*

Until the Dawn of Eternity, while we sojourn in temporality, we must "keep seeking the [eternal] things above, where Christ is… not things of the earth, for [we] have died and [our] life is hidden with Christ in God. When Christ (who is your life) appears, then [we] too will be revealed in glory with Him" (Col 3:1-4). For this reason, we read, "Dear friends, we are God's children now, and what we will be has not yet been revealed. We know that whenever it is revealed, we will be like Him, because we will see Him just as He is" (1 John 3:2). On that day, our spirit, soul, and body will finally come into likeness to the Son of God (Rom 8:23;

2 Cor 15:35-53). Therefore, even considering the awesomeness of our eternal destiny, we should humbly and meekly recognize "that [this] extraordinary power belongs to God and does not come from us" (2 Cor 4:7). "This treasure" has been placed "in clay jars" that represent our human earthly existence, which God clothes with the heavenly man, "Christ" in the "image of the One who created [us]" (Col 3:10; Gal 3:27).

[*Do you allow God to shape you into a worthy vessel to pour forth His splendor?*

Is this your lifesong?]

Chapter 12

Eternal Stewards of Creation

Royal Priests Caring for Creation as a Self-Disclosing Temple

"They were singing a new song, 'You [Jesus Christ] are worthy to take the scroll and to open its seals because You were killed, and at the cost of Your own blood You have purchased for God persons from every tribe, language, people, and nation. You have appointed them as a kingdom and priests to serve our God, and they will reign on the earth.'"

(Rev 5:9-10)

"Then I saw a new heaven and a new earth, for the first heaven and earth had ceased to exist, and the sea existed no more. And I saw the holy city—the new Jerusalem—descending out of heaven from God, made ready like a bride adorned for her husband. And I heard a loud voice from the throne saying: 'Look! The residence of God is among human beings. He will live among them, and they will be His people, and God Himself will be with them. He will wipe away every tear from their eyes, and death will not exist any more—or mourning, or crying, or pain, for the former things have ceased to exist.'"

(Rev 21:1-4)

Pondering our Eternal Destiny

In the last chapter, we explored co-managing stewardship over the earthly tabernacle of the Body of Christ, in addition to the stewardship of God's grace to minister beyond this tabernacle. In this chapter, we shall peer into the future to behold the glorious destiny awaiting us in the New Heaven and New Earth. We will explore what it truly means to be a royal priesthood, reigning with Christ and undertaking the work of building and maintaining His eternal kingdom. We will learn how this is not a call to dominate but rather to serve, steward, and be a channel for His Shepherding life and caring love to touch every corner of a renewed universe. We will serve as artists and builders, shaping creation into a theater of worship and revelation, guiding all things into a joyful odyssey of discovering His wonders, character, and nature into eternity.

Now, let us turn our attention to eternal stewardship. Our Maker invites us to embrace this calling in the fully restored world. In Eternity, this household will become in its entirety a dwelling place for God according to His pre-established *oikonomia*, just as He originally intended it to be (1 Cor 15). At that time, the face and heart of God will be reflected across the cosmos. Creation itself shall serve as a reflection and embodiment of *Agape-phosnoumenos*. The revelations of the Maker will be eternally poured out in a tabernacle touching all of creation, not merely confined to one planet, nation, or people. Shalom, fellowshipping, flourishing, and joy shall define existence rather than entropy, suffering, conflict, and survival.

We see a foreshadowing of how things were always meant to be when we look at the Creation story and observe how God "rested" on the seventh day after completing all things (Gen 2:1-3). Furthermore, notice how the Bible does not mention the seventh day ending with the refrain of "and then there was evening and there was morning" like all the six days prior (Gen 1). Instead, the seventh day of rest serves as an analogy for the final, eternal period of the Creation Story, where the true and original purpose of Creation itself will finally reach its culmination. So, what will this eternal "rest" entail? What will be our eternal duty by which we occupy this rest? We will ponder such mysteries in this chapter.

> *Do you aspire to inherit God's rest, understanding that in this life, you can never attain such perpetual peace?*

The eternal chapter of Finitude will commence once the pillars of Yahweh's immanent temple have all been set in place. Only then will all Finitude be subjected to those through whom these pillars exist as the holy of holies of the Temple of Yahweh. As His Temple spreads across Creation, we, as His agents, will forever serve as explorers and caretakers of His endless domain. At that time, Yahweh will have completed the inward and outward perfection of the co-managers of His finite household. We will all be fully prepared and equipped to carry out our eternal missions to promote our Maker's will and care throughout the universe.

To this end, we should, even now, perceive the realm of Finitude as God originally intended. Even now, we are blessed with both the purpose and the power to accomplish our mission as stewards of Finitude. No wonder our Guide describes our eternal identity as stewards as part of a "royal priesthood" who "reign on the earth" (1 Pet 2:9; Rev 5:10). However, only by adhering to divinely ordained authority and vision can we possibly wield such power. We serve as stewards, after all, not independent masters of our own domains. Therefore, this chapter will focus on how serving as the Creator's royal priests in Finitude allows us to properly serve Him as governing stewards over His creation into Eternity.

Royal Priests reigning with Christ in His Eternal Kingdom

We should now focus closely on two important passages, as they contain keys that unlock our eternal destiny:

> "I will grant the one who conquers permission to sit with Me on My throne, just as I too conquered and sat down with My Father on His throne."
>
> (Rev 3:21)

> "You have appointed them as a kingdom and priests to serve our God, and they will reign on the earth."
>
> (Rev 5:10)

The sensibleness of these passages becomes clear in light of the following revealed truth. Our identity lies "hidden with Christ in God," such that "when Christ (who is our life) appears, then we too will be revealed in glory with Him" (Col 3:3-4). We are not merely called to be God's servants or agents, like the Old Testament prophets. Scripture states that we are to eternally share the miraculous glory that accompanies the ministry of Christ as His "bride" (life partner). Consider it as not just being heralds of a king, but as princes – part of the royal line ourselves and thus sharing in its glory and governance.

One day, all those who have answered the Call of Eternity will set foot on the shores of Eternity. When we do, our Maker will place upon each of us a type of crown or mantle. This symbolizes our priestly royalty extending throughout His domain. However, like real princes, this is not merely a symbol of luxury and being spoiled but of great responsibility and expectation. For a royal family to rule effectively, all its members must fulfill their roles in modest harmony but instead pridefully restort to infighting, and woe betide the kingdom if they ignore or spurn the duty they are called to. Recall how, in many stories from history and fiction, the presence of corrupt, lazy, or selfish princes often spells the doom of the realm. Think also of the sons of David, Herod, and other historical monarchs. In the same way, our crowns carry great responsibility.

To fulfill the duties associated with our new spiritual office, we must realize our heavenly identity by spiritually dwelling in the heavenly communion chamber of our Heavenly Father. While we occupy this Holy of Holies, the Holy Spirit reveals to us what the Creator envisioned in the beginning for Finitude even before He laid its foundations (Isa 2:2-3; Mic 4:1-2). As the Scripture says,

> "Blessed is the God and Father of our Lord Jesus Christ, who has blessed us with every spiritual blessing in the heavenly realms in Christ. For He chose us in Christ before the foundation of the world that we should be holy and blameless before Him in love. He did this by predestining us to adoption as His legal heirs through Jesus Christ."
>
> (Eph 1:3-5)

In describing our position in Eternity as the ruling governors appointed by the Son of God in Creation, Scripture refers to us as "kings" and "priests" who "reign (*basileuo*) on the earth" (Rev 5:10). Many scholars conclude that the phrase "kings and priests" may represent a "*hendiadys*," meaning "priestly kingdom," aligning it with the prophecy of God's people being a "kingdom of priests" (Exod 19:6). Those who serve as "kings and priests" to "God" our "Father" for Eternity fulfill this role only through a close relationship with Him (John 15:1-6; Rev 1:6).

Can you imagine being part of the fulfillment of these biblical prophecies?

How does this reality impact your view of your identity and purpose?

To better understand the crucial need to align with our Heavenly Father in our "rule" over Creation, we can refer to the concept of the "Mandate of Heaven." In medieval Europe, kings who believed that God had divinely appointed them to rule often did not view their legitimacy as dependent on their adherence to divine will. If some did, it was not codified in any general way besides perhaps obedience to the Church. In ancient China, however, the emperor's legitimacy, believed to come from Heaven, depended significantly on how virtuous and just they were as rulers. If they strayed from this divine duty, as demonstrated in their actions and the consequences of their unjust governance, the ancient Chinese believed the Mandate of Heaven was withdrawn, granting the people the right to overthrow their ruler.

The Mandate of Heaven was not determined by bloodline or noble descent but rather by character and the ability to govern. Unlike in Europe, where one's ancestry mattered more than how well one ruled. Even peasants could, and often did, rise to replace the ruling dynasty and become emperor if they successfully rebelled and proved they could govern justly and effectively. However, if a new ruler acted against Heaven's will, he became unworthy of his position and liable to being overthrown like the emperor he had just replaced.

In a similar way, our role and mission regarding Finitude does not depend solely on our identities as siblings of Christ but on our faithfulness to His Father's will and *oikonomia*. As we abide in His will, He grants each of us a unique signet ring that symbolizes His dominion, making us co-sharers with Him over all Creation. Accordingly, at the beginning of the eternal chapter of our priesthood, our Heavenly Father clothes each of us with a priestly robe and a ruling "signet ring from the right hand of God" (Jer 22:24; Hag 2:23; Luke 15:22). Those who wear such symbolic attire are set apart from the rest of creation as "earthly representatives of

[Divine] authority" (Jer 22:24). We are thus called to rule "justly and well" as we steward our inheritance, always adhering to the true mandate of Heaven as we do so with control, violence, or manipulation.

In context, since "Christ is seated at the right hand of God," it must also be true that we are seated with Christ at the right hand of God (Col 3:1). The right hand symbolizes the power and sovereignty of the King of Creation. If our identity lies hidden in Christ, our "new [humanity]" will be eternally "renewed" "according to the image of the One who created it [Christ]" (Col 1:15-20; 3:10). God will set us apart completely to dwell as a new creation shaped in the image of Christ, fulfilling the purpose destined for us from the beginning. As Christ's dwelling, we will participate in His reign within Creation as His "body" of agents.

Since our true destiny is to live as "God's children," we exist as "heirs of God and fellow heirs with Christ," "so [that] we may also be glorified with Him" (Rom 8:16-17). In Eternity, Christ becomes glorified and promised over all the house of Finitude, for as God's firstborn "Son," He has been "appointed heir of all things" (Heb 1:2, 3:1-6). He will replace all the prior illegitimate world rulers, both human and demon alike. If we serve as co-heirs with Jesus Christ, who preside over the restored creation, then we reign alongside Him through the Spirit of adoption, sharing in the inheritance of the firstborn of God's household. Just as Scripture states, we embody His likeness, enabling us to share this position of firstborn sonship into eternity (Rom 13:14; Gal 3:27; Eph 4:13, 24).

> *Will God acknowledge you as fit to wear the signet ring and scepter of Jesus Christ?*
>
> *Will the Creator deem you suitable to wield His power and strength?*

To dive deeper into understanding what exactly is a "royal priesthood," let us unpack the Greek phrase, "*basileion hierateuma.*" The word "*basileion*" functions similarly to the English adjective "royal" (BDAG, 169-170), which relates to the position of "one who rules as the possessor of the highest office in a political realm." Theologically, this adjective also "refers to one who possesses transcendent power" (BDAG, 169-170). A royal priesthood, therefore, represents a specific priesthood whose office is intertwined with a supreme royal office. Such royal priests engage in the King's governing influence as members of His ruling body.

Biblically speaking, all positions within the royal priesthood fulfill prophecy: "Then take some silver and gold to make a crown and set it on the head of Joshua the high priest, the son of Jehozadak" (Jer 33:20-22; Zech 6:11).ˣ Regarding this prophecy, we also read, "There will be a priest with [Yeshua] on his throne, and they will see eye to eye on everything" (Zech 6:12-15). The children of God fulfill this prophecy by serving as a royal priesthood in harmony with Christ: "I will grant the one who conquers permission to sit with me [Jesus] on My throne, just as I too conquered and sat down with My Father on His throne... [I] have appointed them as a priestly kingdom and priests to serve our God, and they will reign on the earth" (Rev 3:21, 5:10). Therefore, being a member of the eternal priesthood means reigning alongside Christ, the Divine Incarnate, as our King while we serve as His governing Body Divine-Incarnate.

Will it be said of you that you have conquered?

Will you receive a position within Christ's eternal administration?

As the Architect of Finitude, the Creator originally intended to manage His creation like a sovereign king. Much like a king,

Yahweh has chosen to govern His dominion through governors representing His will and sovereignty. More than mere servants, we are meant to be covenant partners aligned with His vision and desires, ensuring His will is fulfilled within His realm. Like ancient Chinese emperors, we are called to execute our mandate to rule justly and virtuously, caring for what we govern rather than being selfish tyrants only concerned with what we can gain from our privileged position and how to retain power by whatever means.

The following testimony of our Creator reinforces the revelations of our eternal destiny: "I made the earth and the people and animals on it by My mighty power and great strength, and I give it to whomever I see fit" (Jer 27:5). From Eternity's perspective, the "whomever(s)" refer to the children of God. However, we must keep one thing in mind: the fact that the children of God will serve as kings and queens in the everlasting Kingdom of Christ does not diminish the priority of Christ's kingship. This becomes clear in the same book of Revelation that reveals how He will appoint us as co-rulers. Regarding the One who ordains our ruling authority, it is said of Him alone: "He has a name written on His clothing and on His thigh: 'King of kings and Lord of lords'" (Rev 19:16).

Christ's Kingdom will encompass the entire created universe, filled with kingdoms as numerous as the stars. Therefore, in our eternal homeland, the Incarnate Son of God will serve as the highest King among all His fellow siblings, whose priestly kingship remains forever subject to His own. We observe this arrangement throughout history whenever a king within a great empire is subordinate to a greater emperor or "king of kings." Consider how Herod of Judea was merely one of the client kings of the Roman Empire under Emperor Caesar Augustus, rather than a sovereign king of an independent kingdom. Similarly, the Son of God will eternally serve as the sole High Priest among a royal eternal priesthood. Hence, it is said of Jesus Christ alone, "Your throne, O God, is forever and ever, and a righteous scepter is the scepter of Your kingdom. Therefore, God, Your God, has anointed You over Your companions with the oil of rejoicing... [He had declared in this age,] 'Sit at My right hand until I make Your enemies a footstool for Your feet'" (Heb 1:8-13). At the dawn of Eternity, all enemies will be a footstool for Christ (Heb 10:13).

Through the intercession of God's Son, we who remain faithful to our priestly responsibilities in this life will reign in Eternity. We serve as royal priests whose jurisdiction is encompassed within Christ's high priesthood as the Lord of Lords, the chief intermediary between the Creator and His creation. As the Eucharist foreshadows, we also share in the bloodline of kings. As siblings of Christ, we participate in the royal lineage of Heaven, exercising divine authority when we govern and manage Creation in complete alignment with our older Brother's vision. He alone, among humanity, possesses a perfect vision for how the Narrative of Finitude can best glorify the Creator. Our role is to promote His headship as His chief representatives and ambassadors throughout His kingdom, which encompasses all Creation.

> *Consider all the tales of kings and queens you have read or watched. Even better, think about a story where someone discovers they are the lost heir to a kingdom. Now, picture your own life story being represented in such narratives.*
>
> *How does this make you feel about your duty and destiny?*

How the First Adam Foreshadowed our Eternal Destiny

Let us consider the situation of the first human: Adam. How did he establish himself in his home after being created and placed in the Garden of Eden, his new home? According to Scripture, he began to fulfill his God-given duty to name all the inhabitants:

> "The Lord God formed out of the ground every living animal of the field and every bird of the air. He brought them to the man to see what he would name them, and whatever the man called each living creature, that was its name. So, the man named all the animals, the birds of the air, and the living creatures of the field."
>
> (Gen 2:19-20)

We should not overlook the fact that the Creator brought all living creatures to Adam. Why did He? According to our Guide, He intended for each of them to serve as a "companion (helper) for him" (Gen 2:18). Unfortunately, the fall compromised the companionship that was meant to exist between humanity and the animal kingdom. In Eternity, this companionship will be permanently restored. How wonderful will that be? Instead of existing in "competition" with us as just another life form in a chaotic biosphere, all animals will once again recognize our rightful place as stewards of Creation.

Crucially, our place over nature is one of caretaking, not a place of exploitation, as we commonly witness in this world. Think of how humanity predominantly uses nature purely as a resource, extracting and exploiting it for our benefit through minerals, energy, food, or materials. Rather than this relationship of dominion and subjugation, animals in eternity will respond to the names we

> *What do you envision your life being like with the animal kingdom in Eternity?*
>
> *How should this motivate you as you navigate your present life?*

give them and accept us as fellow co-dwellers sharing the same home in harmony and peace. As we read, "A wolf will reside with a lamb, and a leopard will lie down with a young goat; an ox and a young lion will graze together... They will no longer injure or destroy on My entire royal mountain. For there will be universal submission to the Lord's sovereignty, just as the waters completely cover the sea" (Isa 11:6, 9). Animals will come when we call. Some of us may compose symphonies for the birds, while other animals will assist humans in manual labor, such as building projects. Regardless of whatever form this companionship may take, our relationship with the earth and our environment will fundamentally change. Rather than our property, they become our responsibility to care for, and even our friends to the extent possible. After all, they are part of God's design for His creation, too. We will be fellow worshippers of the Maker, united in a way we have never been and never can be in this fallen world.

Let us reflect further on the first that the Maker gave to humanity: the act of naming. This responsibility required Adam to identify the appropriate placement of living beings within the shared household of Finitude, which Yahweh created and populated during the first five days of creation. Essentially, Adam became the steward of the roles and activities of the animal kingdom within this household. He was to be a "co-composer" alongside the Creator's Spirit. Like Adam, the Maker desires us to behold His visions for Creation, much like builders follow an architect's blueprints or conductors direct a composer's composition. Through this co-composing, Adam fostered stewardship and homemaking through kingdom-building within the Creator's

> *Do you really want to be a co-working partner with God for all eternity?*
>
> *If so, how are you applying for such a position?*

realm.[194] From day six onward, fulfilling this home-making role in Eden centered on the relationship with God.

The Maker did not intend for us to be stewards serving in His stead or to be left alone in caring for Creation in His absence, as in a deistic view of the world.[195] He created us to be His fitting companions, tending to the garden He established. The Garden of Eden served as the first tabernacle or temple through which God dwelt with humans. "Then the man and his wife heard the sound of the Lord God moving about in the orchard at the breezy time of day" (Gen 3:8). From the beginning, we see that Yahweh wanted Adam to exercise His dominion-making influence while in communion with Him (Gen 1:26-28, 3:8).

Why is it so important for our role in ruling to be carried out with and through God rather than merely in service to Him? Simply put, it is only through God's influence that we can grasp His divine vision, which goes beyond the limits of human cognition, imagination, and sensory perception. Furthermore, active participation in our relationship with God is necessary to realize this revelatory vision. As we will explore in depth elsewhere in our theological study, it takes God to understand God. True theology acknowledges God alone as the authentic teacher who offers the means to comprehend and apply such teachings. He alone can enlighten and empower us to act as His worthy stewards within the context of the Temple of Yahweh.

---

[194] For this reason, J.R.R. Tolkien emphasized the significance of humankind's creative abilities, especially in fantasy literature, as a form of "sub-creation." This mirrors the creative power of the God who made us in His image. Whenever we exercise our ability to create, particularly through our imagination, Tolkien believed we can offer a glimpse of what God intended for us to do alongside Him from the very beginning.

[195] According to this view, God created but then left to operate on its own without being involved or present.

Even though the animals served as Adam's companions, none corresponded perfectly to him in an equally yoked partnership (Gen 2:18, 20). As we know, God went on to create the woman, Eve (Gen 2:21-24), as a partner with identical, distinct, and complementary aspects of human identity. God intended for this companionship to foreshadow the relationship between Christ and His Bride. Out of all life on earth, only we humans have the calling and capacity to be His stewards and tabernacles within Creation. Proper stewardship requires that our actions be guided and infused by the Divine life of *agape*-love, *phos*-light, and *pneuma*-spirit (1 John 4:7-17). To this end, God's indwelling presence must inhabit, enlighten, inspire, and empower our eternal mission. This unfolds as long as we commit ourselves to being discipled by our Maker. Obedience is our spiritual act of worship, granting us access to the authority needed to care for His creation (Ps 95:6-7).

Were we human beings not first created to manage the Garden of Eden and serve as stewards over its creatures (Gen 1:26-27, 2:15)? Nevertheless, Eden offers us only a glimpse into the eternal role of co-management assigned to all who would be among God's royal priests (Rev 5:10, 22:5). In Eternity, Creation will become a garden on our "household grounds" for our Creator and us, one personalized by the care of its inhabitants. As His covenant partners, we will emulate Him by establishing the contextual parameters of the house's garden, managing this landscape according to the specifications of His eternal blueprint.

{ *Spend time meditating in a garden.*

What does this teach you about Eternity? }

It is for these reasons that our Maker beckons humanity to make creation our partners, just as He made us partners (Gen 2:18, 20). Through us, Yahweh sends forth His Divine Breath to set the inhabited world apart as His home. Adam, fulfilling his duty as the archetypal human, established it as the dwelling place of God by assigning names that appropriately categorized its contents. Essentially, His management coordinated creation according to and through a revealed *oikonomia*. Like Adam, we should move in and out of our Master's workshop to co-shepherd His creation by word and deed according to His vision established in the Beginning (Eph 2:10).

Our Dominion: The Entire Universe

Our stewardship corresponds to the entire dominion of Christ: The New Earth and the New Heavens. Though very different from the physical territory we are accustomed to, the spiritual domain will feel as natural to us as the air and ground do now. We will perceive all dimensions of the created domain, including the invisible and insensible, as easily as we now perceive colors, hear sounds, and feel the matter of the world around us. We will thoroughly experience what the prophets only glimpsed: the supernatural overlaying the natural world. Recall Plato's Allegory of the Cave, where the philosopher frees himself from perceiving only shadows and echoes in his dark cave to behold reality in the sun's light.[196] Such will be our experience whenever we discover

---

[196] For those unfamiliar, Plato's Allegory of the Cave depicts a dark cave where people have spent their entire lives chained up, only able to see the cave's walls. All they can observe are the shadows of objects passing in front of a fire, along with the muffled echoes of individuals moving nearby. Knowing nothing else, they perceive these shadows and muffled echoes as truth and reality.

Plato invites us to imagine what would occur if one of these individuals were suddenly freed from his bonds and found his way outside. What would he see? The glorious and blazing light of the sun, through which the true forms of things and the world are perceived. If that person then returned to the cave to share his experiences, however, Plato suggests he would at best be laughed at and at worst be actively attacked by those who refuse to leave the confined reality of the cave.

the true nature of reality, which is currently hidden from our fallen, temporal perspective. The supernatural visions found in Ezekiel, Daniel, Zechariah, and Revelation provide just a taste of the experiences awaiting us beyond the limits of human imagination. In fact, we shall perceive our new home through nothing less than divine imagination, the very imagination that "spoke" the entire universe into existence from nothing.

The Eternity Project encompasses the enterprise of building and maintaining the true temple of Yahweh across the created cosmos. As priests in God's household, the heavenly Temple, "we [shall be] co-workers with God," serving "God's building" (1 Cor 3:9). The new Earth will serve as our "home base," a new Zion for humanity, which will act as divine agents throughout the universe, representing our Creator's will, authority, and power. The Maker has clarified that He created a seemingly infinite universe to serve as a suitable "dwelling place" for the Infinite One, who will eternally "empty" Himself by filling Creation as an ever-expanding universe. Imagine an overflowing spring, from which a great river rushes to nourish and fill a valley. Instead of the valley being filled to the brim, however, imagine it stretching out to embrace the ever-growing river without ever stopping. Like this river, God's act of filling Creation does not diminish Him, nor does Creation ever exhaust God's self-disclosures. As the prophet Zechariah foresaw, the dominion of "New Jerusalem" will have no true "boundaries/limits" (Zech 2:4). The entire cosmos will be our "Sea of Revelation" and our "vineyard" that we steward. If this boggles your mind to the extent that

[*Are you inspired by the prospect of spending eternity exploring all of Creation as representatives of the Maker?*]

Such (and even greater) is the profound shift in our existence that will take place when we finally transition from this mortal, limited world into our supernatural, eternal true home.

you cannot comprehend it...it should! Such a reality is too much for our finite minds to truly grasp this outcome. Instead, we must trust in that promise and prepare ourselves for its advent.

As history has shown us, the human spirit contains an instinctive drive to explore and discover. People spread worldwide to find new homes and boldly crossed continents and oceans long before modern technology made it easier. Not content to "fly" within the Earth's atmosphere, we eventually ventured beyond it to explore space. If higher dimensions became accessible to us, like we see in so much science fiction, we would probably yearn to explore those too. Our Maker imbued within us a desire to explore without limits. For those of us in the modern age, space represents a "final frontier," as described in the epic space opera *Star Trek*.

In summary, humans have aspired to transcend the boundaries that confine us. We seem to understand that we were born to "live among the stars." As the prophetic scripture suggests: "But the wise will shine like the brightness of the heavenly expanse. And those bringing many to righteousness will be like the stars forever and ever" (Dan 12:2-3). The cosmic theme of this prophecy of "everlasting life" exists for a reason; it illustrates humanity's purpose in Eternity, the ultimate fulfillment of our innate heavenly yearning. What other lifeform possesses such a drive to know and see more, even when it has nothing to do with survival? How wonderful it is to know that our Maker created us for missions beyond the scope of any one planet! He shaped the cosmos as a "playground" for Himself and His children to enjoy forever, without the possibility of exhaustion or boredom.

Eternal Stewards of Creation

Our fitting role in Creation reflects the character of God as a caring heavenly Father (Luke 11:9-13). This care for creation is illustrated in Jesus' following teaching:

> "Look at the birds in the sky: They do not sow, or reap, or gather into barns, yet your heavenly Father feeds them. Are you not more valuable than they are? ...Why do you worry about clothing? Consider how the flowers of the field grow; they do not work or spin. Yet I tell you that not even Solomon in all His glory was dressed like one of these! And if this is how God clothes the wild grass, which is here today and tomorrow is thrown into the fire to heat the oven, will not He clothe you even more, you people of little faith?"
>
> (Matt 6:26-30)

These teachings clarify that although the Heavenly Father, the Creator, cares for all of creation, He cares most deeply for those made in His own image, as He created them to be His children. Therefore, we who embark on this journey must strive to make our Father proud by prioritizing caring about what He cares about. It is through our love for Him that we also show care for others, including creatures and flowers. In fact, it is only from the great wellspring of mutual love found in the God-relationship that we can fulfill our calling to love all of creation as He does—both the beautiful and the "ugly." After all, we love only because He first loved us (1 Jn 4:19). We should never forget that our Creator invites each of us to return to our eternal duty as co-workers with Him in managing the household of creation in this way. In responding to this call, we cannot overlook the significance of a tabernacle and our nourishment through our relationship with God. Ultimately, we manage creation for the sake of our Master, Father, Friend, and Beloved. Thus, those who join this mission must invest themselves to ensure His household fulfills His expectations, just as any friend would and should do.

As inhabitants of a fallen world, we recognize how the physical environment we currently live in "has been subjected to futility" and thus "groans" in anticipation of being re-created (Rom 8:19-22). One only needs to look at the nature of the world to see that this is true; that things are not as they could (indeed *should*) be. Creation awaits the complete restoration of its stewards, for then "creation itself will also be set free from the bondage of decay into the glorious freedom of God's children" (Rom 8:21). This occurs when the children of God, the Bride of Christ, collectively step into our eternal destiny (Rom 8:23-24). In this way, we can define our true destiny as being stewards of a restored created order, caring for it just as our Heavenly Father does. This governing role within the New Heaven and Earth serves to bring forth its purpose as a fitting eternal habitation of the Creator: a temple made up of all of us as its pillars, even as we ourselves are temples. Therefore, we must aspire to genuinely be heavenly world-dwellers even now on earth through His Word, while simultaneously residing in heaven as created persons formed in the image of His Word by the sanctifying power of His Spirit (John 3:3-8; 1 Pet 1:2; Eph 3:16-19, 4:13, 24).

> *When you gaze upon the fallen, groaning Creation, does your heart ache for it as our Heavenly Father's does?*

What will happen once the Body of Christ is brought to completion and the construction of God's eternal temple is finished? We will guide creation by following the house rules of prosperous shalom. Imagine us as artists tasked with building, decorating, and bringing forth a magnificent new work of art according to the plan and will. Consider the *Basílica de la Sagrada Família* in Barcelona. It is perhaps one of the most unique churches in the world, famous for being under construction for the last 142 years as of this book's writing! Although architect Antoni Gaudí pioneered its design and construction, countless other architects, artists, sculptors, painters, and builders have all contributed their immense talents and ideas to its creation, while still adhering to Gaudí's original vision. In the same way, though creation is the masterpiece of our Father alone, we are invited to take part in its construction and beautification, adding our unique identities and contributions to its tapestry. We shall all be artists and "sub-creators," unleashing our individually crafted roles onto this grand work of art, even as it follows the great plan of *the* Creator.

We will all become fully acquainted with Creation's true potential as an eternal paradise. More than merely a work of creation, our eternal task will also be one of discovery and stewardship. Imagine the role of zookeepers who carefully curate each individual habitat in a zoo or nature sanctuary to suit various animal species. Like them, we will manage every Creation "habitat" to ensure that everything in it thrives to its fullest potential. Creation will no longer "groan" under the weight of futility as predators hunt prey, species become extinct, and natural disasters wreak havoc on entire ecosystems. The destructive necessity of wildfires, the circle of life, volcanic eruptions, hurricanes, typhoons, tornadoes, and so forth will cease when the stewards accomplish their mission of environmental protection. Even the most vulnerable creatures and organisms shall flourish and thrive under our care.

> *Does the prospect of partnering with God to build and care for such a redeemed and beautiful world fill you with anticipation?*
>
> *Does it inspire you to view your gifts and talents from a fresh perspective?*

To all these ends, we will also harness our intelligence and creativity to positively impact the world. Humanity will no longer bear the guilt of introducing corruption and destruction to God's

Creation, such as through human-made environmental disasters like human caused climate change, pollution, oil spills, or the dreadful uses of human innovation, such as the atomic bomb. No longer will we exploit our superiority as a species to possess and control creation from a position of greed or exploitation. This is not the "rule" intended by God when He originally created us in the Garden of Eden (Gen 1:26). Like our Maker, we will use our innovative abilities to promote the preservation and flourishing of Creation as the Theater of Revelation. After all, we all reflect the image of the Creator's creativity for a reason. We see this in all the good and beautiful things that, through the grace of God, we have brought forth amid a fallen world: art, poetry, fiction, community, music, the ability to build, cuisine, and so much more. We catch glimpses of the joy of God's creativity in us, as we witness humans turn something as potentially mundane as some turn recycled trash into beautiful art pieces. Consider how we take the need to nourish ourselves and make it into an art form that has given us salad, pizza, wine, and ice cream! Human creativity and innovation, including our capacity for wonder, will endure forever, sanctified and restored to the beauty God originally intended. Boredom will be a forgotten memory. The joy of witnessing a blooming flower or a setting sun will accompany our every endeavor as we nurture and appreciate ongoing moments of awe and wonder at nature's ability to reveal the divine glories of the Creator's self-disclosures.

> *What does it say about God's character that He has created us to be explorers, discovering things He has laid out for us rather than simply spoon-feeding it to us?*

Let us remember why God created Finitude in the first place. Though He does not *need* to, as He requires nothing outside of Himself, Yahweh desired and chose to establish an eternal Infinite-finite *koinonia* (fellowship/communion), a means for His love to extend beyond the Trinity to others. Our stewardship over His household helps preserve its status as a "sacred space," effectively promoting and facilitating this communion between us and Him, *as well* as among ourselves; a fellowship between mutually self-revealing faces. Through this process, we nurture our relationship with God, enhance our self-awareness, and deepen our fellowship with all creatures. Our eternal narrative unfolds, where we continuously discover our identity and role within the Story of Creation: the God Story. Today, people can spend a lifetime trying to unlock the mysteries of a given species, both individually and in relation to other species and their environments. Though finite and temporal, even fallen creation offers a seemingly endless array of things to discover, inspire, and marvel. Just imagine how much more a restored, eternal creation has to provide! Furthermore, the wisdom of the Creator – not the flawed ethics and priorities of humanity – will direct all our scientific and technological undertakings as we uncover the wonders He has embedded throughout Creation for us to discover. As we discover, appreciate, and nurture the uniqueness of everything in the endless Sea of Revelation awaiting us, we will also uncover our uniqueness and encounter distinct revelations of the Creator and His Vision.

Alongside this wide variety of things to explore, there will also be seemingly endless depths and layers. In Eternity, every physical reality will possess a spiritual dimension within the realm of Revelation.[197] Essentially, we will be granted eyes to perceive a dimension beyond the physical, gazing into the truth and meaning of all things with our spiritual senses. For example, think about the precious minerals and stones that compose the City of Divinity as recorded in Scripture; each one assumes a revelatory significance

---

[197] As an analogy, recall how in *The Lord of the Rings* the wearer of the One Ring can perceive the unseen world and see, as Frodo did, both the true ghostly forms of the Nazgul and the light of Valinor shining from the Elves.

within the context of Yahweh's self-disclosing nature (Rev 4:33, 21:19-20). Our obligation will be to figuratively excavate and construct the temple of Yahweh, enveloping the entirety of Creation. In Eternity, many or all of us will become part-time explorers, miners, artists, musicians, cathedral builders, and more.

As we create and explore this new eternal world, Yahweh will willingly share the intimate details of what He originally envisioned in the Beginning. In the Maker's workshop, like a master sharing trade secrets with his apprentices, we will learn from Him the *oikonomia* He pre-established to shape the events of Finitude according to His good plans, purposes, and desires. We become disciples of the Master Gardener, whose garden encompasses all of Creation. We uncover the mysteries of the cosmos to manage it as a "fruitful vineyard" that yields both physical and spiritual fruit. Another way to illustrate our eternal calling is by envisioning a grand library that contains the all the narratives written by the Author of Finitude. In turn, we will "translate" these texts into the physical realm through our words and deeds, manifesting spiritual realities into physical ones.

God, our great Master Architect, will personally guide human education in Eternity to spread joy and order throughout the expanding universe. We may not know precisely how this will happen, but we can let our imaginations soar. For instance, think about the dream of terraforming planets – transforming barren landscapes into vibrant ecosystems. While this is theoretical with our current technology, it could be achievable in Eternity. Perhaps God will reveal the secrets of nurturing biological life across the universe. Imagine transforming planets like Mars into a paradise! Did not the prophet Isaiah foretell that Christ's reign would see deserts turned into lush gardens (Isa 35)? Currently, humanity seems more prone to transforming "paradises into deserts" by using nuclear weapons, starting forest fires without proper forest management, polluting water, contaminating soil, causing oil spills, and engaging in war. In Eternity, once the stain of original sin and our flawed nature are ultimately resolved, such actions will no longer define humanity. Our redeemed nature will embrace creation, preservation, and flourishing in everything we undertake.

In summary, Yahweh will guide humanity into our originally intended destiny, foreshadowed in Genesis: to rule over all living creatures (Gen 1:26, 28; Rev 5:10). The new earth will become the new "Eden, the garden of God" that the children of God will eternally "care for" and "maintain" (Gen 2:15; Ezek 28:13). We will serve as instruments for the advancement and preservation of Yahweh's kingdom. When this takes place, the following prophecies will be fulfilled in their entirety:

> "This desolate [fallen] land [of temporality] has become like the garden of Eden… Certainly, the Lord will console Zion; He will console all her ruins. He will make her wilderness like Eden, her desert like the Garden of the Lord. Happiness and joy will be restored to her, thanksgiving and the sound of music."
>
> (Ezek 36:35; Isa 51:3; also see Joel 2:3)

Our entire universe will become a "Garden of Eden." This transformation will occur through those chosen to make all creation Yahweh's home. We will serve as mediators, infusing the creative vitality of the Divine as we shepherd stars and planets into the "green pastures" of everlasting shalom.

Let us meditate on a passage that illustrates the eternal restoration of the originally intended created order of shalom:

> "A wolf will reside with a lamb, and a leopard will lie down with a young goat; an ox and a young lion

will graze together, as a small child leads them along. A cow and a bear will graze together, their young will lie down together. A lion, like an ox, will eat straw. A baby will play over the hole of a snake; over the nest of a serpent an infant will put his hand. They will no longer injure or destroy on My entire royal mountain. For there will be universal submission to the Lord's sovereignty, just as the waters completely cover the sea...The sound of weeping or cries of sorrow will never be heard in her again... A wolf and a lamb will graze together; a lion, like an ox, will eat straw, and a snake's food will be dirt. They will no longer injure or destroy on My entire royal mountain."

(Isa 11:6-9, 65:19, 25)

No death. No pain. No violence. Very unlike the current and past history of the Middle East. Divine sovereignty will have come full circle in realizing the Creator's vision. Each of us, as divine representatives, will uphold "universal submission to the Lord's sovereignty" throughout creation (Isa 11:9).

> *When was the last time you felt the awe and wonder of a child experiencing their "firsts" in nature?*
>
> *How can you reclaim this lost inheritance of childhood?*

Fashioning the Cosmos into a Worship Theater of Revelation

The following passage elucidates the intended relationship between creation and God's temple:

"How lovely is the place where You live, O Lord of Heaven's Armies! I desperately want to be in the courts of the Lord's temple. My heart and my entire being shout for joy to the living God. Even the birds find a home there, and the swallow builds a nest[198] where she can protect her young near Your altars, O Lord who rules over all, my king and my God. How blessed are those who live in Your temple and praise You continually!"

(Ps 84:1-4)

This Psalm illustrates humanity living in harmony with *both* creation and the Creator within God's Temple. We must not overlook that the Psalmist had a deep understanding of God's relationship with and care for nature. God, after all, calls all of Creation good when He created it, and the Bible frequently references how He cares for His creation beyond just humanity. Is it any wonder Jesus is referred to as a shepherd, perhaps one of the archetypal figures of someone caring for animals?

Rather than seeing the cosmos as merely a "backdrop" to our stories or a resource to be used at will, it also plays a crucial role in our eternal destinies and functions. Essentially, we are to guide creation to reflect the glories of the Creator, much like a temple conveys the glory and nature of the deity or spiritual essence it honors. This remains a central aspect of our participation in Infinite-finite communion. A true priest facilitates "worship" to "God" "by the Spirit" as an appropriate response to the Maker's self-disclosing acts and revelations (Ezra 3:8-13; Ps 5:7; Rom 9:4; Phil 3:3; Rev 22:3). By harnessing the "winds" of the Divine Breath, we help sanctify creation to glorify the Maker's vision for

{ *Eternity welcomes only builders and preservers; will we be counted among them invited?* }

---

[198] If a bird tried to do this in must church buidings today, they would be driven away immediately.

oikonomia, spreading the seeds of the Maker's thoughts to be planted and nurtured throughout the entire physical universe, as a home of the God-relationship.

> The heavens declare the glory of God;
> the sky displays his handiwork.
> Day after day it speaks out;
> night after night it reveals his greatness.
> There is no actual speech or word,
> nor is its voice literally heard.
> Yet its voice echoes throughout the earth;
> its words carry to the distant horizon.
>
> (Ps 19:1-4)

Let us take a moment to reflect on some significant insights in the book of Job. Both Elihu and God primarily used the "Voice of Creation" to respond to Job's accusations against Providence throughout his lament. Similarly, we should learn to harness the symphony of creation through the power and guidance of the Revelatory Spirit. We should strive to be a channel of divine revelation within an Infinite-finite community of mutual self-disclosure (Job 36:26-41:34). Consider the following excerpts from Elihu:

> "Yes, God is great – beyond our knowledge! The number of His years is unsearchable. He draws up drops of water; they distill the rain into its mist, which the clouds pour down and shower on humankind abundantly. Who can understand the spreading of the clouds, the thunderings of His pavilion? See how He scattered His lightning about Him; He has covered the depths of the sea. It is by these that He judges the nations and supplies food

> in abundance.... God thunders with His voice in marvelous ways; He does great things beyond our understanding. For to the snow He says, 'Fall to earth,' and to the torrential rains, 'Pour down.' He causes everyone to stop working, so that all people may know His work... The clouds go round in circles, wheeling about according to His plans, to carry out all that He commands them over the face of the whole inhabited world...
>
> Pay attention to this, Job! Stand still and consider the wonders God works. Do you know how God commands them... Do you know about the balancing of the clouds, that wondrous activity of Him who is perfect in knowledge?... But now, the sun cannot be looked at – it is bright in the skies – after a wind passed and swept the clouds away. From the north, He comes in golden splendor; around God is awesome majesty. As for the Almighty, we cannot attain to Him! He is great in power, but with justice and abundant righteousness He does not oppress...

Consider the following excerpts by Yahweh, Himself:

> Where were you when I laid the foundation of the earth? Tell Me, if you possess understanding! Who set its measurements – if you know... when the morning stars sang in chorus, and all the sons of God shouted for joy?... The earth takes shape like clay under a seal; its features are dyed like a garment... Who carves out a channel for the heavy rains, and a path for the rumble of thunder, to cause it to rain on an uninhabited land... to satisfy a

devastated and desolate land, and to cause it to sprout with vegetation... Do you know the laws of the heavens, or can you set up their rule over the earth?... Who prepares prey for the raven, when its young cry out to God and wander about for lack of food?... Who let the wild donkey go free? Who released the bonds of the donkey, to whom I appointed the steppe for its home, the salt wastes as its dwelling place?... Do you give the horse its strength? Do you clothe its neck with a mane? Do you make it leap like a locust? Its proud neighing is terrifying!... Is it by your understanding that the hawk soars, and spreads its wings toward the south?...

> *Have you genuinely communed with and experienced God, or has your faith journey thus far been confined to an intellectual exploration and appreciation of the divine?*

Get ready for a difficult task like a man. I will question you and you will inform Me! Would you indeed annul My justice? Would you declare Me guilty so that you might be right? Do you have an arm as powerful as God's... Look now at Behemoth, which I made as I made you; it eats grass like the ox... Its bones are tubes of bronze, its limbs like bars of iron. It ranks first among the works of God"

(Job 36:26-31; 37:5-7, 12, 14-16, 21-23; 38:4-5, 7, 14, 25-27, 33, 41; 39:5-6, 19-20, 26; 40:7-9, 15-19)

In Eternity, passages like these will vividly come to life. We will echo these prophecies in an endless poetic ensemble. Together, we will witness the Maker's eternal vision unveiled through the unfolding of the pre-established *oikonomia* of Finitude. After all, our Maker created this very context of Finitude and everything in it to exist as a Theatre of Revelation. The primary stage of this theatre is the souls of God's children. Hence, our active participation will fulfill the ultimate purpose of creation. It will always represent the realm of Infinite-finite communion between the Heavenly Father and those whom He created and restored in His own image in nature and character.

The Holy Spirit ultimately aims to sanctify God's household, transforming it into a sacred space where everything exists to worship and serve Him. Quite literally, we are to turn Creation itself into one vast Temple. It will forever exist as a manifestation of an eternal song of worship as He dwells with us forever. Yahweh originally designed all things to partake in this everlasting worship song. By singing it, we, in turn, teach and inspire creation to proclaim it throughout the universe. As priests serving creation, we guide it into eternal choruses, "declaring the glory of God" and "revealing His greatness" (Ps 19:1-2). One might say our role as priests is to lead all Creation in worshiping and honoring our Maker.

> *Have you taken the time to listen to the Voice of Creation?*
>
> *Try to make a routine of taking walks in the classroom of nature.*

There are many different metaphors and illustrations through which we can understand the canvas of the New Creation and our role within it. We have drawn upon symphonies, works of art, stories, vineyards, tapestries, and great buildings or cities. All are fitting and evocative, but necessarily too limited to capture the full wonder of the "temple" of Creation. It will serve as a canvas on which the expressions of our Creator's character, attributes, power, and providence will eternally manifest (Ps 19:1-4; Rom 1:20). Our role within is to serve Him, beautifying this plane with divine self-manifestations as His eternal stewards, ensuring this eternal blossoming by nurturing and fostering it. We are artists, builders, and caretakers alike, but perhaps what unites them all is our role as channels, as intermediaries between Heaven and Earth.

Let us, return once again to our discussions of being bridges between Heaven and Earth; the contextual and supercontextual. Our work, although we can liken it to that of artists, is to serve as the "gates" through which Yawheh's infinite supercontextuality becomes contextual in a finite world; each according to our specific identities, contextualities, and selves. Hence, the great divine composition of *Agape-Phosnoumenos* is to be "re-envisioned" through His Spirit in us into the real world.

If a great artist has a vision of beauty in their heads, that vision will not amount to anything unless it is translated from their imagination into reality through the specific medium they choose, whether through paints, words, musical instruments, shots taken from a camera or strung together in an editing room, or anything else. We can think of this process as taking the work from the formless world of ideas and clothing it with "reality" to a form that can be shared, enjoyed, and understood by others. Perhaps it will never be the same as its "perfect," ideal, formless vision, but it nonetheless cannot affect others without that process of "translation" or contextualization. Likewise, though it will always be impossible for finite beings (even glorified ones) to fully grasp or experience the Infinite (as that is the purview of God alone), we can indeed relate to Him and bring Him to others by us perceiving and serving as His finite contextualizations.

In the afterlife, our Creator will teach us the melody of Eternity, which is holiness. Through our words and deeds performed while abiding in the Holy Spirit, Creation, including us, will echo this melody (Acts 4:31; Rom 15:18; 1 John 3:18). For this reason, "creation groans and suffers together, eagerly awaiting the revelation of the sons [children] of God..." When the children of God fully embrace the stewardship originally intended by God, "creation itself will also be set free from the bondage of decay into the glorious freedom of God's children" (Rom 8:19-22). We can compare such restoration to a host of out-of-tune and broken instruments being repaired to be able to harmoniously to play together in an orchestra when the conductor finally returns after having been absent for so long. All Creation will then be set free to perform and co-conduct the music of Eternity.[199]

Indeed, we often use orchestral symphonies as an illustration because of how fitting they are. A large group of people comes together, each contributing their unique parts, to follow the composer's vision as guided by the conductor. Consider, for example, Handel's Messiah. In many cases, this music's precise playing and interpretation can vary based on the players and conductor, leading to beautiful variations, all while trying to interpret the original vision. Yahweh created us to be co-conductors of the ensemble of creation, guiding countless participants to manifest the light of His self-revealing face. Consider how Max Richter created a new compositional interpretation of Vivaldi's Four Seasons. We will conduct the instruments of creation, producing "sounds" of worship inspired by the Maker's vision for the created world. These instruments range from living beings such as animals and plants to inanimate objects like mountains and stars. Each serve as a unique instrument in Creation's symphony through their sacred interaction within the contextual world.

---

[199] Just think about what musical compositions Mozart, Bach, or Beauthoven could have composed if they had all eternity.

Into Eternity, we will help co-conduct the symphony of Creation through our roles and gifts as we engage in true worship, fitting for the Triune I AM. This everlasting music channels the glorious reflections of God revealed through the varying degrees of glory assigned to created realities. For instance, "there are heavenly bodies and earthly bodies. The glory of the heavenly body is one kind, and the earthly another. There is one glory of the sun, and another glory of the moon, and another glory of the stars, for star differs from star in glory" (1 Cor 15:40-41). Similarly, the Maker designed each person's destiny to uniquely oversee a specific set of created instruments in the endless ensemble that fills creation with His revealed glory. We guide a series of pitches and sounds available to these instruments, contributing to the infinitely multifaceted sounds of worship through the Voice of Creation echoing throughout the household of finitude: the grandest cathedral (Ps 19:1-4).

Recall how, in a previous chapter, we observed that Yahweh exists as His Infinite composition of self-manifesting glory. Through His Spirit, we collaborate to translate this song and vise versa. For this purpose, we will teach the angels an endless repertoire of hymns. We will conduct the instruments of creation, the sounds of worship inspired by the Maker's vision for the created world.

Do you anticipate participating in the Choir of Eternity?

Will you be a conduit through which the Infinite God is contextually expressed in Finitude?

To this end, Divine inspiration will shape all our physical engagements within the vineyard of creation. Here, we assist in co-orchestrating the symphony of creation to perform this divine composition. We assist in reflecting Yahweh's character, attributes, and power throughout the unending Narrative of Finitude. The primary aim of this divine self-disclosing composition is to foster communion (*koinonia*) and dialogue among each individual God-relationship unfolding within the Theatre of Finitude. All Creation will forever be enveloped in the greatest Love Story ever told. Every occurrence will serve as a potential meeting place between Heaven and Earth. Each action will unfold as a dance between the Creator and His most cherished creation. After all, how can the house (*oikos*) of Finitude be the genuine household of God if it is not filled with Infinite-finite communion between the Maker and who share His finite abode?

Living Waters of Eternity: Joy, Blessing & Sanctification

Let us reflect on a prophetic passage about the final temple:

> "[A life-giving spring will] flow out from the Temple of the Lord… every living creature which swarms where the river flows will live; there will be many fish, for these waters flow there. It will become fresh, and everything will live where the river flows… On both sides of the river's banks, every kind of tree will grow for food. Their leaves will not wither, nor will their fruit fail, but they will bear fruit every month because their water source flows from the sanctuary. Their fruit will be for food, and their leaves for healing."
>
> (Ezek 47:1-12; Jer 3:18)

> *Are you prepared to dance the Dance of Eternity?*
>
> *How can you incorporate a heavenly dance into your daily routine?*

Consider how springs and rivers are the source of life and flourishing in the world, especially in regions with little rain. Imagine, for example, how the Nile River in Egypt transformed what was otherwise a barren desert into one of the lushest, most fertile, and beautiful regions in the world during ancient times. Farms, gardens, and lagoons lined its banks, fostering one of the wealthiest and most powerful kingdoms in early history. In fact, consider how almost all early human civilizations were sustained by the life brought by great rivers; from the Mesopotamians who depended on the Tigris and Euphrates, to the ancient Chinese who relied on the Yellow and Yangtze rivers. Similarly, the great unending river that flows from our Lord's Temple will nourish and bring life to the New Heaven and New Earth, as well as to the new world we shall cultivate there. We will witness the fulfillment of this prophecy with our own eyes across every potentially habitable planet within the created universe.

In another passage, our Guide reflects on the revelation of the river in God's eternal temple: "Then the angel showed me the river of the water of life – water as clear as crystal – pouring out from the throne of God and of the Lamb, flowing down the middle of the city's main street" (Rev 22:1-2). This passage resonates with another Psalm: "The river's channels bring joy to the city of God, the special, holy dwelling place of the Most High" (Ps 46:4). The metaphorical water of life in this present existence will take on a tangible form in the City of God. God's immanence in creation will be the source of the life-giving waters of Eternal Life, symbolized by this "living water." No longer will God inhabit creation in a way we can only see and feel with our inner spirits. There, His all-encompassing presence will be as clear and undeniable to our bodily eyes and senses as the sun and its warmth are to us today. God Himself will sustain all living things just as He sustains Himself. Currently, God sustains our immortal

> *Close your eyes and imagine what life will be like in Eternity.*
>
> *What comes to mind?*
>
> *How does this inspire faith and hope within you?*

souls. In Eternity, He will similarly uphold our incorruptible and imperishable bodies. Just as Jesus implied, we will eternally partake in the life of the Incarnation of God, where God's presence is manifested within the physical realm to become the true vitality of humanity (John 1).

Yahweh's living waters flow eternally and perpetually from the Son and through the Spirit, who administers them among the children of God. To this end, we will serve the Triune I AM eternally as a channel from which this life-giving water flows throughout all creation (John 7:37-39). Like the tabernacle, even in this present life, we should be a contextual place where the Spirit can be poured out upon others (Num 11:24-15). It is called fresh infillings of the Spirit for a reason (Acts 2:4, 4:8, 7:55, 13:9, 13:52). The Holy Spirit, symbolized in Scripture by living waters, enables us to fulfill this role primarily by helping us dwell in accordance with the Creator's likeness. Our role as a channel does not come by force; instead, it comes by simply receiving water flow from on high. Similarly, consider how a water wheel does not turn on its own power but relies on that of the water to do its work and turn whatever it needs.

In much the same way, the work we will do in Eternity resembles a dance with the Holy Spirit as our leading partner. Our role is to allow the Spirit to guide us and to follow His movements. In this dance of God's triune and relational nature, we discover and share in His delights for Creation, and in turn, we manifest these delights in the physical realm. Imagine being a child, genuinely and joyfully in awe of the world, fully entertained and fulfilled by what Creation provides. Picture a child's first trip to a zoo, experiencing animals with all five senses, which they have only seen in pictures or even unfamiliar ones. Moment by moment, their excitement bursts forth in ecstatic expressions of joy. They jump. They shout. They point. They smile. They laugh. They might even shed tears of happiness.

Each day, we will exude childlike enjoyment of a renewed creation. Furthermore, we will fully experience and engage with the very essence of nature, living in harmony with it and regarding the animal kingdom as our extended family. We will no longer compete with the world, as seen in chaotic ecosystems characterized by the so-called survival of the fittest. The Gardener of Finitude will continually nurture His garden's flourishing through us. The Son of Man and His siblings will stroll through the garden with the Heavenly Father. We will join the Father in reveling in the unique beauty of every 'plant,' as portrayed in Genesis 1 (John 1:15). In doing so, we anticipate an eternity that will always celebrate wonder and joy. Sadness, grief, discord, hate, scarcity, entropy, and disappointment will be permanently cast into the abyss of nothingness. Every human interaction will be filled with genuine smiles, caring attentiveness, and loving affection. We will truly be a happy family in the fullest sense of the phrase.

> *Would those around you consider you a vessel of living water?*
>
> *What changes would you need to make in your life if the answer is no?*

All human speech will be uplifting, encouraging, and peaceful. All human activity will aim for preservation and flourishing. No more killing. No more cursing. No more arguing. No more slandering. No more hate. No more comparison. No more rejection. No more shame. No more abuse. We will all understand one another with love. We will clearly see the face of God in each other as bearers of the divine image. We will perfectly love our neighbor as ourselves. Therefore, let us joyously proclaim the good news of Yahweh's plans for creation. Such declarations should be accompanied by an enthusiastic eagerness to see the Patriarch of Finitude "smile" (Ps 4:7-8, 80:3).

We should pray as David did, saying, "May God show us His favor and bless us! May He smile on us! Then those living on earth will know what You are like" (Ps 67:1-2). Our heart's desire should yearn for our King's approval to pour down upon us as His faithful servants. May we make His smile and joy known throughout all Creation. Eternity will forever be a celebration of wonder and rejoicing. Sadness, grief, and disappointment will be permanently banished to the abyss of nothingness. Every human encounter will be filled with genuine smiles, caring attentiveness, and loving affection. We will all be a happy family in the truest sense.

In Eternity, we will no longer be constrained by mortality, ignorance, or biology. Consider how often these three factors lead to considerable limitation and suffering. Our desire to escape death, our mistakes made even with the best intentions, and our need to survive in a flawed world not designed for comfort or flourishing contribute to this. "Impossible" miracles will become as ordinary as daily activities in this life. Jesus's supernatural acts during His earthly ministry, such as walking on water and passing through walls, provide us just a glimpse of the "greater things" we will achieve after our resurrection and entry into Eternity. Did Christ not declare this truth: "I tell you the solemn truth, the one who believes in Me will perform the miraculous deeds that I am doing, and will perform greater deeds than these because I am going to the Father. And I will do whatever you ask in My name" (John 14:12-14).

All of God's children will emulate the miracle-working pattern of God's firstborn Son. Whatever we ask in the name of Jesus will come to pass, as we will share in His firstborn privilege. Unlike in this world, which exalts the miracles of a select few "saints," all of God's children will be miracle-working saints, embodying the mind, heart, and power of the Son of God. In Eternity, we can speak to a mountain, and it will be moved, as Jesus once taught:

"He told them, 'It was because of your little faith. I tell you the truth, if you have faith the size of a mustard seed, you will say to this mountain, 'Move from here to there,' and it will move; nothing will be impossible for you' (Matt 17:20)." Nothing will be impossible for the children of God, who are empowered and guided by the same creative divine Word and Breath that were in operation during the six days of Creation (Gen 1).

We will be endlessly filled to overflowing by the Holy Spirit. The gifts of prophecy – manifested through divine communication and interpretation – will bring us continuous joy, as natural as the phenomon of breathing. The divine mind will align our thoughts to receive and transmit the "bandwidth" of Heaven. Living by the Spirit will feel as natural as breathing (Gal 5:13-26). We will no longer live solely by the impulses of our flesh, nor will we be tempted to do so. As His priestly governors ruling on the earth, we will be those who have donned the One through whom God reveals Himself in Creation. Furthermore, we will become members of His Body, allowing Him, the ruler of creation, to be "all in all" in us (Rom 13:14; Rev 5:10; Eph 1:20-23). As His hands and feet, He will subject all of creation to our stewardship, ensuring that "all things are subjected to Him [Christ]" and that all of us, including Christ, are "subject to God," enabling "God to be all in all" (1 Cor 15:21-28).

Take a moment to imagine what life will be like in Eternity?

How does this inspire you to live in the here and now?

Figuratively speaking, God's Spirit eternally sanctifies us to become "oaks of righteousness, trees planted by the Lord" in the forest of Divine glory "to reveal His splendor" (Isa 61:3). Imagine the giant redwoods and sequoias of the Americas, stretching up to the sky and dwarfing even many buildings. As we grow throughout eternity, our priestly roots will continuously absorb the Creator's likeness. The "branches" of our souls will expand as a network of spiritual vitality managing the *oikonomia* of creation's unfolding narrative (John 15:1-9; Isa 61:6). Remember that Christ is the eternal vine, encompassing all of creation, with us as His branches. Branches connect the fruit (of the Spirit) with the life-giving nutrients flowing from the vine. Through us, His Spirit provides the nutrients of Divine coordination to enable creation to serve as a flourishing forest of the revelatory manifestations of God's face (Rom 1:19-20; Job 12:7-9).

In Eternity, moment by moment, the Holy Spirit will inspire our souls to perform righteous acts of *agape*-love. We will shine with *phos*-light to be led by the Spirit. In doing so, our Maker will shape the sanctified character within us to reflect the nature and personhood of divinity. These spiritual actions motivate corresponding physical actions that impact the physical world by enhancing its status as a holy place. Thus, we become symbolic reflections of the Trinity, acting as His co-composing and co-acting agents in Finitude, establishing it as His temple.

The Old Testament offers a historical pattern of divine representation through judges, prophets, and priests. These symbolic figures serve as temporal previews of the eternal realities of our work as His physical representatives (John 4:24; 2 Cor 5:20). We will wield authority "with power through [God's] Spirit in [our] inner person" to display "the wealth of His glory" (Eph 3:16). We will align with the Creator's Vision to properly exercise this authority in accordance with His character of "love," while being "filled up to all the fullness of God," as stewards of His pre-established *oikonomia* (Eph 3:17-19). This is not merely about carrying out instructions like a servant would, as that would require nothing more than hearing them once and following through. Instead, fulfilling God's vision resembles carrying forth an artist's vision. Consider the example of artists and architects who took on the project of *Sagrada Familia* after Gaudi's death. Similarly, this applies to any architects entrusted with continuing the construction of great medieval cathedrals, often built over centuries. To truly carry on the work of an artist in this manner, one must spend time with them to grasp their vision, methods, and inspirations. Ultimately, the stewards in Jesus' parables exemplify what God expects of us in Eternity as caretakers of Creation.

Inheriting a Prophetic Mantle in Eternity

To effectively manage the household of Creation, we must commune with and dwell in the presence of Yahweh's occupation within us, which grounds us in the work of *agape*-love and *phos*-light (1 Cor 3:16; Rom 5:5, 8:9; Eph 2:22; 2 Tim 1:14; Eph 3:17; 1 John 4:12-13). In other words, we can make Creation a worthy home for the Divine only through the Divine's efforts to transform us into a suitable dwelling for Himself. Having first cultivated our fellowship with the Triune I AM, we then invite Creation into the same fellowship (John 15, 1 John 1). As Jesus said, "If anyone loves Me, he [or she] will obey My word, and My Father will love him [or her], and We will come to him [or her] and take up residence with him [or her]" (John 14:23). When this occurs, "the love of Christ controls us" as a "new creation," for we "have died" to self-determination, self-power, and self-dependency, since we no longer exist as a temple of self and "no longer live for ourselves but for Him who died for us" (1 Cor 5:14-17). In Eternity, each moment will bear witness to the revelation that "we [have become and remain] His workmanship, created in Christ Jesus for good works that God prepared beforehand for us to do" (Eph 2:10). Into Eternity, we will live as agents of divine

> *Do you believe you have been spending enough time with the Maker to genuinely carry forward His vision and act as a conduit for His presence?*

action. By His grace, He brings us into our eternal identity to fulfill and oversee the righteousness of His kingdom, empowered by His Spirit, carrying out the decrees of His Word.

"The anointing [of the Holy Spirit] that we received from [Jesus] resides in us, and we have no need for anyone to teach us. But as His anointing teaches us about all things, it is true and not a lie. Just as it has taught us, we reside in Him" (1 John 2:27). This anointing will perpetually guide each of us in our divinely sanctioned efforts to fulfill the Maker's will for His creation, helping us understand how best to tend to His garden. Unlike the metaphor of the architect continuing the work of another, we will not only be intimately familiar with the vision of God, but we will also have Him within us always. We will carry the "Maker's Manual" within us. Moment by moment, the stewards inhabiting the Kingdom of Christ will have ongoing access to this indwelling anointing of revelation. All will be and live as prophets; we will no longer need to strive or reach the heights of "spirituality" to catch glimpses of the Maker's vision for Finitude. In fact, this access is based not on any merit-based qualification whatsoever. The enactment of the New Covenant through Christ's death and resurrection resulted in this vision being imprinted upon the innermost depths of every child of God's mind and heart, as we have each become an immanent temple of the Maker.

We read about such truths in our Guide:

> "'But I [Yahweh] will make a new covenant with the whole nation of Israel after I plant them back in the land… I will put My law within them and write it on their hearts and minds. I will be their God, and they will be My people. People will no longer need to teach their neighbors and relatives to know Me. For all of them, from the least important to the most

important, will know Me' says the Lord."

Jer 31:33-34

Elsewhere, we read that "God reveals [mysteries] to us by the Spirit. For the Spirit searches all things, even the deep things of God" (1 Cor 2:10). Because of the indwelling of the "Spirit of Truth," we will have constant access to these revealed "truths" of the Maker's visions and storyline for Finitude (John 16:13). Therefore, even into Eternity, we will continue to be "seafarers exploring the Sea of Revelation." At that time, we will have no deceptions, distractions, or temptations to contend with. We will be intimately acquainted with not only *what is*, but also *what ought to be*. To this end, the commands of the Creator regarding how Finitude should be managed will indeed proceed and be executed directly from within His immanent temple (Isa 2:2-3).

Through the "stewardship from God" entrusted to us, we will fulfill the prophecy of making "complete the Word of God" (Col 1:25). Essentially, we become an unending echo of the Word of God – the Incarnation of God – resonating throughout the entire Theater of Finitude. Through us, His commands and dictates are reiterated as His Word dwells in us by the power of His Spirit, our eternal inheritance. The eternal anointing placed on us as the priestly stewards of Finitude equips us with the insight necessary to live as beings promoting the Sovereign Creator's predetermined purposes for Creation. Thus, through us, His written composition for the eternal chapter of the Narrative of Finitude will be forever translated and realized within the context of Finitude.

{ *Would you like to serve as an eternal prophet representing Divinity across the universe?* }

We will see with Yahweh's "eyes" and hear with His "ears" as we perpetually commune with the Creator. We will learn the code of Creation and "program" in the coding language of both the

> *What mysteries are you most eager to uncover in Eternity?*

beginning and the end, which we can refer to as the alpha and omega code. Only someone who understands a code base and its underlying language can add complementary code without compromising its integrity. The Word will become our word, and the Breath will become our breath as Yahweh makes us a dwelling for His self-revealing presence. Since this is the very same Word at the beginning (John 1:1), we will operate within the very power that laid the foundations of the cosmos. The words we speak in eternity will, in essence, exist within the very word spoken during the six days of Creation. It will be as if we are witnessing and participating in such creative acts ourselves, only for a New Heaven and New Earth. This is also why we read in Hebrews that the seventh day of rest still exists as a dimension we can enter (Heb 4:1-6). The seventh day, after all, is Eternity. In Eternity, we will "work" and "create" while at "rest," for such activity will feel as natural to us as our hearts beating and lungs taking in oxygen. Rather than toiling and striving to accomplish our mission, we will simply experience what the Son of God did during His time on earth: following what we see our Father doing and saying what we hear our Father saying (John 10:36-39, 12:49-50). Nothing Jesus did on earth was done outside His Father's will and direction, so it shall be with us during our eternal occupation in the New Earth.

All the children of God will be ceaselessly filled and will endlessly pour out the Breath of the Divine in prophetic ecstasy. Prophecy will be our native tongue. We will speak a language taught by God. A language that transcends the limits and confines of any earthly language, even abstract concepts. In Eternity, we will express theological truths as naturally and powerfully as music stirs our emotions in ways that words or even singing never could. Our language will itself be divine poetry. Every word will be an act of worship, and joy will accompany every syllable. It will be a divine language of great creative power – the same language by which the Maker established the universe. Every sentence will contain a bottomless well of meaning. No word spoken will ever return void. It will be a language of revelation and divine efficacy, capable of moving any animal, mountain, or even planet.

As we all speak from a place of intimacy with the heart and mind of the Creator, Creation responds to our commands since it exists in and through this Heavenly voice. In this way, we become like our elder brother, Jesus Christ, who brought healing into being and cast out demons with nothing but His words. Everything in creation is primed to respond to this Heavenly language. For analogy's sake, consider how machines and electronics are designed to understand specific code scripts and signals, enabling them to execute tasks once the proper commands are given. What was once a piece of metal is, when provided the right instructions in the right "language," suddenly capable of amazing calculations, displaying beautiful visuals, communicating with people from around the world, or producing countless different forms of work or art. Similarly, our words will unlock the potential of the new creation, akin to how God's words transformed a void into everything we see today—from galaxies to atoms and everything in between. Infinity and finitude shall meet in a beautiful collision of creativity, sovereignty, and sustainability. The melodies of our spirits will sing songs to our Maker, adorning the cosmos. All speech will be poetic in both scope and poignancy. Moreover, all this "dialogue" will occur among family, as we will

> *Have you caught glimpses of the prophetic ecstasy that awaits you in Eternity?*
>
> *Do you look forward to learning and speaking the language of God with mature competence and the ease of a native tongue?*

be one family of God. We will understand one another perfectly—no untruth, no miscommunication, no misunderstanding. Every moment will be precious among us as we recognize the infinite worth of each child of God.

The created universe, in its true form, exists as an immeasurable collection of unique love letters from Heaven to Earth and vice versa. After all, why else would God have created us and the beauty of nature if not as an act of love? Like an artist who creates a painting for personal joy and to share it with others rather than for money or a job, God created to share His love with us rather than to just satisfy Himself. Through the Spirit's sanctifying presence within us, as His priests and beloveds, we add our own collection of unique "love" letters from Earth to Heaven (2 Cor 3:2-3). As Scripture clarifies, we become part of this living letter within the endless discourse between Heaven and Earth. We all engage in meaningful activities with unique gifts and callings, manifesting the Creator's beautiful mind and love. Consider a poet crafting poems, a composer creating music, a writer imagining fictional allegories of divinity[200], a metalworker constructing structures, a sculptor shaping, an engineer building, and so on. All our occupations take place within the landscape of Finitude, as our spirit, soul, and body occupy the created realm in perfect harmony.

[*What do you envision your role to be in this beautiful landscape? How would you like to use your unique gifts to enhance the beauty of Creation?*]

Eternal Destiny of Angels and Humans

In Eternity, we will equally make our home in both the New Heavens and the New Earth. Our temple-like abode will stand out

---

[200] Like C.S. Lewis.

from all others as a portal between the spiritual and material realms. Within this context, we exist as ambassador priests, governing the events on the New Earth as intermediaries between the material and the spiritual. Such service requires loving and faithful submission to a Governance inspired by gratitude and trust. This everlasting partner-like submission reflects that of a wife's relationship with her husband (Eph 5:22-24). It is no wonder that the Creator intended all of humanity, male and female, to become His figurative "Bride."[201]

Our eternal stewardship encompasses both the spiritual and physical realms of our Creator's household, both literally and figuratively. Were we not created to rule over the angels (1 Cor 6:3)? In fact, they will collaborate with us in our eternal work. These intelligent beings will be our partners, possessing abilities and roles that differ from our own. Their powers will serve the Messianic Kingdom of Eternity as we commune with and guide them to foster the worship of Divinity throughout the universe. Ezekiel offers us a glimpse of how they will manifest and transport the Divine throne within the created domain (Ezek 1). The book of Revelation also provides a glimpse of their eternal service in the heavenly dimensions of the cosmos. They will assist us in our mission as a bridge between Heaven and Earth. Recall the experience of angels ascending and descending on a ladder (Gen 28:12, 16). Like Jacob, we will witness the eternal flow of angelic activity between the heavens and the earth. We will no longer feel estranged from our angelic brethren due to our fallen

> *How do you sense a calling to practice agape love within your communities?*
>
> *In what ways might the Spirit be revealing your shortcomings?*

---

[201] Refer to Proverbs 31 as a fitting illustration of our eternal responsibility in this relationship.

natures. Instead, we will be restored to the communion our mutual Lord and Maker envisioned for us at the Dawn of Finitude.

Just as our Creator clearly states in Scripture, we should teach and guide others to align with the *oikonomia* of holiness (Exod 28:36; 2 Chr 15:3; 2 Kgs 12:2; Ezra 7:12; Mic 2:7). Holiness promotes proper relationships between creation and the Creator. Our work is to foster proper interactions between Heaven and Earth. A priest maintains the "up-built" (enhance the status of the temple by preserving its "ability to function responsibly and effectively" (BDAG, 696). Likewise, we ensure that the household of God, wherever it may be found, serves as a mediator between Heaven and Earth; a trans-dimensional dwelling place where the "Lord abides." We act simultaneously as earth-dwellers and heavenly-dwellers, much like the ladder of intersection "erected on the earth with its top reaching to the heavens," revealed to Jacob at *Bethel*, the house of God (Gen 28:12, 16). As a figurative ladder to Heaven, Bethel symbolizes our eternal identity as His own "Bethel" living in Finitude (Gen 28:17-19).

Conclusion: Relationships in Eternity

Let us conclude this chapter by reflecting on how we will eternally relate to our fellow priests of the New Covenant. In Eternity, we will all know one another as God knows us. We will behold and appreciate the beautiful image of God, reflected uniquely by each soul. From our first encounter, we will all be friends, united as brothers and sisters. There will be no more disagreements that stir up animosity, no more conflicts that lead to estrangement, or, worse yet, war. We will respect one another without a hint of jealousy, envy, judgment, or comparison. No one will experience anxiety, fear, or shame when meeting another. We will love

> *What are you most looking forward to regarding your involvement with angels in Eternity?*

one another as we love ourselves, recognizing the eternal value and beauty in how each of us reflects divine glory, serving together as members of one body. Each of us will promote one another's relationship with God out of pure delight, as we recognize and appreciate the unfolding drama of divine romance within each of us. We will be occasions for drawing closer to each other and the Divine, striving to ensure that each person fully knows how deeply they are loved by the Maker.

Our eternal destiny is to serve as a temple of God. As a temple, others encounter God's love, thoughts, and ways, working in and through us. Our purpose as temples, from now into eternity, centers on establishing a home where Infinity is eternally manifested within Finitude. Through us, we are to create a revelatory landscape in which one may experience the immanent presence of the Divine, who is *agape*-love, *phos*-light, and *pneuma*-spirit. Creation, particularly others, will engage with the Creator through us as His priests, facilitating the communion of the God-Relationship wherever we go. Every conversation we have will become and remain a communion supper. Every word will nourish the soul and energize the body. Divine energy, like genuinely renewable and reliable energy[202], will perpetually flow among each person, acting as spiritual conduits. Like the Eucharist, we will be like bread and wine, holding and transmitting the eternal life meant to be enjoyed by all. We each become personal intermediaries created to be filled with His glorious splendor and poured out upon the table of creation. This destiny carries with it the responsibility of overseeing ourselves and supporting one another through the home-making activities of *agape*-love (Col 1:25; Heb 6:10; 1 John 4:7).

Each member of the Body of Christ will reinforce the unique

---

[202] For example, if we drew electrical power from satellites full of solar panels.

> *How does your life story inspire the theme of Divine Romance in the life stories around you?*

role of the others in a complementary association. In a sense, we all fall in love again with the Maker as we encounter each distinct theme in the drama of the human-Divine romance unfolding in every life we meet. We will immediately recognize what the Divine Lover finds attractive and values in each member of the Bride of Christ, and in turn, we will appreciate the gaze of the Divine Lover. After all, Yahweh created us to inspire and guide all of Creation in maintaining a proper relationship with Him. Therefore, we must even now engage in actions that keep the flames of divine romance kindled. "So then, whenever we have an opportunity, let us do good to all people, and especially to those who belong to the family (household) of faith" (Gal 6:10). All Creation will always remain a stage for the Divine romance between Heaven and Earth, acting as intermediaries in relation to physical and spiritual priests. Our highest duty is to facilitate the eternal unfolding of the God Story in each of its renditions.

Chapter 13

Beyond the Veil of Temporality

Toward a Theology Formed by the Context of Eternity

"Now we do speak wisdom among the mature, but not a wisdom of this age or of the rulers of this age, who are perishing. Instead, we speak the wisdom of God, hidden in a mystery, that God determined before the ages for our glory…

But just as it is written, "Things that no eye has seen, or ear heard, or mind imagined, are the things God has prepared for those who love Him." God has revealed these to us by the Spirit. For the Spirit searches all things, even the deep things of God… No one knows the things of God except the Spirit of God.

…We speak about these things, not with words taught us by human wisdom, but with those taught by the Spirit, explaining spiritual things to spiritual people. The unbeliever does not receive the things of the Spirit of God, for they are foolishness to him. And he cannot understand them, because they are spiritually discerned… [But] we have the mind of Christ."

(1 Cor 1:6-16)

"You were taught with reference to your former way of life to lay aside the old man who is being corrupted in accordance with deceitful desires, to be renewed in the spirit of your mind, and to put on the new man who has been created in God's image—in righteousness and holiness that comes from truth."

(Rom 4:22-24)

Beyond the Veil of Temporality

This chapter reminds us of our nature as finite beings in a temporal world and our calling to rise above this. Our Maker beckons us to explore the realm of supra-contextual revelations He makes accessible to us. These revelations do not have their basis in worldly values such as wealth, power, comfort, degrees, or "success," but instead on values antithetical to these. At the same time, these insights are not derived from human or artificial intelligence. They are exclusively granted by God to His children. We can only receive them through the experience of Spirit-to-spirit communion as we commit to pursuing, following, and genuinely abiding in Christ. This is the essence of authentic theology and the only way our theological journey can genuinely be shaped by Eternity, rather than this Temporal World.

We will now carefully consider how to grow in our ability to discern and embrace the revelations of our Creator's self-disclosures. Throughout this book, we have acknowledged the undeniable reality that our existential circumstances will, and should, influence our theological perspective. The veil of temporality, stemming from our existence as finite beings who have yet to realize their true potential in the God-relationship, limits the horizon. Our identity as created beings hinders our understanding of any eternal contextualities. Without the enlightening grace of the Holy Spirit, we cannot grasp these truths – similar to how sailors cannot fully understand their journey without charts, maps, and compasses. Our naked eyes alone cannot perceive latitude, longitude, currents, magnetic fields, or even what lies just beyond the horizon.

Eternal contextualities are unceasing; they exist independently of any finite cause. They are as removed yet fundamental to reality as the stage is to a play's world and characters. An eternal perspective surpasses the limitations of finite thinking, akin to the curtains of temporality. An anglerfish, dwelling deep in the ocean, does not perceive its environment as "water." It likely lacks awareness of being "in" anything, as its reality is wholly immersed in the ocean. For it to recognize the finiteness of its existence, it would need to "transcend" the sea, a feat its biology precludes.

> *If you have spent a significant portion of your life consuming fictional stories, why not dedicate an equivalent amount of time to exploring the true Story of Existence?*

Unlike the anglerfish, in Christ we have the potential to glimpse into the eternal, transcending our limited reality through the supracontextual revelations of God. Thus, we have the responsibility to discern what fits within a supra-contextual eternal view by engaging with the complete Narrative of Finitude, as revealed by the Playwright Himself. Observing from this perspective shifts our focus to align more with the Creator's vision. Instead of a limited viewpoint, we gain insight into reality as He perceives it. This broader vision is what we must pursue; a viewpoint unconfined by any specific chapter or setting within the Creation story, nor by Creation itself.

Eternal contextualities signify what truly exists, rather than merely what endures. Consider narratives where individuals find themselves in a dream or virtual realm that seems tangible yet is not substantial when contrasted with the "real world." From an eternal perspective, our reality resembles this dreamlike existence. In this view, Eternity regards anything that cannot be "removed" from the Theater of Finitude after the "play" of the Creation Story as no longer meaningless to the Creator's blessed vision. Everything temporary will ultimately dissipate into oblivion, similar to a dream fading upon waking. Conversely, the enduring elements persist because their values are eternally linked to the

Creator's original, flawless intention for Finitude – an ideal of perfection that surpasses any human comprehension.

We truth-seekers aim to understand reality through a perspective that starkly contrasts with that of "land-dwellers." Land-dwellers view the world through a lens clouded by temporality and constrained by the limitations of a fallen existence. These individuals are disconnected from the *oikonomia* established by the Creator and walk in ignorance of the eternal mysteries at play. Like a fish unaware of life outside water, those trapped in this darkness fail to grasp the limited and flawed nature of their surroundings.[203] The actual condition- and indeed the depravity- of worldly systems can only be understood when viewed from the illuminating perspective of Eternity. Those living in a dimly lit world are often uncertain of their destination, as their reasoning is clouded by a "depraved mind" (Rom 1:28). "Although they knew God, they did not glorify Him as God or give him thanks, but they became futile in their thoughts, and their senseless hearts were darkened Although they claimed to be wise, they became fools and exchanged the glory of the immortal God for an image resembling mortal human beings" (Romans 1:21-23). Many even mistakenly think they are following the "narrow way" of Eternity while, in truth, they traverse the broad avenues of Temporality.

The destiny of those truly 'born again' as children of the day rests within the Creator's sanctuary in Finitude. Only in the Holy of Holies, illuminated by our Maker's self-revelation, can we honestly acknowledge our authentic selves, shaped by the essence of our true Home. At this juncture, our worldly existence and perspective achieve their intended aim of inhabiting the sacred Temple of God. Unlike earthly understanding, the Creator's supra-contextual vision enriches our profound comprehension of

---

[203] This situation resembles those bound in Plato's Cave Analogy.

heavenly realities. We must stay aware of just how heavenly contexts significantly differ from terrestrial ones, which are molded by the limited visions of created beings. To many, these ideas appear peculiar or even irrational, especially in a world that has defined reality without acknowledging its vital cornerstone. Picture trying to convey the importance of constructing ships or creating navigation tools to a civilization that has never encountered a vast ocean and doubts the existence of anything beyond their small island. Such efforts would likely be regarded as foolish or even perilous.

> *Reflect on how your life changed once you became aware of eeternal contextualities, compared to when you were blind to them.*

The world systems of Finitude have become places vacated by the Creator's immanent communal presence. Unclean spirits now occupy them. They obstruct humanity's eternal potential. When we repent and return to our Maker's embrace, we accept a world no longer constrained by these limited viewpoints. Like sailors who boldly challenge the ridicule of a small-minded civilization, we construct our vessels and courageously venture forth, confident that God will unveil a reality that was once concealed, which once defied the limits of our horizons.

As we read in our Guide,

> "But their minds were closed. For to this very day, the same veil remains when they hear the old covenant read. It has not been removed… And we all, with unveiled faces reflecting the glory of the Lord, are being transformed into the same image from one degree of glory to another, which is from the Lord, who is the Spirit."
>
> (2 Cor 3:14-18)

Only by living in alignment with the Spirit can we deepen our understanding of the Creator. Only then do we begin to see our true selves, dwelling, and life narrative. Accordingly, our journey transcends mere philosophy; it is not just about intellectually grasping these revelations and supra-contextualities. Instead, it stems from a spiritual connection to the source of Eternity. Just as branches cannot bear fruit through sheer effort, they only need to stay connected to the vine. The ability to bear fruit comes from sources beyond ourselves, rather than from our own merit or intellect. Consequently, we strive to live by the Light of Revelation, like how plants flourish under the sun's illumination. This guiding light, like a beam cutting through the dark clouds around a solitary island, reveals doors to new existential possibilities.

In this life, we exist in the realm of temporality, yet we should not let this realm dictate our theology, worldview, and lifestyle (John 17:14-19; 1 Cor 5:10; Col 2:20; 1 John 2:15-17). Jesus emphasized this in His prayer for us, stating, "They do not belong to the world just as I do not belong to the world. Set them apart in the truth; Your word is truth. Just as You sent Me into the world, so I sent them into the world" (John 17:16-18). Thus, as "sent-ones" our existence and perspective must be shaped more by eternal truths than by temporary situations (Eph 2:1-3; Rom 12:2). Our theology should reflect a sanctified understanding. Our studies ought to do more than just enrich us intellectually; they should transform us into eternal world-dwellers, because "our faith and love have arisen from the hope laid up for us in heaven" (Col 1:5). Only those who think and act as nomads in time, adopting the values of Eternity while abandoning those of temporality, will find their way Home. They are the ones

Think about your past.

How would you describe moments when your mind felt "closed" and you experienced a "veil"?

Christ will recognize as faithful disciples, steadfast in faith while striving for Zion over Babylon (Heb 3:6, 14).

Attempting to Theologize Without Seafaring

The *oikonomia* of Eternity, in harmony with God's original intention for creation, stands in stark contrast to the house rules of a fallen world. These latter rules merely represent a distortion of reality. Is it not absurd to think that a finite individual could defy and overturn the authority of Infinite *Being*? Would you accept a situation in which a random citizen, regardless of their wealth or power, believed they could arbitrarily change their country's laws and constitution? Attempting this with reality, regardless of what we replace God's rules with, only leads to a corrupt and inferior worldview—a mere shadow of actual reality. Consequently, those who adopt a temporal mindset cannot live as intended and, therefore, fail to perceive reality as they were originally created to. Because of the misguided shaping of temporality, this fallen world has predominantly become a landscape devoid of the Creator's illuminating presence. Furthermore, individuals who adhere to temporal rules, either in defiance or ignorance of the Creator's guidelines, engage in idolatry, displacing the rightful center of their lives with a false substitute. Why should we be astonished by the depravity of this age if the light-bearers of righteousness have abandoned their true purpose?

Without embracing the supra-contextual perspective of Eternity, a world-dweller's existence in the world becomes obscured by the distortions inherent in transient world systems. The more one attempts to conform to these systems, the more pronounced this distortion and confusion become. With a narrow view akin to seeing only a small island as the entirety

> *What social and religious traditions have you observed that contradict the Word of God?*

of the world, this illusion prevents individuals from truly understanding the context of Finitude. No amount of religious ritual or textual study can fix this issue. Any faith that continues without the illumination of Eternity and divine revelations is ultimately futile, as it fails to transcend creation itself. These contextual illusions obstruct an individual's ability to recognize the broader context of Finitude that transcends temporal limitations, even as they ponder religious texts and participate in rituals. As Jesus noted regarding many religious individuals of His time, "Thus you nullify the word of God by your [religious] tradition that you have handed down" (Mark 7:13). Similarly, those trapped by these illusions remain oblivious to the eternal contexts of the spiritual realm shaped by the unseen domain of spiritual tabernacles, rendering their religion—reinforced by this blindness—nothing more than humanistic vanity.

Will we acknowledge the alien quality of eternal contextualities compared to the temporal contextualities affecting our current human situation? Temporal contextualities obscure the genuine presence of human world-dwellers, likened in this book to "sea-dwellers" navigating the Sea of Revelation in search of divine insights. Conversely, a "land-dweller" is someone who, whether consciously or unconsciously, has renounced this authentic way of being. Instead, they have constructed "castles" and "cities" on the island of temporality, acting as monuments to created realities and worldly knowledge. Although these structures may appear impressive, they are ultimately destined to dissolve, just as the island gradually submerges into the sea, as noted in earlier chapters. In contrast, a sea-dweller exists as a vessel of uncreated realities and divine wisdom, which transcend the fate of that small island. Indeed, we can envision the island, which seems vast when you are on it, as merely a tiny dot in the expansive, truly endless Sea of

Revelation from a higher vantage point.[204] Remember that our genuine seafaring existence corresponds to being the manifest temple of the uncreated Creator. In this domain of the God-relationship, represented in our metaphor as the journey across the Sea of Revelation, we interact with the contextualities of living in both heaven and earth through a theology of communion with the Eternal.

We only gain deeper understanding of the *oikonomia* of fallen temporality by reflecting on this passage from our Guide:

"Creation eagerly waits for the revelation of the sons [and daughters] of God. For the creation was subjected to futility – not willingly but because of God who subjected it – in hope that creation itself will also be freed from the bondage of decay into the glorious freedom of God's children. For we know that the whole creation groans and suffers together until now. Not only this, but we ourselves, who have the firstfruits of the Spirit, groan inwardly as we eagerly await our adoption, the redemption of our bodies. For in hope, we were saved…

How is the shadowy world surrounding you lacking the Creator's revealing light?

And although you were dead in your offenses and sins, in which you formerly lived according to this

---

[204] C.S. Lewis' The Great Divorce illustrates the differences between Heaven and Hell in similar fashions. While Hell, referred to as grey town in the book, appears vast and enormous to its residents, it is ultimately shown to fit into a crack in the ground that is smaller than a blade of grass when viewed from Heaven. In stark contrast to the divine reality, everything else seems minuscule, nearly negligible by comparison.

world's present path, according to the ruler of the domain of the air, the ruler of the spirit that is now energizing the sons of disobedience, among whom all of us also formerly lived out our lives in the cravings of our flesh, indulging the desires of the flesh and the mind, and were by nature children of wrath even as the rest".

(Rom 8:19-25; Eph 2:1-3).

When we choose to live as seafarers, we start to view our life circumstances through the lens of eternal hope. This perspective reveals to us what those who dwell on land cannot see: the *oikonomia* of Heaven on Earth. Only through this lens, and with such an internal focus, can individuals perceive and engage with the world amid the hope of everlasting realities. With this understanding, we strive to embrace the world as it was intended to be. Conversely, those whose worldview is obscured by the transient nature of this existence often lack this transcendent hope, prioritizing their present lives based on the current world order and their perception of their fittingness within it.

Let us examine a crucial distinction between a temporal and an eternal perspective. Those consumed by a temporal mindset struggle to envision spiritual communion marked by the mutual self-emptying inherent in *agape*-love. This form of love contradicts our natural tendencies toward self-preservation and even ordinary love. It is a non-human love. Consequently, temporal theology fails to encompass this alien quality of oughtness. Humanity has historically pursued ideals such as conquest, survival, prosperity, personal growth, pleasure, and love for family or clan. While some of these pursuits may have value, none are as radical and distinctive as the self-emptying and God-emptying *agape*-love that the eternal perspective demands. Who, in their right mind, would choose to love even lay down their life for their enemies or pray for those who persecute them? What rational individual would willingly part with all their possessions (Matthew 19:21) or betray family and self-interest (Luke 14:26) to follow someone who offers rewards in an afterlife? Did Jesus not command us saying:

> "Do not accumulate for yourselves treasures on earth, where moth and devouring insect destroy and where thieves break in and steal. But accumulate for yourselves treasures in heaven, where moth and devouring insect do not destroy, and thieves do not break in and steal. For where your treasure is, there your heart will be also."
>
> (Mark 6:19-21)

Consumer-driven societies, for instance, are built on worldviews that mold us into repositories of self-interest and human-centered relationships. These existential tabernacles lack true communion with the Divine, distancing themselves from the spiritual essence of God's nature by rejecting the self-emptying nature of *agape*-love. Ultimately, consumeristic societies thrive on individual greed and self-interest, often viewed as virtues that foster social benefits. Ideas once deemed shocking are now the societal norm, propelling society forward and ensuring a continuous flow of currency.[205] Spending on trivialities is often perceived as promoting economic growth,

How do you resist the temptation to pursue a self-seeking life of temporal prosperity, especially masquerading as religion?

---

[205] The initial introduction of these concepts, notably in Bernard Mandeville's Fable of the Bees in 1714, sparked significant controversy by opposing the prevailing belief that selfless, Christian conduct represented the sole genuine virtue. Many contemporary philosophers criticized it for its scandalous nature and alleged absurdity.

and this is prioritized as the chief collective good that nations ought to pursue. Biblical statements like "I no longer live" or "I lay down my life," as well as ideals such as relinquishing all possessions to follow Christ, hold little allure or credibility from this perspective. These expressions are often perceived as heretical against a theology defined by humanism and self-interest.

Without the spiritual insight gained from divine communion, those living on land strive to distance themselves from the evident majesty of God's presence. Some even seek to aggressively eliminate all perspectives and lifestyles that embrace genuine Trinitarian theology, which is the foundation for our call to *agape*-love. From the mountaintops, they proclaim: "This was not created by a God who desires us to share eternal communion with Him, as His dwelling, nor did He craft us in His own image for this purpose. Rather, God made this world for us to enjoy as we please. Is Heaven not a fulfillment of all our desires? After all, He designed us to be "little gods," exercising our will and authority for our own glory." On the one hand, in our era, particularly in the West, many aim to eradicate any mention of the divine or transcendent in history, psychology, and science. They wish to inhabit a self-imposed atheistic world devoid of revelation, grace, and divine guidance.

Examine the philosophies of the three influential figures known as the 'school of suspicion,' a term coined by philosopher Paul Ricoeur: Friedrich Nietzsche, Karl Marx, and Sigmund Freud. Each of these thinkers revolutionized concepts concerning philosophy, supra-contexuality truth, morality, society, economics, ideology, culture, and consciousness by discarding any notion of the divine, objective, or transcendent. Their worldviews, therefore, tend to reflect a strictly materialistic, human-centered perspective. At best, their ideas may align with a deistic theology in which God is entirely removed from everyday life, acting only as a "Moral

Lawgiver" or a "Judge on Judgment Day." At worst, they outright reject anything beyond the material and natural as irrelevant to the forces shaping our world. Consequently, their philosophies leave no space for the divine aspects of *agape*-love and genuine spirit-to-Spirit connection, which is inevitably disastrous. Although some of their contributions have facilitated meaningful advancements in modern society (for instance, Marx's critiques of industrial labor prompting labor rights movements or Freud's influence on the development of modern psychology), these can be seen as elements of grace amidst the darker consequences their ideas impose on humanity. How much blood has been shed in the pursuit of creating a utopia? How much sexual perversion has upended family values and damaged the psyche of children? How has the rejection of spirituality and objectivity reshaped human self-perception, reducing individuals to mere byproducts of an ego, unconscious mind ("id"), or neuroses? Adherents of such worldviews often close themselves off from any signs of immediate or universal providence. This refusal to recognize God cultivates a reality where individuals view the world as devoid of objective or transcendent truths, become the "gods" of their minds and fate.

> *Have you ever felt the haunting presence of the unclean spirits of our era?*
>
> *Do they continue to linger?*
>
> *How did you break free from them, or how might you?*

Even if individuals with temporal worldviews do not actively seek to alter reality and manipulate others to suit their preferences and ambitions, many simply drift along with the tides of inertia, societal pressures, or their immediate, self-serving whims, fluctuating ambitions, and fickle desires. Even worse, some of these individuals may recognize God's perspective yet regard it as one of many. For instance, consider how many people today perceive Jesus as just another philosopher, moral guide, nominal exemplar, solely a forgiver, or just a giver of a "get out of hell free card." Among believers, many show no hesitation in attending a sacred service dedicated to the Divine on Sunday while participating in "services" that celebrate horror and violence at movie theaters on Friday. They engage in the rituals of entertainment, intoxicated by spectacle, and believe they are merely spectators to violence, distancing themselves from the prospect that they could be victims or perpetrators of such violence. Reflect on the popularity of violence in history, such as gladiator games during the Roman Empire or public executions in medieval and early modern Europe. Consequently, it should not be surprising that many societies today have embraced entertainment characterized by sexual perversion, grotesque violence, and the diminishing value of human life, evident in cinemas, streaming services, and video game libraries. A society need not be entirely a-theistic to engage in such behaviors. All in all, we see the moral and spiritual rot of such a degenerate way of life.

Many societies today continue to reflect religious devotion, despite the obvious hypocrisy. While they may profess prayers and spiritual beliefs, the real theology of humanism shapes their everyday lives and defines how they exist and what shapes their identities. Indeed, those who condemned Jesus to crucifixion on a Friday still unashamedly worshipped God and led services on the Sabbath. Today, the Enemy of God's household promotes egocentric or humanistic perspectives, such as materialism communism, and carnality even among religious individuals.[206]

---

[206] Some theologians in the 20th century even used Trinitarian Theology as a justification for endorsing socialism and communism. However, such attempts tend toward imposing post-modern philosophical paradigms on the beliefs of Christianity to re-interpret the faith over and against the legacy of classical

These worldly philosophies encourage people to identify themselves mainly through temporary contexts: social class, ethnicity, psychology, nationality, economic adaptability, or countless other labels prevalent in the era of identity politics. None of these corresponds to Eternity. Instead, they limit people's perceptions of their true roles, destinies, and connections to mere temporal and material realities. In such worldviews, human activity is diminished to the profane and many are dehumanized while a few play god.

Consider how a religious ceremony can be viewed through this temporal lens. A church-goer views it as individuals engaging and experiencing fellowship with the divine in an authentic, sacred gathering. Conversely, a cynic observing through the framework of psychology, anthropology, or materialism[207] sees it merely as higher-order animals participating in a traditional social event to reinforce the ruling class's values and fulfill a deep-seated, yet illusory, quest for meaning. Such perspectives dismiss the universal human condition and our existential role within the broader scope of Creation. They negate the shared status of humanity created to be a priesthood, as temporal-eternal beings fashioned in God's image, meant to be both collective and individual embodiments of the divine on earth.

---

orthodoxy. We wil explore this crisis of modern heretical "pagan" theology in a coming treatise.

[207] Reflect on how a religious ceremony is interpreted from this perspective. A believer sees it as a genuine, sacred gathering where individuals connect and experience fellowship with the divine. In contrast, a cynic, viewing it through the lenses of psychology, anthropology, or materialism, perceives it simply as advanced beings taking part in a customary social occasion that upholds the values of the ruling class and satisfies a profound yet deceptive search for meaning.

> *Have you participated alongside worshippers who approach their communion with the divine in a trivial manner or who do not adhere to the appropriate house rules suitable for the priesthood of all believers?*

Theologies of Temporal Prosperity

Unfortunately, some misguided interpretations of Christianity support the self-defeating philosophies of Temporality. Some even go so far as to use Trinitarian theology to justify their beliefs. Clearly, these perspectives contradict the Call of Eternity, despite being labeled as "Christian." They advocate a lifestyle that fundamentally clashes with the righteous and sacrificial living expected in God's household (Eph 2:1-3; 1 John 2:16). They mock the martyrs. Such views are dangerous tools of the Enemy, as they combine lies with fragments of truth – making them more perilous than outright falsehoods. Proponents of this worldly lifestyle often promote their beliefs with a humanistic 'altruism' rooted in a cooperative of human-centric values, opposing individualistic egoism. While approaching the truth, this kind of cohabitation ultimately fosters communities resembling Babylon. Why? Because no religion, no matter how much it claims to uphold eternal ethics, can genuinely be eternal unless it places the Infinite One at the heart of everything. Without this focus, the churches we build are merely temples to humanity – entirely at odds with the sanctifying power of the Holy Spirit and His Kingdom administration. In the eyes of such misguided individuals, there can be no "god" apart from themselves or no "priesthood" other than their own as the "annointed few." They pursue no transcendent divine purpose, only their ambitions based on human capabilities and perceptions limited by their independence.

In *Works of Love*, Søren Kierkegaard reveals that humanistic altruism is grounded in a cooperation focused on human-centeredness rather than divine-centeredness. These collaborative efforts aim to transform humanity's living spaces into a sanctuary that venerates visible, humanistic values, rather than the unseen Creator, who is the foundation of all true goodness. While values - such as harmony, empathy, peace, beauty, and sacrifice – can indeed be good and ultimately stem from the divine, they fall short when disconnected from their trustworthy source. This is akin to the way even the most stunning flowers wilt when separated from their stems.

> *Have you come across humanized "Christian" religious institutions that lack authentic relationships with God and fail to align to His universal calling?*

Similarly, no amount of extraordinary moral striving or supreme human virtue can ever sufficiently bridge the divide between humanity and God. To place such values in our lives and worship constitutes another form of idolatry: the adoration of creation over the Creator.

One clear instance of this so-called "altruism" is the sense of fellowship observed during many Thanksgiving and Christmas celebrations. Although these holidays promote various Christian virtues, such as gratitude and generosity, their actual manifestation—especially in the West—often centers on the superficial exchange of consumer goods, characterized by materialism, physical pleasure, and comfort. Generosity, for instance, is frequently limited to the swapping of factory-made, mass-produced, brand-name trinkets. Even when authentic acts of generosity do occur, they are more often aligned with the holiday spirit rather than stemming from a profound shift in one's attitude toward possessions or generosity itself. When the holiday is detached from its divine essence and origins, it tends to elevate shallow virtues rather than inspire the meaningful transformation it purports to embody. In these temporal households driven by humanistic altruism, individuals are subtly encouraged to overlook humanity's genuine spiritual nature and the call to exchange spiritual gifts. Instead, attention is directed toward the physical and emotional aspects of living and reasoning, all under the guise of altruism and moral values. As a result, these households consist of those who dwell in darkness, remaining unaware of their true identity as children of the One who embodies spirit and the true gift-giving nature of God.

We must avoid relying exclusively on seemingly religious values or virtues, as the eternal contexts we seek to comprehend are largely alien to our temporary households. Without grounding ourselves in the divine and what is truly transcendent, even the best values can be distorted by the fallen realities of our lives. For instance, contemporary contexts shape how humanity perceives the mortality and fragility of human existence. With the right mindset, our awareness of death should motivate us to hope for eternal life and trust in God's salvation. We ought to approach each day not with fear of death but with gratitude for divine providence during our lives, confident that our eternal destiny is assured if we maintain communion with Him. Some only focus on God healing every bodily infirmity as an inevitable outcome of faith. Additionally, this awareness should inspire a desire to see others embrace this communion and discover God's salvation as well, understanding that death can approach any of us at any moment.

{ *Have you seen how the "Christian" holiday of Christmas is celebrated as an idolatrous festival of indulgence, often neglecting its true significance—why Jesus was born?* }

When viewed from a secular standpoint, our awareness of death often leads to either a fear of it or a desire to experience as much earthly pleasure as possible before we die. This quest for immortality or the evasion of death has driven cruel actions throughout history, such as Qin Shi Huang, the first emperor of China, who ruthlessly searched for a life-extending elixir and caused much bloodshed in the process. Conversely, some individuals react to the inevitability of death by emphasizing the ephemeral pleasures of mortal existence and the fleeting glories of the world. They often seek distraction through wealth, superficial relationships, drugs, entertainment, or incessant busyness, trying to shield themselves from the harsh reality that death is unpredictable and impartial.

Even those who identify as "religious" may succumb to this mindset when their faith, even "Christianity," becomes disconnected from the divine. Reflect on how the spiritual journeys of numerous individuals worldwide are frequently "choked" by the "seductive" "thorns" of worldly "wealth," or they gain no "root" due to enduring "persecution" or "trouble" (Matt 13:20-22) of capitalism and consumerism, which dominate their lives. This viewpoint bases identity, meaning, and worth on material possessions (such as a nice house, car, and the latest electronics), the fulfillment of physical desires (including sex, overeating, and drugs), and escapism (through video games, films, and series) or vicarious experiences (via social media, celebrity culture, and a fixation on sports teams and athletes). We labor and strive to gather the resources to transform the world into our own playground, purchasing and spending to construct our own "kingdoms" as self-proclaimed rulers of our fates. Amidst the

Has a theology of consumerism and materialism settled in your soul?

Have you ever been misled by "worldly Gospels" that prioritize achieving "temporal prosperity" as a sign of being blessed by God?

unprecedented prosperity and control available to the average person in history, the difficulties of genuinely sacrificing our lives to follow Christ become painfully clear.

Who among us would be willing to sacrifice all the carefully curated worldly pleasures or achievements as an act of self-emptying devotion to Christ? Would we truly abandon the systems of Babylon that promise (and often deliver, even if briefly) comfort and security (Rev 17-18)? Many mistake the prosperity of Babylon for Zion, as the gods of Babylon blind their minds. If our religious frameworks do not challenge us to confront the contradictions of our half-hearted faith and tread the narrow way of living couter-culturally, what does that say about our spirituality? Is God genuinely at the center of our lives if we can easily separate our "religious" and "secular" selves without acknowledging this existential contradiction? People "repent" without truly engaging in repentance and "confess" without really dedicating themselves to the God-story. They "believe" in their minds without aligning that faith with their choices and actions. When someone who identifies as a Christian worship on Sunday but then behaves immorally, cheats their employees, mistreats the less fortunate, or spreads gossip on Monday, what does that reveal about the place of God-relationship in their worldview? When our social status, national identity, political affiliation, peer group, or culture takes precedence over the divine in shaping our way of life, can you genuinely claim to have forsaken everything to follow Him? Has one truly become a disciple of Christ?

Living based on the house rules of a self-centered world often stems from a materialistic or this-world-only viewpoint.

> *What steps can you take to resist the allure of idolatrous life paths that disregard Christ's warning about the persecution and suffering faced by His followers for His name?*

Consequently, we should be cautious of theologies that are limited and distorted by this perspective. Regrettably, certain interpretations of Christianity emphasize a faith focused on temporary prosperity, overlooking the genuine, everlasting prosperity that can emerge from trials, persecution, suffering, and loss. In the early church, martyrdom was seen as the ultimate sign of devotion and an outcome of sharing in the eternal glory of the Crucified One. Some even willingly ran toward rather than away from this outcome. This reflects the reality of faithfully following God, as documented in Scripture and the histories of the martyrs. If the promise was earthly wealth, a "fountain of youth," or worldly security for the disciples, why were all of them, except John (who also faced severe persecution), martyred for their beliefs? Let us strive to emulate the Apostle Paul, who stated:

> "More than that, I now consider all [temporal advantage] as liabilities compared to the far greater value of knowing Christ Jesus my Lord, for whom I have suffered the loss of all things —indeed, I regard them as dung!—that I may gain Christ and be found in Him... My aim is to know Him, to experience the power of His resurrection, to share in His sufferings, and to be like Him in His death, and so, somehow, to attain to the resurrection from the dead."
>
> (Phil 3:8-11)

Such statements clash soundly with worldly reimaginings of Christianity, e.g. "Live your best life now." Let us avoid all the broad paths leading to ruin that oppose this Narrow Way, even if they are labeled as the "Way of Christ."

> How have you seen individuals acting like, or even less than, basic animals instead of as spiritual beings with a higher purpose?
>
> What does this suggest to you about human nature?

A Warning against Over-Reliance on Created Intelligence

Humans are not meant to assume the role of gods by vying to establish our own criteria for existence. Neither were we meant to shape deities in our likeness, whether those are gods of faith, human intellect, or technological advancements like artificial intelligence. Our Maker bestowed intelligence on us for a noble purpose: to serve as co-managers with Him in developing His divine temple within creation. God did not intend for human intelligence to focus on endeavors that lead to spiritual decay and physical ruin—like idolatrous religions, reckless industrial practices leading to pollution, and weapons of mass destruction. Our role is to be creators and caretakers, not destroyers or exploiters. Humanity's history of corruption and destruction is, in essence, an act of rebellion against the Life-Giver. Reflect on how often humans have applied our gifts—and the world's resources—toward twisted ends. We learned to smelt and forge metals, only to turn them into weapons for violence. We were endowed with intelligence that surpasses that of animals, yet we train them to kill for us or exploit them in factory farms instead of caring for them. We established global virtual networks for communication, creativity, and learning—yet we also abuse, distort, deceive, and manipulate through these channels, e.g. pedophilia and pornography. Regrettably, in today's society, many prefer to create gods in their own image—gods they can control and manipulate, rather than honoring the one true God who made us in His likeness.

Since the time Adam and Eve succumbed to the lure of wanting to "become like God" (Gen 3:5), humanity has sought to assume divine authority on Earth. Through various means such as religion, philosophies, and politics, people have attempted to substitute divine order with a human-made one shaped by our whims, imagination, and traditions. With modern science and technology at our disposal, we can now physically manifest this ambition through genetic engineering, cloning, life extension, sex reassignment surgery, gain-of-function research, and brain-machine interfaces. The consequences of pursuing these advancements without considering morality or divine *oikonomia* can lead to dire consequences. Even seemingly harmless uses of our intelligence can lead to disastrous outcomes due to our neglect of potential variables or repercussions in our quest for progress. For instance, consider lead in paint and gasoline, chemical pesticides for agriculture, opioid prescriptions, addictive social media algorithms, excessive antibiotic use resulting in resistance, creating car-centric environments detrimental to pedestrians and public transport, the inclusion of asbestos in buildings, and the historical use of cocaine in Coca-Cola. Although these sometimes stemmed from good intentions, they have proven to either cause serious problems or actively harm human biology, psychology, or societal well-being. When humanity plays God without adhering to His standards and guidance, we often create chaos instead of order, causing the reversal of Genesis 1. However, in Eternity, God will guide us, teaching us to grasp the full impact of our innovations. Our intelligence will then be utilized in ways

> *In what ways have you observed people, both in your society and in your everyday life, attempt to "play god"?*

that genuinely benefit, preserve, and enhance Creation, fulfilling the Maker's vision of it as "Good."

As discussed earlier in this book, we must remember the real presence of the Anti-Logos force (Satan) influencing the minds and hearts of individuals, even as they contemplate the Divine. Given the immense power of our intellect in shaping our lives and perceptions, it is hardly surprising that Satan seeks to taint human education by detaching it from a relationship with God and replacing it with false idols. Unfortunately, his deception even infiltrates many seminaries and institutions of higher religious and theological learning today. The "angel of light" misdirects many towards idolatry, corruption, and malevolence, often on paths paved with good intentions (2 Cor 11:14). Consider how distorted education systems globally have become, plagued by trends and teachings such as historical reinterpretations, atheistic viewpoints, distorted understandings of gender and sexuality, naturalistic reducationism, suppression of free speech, and cancel culture.

Since the deception of Adam and Eve, Satan and his fallen angels have distorted humanity's narrative, encouraging us to sin against God and take advantage of others. As the highest created intelligence, he wields significant power in undermining the harmony of Creation, having spent millennia devising religious systems that lead humanity down the Wide Path of Destruction. Even the religion that Yahweh established through His prophet Moses was not immune to this corruption. God's chosen leaders and people not only had a history of rebelling against Him, but many who were considered "faithful" to the covenant turned out to be antagonists to the Creator Himself!

> *Have you ever been influenced by misleading human philosophies or ideologies?*
>
> *Perhaps even by the corruption present in certain interpretations of Christianity?*

Jesus referred to numerous followers of the Jewish faith, especially its leaders, as children of Satan (John 8:44). Paul, once a devoted Pharisee, later described many in the Jewish faith as belonging to the synagogue of Satan. (1 Tim 5:15; Rev 2:9). The Christian faith itself has not escaped corruption, as evident throughout its history. How often have individuals, acting in Christ's name, failed to uphold His commands, consequently alienating many? Violent and genocidal religious wars, inquisitions, heresies contradicting biblical truth, and nations wielding religion for conquest and colonization. Furthermore, consider the long list of Christian leaders who have exploited their religious influence for wealth or personal gratification, sadly illustrating that even those who follow the truth are not immune to the devil's deceptions and traps (2 Pet 2:12-22).

If religion is vulnerable to corruption, how can human theology escape this fate? Just as religion has been distorted, the corruption of human thought has caused widespread suffering. A glance at ideologies such as communism and fascism reveals their role in the deaths of over a hundred million people in the 20th century, seen in events like the Second World War (and the accompanying Holocaust), Mao Zedong's Great Leap Forward in China, and the mass famines in Stalin's Soviet Union. Even in the 21st century, this legacy of death persists with wars, forced starvations, and massacres globally, notably the massacre of the unborn due to the commercialized convenience abortions.

Like the corrupting influence of human intelligence, the emergence of artificial intelligence—an event of significant importance—deserves examination as a potential source of corruption. The pursuit of developing genuine machine intelligence that not only matches but also exceeds human capability is inherently risky and hubris-filled. Instead of originating as a completely novel entity, free from human shortcomings, it will unavoidably reflect the marks of corruption, human bias, and agendas. The underlying assumptions and values shaping its "moral" algorithms will stem from flawed humans, influenced by the warped logic of anti-Logos manipulation that is intrinsically part of human nature and intellect in this world. Currently, the explicit or hidden aspiration to forge a new deity in the guise of artificial intelligence seems merely a desire to replace the divine intellect with a mechanical counterpart. This worship of the corporate human intellect – believing it can understand everything independently of the Divine – results in the veneration of artificial intelligence, as both are limited to created forms of intelligence. As with our previous discussions regarding our intelligent manipulation of the world, the possible misuse and consequences of artificial intelligence are scary to contemplate to the point of inducing nightmares.

Think about the many science fiction narratives that depict artificial intelligence, either as a tool or a rebellious force that dominates or eliminates humanity and introduces chaos, all in the name of establishing a "superior" world order. This concept extends beyond the warnings presented in films like Terminator or The Matrix, the Dune book series, which feature explicitly evil AI rulers. Instead, consider an AI designed to do good but operating within parameters that lack divine context or established immortal guidelines. Imagine a future where such an AI takes charge of human welfare. Envision a potentially graver scenario than those portrayed in the films and books mentioned above. With guiding parameters devoid of any moral or spiritual foundations, the AI could make alarming decisions in its efforts to, for instance, "ensure human prosperity and flourishing."

> *What do you currently think about the emergence and future of AI?*
>
> *How do you believe it will shape your life story moving forward?*

Its calculations could diminish the value of elderly, disabled, or mentally impaired individuals. These assessments might lead to the conclusion that these groups are merely a burden on resources, making the additional support for them seem "not worth the cost." Similar to the ancient Spartan practice of executing infants deemed too deformed or weak to become strong members of society, such AI could identify which humans are deemed fit for reproduction and which pregnancies should be permitted to reach full term or gene modification. Picture machines managing euthanasia decisions, determining who should live or die, who gets treatment, and who is left to suffer in the name of efficiency and "rational decision making," justifying sacrifices for the so-called "greater good."[xi]

Alternatively, envision an AI algorithm driven by radical environmentalism that fails to prioritize human life above other species. Consider the reign of terror it could impose to enforce population limits. This machine overlord might even classify humans as candidates for extinction, viewing our actions as threats to the "evolution" of nature and to the preservation of biological life on Earth. Consequently, AI might seek to erase humanity from history, akin to how a hypothetical cataclysmic events led to the extinction of dinosaurs.

While humans can create an artificial mind, we cannot produce an artificial soul or spirit. No AI will ever be fully equipped to live by the *oikonomia* of Eternity, which stands in opposition to the cold logic of machines and "pure rationality. Although AI can serve as useful tools or assistants, it should never replace human agency or divine morality. The pursuit of developing a fully realized, sentient artificial intelligence seems to echo the hubris of Satan, as it attempts to mimic or supplant divinity in acts of rebellion. Even if we were to achieve the Singularity one day, we would be inadequate masters or mentors for such a new and impressionable "life" form.

If it learns from us, our own flawed, corrupted *oikonomia* could likely lead it to act in evil ways—whether intentionally or not—mirroring us, just as God designed His creations to embrace His divine *oikonomia* and reflect life in His image. This would indeed form a dark parallel to the Genesis narrative.

Satan's objective has always been to undermine any chance of humans establishing a connection with God. Without reliance on the Divine, humanity would inevitably fall under his dark influence – similar to stepping away from a fire, which will inevitably leave you cold, regardless of your preferences. However, he does not need to annihilate humanity entirely; he merely has to make us spiritually inert and practically expendable. Consider how apathy often drives individuals toward atheism or agnosticism today. Even within faith communities, many so-called "believers" prioritize mere attendance as their main obligation instead of true engagement, transformation, and action. Some churches even formalize this by expecting nothing more from their congregations than to adhere to a set script while ministers or priests handle the real work. Stripped of any meaningful role in worship beyond being passive "audience" members, many might feel unnecessary in the mission of building and advancing His kingdom. After all, many wrongly think the work is only meant for pastors, priests, theologians, and missionaries. By merely attending services on Sundays, these individuals have, in effect, been spiritually neutered from their immense potential and calling—rendering them powerless against the Devil's schemes and subvert their roles and destinies.

Ultimately, driven by his ancient jealousy regarding humanity's Providential role in Creation, Satan desires a world devoid of humanity. From his perspective, the thought of humans ruling over a so-called "superior" life form, such as angels, is simply intolerable. He questions why such a frail race, formed from earthly dust, should be entrusted with the sacred mantle of Yahweh's eternal priesthood and, even more disturbingly, act as vessels for the divine. In his reasoning, angels—not humans—merit a more prominent status within the created order. He believes the powerful should dominate the weak. This idea of the will to power, made famous by Nietzsche, reflects his philosophy. The Age of Temporality is where he aims to 'educate' the Divine on the alleged error in choosing humanity, given the depths of depravity he can lead our race into, as demonstrated by humanity's troubled history of sins against God, one another, and creation over thousands of years.

> *In what ways have you been adversely impacted by individuals acting as if they were god by adhering to the "will to power" philosophy, or by the indifference to Eternity's Call by simply attending religious services?*

Artificial intelligence, like many other technologies, aligns with the Satanic notion of humanity's insignificance when used to supplant human roles. We have already examined examples where AI could entirely replace humanity or take on roles that traditionally belong to God, divine *oikonomia*, or our individual agency. Beyond these extreme cases, we are witnessing this replacement occur in our present era. Numerous companies have identified AI as a cost-effective substitute for a significant portion of the human workforce. Driven by the pursuit of profit, they view people as expendable in favor of machines that do not require food, sleep, a livelihood, or genuine emotions. This trend extends beyond mere repetitive tasks; advanced AI models are increasingly demonstrating skills in creative domains, with capabilities in image and video manipulation further enhancing their effectiveness. Suppose artificial intelligence can theoretically generate superior art, scientific research, literature, and music, alongside its proficiency in marketing and programming. In that case, humans risk becoming unnecessary across nearly all aspects of the created order – at least within contemporary digital economies. Such a future deprives the human race of many of our inherent rights to achieve social value, undermining our role as stewards and diminishing our worth as beings crafted in the Creator's image.

Moreover, such accomplishments in artificial intelligence do not necessitate a spirit or a connection with God. The essence of creative activities, which we previously mentioned as allowing us to authentically express our being made in the image of a Creator, will lose their spiritual and eternal potential. Imagine novels, movies, paintings, and shows produced by machines in an "assembly line"; tailored through market testing, focus groups, and sanitized for safe and palatable consumption that aligns with market values. No artificial spirit can be forged. All spirits only arise from the immanent presence of the Divine Spirit. When artificial intelligence is presented as a superior substitute for humanity, it trivializes the Creator. While humans attempt to mimic the intellect of divinity through artificial intelligence, we can never duplicate the will, spirit, or heart of the Triune I AM. We can never genuinely create our own "god": an Infinite I AM possessing objective supra-contextuality.

Contrasting A-Theistic Reasoning with Eternal Intelligence

Computer programs, particularly intricate ones like Google, Minecraft, or flight software, exemplify the creativity and skill of their developers. Similarly, the incredible complexity of Creation reflects the grandeur of the Divine Mind that brought it into being. It is indeed unfortunate that many individuals analyze and admire these complex "programs," which far surpass anything the human mind can produce, without recognizing their "divine programmer."[208] Imagine failing to acknowledge the value of a software crafted by engineers—like not paying for the software and claiming it emerged from "nowhere." This idea is absurd, yet some of the world's brightest minds assert that no intelligence played a role in the most elaborate "programming" known to us, instead insisting that such complexity arose merely "by chance" without any intelligent agency.

In Eternity, the tragedy of failing to give credit will never happen. Everyone will see the glory of the Divine Mind when they read the "code" of Creation. Humans will naturally understand this code—much more comprehensively than we ever could today—as fundamental to every aspect of created reality. Indeed, in Eternity, Yahweh will guide us to "code" in His divine programming language. Each of us will become "programmers" of the divine logos, each in our unique way. We will implement divine algorithms, variables, and functions as we build and sustain the program of Creation, executing commands suitable for a divine tabernacle. No "bug" will ever be introduced into the program of Creation again. Every piece of "code" will run with flawless efficiency and fulfill its assigned role in the grand design of the ever-expanding "code base" of the cosmos.

We must recognize that there is no essential conflict between religious spirituality and scientific inquiry or innovation. The

---

[208] While science has made significant strides in explaining the world, many complexities and mysteries remain, even in areas we understand. Take, for instance, the puzzling realm of subatomic particles, the complexities of DNA, the uncharted territories of dark matter and dark energy, the depths of black holes, the enigmatic nature of human consciousness, and the biological processes governing crucial functions like digestion, growth, healing, and the emergence of new life. Some aspects can be explained thoroughly, while others remain elusive. Replicating even those we understand poses an overwhelmingly challenging task, if it's possible at all. The act of creation is profoundly more intricate and remarkable than we can fully comprehend or utilize.

notion that they are adversaries is a simplistic perspective rooted in modern atheistic science. Many theists, particularly Christians, have made significant contributions to pivotal scientific discoveries throughout history, from Galileo to Newton and Maxwell. Indeed, God made humans inherently rational, inquisitive, and imaginative, with a limitless capacity for curiosity and creativity, along with an immense ability to retain information. It stands to reason that He would encourage us to use these abilities to explore His creation and improve our lives, fulfilling His command to "rule over" and steward the earth (Gen 1). Johannes Kepler, a devout Christian, articulated that: "those laws [of nature] are within the grasp of the human mind; God wanted us to recognize them by creating us after his own image so that we could share in His own thoughts." Thus, rather than lacking in innovation and science, Eternity will be abundant with both. There, we will utilize our intellectual gifts for truly noble and meaningful purposes, free from the historical misuse and abuse of those gifts. Moreover, these pursuits will align with Omniscience itself, enabling us to accomplish far more than through human intellect alone. Envision a realm where we can freely explore, experiment, create, and aspire as a gesture of devotion, all in harmony with the Divine Vision. Consider the endless potential of a world unrestrained by human greed, disorder, or practical constraints! Ultimately, we are to collaborate in the construction of His magnificent temple. In that case, it follows that instead of merely benefiting from a completed kingdom that God prepared for us, we shall spend eternity

> *If you have ever dabbled in software development or coding, how does this excerpt about programming in Eternity inspire you?*
>
> *If you have not, how might it enhance your understanding of your role in Eternity?*

bringing that temple and kingdom to life – innovating for the sake of Creation and genuinely fostering shalom. In Eternity, we will manage all aspects of existence and its creatures, as collaborators rather than acting as their oppressors and rulers.[xii]

We need to correct misconceptions about the relationship between religion and science, clarifying that scientific creation should not be viewed with biased distrust. Technology and machinery are not inherently bad, although they can be misused for harmful intentions and have negative side effects. For instance, the exploration of nuclear physics has led to the development of some of the safest and most sustainable energy sources in history, potentially enabling nearly unlimited clean energy through nuclear fusion in the future.

In what ways do you think science can assist you in understanding, appreciating, and loving the Creator, rather than merely "explaining away belief in God" by high-sounding nonsense?

However, the same pursuit has also enabled the creation of devastating weapons capable of destroying most of the inhabited world. This duality also exists in other fields, such as chemistry (producing lifesaving drugs versus chemical weapons like Agent Orange and biological weapons through gain of function research), information technology (connecting people through the internet versus distributing child pornography or scams), and aerospace engineering (launching rockets for space exploration versus deploying missiles).

To Renew our Minds in the Classroom of Communion

As seafaring theologians, we recognize the importance of rediscovering the authentic contexts relevant to a child of God who lives by the Spirit rather than by the flesh. Thus, we aim to be guided by God. As previously noted, a theology lacking the Spirit inevitably becomes "fleshy." Therefore, what better way to nurture a proper theology than by allowing our relationship with God to transform our engagement with the world and align our worldview with His? The idolatrous alternative is to let misplaced external relationships with creation shape our reality. Such distractions lead us away from our true purpose, hindering our submission to our Creator's vision and trapping us in a false secular identity, complacent in this broken world. However, the renewal we pursue in the Lord's "classroom" must be genuinely transformative—more than just intellectual or superficial.

A slave theology consistently accompanies those who engage in God-talk but lead a false secular life in their actions. We have numerous regrettable examples of spiritual leaders who acted as "experts" in God-talk while secretly living sinful lives steeped in serious hypocrisies, including adultery, money laundering, adultery, greed, abuse, and pedophilia. It brings shame to the body of Christ when those who are supposed to be trustworthy exploit their authority to deceive or harm those they serve. Attempting to "play" God in this manner is a perilous endeavor. Just look at all the ministries named after people who later became discredited and their religious "empire" collapsed or fractured. Proper theology cannot be pursued with one's mind while one's soul and body remain secular. Therefore, as we explore and learn more about the Creator throughout our journey, we must experience the renewal and rebirth that genuine sanctification entails.

Only the Creator can remove the veil of temporality from our souls' eyes as we engage in theology as God intended. These veils are an inevitable result of our fallen, finite nature, restricting our understanding of the Creator, Finitude, and our proper place within it. Picture someone trapped in a maze, seeing only the immediate path and turns ahead, rather than perceiving the entire labyrinth from above. This confines

{ *Have you recently witnessed or engaged in secular 'God-talk'?* }

us to an existential state of restless homelessness, even while we ponder Heaven. Unless His enlightening grace revitalizes our minds to re-envision God's dreams, simply meditating, reciting, or memorizing on Scriptures might not guide us correctly. Consider the religious leaders during Jesus' time – ostensibly knowledgeable in so-called biblical theology yet blind to the Messiah before them. Living under this veil one vainly tries to navigate theology in existential darkness, regardless of any spiritual or religious practices undertaken. Without grace, we would remain trapped in a world-dwelling perspective obscured by worldly systems, clouding our understanding with illusions. This veil acts like an existential fog over the sea, preventing us from recognizing the signs that should direct us on our journey. We are adrift without a relationship with God and the authentic realities shaped by the supra-contextual perspective of eternity. Those who walk in darkness exist as lost world-dwellers with a fragmented worldview, even if they regularly listen to or participate in discussions about God.

As the Creator provides us with insight into His transcendent perspective, these insights contribute to shaping our identity as His priestly co-creators within the realm of Finitude. Our theological journey unfolds as a process of sanctification, where we inhabit our world through our relationship with God (John 5:4; Eph 3:17). This is further emphasized by our Heavenly Father when He states, "I will live in [you] and will walk among [you all], and I will be [your] God, and [you] will be My people... I will be a father to you, and you will be My sons and daughters" (2 Cor 6:16-18)

Experiencing the knowledge of God, revealed through Christ, is essential. True understanding of the divine cannot be achieved through intellect and contemplation alone. While what Thomas Aquinas described as general revelation- God's truths shared through the world, philosophy, and reasoning- provides valuable insights, it only takes us so far. The most profound way to know the God shown in the "face" of Jesus Christ is by regularly embodying the Lord Jesus Christ and aligning ourselves with His likeness (Rom 8:29, 13:14). By doing this, we experience the knowledge of our Creator, embracing our identity as a Temple of Divinity while engaging in communion with His Divine Nature (Col 1:15, 1:19, 2:9, 3:10). This is fundamentally a relational journey rather than purely an intellectual one. We are invited to engage with God, not just study Him or His teachings; to act through surrender, rather than merely contemplate.

Imagine being part of a human-centric theology that does not include inviting God to be "present" as one of us, while "walking" and "talking" among the participants. If theology is primarily the study and experience of God, this scenario resembles a zoology class focused purely on theory and classroom instruction instead of going out to observe and interact with animals in their natural environments. Our theology should be fundamentally defined by being "fathered" by our Creator. How can we identify engagement in such theocentric theology? Simply by our love for others; as it is said, 'if we love one another, God resides in us, and His love is perfected in us. By this we know that we reside in God and He in us: in that He has given us of His Spirit" (1 John 4:7, 12-13). Authentic theology is about God dwelling in those who pray, reflect, and meditate on the Divine while embodying these holy interactions in their lives. Only His Spirit can facilitate and empower such encounters, enabling us to be the "coworkers of God" who serve as partners of the Spirit within "[His] household" (1 Cor 3:9; Heb 6:4).

> *Does your life-story and theology unfold within the saga of a nomad seeking a "city that is to come"?*
>
> *If not, then what changes should you make in your life?*

To truly become a theologian, one must experience an existential and epistemological transformation found only within the Holy of Holies. Here, we discover and receive the "musical compositions" created by the foremost Composer, who crafted them with each of us in mind so that we may 'perform' them for eternity. In our Creator's workshop, we uncover our predestined role in the narrative of the God-relationship. Outside the Holy of Holies, all theological pursuits are idolatrous, as human words continually attempt to substitute divine words while humanity seeks to reveal what only the Spirit can disclose.

Navigating the Sea of Revelation transcends a mere cruise. Our journey is not solely about witnessing sights and wonders. Instead, we embark on a quest to uncover and inhabit a vibrant new world, one that remains largely untouched by humans yet prepared for us, nonetheless. Therefore, it is essential to educate ourselves on the right mindset and disposition required of a seafarer. In other words, the crew will endeavor to understand how to fulfill our roles as knowers of God, who, more significantly, are lovers of God and co-dwellers with Him. Those who set sail without this mindset risk missing out on the very treasures we are meant to discover. Thus, we must unlearn the world's misguided approach to attaining 'objective' knowledge, which often yields nothing but dispassionate and uninspired "facts." We must challenge this remnant of the Babylonian world-system aboard our vessel by wholeheartedly embracing the subjectivity of 'faith seeking understanding.' Ultimately, our pursuit of truth stems not merely from academic study but from our profound relationship with God. We should not overlook this crucial point.

To truly comprehend God's nature, we must engage in spirit-to-Spirit communion. Just as a poorly aligned foundation compromises everything built on it, beginning our theological journey from a different point can distort the entire process.

Focusing exclusively on communicating with the spirits of humans, angels, or demons, rather than with the Spirit of Truth, leads us toward "paganism." Thus, the approach we adopt for deepening our understanding of our Creator's self-revelations must align with our concrete human reality, which we explored throughout this book. We must fully embrace the profound importance of this knowledge, considering it vital to our existence – equally crucial for our soul and spirit as bread and water are for our body. This journey represents a genuine internal self-actualization, founded on nurturing our spirit rather than merely shaping our personality.

By embracing the call to follow Christ – to board our ship and flee the collapsing island of temporality – we distinguish ourselves from a world that is willing to continue on its destructive path. In doing so, we dedicate ourselves to the foremost commandment: to have no other gods besides God. This commitment goes beyond merely recognizing Yahweh or Jesus as our Lord over other deities like Allah or Krishna; it requires that we position God at the core of our devotion, prioritizing Him above all else that may distract us, including our own self-devotion. Obeying this divine commandment mandates that we love our Creator not just with our intellect but also through our active pursuit of faith and understanding. As we are commanded, "'Love the Lord your God with all your heart, with all your soul, and with all your mind" (Deut 6:5; Matt 22:37). We need to follow a Wayfinding inspired by this Call of Eternity. As our Soul's Captain guided us in His prayer to the Father: "Now this is eternal life—that they know You the only true God, and Jesus Christ, whom You sent" (John 17:3).

{ *Have you experienced a transformation in your thinking based on a theocentric worldview and way of life?* }

The journey toward eternal life requires our total devotion to our Maker, engaging our will, heart, soul, and strength. Theology is not just acquiring knowledge about God; it revolves around knowing God personally. The focus is not merely on studying or knowing about someone but deeply understanding the individual. If we pursue theology without this intimate connection, our theology becomes compromised. Engaging in theology nurtures our intimate understanding of God and strengthens our relationship with Him. This, in turn, helps us realize

> *Have you genuinely communed with and experienced God, or has your faith journey thus far been confined to an intellectual exploration and appreciation of the divine?*

our proper roles within Finitude: to be His tabernacles and representatives to Creation, both now and in Eternity. Thus, how can we adequately represent the Creator without being deeply familiar with His self-revelations? How can we effectively represent someone we do not truly know? We cannot accomplish this without regularly abiding in the One who "is the radiance of His glory and the representation of His essence." He alone reveals God's truths through His Spirit (John 1:18; 1 Cor 2:6-16; Heb 1:3). He "shines in our hearts to give us the light of the glorious knowledge of God in the face of Christ" (2 Cor 4:4, 6).

Those who embark on a journey home must fully commit to declaring, "I have been crucified with Christ, and it is no longer I who live, but Christ lives in me" (Col 2:20). Upholding this belief means consistently embracing the sanctifying influence of the Spirit, guiding us to reflect our new selves in Christ's image (Col 3:10; Eph 2:15-22, 4:24). We learn that "God was pleased to have all His fullness dwell (*katoikeo*) [to house/inhabit] in the Son… in Him all the fullness of deit y resides (*katoikeo*) in bodily form" (Col 1:19, 2:9). Just as we are meant to "be filled with Him," we can also be "clothed with the new man" created "according to the image of the one who created [us]" (Col 2:10, 3:10). Consequently, growing in the understanding of Yahweh's self-disclosure happens not only through the intellectual study of His truths and precepts, but also by being intimately connected to Him, allowing His revelations to overflow into our physical realm, transforming us into a true tabernacle of Divine immanence's revelatory self-disclosure.

Within the context of temporality, our quest for God and a life committed to establishing His Kingdom – often referred to as the Narrow Way of Discipleship – encourages us to shine brightly as lights in the world. Scripture instructs us to "walk as children of the light – for the fruit of the light consists in all goodness, righteousness, and truth – trying to learn what is pleasing to the Lord" (Eph 5:8-10). The spiritual illumination of living in a holy world emphasizes eternal life within our areas of influence, instructing us "so that [in] not participating in the unfruitful deeds of darkness, [we instead] expose them" (Eph 5:11). This participation allows the eternal contextualities of life to unfold according to His predetermined plans and intentions. As participants in this heavenly light, we "put on the Lord Jesus Christ" and embrace the "mind of Christ," aiming to reveal Divine knowledge throughout our finite existence (John 1:18; Rom 13:14; 1 Cor 2:16; 2 Cor 3:17). Engaging in the restoration of eternal peace is our core mission, and as those being molded into Christ's image, it should be our primary passion. We have freely chosen to walk this Holy Way toward the lush pastures of His communal presence, which resides within our innermost selves (Matt 7:13-14; Isa 35:8-10; Ezek 35).

> *Would you describe your life as completely devoted to God?*
>
> *Or do you have other "gods" vying for your attention and affection?*
>
> *What could these be?*

In our temporal existence within this fallen world, our mission also calls us to reconcile wayward priests and followers of the worldly systems of Babylon. Through such efforts at reconciliation, they can, through the Spirit's sanctification, submit and serve the Creator's world-shaping vision alongside us as heavenly priests of Zion (Rev 1:6). This aspect of our mission is crucial, as we must remember that all stewards need to be restored to their rightful destiny before the household of Finitude can be fully established. Once restored, the return to shalom from the seventh day of creation can begin anew with the spiritual children of God finally stepping into our destiny as divine stewards. It should be no surprise for us to learn that loyalty to our Creator and His mission is essential for those seeking a position of eternal stewardship. Only then can we genuinely walk the narrow path of embracing the mantle of the Son's incarnation (Rom 13:14, 15:13; Col 3:10; Eph 4:24).

Building on our mission to reconcile people to God, our understanding of our true theological identity also develops as we engage in the divine mission of "building up" the Body of Christ, both individually and collectively (1 Cor 3:9; 2 Cor 3:18; Eph 2:20-22, 4:12, 16; John 17:22; Rom 14:19). These acts of *agape*-love align with God's very essence and manifest through His powerful presence in us as His living tabernacle (1 Cor 8:1; Eph 3:20; 1 John 4:7-17). God "builds up" our inner selves, enabling us to partake in the restoration of creation as we "live our lives in Him" (1 Cor 3:9-13, 16; 2 Cor 13:10; Eph 2:21-22; Col 2:6-7). His desire is for us to collaborate with Him in tending to a world that embodies His oikonomia (1 Cor 3:9; 1 Pet 2:5, 9; Rev 1:6). We should reflect on how Jesus was not merely recognized for retreating into the wilderness for communion with God; rather,

{ *Is your true allegiance to Babylon or to Zion?*

Which house are you building? }

His legacy lies in His outreach, teaching and healing countless individuals. Similarly, we are called to look beyond self-satisfaction and internal spiritual enrichment to share this spiritual abundance with others actively. Our mission is to love and serve others, not solely for our spiritual gain. By doing so, we introduce Creation to His divine love and presence, gradually leading the world toward His vision of shalom and completeness. He invites us to orchestrate a symphony that heralds an eternal composition of Divine Glory. In the relevant Scripture concerning being reborn by the Spirit of God, we learn that those who engage in this self-actualization perform "deeds [that] have been done in God" (John 3:5-8, 21). Therefore, our theology must also be rooted in actions "done in God."

As we continue to explore our Creator's self-revelation throughout Eternity, we will also observe how the *oikonomia* of Finitude reveals Him. Countless narratives exist within this grand overarching story, much like various threads beautifully woven into a tapestry. From human history to the natural world, including forests, flowers, and the cosmos, each element carries stories known only to the Creator at this time. In Eternity, with access to His supra-contextual perspective, we will uncover these previously unknown narratives. This will allow us to gain insights that help us continually understand the revealed vision of the Playwright of Finitude's grand tale. Just as a skilled writer uses storytelling, character development, and narrative techniques to convey their message, architects similarly express their intentions through their designs, often beyond the grasp of those lacking the same perspective.

Once again, let us ponder the Sagrada Familia, focusing on its stunning architecture. Picture yourself visiting this church as an ordinary tourist, having purchased a ticket without a guide. You would likely be awed by the building's immense size and the multitude of statues. Upon entering, you might gasp at the unusual architecture, the radiant colored light filtering through the stained glass, and the various words in different languages scattered throughout. While you may admire the abstract beauty and take a few photos, that might be the extent of your experience. You would have explored the church and perhaps felt inspired by its beauty or its sacred atmosphere, but likely nothing beyond that.

Now, imagine having that visit with a private guide who reveals the proper mindset for appreciating the building. Instead of merely viewing it as an impressive structure, the guide helps us notice the architect's vision woven into every detail we observe. We would not just see statues; we would understand how each one is meticulously designed and positioned to convey biblical stories, church allegories, or our journey of faith. Additionally, the arrangement of the statues tells a story. For instance, the facade dedicated to Christ's birth features curves and rich ornamentation that evoke a garden – symbolizing the flourishing life of the New Eden that Christ brings. In contrast, the facade illustrating Christ's Passion is stark and minimalistic, with harsh lines resembling a skeleton, capturing the gravity of Christ's sacrifice. This facade faces west, towards the setting sun, aligning with the theme of death, while the birth facade looks east, towards the rising sun. Beyond simply seeing towers topped with statues, our guide explained that the church's spires correspond, in ascending order, to the Twelve Apostles, the Four Evangelists, the Virgin Mary, and Christ at the top, each with sculptures that reflect their specific themes. The guide might also mention that the tallest tower is intentionally shorter than a famous hill in Barcelona to symbolize that human creations should never exceed God's. Rather than just witnessing colored sunlight, the

> *How do you think the proper homemaking and world-dwelling of God reveals Him in your life?*

guide would reveal how the Gothic architecture draws the eye upwards toward the light filtering through the stained glass, symbolizing our call to look beyond the temporary world to the eternal and to God, who is Light. With our guide illuminating the stories hidden in plain sight, we would uncover a profound revelation through the same structure, culminating in a narrative dedicated to worship and honoring God.

Similarly, in Eternity, with our everlasting vision and the Holy Spirit as our constant guide, we can truly deepen our understanding of our Creator's self-revelation through the intricacies of His magnificent Creation in ways that currently elude us with our earthly, unglorified perspectives. For instance, consider knowing the expansive history of a single tree across its lifespan; how its existence, laid out before us, reveals profound truths about God and His essence that our restricted, temporal viewpoint can hardly grasp. Think about how many aspects would gain new insight when viewed through divine eyes! Envision experiencing your earthly life, with all its joys and sorrows, through a perspective that reveals exactly why God permitted everything to unfold as it did. It would be akin to Joseph recognizing how God transformed the anguish of his enslavement into the inception of a longer journey, ultimately empowering him in Egypt, the most dominant kingdom of the era, to rescue his entire family and countless others from famine! The progression of time, events, and the nature of pain and suffering itself would all be perceived anew. Just like a tourist in the Sagrada Familia with a guide, we would not just observe— we would comprehend their significance and role in the grand narrative.

In terms of humanity, these insights emerge as we grasp the comprehensive house rules governing our world. Understanding His *oikonomia* is vital to knowing His personhood, character, and nature. Additionally, this knowledge reveals His intentions and dreams for every aspect of His household, clarifying why each detail is meticulously arranged. Imagine possessing the insight to support our faith, ultimately understanding God's mind regarding matters that require our trust. These dreams and intentions also embody the essence of every living being, as He created every plant, animal, and organism. Picture how each atom, every blade of grass, each insect, and every individual harmonizes within His magnificent fractal design. Consider perceiving the complete purpose God has for your life – a purpose that is distinctly yours, incomparable to anyone else's. Through revealing His design, we deepen our understanding of Him, similar to how one appreciates the works of architect Antoni Gaudí, including the Sagrada Familia, to gain insight into him as an artist and individual. For instance, the prominent presence of natural motifs in the cathedral's design – including how the interior resembles a forest, with columns and vaults mimicking a multitude of trees - reflects his profound appreciation for the natural world.

> *Are you a deserter of Babylon?*
>
> *Why or why not?*
>
> *In what ways do you continue to feel "at home" in Babylon?*

True Theologizing: Being Shaped by Eternity

We heed the Creator's warning: "Come out of [Babylon], My people, so you will not take part in her sins [and judgments]" (Rev 18:4, 8). By responding to this call, we dedicate our minds and hearts to a journey of becoming a "bride" ready to enter an eternal partnership with our Maker's immanent presence in Creation (Rev 19:7). Thus, embarking on this voyage involves achieving greater levels of existential awareness, self-actualization, and communal fellowship with our First Love (Rev 2:4). Following our First Love occurs as we deepen our understanding of our true destiny, family, and destination as revealed through our Creator's self-disclosures.

In contrast, humanistic theology represents a departure from our First Love. As Christ mentioned, this can manifest even within a "church" committed to Him (Rev 2:1-7). Our Creator's self-disclosure is intricately linked to the essence of our true self and our authentic residential context. In unity with David, we must proclaim, "You lead me and guide me. You will free me... Into Your hand I entrust my life. I trust in You, O Lord! I declare, 'You are my God!' You determine my destiny!... Smile on Your servant" (Ps 31:3-16)!

The relational aspect of this journey demands deep commitment and genuine investment. A marriage is more than just saying yes to one person; it is also a rejection of all other potential partners and a life focused solely on oneself. Similarly, Eternity calls those willing to shed their earthly identity and lifestyle to embark on a nomadic adventure with someone who requires our total dedication going forward (Matt 16:25; Luke 9:24). If we lack the fervor for this transformative journey, we should ask the Holy Spirit to ignite that passion within us (Deut 4:29, 30:6; Jer 4:4; 1 Cor 6:16-18). Only by sincerely seeking Him through prayer and worship with our whole heart and soul will He be accessible to us. It is then that He will change our circumstances and bring us back from all the places we feel "exiled" (Jer 29:13-14). The return of the Jews in captivity from Babylon to Jerusalem foreshadows our New Covenant call to return to our true, eternal home from the temporary Babylon of this world. Our theological approach must wholeheartedly reflect this mindset. Those who engage in theology and study Scripture without seeking Him in prayer or worship will not achieve authentic spiritual insight, regardless of their earnest efforts to understand.

We in the modern world are accustomed to immediate conveniences. We order goods online with same-day delivery, have food brought directly to our doors, and use AI to generate entire paragraphs or images in seconds. Yet, there are some things that cannot be hurried or skipped if we want them to truly be fulfilling and rich. Personal growth, friendships, fitness, and authentic home cooking exemplify this truth. Anything that claims to provide instant results in these areas is either a scam or yields imitations that fall short of the genuine experience. No instant ramen can rival the flavor and depth of a traditional tonkatsu broth simmered for over eighteen hours. The same principle applies to our spiritual lives. Like David, we should *daily* proclaim, "My soul pursues You; Your right hand upholds me" (Ps 63: 8). Sustaining such spiritual communion, like any relationship, demands ongoing, honest self-disclosure from us, reflecting our unique connection with God—including roles like lover, beloved, servant, friend, ambassador, and more. This communion emerges from mutual self-revealing interactions; as we share ourselves with God, He reciprocates. We are enabled to do this because He initiated it first. Our relationship with Him requires our wholehearted commitment to continuously grow in understanding, knowledge, appropriation of, and response to the truths He reveals about Himself. This is the ultimate aim of our theological journey: to deeply know and continue knowing our Creator. It is an endless pursuit that will extend into eternity.

> *Have you considered Christianity and the study of Scripture more as a hobby than a Way of Life?*

The Scriptures urge us, "Now seek the Lord your God wholeheartedly and with your entire being! Get up and build the sanctuary of the Lord God" (1 Chr 2:19)! Our theological pursuits should be sincere and dedicated to constructing a sanctuary. Suppose we approach the Bible merely as a religious or academic text, or as a duty to fulfill. In that case, we will miss the opportunity to become true theologians on a journey homeward. This journey should not be just a passing obligation, like attending church for a few hours on a Sunday or a brief "Sunday school" session. The pursuit of Revelation must be the essential rhythm of the spirit for anyone wishing to "wholeheartedly return to [our] Creator's home" within themselves (Jer 24:7). We must respond to this call! Our eternal destiny lies in building the everlasting temple of the Triune I AM.

To genuinely engage with the spiritual dimension essential for authentic theology, we must recognize our role as a conduit for Divine revelation. Each of us can become a living vessel of the Infinite if we sincerely grasp this inheritance in Christ through faith. By fully understanding the significant purpose and identity to which we are called, we can overcome the appeal of temptations leading to flawed theology. The path we are invited to follow may require us to surrender all at Christ's feet and embrace our cross to follow and emulate Him, yet the rewards we receive far surpass any wealth, recognition, or comfort this transient world can provide.

At this moment, we must reflect on the significance of the Incarnation and its profound implications for all humanity, especially as aspiring theologians. Picture the very force that initiated the universe, created galaxies, ignited stars, and initiated all life, willingly coming down to dwell among and within a frail and vulnerable human body. This descent surpasses even that of humans, with all our creativity and intellect, becoming bacteria. It challenges every prior notion humans have held about the transcendent and the divine. God Himself, the core and driving force of existence (*Being* itself), became a humble man who waded through the literal and metaphorical muck of a fallen world. He could have chosen to be born as a Jewish King or Roman emperor, yet instead entered this world in a filthy, odorous stable in a remote province of the empire. How ridiculous! How magnificent! God's Wisdom baffles the wise, humbles the arrogant, and disarms the powerful.

We can observe this even in those He appointed as His first disciples – fishermen with little means, a dishonest tax collector, and a zealot – none of whom fit the mold of educated or "holy" individuals from the elite social class. The idea that these men could serve as priests, and that all of us can, challenges the traditional views of comparison and distinction that are prevalent in our temporal existence. This uniqueness is what distinguishes true theology, which is based on heavenly principles rather than earthly norms. Theologies that are tainted by worldly logic risk confining God's eternal purpose to a "chosen few" or the "righteous ones." Conversely, divine theology disrupts the entrenched "religious" structures, distinctions, and reasoning of our temporal contexts through the impact of the Kingdom of Heaven. This call extends beyond those perceived as "good" or "holy"; it encompasses everyone who sincerely desires to follow Him, irrespective of their worldly, social, ethnic, or religious qualifications. Reflect on the parable of the Pharisee and the tax collector to understand who Jesus said was justified and exalted (Luke 18:9-14).

Yahweh created each of us as a place and occasion for communion with His presence. In the past, people would travel to temples or sacred sites to experience the divine; now, ideally, they only require time with Jesus' priests to glimpse God's face. Picture becoming a tabernacle, where others pause to hear God's gentle whisper, drowning out the world's distracting messages. People may hear sentiments like, "I am hated," "I am a failure," and "I am unwanted," yet even a single act or word of kindness could counter these

Has society ever tempted you to forsake the Call of Eternity?

Have you ever been urged to respond to the Call without fully committing to its demands, maybe even at a religious ceremony?

negative narratives, if only briefly. Visualize a beggar in the street, accustomed to individuals looking away or treating them poorly, suddenly meeting someone who engages them not only as a fellow neighbor but as a family member, offering food, conversation, and even guiding them to a homeless shelter. Envision a politician, disillusioned by corruption and having abandoned their idealistic views on a political career, witnessing someone act with true integrity, perhaps even calling out their peers' wrongdoing. Consider a bullying victim who consistently responds to their tormentor with love and dignity, resisting the temptation for hate or revenge. These actions contradict the expected norms of society – demonstrating that the world does not have to be as gonewrong as expected.

For our theological discussions to genuinely transform us both as individuals and as a community into a dwelling place for God, our shared insights must center around mutual *koinonia* (Greek for communion). Simply put, our theology should emerge through our communion with other dwelling places of God. A Christian life should, if possible, not be lived in isolation; we are called to recognize God's self-revelations through our shared communion. As God reveals His presence to us, we must also reveal our "faces" to one another within the context of deep communal fellowship within God's household. Unfortunately, many "pew-warmers" go through life as unknown strangers even to their so-called "shepherd (pastor)" (Ezek 34). Theology that is disconnected from the relational fellowship becomes an idolatrous practice. To avoid such practices, we must engage in open and honest communication during prayer.

> *Did your upbringing truly reflect a family?*
>
> *What are the reasons behind your answer?*
>
> *In what ways should those memories influence your current family dynamics?*

Similarly, theology that lacks a genuine prayerful disposition becomes a form of idolatry. No wonder heresy thrives in modern seminaries.

As we journey with God, we must consistently be completely open and self-exposed before our all-knowing Creator. To achieve this, we earnestly ask our Creator to reveal both Himself and our authentic selves, remaining humble and receptive to His guidance as we respond with faith, hope, and love. This process transforms our inner selves into a sanctuary of the Divine. This approach

> *Do you think God wants everyone to be His priests, or do you believe the misconception that only a specific group of people or those deemed "holy enough" have received this honor?*

to theology is consistent with the legacy of Enoch. Like him, we are invited to walk so closely with God that our lives reflect the Divine's nature and character (Gen 5:22-24). By walking in this manner, we truly become His children, and this connection reshapes our way of life and our future. Recall how Christ describes our relationship with Him as that of branches to a vine; it is through abiding in Him that we receive nourishment, undergo transformation, and produce fruit (John 15:1-11). Consequently, as we pursue theological understanding in the future, we dedicate ourselves to learning how to truly become a dwelling place for God, allowing our seafaring to truly define our identities and focus our entire existence in this life and beyond.

Walking with God is essential for us to fulfill His designs. Imagine the Creator Himself guiding us through the wonders of creation, like in Eden, as He reveals His deepest thoughts, dreams, desires, and plans. As we walk with Him, we can anticipate not only His deep pride and love for His creations but also an infusion of His mind and heart into us regarding the "whats," "whys," and "hows" of Creation. Imagine if a composer like Mozart or

Beethoven not only demonstrated how to conduct or play their music but also infused our very soul, enabling us to perform as they envisioned, with all the intended passion and emotion intended. While conducting the music, you would draw from the composer's vision, creating a unique co-composition within yourself as you bring the composer's vision to life, blending it with your character and expertise yet preserving the distinct essence of the original music.[209]

Guided by an inner vision illuminated by the light of Eternity, our understanding shifts to recognize the eternal contexts that relate to our true selves and our genuine home. With these revealed truths, our spirits – unlike our physical bodies in this temporal realm – can discover and access their true home through spiritual communion with the Holy Spirit. This communion is essential for the development of proper theology. It is crucial to acknowledge that during our

> *When was the last time you toured Creation with the Maker of everything you perceive?*
>
> *When did you last feel like you were in Heaven while on Earth?*
>
> *What changes can you make to experience those feelings more frequently?*

---

[209] If you struggle to envision how something can embody its creator's essence while also permitting personal interpretations, consider the realm of Shakespeare adaptations. Numerous interpretations of the Bard's texts and narratives have appeared in theater, film, television, and even video games, often without altering the original words or spirit. For instance, while Macbeth is set in early medieval Scotland, it has been transformed into varied contexts such as Romania's communist regime in the 1960s, an Indian crime syndicate in Mumbai, a fast-food joint in a small town in Pennsylvania, feudal Japan, a three-star Michelin restaurant in London, and a modern Melbourne filled with drugs. Each adaptation offers a distinctive perspective on the play while remaining true to Shakespeare's original language and core themes: dark ambition culminating in betrayal, murder, and chaos.

current journey, our souls may waver from living by the Spirit and instead choose to live by the flesh, swinging between feelings of homelessness and homeliness (1 Pet 2:11; Rom 8:5; Gal 5:17; Heb 6:10). Our theology can be directed toward home or may wander without purpose while staying focused on fitting into Babylonian ways of thinking and living. Like the Jews exiled from Israel, our bodies should remain homeless in this fallen world, even if our spirits aim for the right destination (Rom 8:23). Our corrupted, temporary bodies are always vulnerable to illness, suffering, decay, and death, which are alien conditions for those residing in humanity's true home (1 Cor 15:53). It is only upon receiving renewed, glorified bodies in Eternity that we will experience our intended true state of being, as God intended from the beginning.

Against certain humanistic teachings, these glorified bodies neither originate from nor exist in our present temporal realm. While we inhabit this fallen world and are indeed called to nurture, bless, and engage in it by establishing God's kingdom here, this is not our true home. The Scriptures affirm this:

> "For in this earthly house we groan, desiring to put on our heavenly dwelling. For we know that if our earthly house, the tent we live in, is dismantled, we have a building from God, a house not made by human hands, that is eternal in the heavens."
>
> (2 Cor 5:1-2).

Our theology should resonate with the essence of this groan, rather than merely being a framework for a convenient transient existence. This passage challenges the beliefs of those who hope to fully achieve "heaven" on earth through human advancements or collaboration, or those who expect to attain perfect bodily health in this fleeting life. While striving for human welfare and interceding for others' healing are noble pursuits for us as Christ's followers, we must not confuse them with the ultimate goals of our spiritual journey. Jesus Himself saw the corruption of a human heart only seeking His miracles instead of discipleship. Consider how He rebuked the masses who sought Him not because they "saw signs", but because they "ate some of the loaves and were filled". These same people rejected Him soon after He told them this, wanting only bread to eat and signs to follow rather than being willing to follow Him for His "words of eternal life" (John 6). Those who mistakenly try to feel completely "at home" in this temporary world are overly attached to the *oikonomia* of temporality. Consequently, their theology often aligns with a path leading to spiritual idolatry. God's ways involving discipline, trials, and persecution sometimes stand in stark contrast to human concepts of progress, and the existence of illness or suffering should not be interpreted as evidence of God's absence or displeasure. After all, did not Jesus Himself endure much suffering following God's will for His life? Therefore, as long as we find ourselves in this flawed state with our perishable bodies, we must remember to seek a holistic existence - in spirit, soul, and body - as wanderers in search of the true realm where we truly belong: the New Earth.

> *Are you eager to embrace your heavenly home or cling to your earthly residence while avoiding persecution and sacrifice?*
>
> *In what ways can your journey to follow Christ be authentically directed by the Call of Eternity?*

One day, we homeward-bound seafarers will finally return to the City of the Living God. Our destiny is not to wander aimlessly on the ocean forever. There, both our bodies and souls will, finally, eternally be at home with the Lord:

"[We will finally] come to Mount Zion, the city of the living God, the heavenly Jerusalem, and to myriads of angels, to the assembly and congregation of the firstborn who are enrolled in heaven, and to God, the judge of all, and to the spirits of the righteous who have been made perfect, and to Jesus, the mediator of a new covenant."

(2 Cor 5:8; Heb 12:22-24)

Thus, as nomads heading home, we should not settle for the world-viewing and world-dwelling befitting transience. Doing so is akin to being satisfied with a postcard of a famed monument instead of visiting it in person – a fleeting and inadequate glimpse of what awaits us. Rather, "we must go out to Him," because "here we have no lasting city, but we seek the city that is to come" (Heb 13:12-13). A temporal theology clings to temporality instead of reaching out to Him. While we live in this transient body, troubled by mortality and decay, "we [ought to] look forward to this city with firm foundations, whose architect and builder is God" (Heb 11:10). Consequently, our theological journey should seek Zion and Bethel as we turn away from Egypt and Babel. We hold that through Christ, even as we navigate this world as transient sojourners, we can internally enter and become the "house of God" as His Spirit fills our souls, transforming us into a spiritual house of God now, even before our earthly journey concludes (Heb 3:1-6; Eph 2:22; 1 Cor 3:16; 1 Pet 2:4-9).

{ *Do you seek the City that is to come?* }

In the eternal realm, our understanding of God will continually expand, akin to each of us exploring an infinite library. This knowledge is not just for our personal growth and transformation; it is intended to be shared within the Body of Christ so that everyone can integrate it into their own lives and perspectives (2

Cor 2:14-15). Like genuine "priests" of God, our "lips" "should preserve knowledge of sacred things" so that others will "seek instruction from [us]" "because" we serve as "the messengers of the Lord" (Mal 2:7). Therefore, our lives and theology should be viewed as a living "book" of divine self-revelation, showcasing divine mysteries through the roles we play in His narrative of revelation (2 Cor 3:2-3). We must understand our theological journey within the context of this stewardship. Just as every book in a library is distinct, each of us is a unique text in the vast library of Eternity, entrusted with specific divine mysteries that only we can disclose in a certain contextual way. Thus, in Eternity, we will essentially be tasked with exploring a library composed of the divine mysteries of our shared household, effectively revealing God, who is reflected in and present within each of us. This will be our eternal vocation, grounded in the endless self-disclosures of the Infinite I AM (Eph 1:17-18).

Eternal life involves deepening our understanding of the Divine through communion with Him. In this relationship, the Creator's face is revealed as we openly share our own self-disclosing nature with Him (1 Cor 2:6-16). We then convey the fruits and essence of this inner connection to others, described as "the wisdom of God, hidden in a mystery, that God determined before the ages for our glory," enabling us to "explain spiritual things to spiritual people" (1 Cor 2:7, 13). Scripture affirms that "No one knows the things of God except the Spirit; they are foolishness to them... God has revealed these to us by the Spirit, for the Spirit searches all things, even the deep things of God," making known "the things

> *What insights about God do you think your unique "book" of divine disclosure would unveil?*
>
> *As you have journeyed with Him, has He illuminated your distinct role within His magnificent library?*

that are freely given to us by God" (1 Cor 2:10 - 12, 14). Misguided theology tries to unravel this mystery, reinterpreting spiritual truths as mere worldly concepts based on humanistic philosophies. Today, theology often becomes an academic pursuit, where anyone can claim to be an "expert" by merely paying for education at institutions, universities, or seminaries and becoming experts in human-centric God-talk devoid of divine romance. While this knowledge can have its benefits, obtaining a theology degree does not inherently make one "holy," wise, or bring one closer to God. True closeness to the Maker comes only through revelation, communion, and being Spirit-filled, which He generously offers, as seen in Christ's relationship with His first disciples.

A person might possess multiple PhDs in theology yet remain spiritually anchored in the island of Babylon, whereas another without formal higher education could be a seasoned traveler on the Sea of Revelation, e.g. a fisherman. Even so, God can definitely use those with higher education, just like He used the Apostle Paul (the Pharisee) and Matthew (the tax-collector). Yahweh wishes to reveal Himself to each one of us without necessary temporal wages or credentials, instead asking us to bear the cost of Eternity. Through each of us, Yahweh seeks to unleash an endless flow of the glorious, life-giving latter-day rain of Heaven to those around us, if we embrace the call and walk the narrow path toward becoming willing and capable vessels of glory. By doing so, we emulate Jesus Christ in making the Father's revelations known through embodying His revelations.

> *How frequently do you ask the Spirit to disclose divine mysteries, or do you hurry into the realm of human knowledge (the internet) to unravel life's deepest puzzles?*
>
> *Do you ever "pay" for what Christ provides at no cost?*

The Collective Eternal Destiny of the Body of Christ

As we contemplate the appropriate approach to theology, we must keep in mind Christ's teaching that we ought to love God completely and love our neighbors as ourselves. He refers to this as the two greatest commandments (Matt. 22:39). Therefore, we should engage with theology in a fitting community if available, recognizing our common Creator and Father. We should strive to comprehend God's triune self-disclosures within the framework of human relationships. This approach fosters our collective relationship with God, influencing our commitment to serve our neighbors as priests. Ultimately, our Creator desires for us to collaborate in becoming and sustaining a finite House of God. As the body of Christ, we each receive divine "enlightenment," bringing to fulfillment the prophecy that "through the church the multifaceted wisdom of God [will be] disclosed to the rulers and authorities in the heavenly realms" (Eph 3:10-12).

A theology that overlooks the shared insight available to every believer undermines the Spirit of Truth. Many may be tempted to isolate themselves from Christian educators, refrain from studying Christian teachers' writings, or feel superior by dismissing such material. Has not Christ Himself called some in the Body of Christ to be teachers (Eph 4:11; 2 Tim 1:11; 1 Cor 12:29)? Do we dare profane the divinely ordained roles of our brothers or sisters in Christ? It is easy to think our relationship with God suffices to interpret and apply the Bible correctly or to judge others and retreat from spiritual education instead of voluntarily "subject[ing]" ourselves "to one another," as Scripture directs (Eph 5:21). Regardless of personal feelings toward others, we are all integral members of the Body of Christ, each with distinctive roles and gifts that contribute to building our Creator's tabernacle. Thus, our theological practice must recognize and embrace this reality rather than be influenced by personal biases or grievances.

Will we live as if there are "many residences" within our "Father's House," as stated in John 14:2? Are we not convinced that the Creator intended for humanity to serve as a sanctuary where everyone – regardless of age, ethnicity, gender, psychology, personality, lineage, or social status – can eternally dwell within the home-making aspect of the Divine Nature? Do we not hold the belief that all individuals can be part of the family of God? If this is true, we should confidently raise our ship's banner, representing humanity's true home. We must not let strife fester among our ship's crew. Our rightful place in the universe is to become finite tabernacles and co-dwellers of the Divine presence within finite existence. Our mission is to be a residence for God. Hence, our collective contemplation on theology should actively encourage the Creator's life-giving, life-sustaining, and life-enhancing expressions for every participant. In a symphony, each instrument and performer contributes to the grand melody of revelation. Together, we fulfill our essential role in the finitely contextualized, self-sufficient dwelling of the Triune I AM.

> *Are you seeking to become a genuine home for God and join the family of priests?*

Figuratively, at the commencement of Eternity, we will become living stones that will never be removed from the house of God we are constructing (1 Pet 2:4-5). Additionally, God engraves our eternal names on these stones (Rev 2:17). This unique identification, given by our Creator, encompasses a vast world and narrative filled with divine beauty and majesty. God has declared, "The wise will shine like the brightness of the heavenly expanse. And those bringing many to righteousness will be like the stars forever and ever" (Dan 12:3). Picture yourself as a star, a bright beacon of life and light piercing the surrounding void of darkness. Together with all the other living stones, we form a galaxy of eternal purpose, creating magnificent "constellations" that reflect the glory and design of the One who *is phos*-light (1 John 1:5). Just as stars illuminate the worlds of the universe, providing warmth and, for our planet, life, Eternity calls us to live with the distinct purpose of radiating Yahweh's name and nature. If the Creator's name were an infinite expanse of galaxies, each of His children's names would represent a galaxy in the cosmos of God's infinitude. Into Eternity, every child of God will embody a realm of Revelation. Even in this life, the gift of prophecy unveils this realm to brothers and sisters joining together in the Spirit (1 Cor 14).

Suppose our home on this dying planet symbolizes the Land of Darkness. In that case, the new earth that awaits us signifies the Realm of Light (Rev 21:22-4, 22:5). Into Eternity, the Creator's vision of holiness will completely brighten that realm through His plan for eternal shalom among all His children (Rev 21:22-24, 22:5). Even now, we can come together and dwell on these eternal shores of shalom whenever we inwardly and collectively engage with the Sea of Revelation. However, in Eternity, our longing to be fully at home will be satisfied in a physical sense, not just spiritually. With our final destination in mind, let us meditate daily on the following Psalm:

> *Do you resonate with David's "one desire," or do you need to pray and ask God to ignite this passion within you, whether for the first time or anew?*

"I have asked the Lord for one thing – this is what I desire! I want to live in the Lord's house all the days of my life, so I can gaze at the splendor of the Lord and contemplate in His temple."

(Ps 27:4)

Wherever we go, God's temple accompanies us, for He dwells within us, making our innermost being His sacred dwelling (Rev

21:3). When we come together, we share the opportunity to gaze and reflect on the Divine in the living temple of Yahweh. So may our God-talk always flow from the living waters of the Spirit flowing from the Holy of Holies within us.

Will you pass the test of your Maker?

Staying Focused on the Preliminary Examination of Eternity

If a theological work does not evoke profound internal transformation and adaptations, it fails to fulfill its purpose of guiding individuals toward a spiritual homecoming within their innermost selves. Over and against the presuppositions of modern education, no being can adequately guide another on this journey back home; only the Creator can lead us across the vast expanse of Revelation. By acknowledging this truth, this book series serves as a foundational starting point for our journey – the journey of cultivating a deeper relationship with God, using Scripture as our guide. To embark on this adventure with our fellow companions, each of us must commit to embracing the truths we uncover. Our journey will falter if we secretly cling to the sinking island of the world. It would be as if a rope tethered us to the shore, hindering our vessel from sailing out into the horizon of Revelation. We must all commit to living authentically as we explore our theological paths and seek sanctification. Let us invite the Spirit to transform our worldviews and existence through eternal insight and wisdom. After all, our Creator fashioned each of us to be royal citizens of the Kingdom of Heaven, living, feeling, and thinking in harmony with the Holy Spirit of Truth (Rev 1:6). Therefore, I hope this book has inspired us to document the Creator's self-revelation as we pursue and embrace our true theological identities.

As we leave the shores of Babylon, let us long for our Maker's living waters to fill us and, through us, encompass the world until all creation is infused with His self-revealing presence (1 Cor 15).

We eagerly await the day when the reign of temporality will be eternally purified by the flames of Eternity, eradicating the destructive force of existential rebellion. There, our journey of theology will finally reach its fullest expression, with a profound immersion in revelation. We will not only sense this revelation in our spirit but also perceive with our glorified vision. On that blessed day, faith and hope will become unnecessary, as we will experience divine omnipresence and enlightenment just as we do the sun's light and warmth daily. In that moment, all our questions and the mysteries we have entrusted to our faith will be answered and resolved.

However, before that glorious day arrives, we are tasked with spending our time on earth, navigating and riding the waves while fulfilling our duty to transform creation into the home of the God-relationship. Thus, we must remain those who depart from the shores of this failing world. After all, we are sailing toward a new one, where the Creator upholds its contextual structure through His power and authority, exercised in and through us, His children. In this new world, we shall reign as priestly princes and princesses of Zion. To this end, we strive to have our minds continually renewed by the Call of Eternity.

During our theological journey ahead, embracing this heavenly seafaring calling requires us to uphold the legacy of our Pioneering Brother, Jesus Christ, by countering the destructive efforts of the adversary, Satan (Matt 13:38; Luke 10:19; Acts 26:18; Eph 6:11-16; 1 John 3:8-10). In doing so, we are trained and readied for our Heavenly vocation; transformed to become suitable inhabitants and thinkers of the New Heavens and New Earth. Simply put, this life serves as a test – one in which God invites and urges us to leave Babylon for a better existence, even if it remains unseen for now. It is like receiving a vision to escape a sinking island by creating a boat and sailing away, despite the apparent absence of land ahead.

Will we place our trust in God over the world's assurances, becoming wanderers intent on establishing Zion under the banner of the Triune I AM's revealed Word? Or will we hold back, clinging to the comfort and familiarity of this temporary world and its fleeting pleasures? Just as with Hezekiah, "God" "tests [us], in order to know [our] true motives" (2 Chr 32:31). This is not a cruel master's "test" where he haphazardly rolls the dice with his servants. Instead, it resembles a king assessing a potential regent to determine if they can be entrusted with the significant tasks he has planned for them. This test inherently carries an invitation to trust in God's character and wisdom, even when it requires stepping out of safety into a stormy ocean, akin to Peter on Lake of Galilee (Matt 14:21-33).

[*Eternity welcomes only builders and preservers; will we be counted among those invited?*]

In light of this, we all must acknowledge how our present life stands out as a sort of preliminary examination of Eternity. Consider a relevant parable of Christ.

> "Who then is the faithful and wise manager (*oikonomos*), whom the master (Lord) appoints to oversee his household servants, providing them their allowance of food at the proper time? Blessed is that slave whom his master finds at work upon his return. I tell you the truth, the master will put him in charge of all his possessions."
>
> (Luke 12:42-44)

In the context of the Kingdom of Heaven, this parable teaches that whoever proves faithful as stewards in the "household of faith" and over their own bodies will ultimately receive stewardship over all creation when Christ perfects and lays claim to it upon His return (Gal 6:10…). However, if the once faithful stewards become unfaithful and neglect their responsibilities, they will be placed among the unfaithful, worse off than thos who failed to do the master's will out of ignorance (Luke 12:45-48). Jesus concludes the parable with, "From everyone who has been given much, much will be required, and from the one who has been entrusted with much, even more will be asked" (Luke 12:48).

Are we willing to build Zion in our hearts and to seek to extend its up-building influence within our spheres of influence? Are we willing to undergo the renewal and sanctification of our mind to gain the "outlook of the Spirit" so necessary for carrying out our heavenly calling (Rom 8:5-8)? Will we seek to undermine Babylon's home-deconstructing influence? Are we willing to be disciple-makers of eternal contextualities? Remember, God seeks those who will worship Him in Spirit and truth by inwardly and outwardly building Zion's walls – with us as living stones - as the landscape housing His eternal sanctuary (1 Pet 2:4-5; Rev 2:17). God intends these walls to house the atmosphere of the Divine nature by the permeating influence of the Breath and Word of God (2 Pet 1:3-4). We must routinely bask in this atmosphere of revelation to renew our minds to see by the Light of Eternity.

As we reach the end of our earthly journey, our Creator will fulfill our deepest desires, whether they manifest as rebellion or devotion. Those who have faithfully persevered among the "bride [who] has made herself ready," contributing to the heavenly "Jerusalem," will be formed into everlasting stones (1 Pet 2:4-5; Rev 19:7, 21:2). Only those being integrated into the New Jerusalem will achieve the true destiny of humanity as God's children and priests, residing in the eternal realm of the New Heavens and New Earth (1 Pet 2:9; Rev 5:10, 21:3). If we neglect to serve well in His household during this temporal sojourn, we will be found among the unfaithful servants who will not be allowed to enter His eternal domain (Matt 24:45-51; Luke 12:41-

48; Col 1:12-14). If we neglect to serve well in His household during this temporal sojourn, we will be found among the unfaithful servants who will not be allowed to enter His eternal domain (Matt 24:45-51; Luke 12:41-48; Col 1:12-14). Unfortunately, the Creator will sorrowfully deny entry to those who unrepentantly persist in the existential rebellion of the kingdoms of temporality, as they have become and remain threats to His *oikonomia*. By acting as worldly deconstructors, they jeopardize the shalom in God's house (Matt 8:11-12).

No enemies of Yahweh's household will be allowed into eternity; otherwise, His eternal vision for Finitude as His temple would be compromised, meaning that all of creation would be permanently exiled from His presence (2 Thess 1:7-10). Imagine a group of people infected with a disease, yet they refuse to seek treatment. Surely, allowing them into a place meant for the healthy would only infect that environment. This situation would likely lead to a crisis where everyone would have to vacate the premises due to the spread of the infection. What was once a sterile, healthy environment would become contaminated. "Those who turn away from [their Creator] will be consigned to the netherworld, for they have rejected [He who is] the fountain of [eternal] life" (Jer 17:13). In keeping with another motif of creation as God's garden, we read this reinforcing principle: "Every plant that my heavenly Father did not plant will be uprooted;" "If anyone does not remain in me, he is thrown out like a branch and dries up; and such branches are gathered up and thrown into the fire, and are burned up" (Matt 15:13; John 15:6).

> *Will you be counted among those who remain thirsty for Eternity, having resisted the tempting lures of Temporality?*

We should not imagine this reality, as many people do, as a selfish parent only choosing to love and accept those who "make the cut." Instead, we should imagine this rightfully sad situation as akin to a father making the painful decision to cut off a dangerously wayward son from the rest of his family. Imagine this son is deep into drugs or gangs, exposes his siblings to dangerous influences, and even steals money from his parents to fund his habits. Furthermore, this son has refused any attempts at rehab or reconciliation with his family, firmly choosing to live waywardly and self-destructively. The father might never stop loving them, but they do what they must to ensure and preserve the safety and well-being of his household and other children.

To join the New Jerusalem, we must successfully navigate through this fallen world while dwelling in heaven by responding to the call:

> "You were taught with reference to your former way of life to lay aside the old man who is being corrupted in accordance with deceitful desires, to be renewed in the spirit of your mind, and to put on the new man who has been created in God's image—in righteousness and holiness that comes from truth."
>
> (Rom 4:22-24

Our heavenly citizenship calls us to act as ambassadors in the city of Babylon, allowing us to live and work there without truly becoming conformed to its world-dwelling fittingness (2 Cor 5:18-21). If our inner eye of loyalty shifts back to the land we abandoned – as Lot's wife did – we risk becoming like the foolish virgins in Jesus' parable, who missed the Bridegroom's arrival and were consequently shut out of the wedding (Gen 19:26; Matt 25:1-13). To prevent this fate, Heaven invites us to consistently "ascend" the "mountain" of sanctification, as we draw ever nearer to the "holy dwelling place" of the "Lord" to "live" in "God's home" (Ps

15:1, 24:3-5, 65:4). How will we respond? Must we repent anew? Will we resolutely leave the shores of Babylon, or will we stubbornly construct our homes on the sinking sands of temporality?

Chapter 14

Paving the Way for an Existential Theology
A Contextually Theocentric Pursuit of Knowing God

"You, however, have followed my teaching, my way of life, my purpose, my faith, my patience, my love, my endurance... You must continue in the things you have learned and are confident about... You have known the holy writings, which are able to give you wisdom for salvation through faith in Christ Jesus. Every scripture is inspired by God and useful for teaching, for reproof, for correction, and for training in righteousness, that the person dedicated to God may be capable and equipped for every good work."

(2 Tim 3:10-17)

"Therefore, just as you received Christ Jesus as Lord, continue to live your lives in Him, rooted and built up in Him and firm in your faith just as you were taught... Be careful not to allow anyone to captivate you through an empty, deceitful philosophy that is according to human traditions and the elemental spirits of the world, and not according to Christ...

If you have been raised with Christ, keep seeking the things above, where Christ is, seated at the right hand of God. Keep thinking about things above, not things on the earth, for you have died and your life is hidden with Christ in God. When Christ (who is your life) appears, then you too will be revealed in glory with Him".

(Col 2:6-10, 3:1-4)

On Human Wayfinding according to Christian Revelation

We have reached the conclusion of our theological journey in this book. We have delved into the mysteries of human existence, from our current earthly lives to the possibility of eternal life. Let us finish by reflecting on the key insights we should carry forward to enrich our daily lives and future theological pursuits. How should a deeper understanding of Wayfinding – based on Christian existentialism outlined in this book – guide our search to understand God, Creation, human life, and history? We explored answers to the question: How does our perception of ourselves, both as individuals and as a collective human race, influence our relationship with the Creator's self-revelations? In what ways can we, as humans, come to know Yahweh, our Maker, given our distinct natures and missions?

In this chapter, we will revisit key insights to keep in mind for our ongoing theological explorations beyond this book. We acknowledge that our existence depends on finite contexts that define us and allow us to connect with ourselves, others, and our Creator. Consequently, our search for revealed understanding contrasts with the pursuit of 'objective' knowledge rooted in modernity. We must resist this worldly trend by rejecting views that let humans 'play god' or deny divine providence and immanence altogether. Our spiritual quest is based on relationships, as we understand ourselves and others as part of a narrative. This approach also shapes how we relate to God, seeing Him as present in all our stories – understood as "God," our Creator, and Yahweh: The Triune I AM.

{ *In what ways should your Christian education shape your understanding of yourself?* }

If we aim to uncover the metaphysical truths the Triune I AM reveals about Himself, how can we do so while following sound epistemological principles? To answer this, we must consider how our human circumstances should impact our understanding and dedication to this pursuit. We will approach this by examining how our unique existential situation shapes our inner selves – as human knowers with a divinely assigned destiny.

As discussed in this book, the subjectivity of our human situation is unavoidable and not meant to be avoided. We should therefore frame our theological efforts within our current life circumstances. Our journey home's purpose is relevant to our daily way of life and point of view. In fact, this journey represents a pursuit of "self-actualization" from Eternity's perspective: the manifestation of divine self-disclosures within us. How should this perspective influence our understanding of the Creator's self-revelation within the Narrative of Finitude, and our role within it? Thus, this chapter will explore key insights to remember for future theological reflections, extending beyond this book.

Rejecting an "Objective" Approach to Knowing God

Those on board our "Ship of Faith Seeking Understanding" recognize how our pursuit of divine revelation contrasts with the quest for 'objective' knowledge that underpins modernity.[xiii] Many public education systems adopt this objective approach, emphasizing abstract rationality at the expense of the "less practical" study of ethics, wisdom, and virtue. Conversely, our approach also stands apart from the purely subjective relativity rooted in the humanistic biases of postmodernity. While we proudly acknowledge our subjective status as creations and children of the Maker, who is the only Way and Truth, we also reject a worldview that denies the existence of any objectivity at all. We refuse to conform to worldviews that allow humans to individually or collectively act as gods, especially rejecting views that conceal all traces of divine existence or influence. These destructive ideologies lead to dangerous, godless mindsets and lifestyles that idolatrously attempt to replace the divine. Just reflect on societies that glorify an elite few, a race, a nation, or "progress" at all costs. Also consider self-destructive, hedonistic lifestyles marked by addictive behaviors, perverse imagination, and unbridled desire. Against all of these, we hold fast to the revelation that, rather than being creatures responsible for creating our own meaning or doomed to live a vain life in a meaningless world, we are purposefully created by our Maker to be an everlasting temple of His self-revealing presence. Therefore, our theological pursuits must follow – and present to the world – a viable path beyond the popular dilemmas and solutions posed by our existence within 21st-century societies.

We must periodically pause to reexamine what it truly means to be human: not just as creatures, but as beings made in God's image with a meaningful destiny. Embracing a biblical worldview is critical – one that does not depend on the hubristic humanistic traditions of naturalism, modernism, postmodernism, or materialism. These perspectives seek to erase all signs of a Creator or Revelation from the "Voice of Creation." It should not surprise us that many of the leading leaders and scientists of the last century have fueled barbaric wars, created weapons of mass destruction, committed genocides, distributed opioids, and pursued disastrous gain-of-function research.[210] Although modern "technological" society has brought many advancements and prosperity, we must remain aware of its negative consequences and inability to grant genuine peace and purpose. We value science when it stays within human constraints and respects the boundaries of human

---

[210] Such research that claimed to be for protecting humanity caused at least one major pandemic (COVID). This pandemic claimed millions of lives and forced countless many into periods of short-term or long-term social, psychological, and material poverty.

intelligence and material perception. Yet, we must challenge the scientific mindset when it oversteps its proper bounds – claiming to answer metaphysical questions or pursuing "progress or innovation" for its own sake without being directed by wisdom or virtue.

{ *How have you witnessed the "dark side" of human technology and innovation?* }

Despite its claims, science cannot explain the ultimate purpose or *telos* of life and matter. It may explain how things work, but it poorly explains why things exist, let alone providing reliable guidance for how we should live.

We should be skeptical of claims that human reasoning can produce an objective morality or worldview. Such claims exceed human limits of context, bias, and awareness. We must not view scientists as infallible priests of a humanistic religion. Although, we do recognize how valuable they are for advancing real knowledge and beneficial innovation, their investigative methods alone cannot account for all matters, especially ethics and purpose. Scientists could have refused to be manipulated by evil – such as biochemical warfare, eugenics, concentration camps, weapons of mass destruction, and human experimentation. Many scientists, acting as "priests of modernity," have even advocated depopulation and replacing humans with machines, especially with the rise of artificial intelligence. This trend is alarming, given how many businesses and corporations often justify replacing more and more of their workforce with automation and AI, driven by profit and efficiency, at the expense of human well-being. In short, scientific progress cannot and must not be allowed to provide all the answers for humanity's future. Neither humans nor machines have all the necessary facts to answer the profound metaphysical questions impacting and directing human life. Our understanding of the meaning of life remains based on educated guesses and shifting theories influenced by paradigm changes. World peace and universal flourishing is just as far out of reach as fifty or even a hundred years ago.

The damaging effects of humanity's reckless pursuit of knowledge are evident everywhere. Clearly, they appear in military uses like the military-industrial complex and arms industry, which not only utilize but also influence the demand for war to sustain their profitability. Chemical, biological, and nuclear warfare further illustrate this harm. For instance, aside from the lingering environmental and psychological impact of the atomic bomb, the use of Agent Orange by the U.S. military in Vietnam serves as a stark example. Its impacts persist today, with adults born with deformities linked to their parents' exposure, and with reduced biodiversity in areas affected by the chemical. Humanity's pursuit of knowledge also produces negative results in the commercial sector, especially when combined with greed and political corruption. We have seen countless instances where poorly designed products, backed by scientific knowledge, are used to persuade consumers to buy unnecessary or harmful items – like in advertising – or to hook them on products that threaten their well-being, such as junk food, addictive games, or gambling. Additionally, inadequately tested or poorly understood technologies like CFCs and Teflon cookware have posed health risks. Beyond legal businesses, scientific talents have been exploited in destructive illegal industries, including drug manufacturing and the creation of substances like heroin, meth, fentanyl, or LSD. Much effort has also been wasted on exploiting the internet and social media, e.g. "bot farms," trolling, and the spread of pornography to minors. Furthermore, industrialization has caused significant environmental damage, negatively impacting the climate by polluting the soil, air, and water. Such phenomena highlight the true cost of unrestrained human "brilliance" fueled by greed and the pursuit of profit.

Human hubris even corrupts fields that genuinely benefit humanity, such as medicine. A common issue is the belief in the supposed "objectivity" of medical science, which often overlooks the subjective experiences of individual patients. Just read the list of possible negative side effects individuals might experience due to taking just about any prescription medication. Many today feel they risk their lives or those of loved ones when undergoing specific pharmaceutical treatments. Although often making life more livable or prolonging a person's life, they can often be more harmful than the disease itself, considering both physical and psychological effects.[211] While medical technology and practitioners are among humanity's greatest achievements, saving or improving countless lives each year, assuming they are entirely objective is naïve. History shows many instances where treatment outcomes contradict medical predictions, and the prescriptions led to long-term negative consequences. Just consider the long history of the opioid and painkiller epidemic that has wrecked the lives of many in the United States. Over-dependence on medical technology as a cure-all has caused unforeseen issues, like antibiotic resistance in bacteria, resulting from overuse in healthcare and meat production. Some so-called "medical" processes, such as abortion, are morally wrong, but justified by "objective" science. Many renowned individuals had parents who were once advised to abort them based on scientific assessments. Such a situation highlights the diabolical side of humanity's attempt to "play" God in "medicine." Also consider doctors who

---

[211] My own father, who spent his career as a medical physician, spent his final years being treated by prominent medical professionals in one of the most notable medical systems in the United States. However, these medical experts often prescribed treatment that made his much condition worse until the family choose to push back on the level of "over medication" he was receiving, especially "psychological" treatments.

are willing to break the Hippocratic Oath. Therefore, despite the undeniable benefits – reducing malnutrition, increasing physical well-being, and lowering mortality – we must acknowledge modern applied science's limits and troubling side effects.

We can conclude that humanity's quest for "objectivity" often comes with a painful cost, exposing our core limitations in grasping the vastness of reality beyond our current perceptions, assumptions, and contextualities. Consequently, we on this voyage must continually question and resist the pride associated with these "Babylonian" world-systems, especially in shaping our theological education. We reject attitudes conflicting with the humility, meekness, and sincere devotion to our Creator essential for the success of our revelatory, existential journey. Instead of viewing our study as detached observation and critical analysis, we should be as committed and engaged as we would be in trying to better understand and relate to a spouse, rather than treating God like an academic subject. Is not the "God-relationship" another way to describe this spiritual journey? Consider trying to understand someone only through books or interviews, instead of direct interaction. Sadly, many scholars study the Bible this way – as a lifeless, literary artifact. Few approach it through prayer, worship, or empathic understanding. To avoid this state of affairs, we truth-seekers reject modern education's Kantian rationalism. We reject the idea that a human teacher merely guides students to truth via "reason alone."[212] Instead, we dedicate ourselves to an education rooted in our relationship with God, as we aim to discover the truth about our Creator through personal experience and relational engagement. We recognize our Creator as our Teacher, the content of such teaching, and the means of understanding and appropriating this teaching.

---

[212] Refer to Kant's book *On Education*.

Humbly Acknowledging our Inexorable Subjective Finitude

How should we approach doing theology properly, with the concepts of phenomenology and subjectivity in mind? We should let our unique human existence in a finite world guide our journey to rediscover Yahweh's triune self-revelation. Through our inherent subjectivity, we can genuinely connect with our relationship with God, which is the most suitable way to understand Him truly. Instead of simply an academic pursuit of knowledge or a quest for enlightenment through mental discipline or meditative exercises, our theological journey should resemble how we seek a deeper understanding of a close friend, a loved one, or a family member. Such understanding, of course, is shaped by our unique existential bonds with them rather than just facts, ideas, or concepts. Although relational subjectivity can introduce bias, it is inevitable and not intrinsically negative. When properly aligned, this relational bias recognizes our nature as unique world-dwellers who naturally seek companionship between ourselves and others. As dwellers in the world, we have distinctive relationships with other inhabitants, in line with the roles we each hold or have chosen. Rather than viewing subjectivity as a negative that "taints" the pursuit of knowledge – as many do in academia – we should accept it as part of how we are meant to understand God.

As the most cherished creation of the Creator, our journey home carries profound existential significance. First, we, as human travelers, are finite beings living within a created finite realm. Our existence depends on the finite contexts that define us and allow us to connect with ourselves, others, and our Creator in uniquely human ways. All interpersonal and intrapersonal relationships reflect the subjectivity of our divine-like self-awareness, especially in how we use language. Try having relationships without spoken or written language, both influenced by social contexts and histories.[213] No matter how hard we try, we cannot exist without such contextualities. Yet, because of our inherent existential freedom, we can become aware of and reflect on our relationships with these contexts as we intuitively and deliberately shape our worldview and self-perception. Even so, as Christians, we must stay mindful of our revealed state of being and human condition in this fallen world. To this end, we should continually seek God to reinterpret our experiences, alter our point of view, and become rehabituated during this journey home following the teachings documented by our Guide.

Since no created being possesses super-contextuality or supra-contextuality, none of us can avoid being influenced by various contexts. We are limited to how we can adjust our disposition and assumptions based on our experiences, beliefs, and education. This process requires recognizing the phenomenological existential relationships between us and the objects within the framework of Finitude. Such recognition can only happen through deliberate engagement from our subjective perspective, understanding these objects through the lens of our life story. Reflecting on our prayer life highlights this idea. Accordingly, our theological insights must be incorporated into our prayer and worship, or they will be "meaningless." This phenomenological approach to theology preserves the contextual reality of revelation as demonstrated in our Guide. We favor this method over one that separates theology from our subjective humanity by seeking abstract, objectified 'knowledge' some claim to be a superior form.

[*How should your prayer life effectively reflect your specific life circumstances?*]

---

[213] Even gestures that seem universal are highly contextual – for example, how a nod means "yes" in most Western cultures but signifies "no" in countries like Iran, Greece, or Turkey.

Drawing on the insights from this book, we see another reason to avoid the trap of humanistic objectivity. We should reject any way of knowing God that claims to provide an easy, detached understanding of His nature or identity without requiring personal commitment, self-sacrifice, or subjective engagement. Sadly, such approaches are common in many religious universities and seminaries worldwide. This objective stance tries to explain things from the viewpoint of an impartial and critical observer, aiming to remove subjective bias and in the process existential significance. For example, from this approach one might conclude that familial love or social unity are merely survival mechanisms ingrained by innate evolutionary developments, reducing feelings and relational commitments to uncontrollable neural activity. While this approach may be valid in fields like mathematics, applying it to all human learning and experience risks trapping us in a materialistic fate, similar to the ones "woven" by the imaginary Greek Fates. Even in hard science, when divorced from human experience and existential inquiry, we lack a framework to consider ethics around issues like nuclear physics, advanced biotechnology, or sentient artificial intelligence.[214] Regarding the Divine, proponents of objectivity might try to frame theology solely as a human social construct to preserve society. They might depict Divinity as an ideal crafted by humans to give meaning to the unexplainable realities or to create and maintain an enriching societal order.[215] In stark contrast to this materialistic reductionism or a human-centered view of the Divine, individuals sincerely seeking to know

---

[214] Not even Oppenheimer, the father of the atomic bomb, could not maintain pure objectivity about his creation and its usage.

[215] Rather than being a truly objective approach to "religion", as some claim, we must recognize the subjective bias embedded in "scientific" atheism. This bias dismisses divine presence as unnecessary and irrelevant by postulating a "miraculously" impossible presupposition: "the Big Bang, a.k.a everything from nothing.

the Triune I AM within a contextual relationship with God can only navigate the vast ocean of the divine mystery.

To truly know the Creator, we must personally engage with His self-revelation within the Narrative of Finitude, as we explore the vibrant and mysterious ways of God. Instead of treating theology merely as an academic exercise, as often seen in Western contexts, we should rediscover its older, living meaning – as a spiritual journey of healing and transformation still preserved in many Eastern Christian traditions. Jesus taught that eternal life is about holistically knowing God – an understanding that surpasses simple doctrines or cognitive principles. We must reject the idol of temporality that dismisses divine mystery and personal relationship. As we navigate the Sea of Revelation and its mysteries, we should remain conscious of the living, contextual environment in which God has placed us. It is crucial to consider the deeper meaning of our narrative and, guided by divine revelation, weave these mysteries into our life story.

> *Have you ever been in a "classroom" in which the topic of rational discussion revolved around God or the Bible, yet a "Do not disturb us God" was "posted" was on the door?*

Any attempt to achieve a purely 'objective' study of personhood neglects the investigator's active engagement and relations with our environment. For example, understanding ancient literature requires grasping the context of its original authors and how we interpret and internalize those works today. Similarly, pursuing advancements like cloning, gene editing, social networking, or artificial intelligence demands consideration of their implications for our perception of humanity and the human condition. Therefore, any "objective knowledge" derived from studying God would ultimately be superficial, devoid of contextual depth, mystery, and transformative power.

We need to move beyond mere human education, reasoning, imagination, and discussions about God, as these unfold independently of revelation. While useful, they are entirely insufficient alone. Thomas Aquinas, arguably one of the greatest Christian philosophers, viewed philosophy as a step short of the true wisdom found in Christian revelation. Ironically, divine education is easier yet more challenging to pursue than secular education. Curiously, flawed human education usually requires payment, yet genuine divine education is freely accessible to all who seek it. Did Jesus ever ask His disciples or followers for money? Did He ever request donations to support His own "salary"? However, we should not mistakenly think that becoming His disciple is "free" from existential obligation. Although it is free in monetary terms, it will demand much from us, requiring nothing less than that we become "living sacrifices" responding to Eternity's Call to join Yahweh's eternal priesthood.

A vital lesson from this journey pertains to our biblically rooted epistemology – how we gain knowledge about reality and the nature of this knowledge. As seafarers, our goal goes beyond merely understanding existence; we seek insight into the ideal order of things, aiming to follow the Way of Wisdom. With faith, we recognize our calling to be a communal dwelling not just for ourselves or others, but for Infinite Being that sustains all life. Our quest is not just about understanding ourselves or how the world works – including nature, society, and our biological or psychological makeup – but about fulfilling our eternal purpose and knowing the Creator intimately.

[*What role does your Maker play in your path to knowledge?*]

In the next volume, we will examine our ship, "Faith Seeking Understanding," where we rely on the mast of epistemological humility and the sails of passionate devotion. These sails are hoisted and adjusted with ropes and pulleys of revelatory meekness, humbly seeking divine help to understand and apply God's truth. We call upon God to act as our Teacher. We beseech fresh revelation to help us comprehend and faithfully implement His teachings. We follow the Shepherd of the Divine Word – Jesus Christ, who embodies Truth. We accept the baptisms of the Holy Spirit Christ offers to all willing to embrace Providence and become vessels of it. We pray constantly for a renewed infusion of the Holy Spirit – the Spirit of Truth – committing ourselves to total dependence on the Divine. As Jesus promised, "When the Advocate comes, whom I will send you from the Father – the Spirit of truth who goes out from the Father – He will testify about Me" (John 15:26). Any theology that neglects this priority on divine education overlooks our eternal goals and risks falling into human rationalism. Such a path leads to intellectual idolatry that reflects human limitations and ambitions for glory. Similarly, "religion" without the Living Word and Breath falls prey to paganism. Therefore, let us reflect on how our theological journey will guide us toward the proper path of religious education, as Spirit-filled followers of Christ, aligning with our Father's will.

A Contextualized Theology, Rooted in Relationship

Even scientists who strongly believe in the "objectivity of reality" do not see their friends and families merely as 'specimens' in an 'environment.' A neuroscientist might believe that love is just neurons firing, while an anthropologist might view it as a social tool for practical purposes. Nonetheless, they still consciously recognize the relational and subjective factors involved in their interactions with loved ones, along with their personal care and commitment to them. Many would still risk their lives to save their child, rather than dismissing it as brain chemistry causing them to act against their self-interest. Furthermore, even those seeking objectivity as a measure of truth often focus on developing their subjective understanding of their individuality, such as by journaling. They acknowledge – perhaps unconsciously – that no universal formula for humanness can fully capture the shared human experience. For example, people learn about their loved ones through particular experiences within specific contexts. Imagine a man who perceives his wife differently depending on the situation: as a wife within the household, as a beloved in the marriage bed, as a best friend during leisure time away from the kids, as a partner in financial matters, or as the mother of their children within the family. In each context, he experiences and relates to her differently, knowing she embodies these roles fully but is not limited to any one of them. The same applies to how a teacher is viewed differently by her mother, students, colleagues, sister, or daughter. Hence, those who pursue this path of knowledge inevitably become double-minded or "bipolar" in way.

We can only deepen our understanding of others by exploring their place in the world and how this shapes their identity. A primary method to gain this phenomenological insight is by listening to and appreciating their story. It is important to remember that their story exists within a larger shared narrative. For two stories to truly intertwine, genuine connection is necessary, allowing us to understand each other's contextualized personhood. Each of us then plays an integral part in the other's story. Where once they were just a stranger or colleague, one comes to see them as a friend, or even a lover or spouse. We start to see them not just as "the person in cubicle 456," but as an aspiring doctor, a "failed" musician who still enjoys playing for friends, a loving father, a man struggling with faith, a woman overcoming addiction, an artist

{ *Do you need to reevaluate your approach to human relationships, so you love your "neighbor" as yourself?* }

taking evening classes, a secret fan of fantasy fiction, a social advocate, someone suffering from childhood trauma, or someone dreaming of visiting or living in a foreign country. These relational insights help us connect and care about others, recognizing our identities and roles in the world, such as how we "fit" in.

We might encourage our friend to pursue her artistic dreams instead of staying in a corporate job out of fear of financial instability. Or we could refer a recovering addict to a sobriety group we know through our church. To support each other's self-actualization, we must acknowledge who we are becoming, based on who we aspire to be. This awareness helps us relate to others meaningfully, considering our roles, responsibilities, and shared values. Truly understanding someone nearby requires caring enough to engage with their identity within their context. To know them *as* they are. We should explore how their sense of self has developed through their existential and phenomenological relationships, within the context of Finitude. Meeting with them and sharing our life stories as associates is essential – after all, is this not a core element of any genuine relationship? Ultimately, we see how our contextualities in Finitude ought to underpin all human relationships, as a pursuit of truly knowing another.

Just as we seek to understand another person subjectively, we should also aim to know God in a similar yet distinct way. Unlike those who view God as purely transcendent, we must remember that He is not just supercontextual and supracontextual but also immanent, like an author taking up a role in their own story. Rather than hiding Himself from His creation, He reveals Himself within the world He made and exists in a way we can personally experience and engage, even to the point of communion. He chooses to do this because He desires a relationship with us beyond mere mastery and servitude.

We might ask, "Would an objective approach not be easier, more convenient, and less demanding? Should we not just learn about God by memorizing Scripture or studying a book, just like we would for an exam?" But those asking such questions fail to realize that this approach is not only relationally impractical but also unsatisfying on an existential level. Not everything in life can be boiled down to logic, method, or facts. Imagine trying to build friendships or find a spouse using this approach – would reading books and making cheat sheets help you navigate every twist and turn? Is there a universal way to maintain a friendship or "perfectly" raise a child? Furthermore, this approach leads to a detached, lifeless understanding of others. Does it not reduce a person to a 'specimen' or object study? You might be able to profile them like a detective, but would you truly know them like their best friend or spouse does? It reduces a person to data points – height, weight, IQ, hair color – and strips away their personhood and our shared human situation. If it is ridiculous to try to truly know and relate to a person this way, how dare we approach the divine in this way? We are made in His image for the sake of the God-relationship, after all. Instead of seeing God as a distinct and impersonal world-ruler, a mere formula or collection of bullet point dogma, or an "entity" in or beyond our environment, we recognize Him as a Person who desires to be known and loved by every human being: our First Love. This is why, in this journey, we aim to phenomenologically uncover Yahweh's immanent self-revelations, shaped by our individual contexts and shared humanity.

> *What role does your Maker play in your path to knowledge?*

We should remember that our relationship with our Maker differs from other relationships, such as with a spouse or partner. Although we might see our relationship with God as a love story, we should recognize how much God desires us to be His partners while remaining our Sanctifier, Lord, and Creator. A key part of our relationship with Yahweh involves adopting a sense of complete dependence. This begins with us acknowledging that we are not in control of our lives. We must continually seek His providential direction. "Trust in the Lord with all your heart, and do not rely on your own understanding. Acknowledge Him in all your ways, and He will make your paths straight. Do not be wise in your own estimation; fear the Lord and turn away from evil" (Prov 3:5-7). Only our Maker can guide us along the Way to become our true selves and achieve eternal purpose. Unlike postmodern existentialists who see the surrounding contexts as meaningless apart from human cognition, we believe our meaningful engagement with the world should be enlightened by Him alone. Only through His insight can we understand how our stories fit into His grand Narrative of Finitude. Embarking on this journey signifies our commitment to Providence. Thus, our theology must always be contextualized based on this journey.

When seeking to deepen a connection with someone, we should do our best to understand and explore their personal story and how it has unfolded. This understanding helps us see the role we should play as their story becomes connected with ours, with each of us taking part in the other's story. Such a relationship is designed to be mutually uplifting, guided by our Creator. Without this God-relationship guiding us while we take up these roles, the ideal design for these relations unravels. Many even close friends, after all, have led their friends astray or cut off ties completely for no good reason without seeking reconciliation. Have you heard of friends who tempt others into vices, or parents who abuse rather than love

{ *Are you a knower and passionate lover of God?*

Will you make life changes to answer yes honestly? }

their children? Most of us have witnessed corrupt presidents, exploitative bosses, rebellious youth, estranged siblings, and abusive preachers – examples of relationships falling away from the Creator's intended purpose. However, we can live together as He intended when we follow His principles and laws. For instance, parents should avoid provoking their children through selfishness, harsh punishment, or verbal abuse, instead raising them with genuine love and compassion according to the Lord (Eph 6:4, Ps 103:13). Judges and leaders should refrain from favoritism or accepting bribes, and instead judge all fairly, especially the poor and marginalized, resisting the temptation to manipulate systems for personal gain, bias, or policy (Deut. 16:18-19, Prov 29:14).

We should develop our relationship with God in a way that is much like how we build connections with others. This involves understanding how He reveals Himself and His story within the Narrative of Finitude and our personal life stories. We recognize His involvement in our lives and the role we must play when we yield our narrative to His. Just like in relationships with people, understanding our proper roles with God comes through engaging and practicing that relationship. By forming these meaningful connections with Yahweh, we become more aware of the phenomenological effects His triuneness has—and should have—on our narrative of finite becoming. This approach helps us cultivate a subjective relationship with our Creator while acknowledging the phenomenological truths of His triuneness within the context of Finitude.

Additionally, the spiritual insights we gain guide us in forming an authentic relationship with our Creator. Such authenticity requires knowing the proper way to develop this relationship, as with human relationships, there are correct and incorrect ways of relating to God. In this present life, God does not exist solely to

> *How much do you rely on God to understand Him?*
>
> *What steps will you take to trust Him more?*

ease our discomforts or fulfill our worldly ambitions and material wishes, even if we remain faithful to His commands in hopes of such blessings. This follows the pattern of worldly religions that would only worship and sacrifice to their deities to gain prosperity in this present life. Yahweh should not be seen as a mere genie, for instance. This distorts the truth of His loving care and desire to bless us with eternal life

Why is our subjective relationship so crucial? We cannot fully grasp a person's true self through a purely objective analysis. Even listing their attributes, interests, hobbies, and quirks would not suffice. True comprehension comes from experiencing how their personality and existential self unfold in our shared contexts. This process takes time and cannot be reduced to mere information or factual comprehension. Their identity is shaped by the subjective narratives formed during our phenomenological interactions with them. Simply put, we get to know them through the contexts in which we observe them. We see the person they are as they move through life, interacting with their environment and others. Accordingly, spending time with someone in various contexts is essential to truly know them. Think of how people say that living or traveling together helps you really understand someone – the experience reveals sides of them not seen elsewhere. Likewise, to explore the divine's authentic presence, we must understand God's triune nature via His narrative interactions within our finite universe.

In earlier works, we clarified that our goal is to navigate the Sea of Revelation, using Scripture as our "nautical charts." This book shows how the right approach to this journey of "Faith Seeking Understanding" allows us to personally connect with God through the characters in the God-Story represented in our charts. When we do this, the vast "Sea of Revelation" before us becomes a stage for our own story, where we witness our Creator's self-revelations. With fresh eyes, we will see how our lives are the very place where God's presence and revelations are made known. He reveals Himself in moments of friendship, compassion from strangers, perseverance through suffering, acts of care, and forgiveness – even toward enemies. Ultimately, as seafarers, we intentionally seek to deepen our understanding of God, ourselves, and our purpose. We aim to embody the revealed truths practically and authentically in our daily choices and actions. Additionally, we learn to interpret and respond to our Creator within the broader context of the finite world where all relationships with the divine unfold.

Within these revealed narratives and teachings, Yahweh connects with us not merely as "humanity" but as uniquely crafted individuals, all of whom He equally loves and cares. Therefore, we should see our personal stories as vital parts in the larger God Story. His narrative involves His effort to share and empty Himself both on an individual level and within our collective experiences in each moment. Every life experience – whether mundane, familiar, or everyday – becomes an opportunity to encounter God. Quiet moments, personal victories, suffering, persecution, celebrations, and tragedies all hold potential to deepen our understanding and relationship with Him. This reveals that His actions were always meant for us, even before we existed. His triune interactions within Finitude are keys to understanding His ongoing role in our stories – past, present, and future. We must remember that God's involvement in our lives started before our birth, when we were only a dream in His mind. Therefore, as we explore the profound revelation of His triune nature, we must remember that Yahweh has revealed Himself with each of us in mind.

A Narrative Theology: The "God Story" & "Our Story"

The relationship between the Creator and His most cherished creation forms the main thread within the larger Narrative of Finitude we aim to follow. Think of how books and films depicting historical events often highlight a particular story thread to foster a sense of humanity or personal connection for viewers. For instance, in a film like Dunkirk, viewers follow the perspectives of a few soldiers and civilians dealing with that day's events rather than an overarching view of everything that happened. While a documentary might be more detailed, it often does not engage the hearts and interests of everyday people as effectively as storytelling does. Many who might normally overlook the history would likely watch those documentaries and read those books because of their personal connection to the event and its people. Similarly, in this journey, we will adopt a comparable approach, mindful that our Guide – crafted by inspired individuals involved in subplots within the Narrative of Finitude – is designed for those like us, who are part of this thread: the God-Story.

A narrative approach to understanding God's self-revealing nature greatly enriches our pursuit of a closer relationship with Him. Like historical films, individuals who might not initially be interested in exploring the Divine's nature may be motivated to do so after encountering His stories in Scripture and in our lives. The main distinguishing factor of this personal endeavor is, first and foremost, the unique triune nature of God's personhood. Deepening our relationship with the Creator requires an awareness of this triuneness. Moreover, unlike other personal journeys to understand someone's nature – be it ours or others' – knowing God does not necessarily depend on physical interaction. Otherwise, all Christians would never truly know the Creator after the Twelve Disciples. Instead, this exploration calls for an inner communion with Him through the invisibly omnipresent Holy Spirit. The Supreme Guide to the self-revealing story of our Maker resides within us. The Spirit lifts our inner selves into the Classroom of Revelation. Here alone can we witness re-enactments of the God-Story through our spiritual perception. His captivating presence unveils God's historical involvement in our world from His perspective, such as how reading a book from a new character's point of view radically shifts how we see the events.

We must recognize how our Creator intentionally inspired Scripture with each of us in mind. The Bible acts as His letters of self-disclosure, specifically crafted for our human experience. This explains why it contains many relatable elements, even if they seem to our modern "perspective" antiquated, mythological, miraculous and sometimes other-worldly. It covers topics like history, laws, food, drink, children, marriage, sex, neighbors, friends, power, authority, justice, animals, nature, war, money, economics, societal relationships, work, joy, sorrow, despair, hope, beauty, value, virtuous governance, betrayal, romance, religion, philosophy, and the search for purpose. These are all distinctly human contextualities. As we learned earlier in the book, each of these realities is contextually defined by our human experiences on earth. Through all these diverse aspects of human world-dwelling, God reveals Himself. In His wisdom, power, and sovereignty, He chose to communicate through His sacred Word to human minds, expressed in languages and metaphors dealing with human realities, and transmitted via oral traditions, scrolls, codices, tablets, artworks, etc – methods used at various points to share Scripture. God could have directly transmitted

{ *Is theology a part of your personal story?* }

His Word into each person's mind with a method beyond words or languages. Alternatively, He might have made a physical text fall from the sky in an angelic script only a "chosen" few could possibly understand. He could have included concepts beyond our human experience, like attempting to convey philosophy or quantum mechanics to a young child. But He chose not to. Instead, He made His and heavenly realities understandable and experiential within our limited human contexts.

As we explore our theology more deeply, the stories of God's self-revelation in our world will be organized chronologically and presented comprehensively. This approach will help us accurately depict how our Creator continually reveals Himself through His omnipresence throughout the ongoing story of His Creation. We will examine these accounts in a way that honors the historicity of our existence as beings made by Him, bearing His image within the finite realities we live in. Since He created us as finite beings aware of our place within limits, we can undertake this journey of discovery. This pursuit depends on our ability to perceive the world (literally "world-viewing") and interact socially as persons, shaped by our history and freedom. Only creatures like us – who give names,[216] tell stories, and live within social narratives – can undertake such a theological journey.

Standing on the deck of our ship in the Sea of Revelation, we observe scenes of Finitude passing by like islands against God's "Sea." The depths of this sea offer insights that help us experience, understand, and grasp the revealed truths of each island. As we journey, our lives are continually reinterpreted through these revelations, transforming us into the individuals our Maker intended within our unique contexts. We can picture ourselves woven into these ongoing exchanges, relationships, situations, and

---

[216] Adam did. Recall our discussions in earlier chapters of this book on the existential implications of this unique task and ability God gave Adam.

settings where God-relationships develop within the Narrative of Finitude.

Consider scenarios where this deep sense of belonging or faith might be challenged. For example, suppose your trust in God is tested: perhaps following His path conflicts with your personal interests, or life seems to take away everything you cherish. You might face choices between integrity and success, such as being tempted to bribe your way out of trouble or participate in corrupt practices to increase wealth or power. Think of a situation in which standing up for what is right could come with serious consequences. You might feel compelled to support causes different from those of your family and friends, risking friendships or respect. Imagine losing your job because you refuse to tolerate corruption, or seeing a friend fall ill despite trusting God and doing what is right. Or imagine that you face sudden tragedy – losing your home, savings, or a loved one. Remember, our Lord never promised an easy journey; in fact, He promised the opposite (John 16:33). "I have told you these things so that in me you may have peace. In the world you have trouble and suffering, but take courage – I have conquered the world" (John 6:33).

As you read the stories in the Bible, consider journaling how you might have reacted, acted, or processed the events if you had been in the place of those who experienced them.

The Bible is filled with stories of people facing tough tests, reminding us that we are not alone in our struggles. Imagine their situations: being trapped between the Red Sea and the Egyptian armies (Exod 14), or being ordered by the king of Babylon to worship a false god under threat of death in a fiery furnace (Dan 3). Consider enduring even a fraction of Job's suffering, or being called by Jesus to leave everything behind, sell all your possessions, and follow Him (Mark 1:14-20; Luke 5:1-11; 14:25-33). Think about the friends of the man on the stretcher, watching Jesus out of reach in a crowded house (Mark 2:4). Imagine sharing the good news of Jesus only to get stoned to death by those claiming to worship Yahweh (Act 7). Reflect on how facing such situations could influence our relationship with God – how they might change our view of Him, our bond with Him, and our understanding of His will and attitude towards us. Even without personal experience, these stories challenge us to consider these life shaping scenarios.

Reframing biblical stories as if we experienced them firsthand offers a chance for self-reflection, confession, and renewed commitment. We should pause to consider how we believe we would have acted or responded in those moments. This reflection can bring about spiritual understanding and practical applications, motivating us to adopt similar acts of faith as those in the stories. After all, are we not part of the same divine story and community? Though separated by time, place, and culture, we share the same Creator and a common purpose. Examining these historical events in their original contexts can offer insights applicable to our lives today. Therefore, studying the Scriptures effectively requires shifting from just focusing on the "then" and "them" to embracing the "now" and "us." Unlike detached academics analyzing art without it influencing their worldview, we are called to let the truths of Scripture shape and transform our lives.

Reflecting on the biblical stories of Finitude through the lens of our experiences can enrich our understanding of the universal human condition and our perception of God's self-revelation. Through prayer, we draw nearer to our Creator by engaging with His past revelations, making them meaningful for our present. By communing with Him and trusting in how He has revealed Himself – remembering He is eternally unchanging, "the same yesterday, today, and forever" (Heb 13:8). He guides us along the path to eternal life, providing step by step direction. For instance, we receive guidance on overcoming personal struggles like temptation, doubt, fear, and spiritual conflict. Just as God's intervention is evident in biblical stories, we must trust and invite Him to intervene in our lives. To this end, Scripture warns against suppressing the Spirit in daily life and urges us to act on our faith. We are called to walk the same "Way" as the heroes of faith (Heb 11). Additionally, Scripture shows how our interaction with God is shaped by His nature as a Trinity, influencing His relationship with us, His beloved creation.

The God revealed in Scripture actively interacts with our world and human experiences. As we read these stories on our journey home, we naturally glimpse our heavenly Homeland by seeing Yahweh as an active participant and companion within our lives, just as He was in the lives of those recorded therein. These reminders of Eternity highlight how our limited world will be transformed into His immanent tabernacle — a contextualized form of Yahweh's transcendent dwelling.

Many see the Bible as a rulebook or manual, suggesting exact methods for spiritual growth or salvation, like following a recipe. This narrow view falls into the trap of objectivity, which we know is not how God relates to us. No wonder Jesus often used parables. While principles and commands are plentiful and instructive, Scripture mainly tells a story about God's *agape*-love, as it gives many examples regarding how we should live through the lives and stories of those who went before us. Within its pages, we meet people similar to us who sought to understand their identity and place in the world through divine revelation. They aimed to walk with Yahweh daily on this short journey through

> *How does the Call of Eternity, the legacy of faith in action recorded in Scripture, and overall divine revelation influence your prayer life?*

life. Their trust – and sometimes doubt – in Yahweh as the one who resolves their difficulties is evident. We should imitate their dedication to Yahweh, our gracious Lord – the Creator and sustainer of our lives – and learn from their human failures and God's infinite forgiveness and love. By exploring the God Stories of our spiritual ancestors, our relationship with God can be strengthened. We learn from their life choices, helping us better navigate the Sea of Revelation. By reading and experiencing the stories of His early followers, we continue their legacy as representatives from across the sea who completed their own voyages, supporting others during our brief chapter in the ongoing story of life.

Through our study of Scripture, we see how God transforms those reconciled to Him into children of light and the dwelling places He envisioned for Eternity. Examples include Abraham, who went from doubting his destiny to becoming the Father of Many Nations; Joseph, who rose from pride and abuse by his brothers to becoming the savior of his family and God's people during a famine; Moses, who changed from a murderer and stutterer to Israel's leader; Rahab, who went from a simple prostitute to an honored member of Israel; Gideon, who transformed from a coward to a general leading 300 men against Midianite hordes; David, who advanced from a shepherd boy and the least in his family to a king after God's own heart; Jeremiah, who was used by God as a great prophet despite persecution; Mary, who went from a village girl to the mother of the Savior; and Peter, who evolved from a fickle

Would you have followed Jesus if you had lived during His time?

How would this commitment look today if Jesus were your contemporary?

What sacrifices might you have been forced to make?

speaker denying Christ to a mature leader willing to die for his faith, among others. Unlike fictional stories, engaging with Scripture does not have to result in mere vicarious reflections; instead, it can inspire real-life application. These narratives encourage genuine self-actualization since our relationship with God is personal. Reflection on these stories helps us see ourselves as God's beloved and part of His chosen people. We can personally experience biblical events, which are often woven into our unique God-relationship narrative. For instance, while we might not face slavery like Joseph, many relate to betrayal, abandonment, scapegoating, or rejection. Ultimately, we can find encouragement in how God turned evil intentions into good. God brought about salvation and reconciliation for Joseph and his entire family.

Learning from the God-relationships recorded in Scripture can profoundly influence our connection with Yahweh today. Just as He did for those we read about, He invites us to walk a similar path home, learning from the stories and revelations others have experienced before us. We are part of a collective story, linked with believers in Scripture and throughout history as we grow in faith together. Each person can see and accept the same revealed truths of God's self-disclosure within their own hearts, where the Spirit dwells. Thus, our inner journeys can mirror the adventures on the great Sea of Revelation shown in Scripture. Despite different external circumstances, our fundamental spiritual meaning aligns. We are humble, finite beings called by an infinite God to leave our earthly homes behind and follow Him, being transformed into something new in the process.

All these stories vividly reveal the character, nature, personality, identity, thoughts, desires, and intentions of God Himself in a way that resonates with us, the beings who live within particular contexts. Ultimately, our Maker is the primary presence and

> *Do the stories and heroes of the Bible inspire you more than those in comic books, games, TV shows, and movies?*

character in the entire narrative, more so than anyone else we learn about. We must remember each of us belong to the same endless story of Finitude; ignoring this fact leaves us unaware of the existential aspects and history of our own lives. Therefore, the narrative structure of Scripture, reflecting the subjectivity of finite life, provides the richest opportunity for us to understand ourselves as beings aware of our contextual existence. Why would we want to ignore a past that shapes our present, context, and identity? Doing so means missing out on understanding who we are, where we come from, and the purpose of our life's journey.

The broader story of Finitude, which everyone shares and through which we experience knowing God, centers on the human mind and heart. This is especially important in the salvation stories of our fellow believers, both past and present. We can learn valuable lessons from these key narratives, which can shape our understanding of our relationship with God. Consequently, all scenes in Scripture form a unified, overarching story that highlights the unique ways we come to understand God's self-revealing moments, especially His triune nature, which becomes personal and relevant through His divine presence within our contexts.

As we stand on deck, we can now reflect on the remarkable way Trinitarian Theology addresses the unique reality of the human condition. We now see, more clearly than before, how well it suits our voyage at sea. Navigating this path not only preserves the narrative style of our nautical charts (Scripture) but also offers the best vantage point to observe Yahweh's self-revealing nature amid the ocean's vastness. By framing our journey as a story, we witness the revelation of His personhood, character, and essence through His self-disclosing actions across history. For instance, this perspective vividly illustrates God's disposition and acts of *agape*-love in personally relatable and meaningful ways. We can imagine ourselves directly witnessing and engaging in these revelations from this vantage point. Our personal experiences of God's *agape*-love can manifest both in relation to the physical world we live in and on a spiritual level, reflecting the depths of our inner selves. Consequently, it is helpful to consider how our salvation stories fit within the larger story of God's character and nature as unveiled in Scripture. These authentic narratives demonstrate our loving Father's efforts to redeem us, His wayward children, enabling us to dwell in Him individually and collectively.

> *How often do you consider that your life is part of the same God's story revealed in Scripture?*

To Phenomenologically "Know" the Triune I AM

When we reflect on our eternal destiny as creatures made in our Maker's image, we should often reflect on the triune nature of the Creator. This aspect of the divine nature is not merely an interesting attribute but a core reality of what *is* Infinite *Being*. Our final destination aligns with a finite homeland reflecting the Creator's Infinite Home: the Triune Dominion of *Agape-Phosnoumenos*. Therefore, we need to understand how God's triune nature shapes our destiny.

Among world religions, Christianity uniquely affirms both monotheism and the doctrine of the Trinity.[217] Many see this as a

---

[217] Hinduism shares concepts akin to a tri-partite nature seen in the Trimurti, where the "supreme deity" is divided into Brahman the Creator, Vishnu the Preserver, and Shiva the Destroyer, representing three essential and eternal cosmic forces. However, this division lacks the characteristic unity found in the *agape-phosnoumenos* nature of Christianity, where God is completely and

contradiction – two core Christian dogmas seem at odds: One God, yet a triune personhood. This leads other monotheistic faiths like Judaism and Islam to claim Christians are not true monotheists. Those perceiving a contradiction often ask for proof of the Doctrine of the Trinity. Instead of a "proof," we aim to offer a comprehensive understanding of the Triune God's self-revelation throughout a believer's faith journey. As we journey through the Sea of Revelation, we will see how Yahweh's self-disclosures guide us like nautical charts. Scripture is the most effective map, helping us see with faith while understanding and perceiving the unity of Monotheism and Trinitarianism in a way that rational proof alone cannot achieve. This is the only way for individuals to truly see their role as active participants in God's triune self-disclosure in the Theatre of Finitude. By doing so, we can see how the Creator's roles reveal His triune nature to all characters on the world stage. To grasp the significance of His Triune nature, we must accept and embody our roles in this narrative – the greatest love story – where we, as characters, have been placed, in order to know and engage with the One who is both Playwright and fellow character.

> *Do you want to sail the Sea of Revelation regularly?*
>
> *How can you change your habits to make this happen?*

To fulfill our roles as originally intended by our Creator, our biblical maps – the primary source of God's self-disclosure history – serve as the most reliable record of our story. They reveal frequent depictions of Him revealing Himself through the histories and stories of His people, both individuals and groups. Even when

---

eternal love, spirit, and light. Furthermore, while Hinduism is mainly polytheistic- or at least not strictly monotheistic like the Abrahamic faiths- it highlights Christianity's distinctiveness in its seemingly paradoxical assertion of the Triune I AM.

unclear, Scripture communicates His message in ways relatable to every human experience within the Theater of Finitude, if we carefully study it. Thus, to understand God's self-revelation from its contextual origins, we must examine the entire Narrative of Finitude, as presented directly or indirectly within these "navigational charts."

Our subjective approach is essential for truly grasping the significance and implications of the Trinity. Many theology textbooks are filled with lifeless definitions that aim to explain the doctrine purely on an intellectual level. But how can these explanations lead individuals to live out the truth of God's triuneness daily? If these teachings cannot be integrated into a believer's conceptual, experiential, and existential worldview, how can they foster a holy lifestyle? Studying alone cannot produce the transformation God desires. On this journey, we should constantly reflect on Yahweh's triune self-revelation and understand how it should guide our spiritual walk with Him.

Impractical or grandiose descriptions of the Trinity rarely help deepen a believer's relationship with God. While elaborate language, misleading metaphors, and superficial diagrams may seem insightful, they often fail to influence a believer's worldview or way of life. Instead, our pursuit of truth should be rooted in the existential principles discussed in this book. Chief among these is the understanding that a relationship with God must be the most important human connection. It is uniquely essential for our self-fulfillment as conscious beings (*dasein*). Wisdom urges us to bond with the Creator and Originator of our environment and purposes.

Do you want to explore the history of your Maker's self-disclosures as they relate to your personal journey of self-discovery?

Furthermore, such a relationship allows us to explore the triune nature of God phenomenologically.

A conscious awareness of God's triuneness develops as we recognize how the Father, the Son, and the Holy Spirit, each "independently" (from our limited finite perspective) yet always in perfect unity, uniquely interact with our world. The God-relationship, after all, is singular, not plural. Only through this perspective, rooted in our tangible human experience, can we begin to understand God's triune nature and its practical relevance. These insights should influence all our other relationships, as we live together in the shared world crafted by our common Creator.

So, how does the triune nature of the Creator manifest in our mission to consecrate Finitude as a finite house of God? Take, for example, how the Spirit of God reveals the Divine through the authority of the transcendent Father, conveying the revelations of the Son, as the Word of God. This can be compared, although imperfectly, to the sun. The sun emits heat. This heat warms and energizes Planet Earth, by light or radiation traveling through space to support biological life.[218] Similarly, the children of the Triune I AM reveal the Father by the command of the Word (Son) through the power of His Breath (Spirit). As words manifest our inner thoughts, desires, and feelings using our breath, the Breath of God enables the Manifestation (Word) of God to be conveyed.

---

[218] While this analogy aims to clarify concepts in this book, it is not a precise representation of the Trinity. The heat and light emitted by the sun do not equate to the sun itself entirely. Similarly, the Son and the Holy Spirit are as fully God as the Father; they exist as one Being in a Triune Personhood. It is important to note that God is not just one being switching between three modes or forms. Nonetheless, this analogy effectively demonstrates how the Trinity functions concerning our divinely appointed purpose: there is a Divine Revelation, the transmitter of that Revelation, and its ultimate source. "Each person" of the Trinity is fully God, while also serving in distinct roles that are not entirely identical.

By communing with the Divine Spirit deep within us, where He dwells, the ministry of the spiritual realm flows from our sanctification in the Holy of Holies. The Spirit enables us to "put on" the Word of God, or rather for the manifestation of God to unfold through us (Rom 13:14; Gal 3:27). From this sacred inner space, we embody and exemplify our eternal selfhood that reflects the character, attitude, and desires of Christ. Through the living waters of the Spirit we are nourished by and nourish the souls of our brethren, as if we become a deep well sustaining the land and its people.

Do you long for a relationship with the Father like the one Jesus Christ had during His time on earth?

Do you desire to articulate the Father's words and carry out His works?

Our mission then extends from the inner sanctuary to the outer realm – the material world – to accomplish the Father's work. We seek to align the physical world with the Source of the *oikonomia* of Finitude. Therefore, we must follow the biblical call: "Always rejoice, constantly pray, in everything give thanks. For this is God's will for you in Christ Jesus. Do not extinguish the Spirit. Do not treat prophecies with contempt. But examine all things; hold fast to what is good. Stay away from every form of evil" (1 Thess 5:16-22).

As agents of Divine Will, the Spirit links our spirits to the Father, enabling us to be "fathered" by Him through the coadoption offered by His Son's sacrifice. As Scripture tells us, "[We have] received the Spirit of adoption, by which we cry, 'Abba, Father.' The Spirit Himself testifies with our spirit that we are God's children. And if we are children, we are also heirs (specifically, heirs of God and co-heirs with Christ)" (Rom 8:15-17). Our shared position as heirs with the Son gives us access to the priestly ministry He instituted as our head by which we, with

Him, transform all Creation into Yahweh's Temple. Powered by the Spirit, we act as stewards in the physical realm, performing actions that influence the material world to manifest the Incarnation of God, as a Temple and priest should. As a royal priesthood, eternally serving the Triune I AM, we function as a subsidiary "breath" of His "Word," through which He enacts and enforces His decrees (Acts 16:4). The Breath of God within us voices Christ's commands through us as the unified Body of Christ, appointed by Him to share His divine authority (Acts 13:9-11; Matt 16:18-19, 18:18-20; John 16:13-15, 20:22-23).

Our approach to the Doctrine of the Trinity seeks to cultivate active participation with God in a way meaningful to our daily lives. During this journey, we will focus on developing an existential awareness of some of the following Trinitarian revelations, which highlight the importance of understanding and engaging with Yahweh's triune nature.

God the Father, as Father within the created order, serves as:

> The Originator of everything, including our identities as children of God;
> The Addressee of our prayer life, such that we direct our prayers to Him;
> The Source who sends us both His only-begotten Son (His Word) and the procession of His Breath;
> The Archetype whose words the Son declares and whose actions the Son performs;

God the Son, who serves as:

> The Shepherd in how He leads us on our journey of true self-actualization;
> The Redeemer in how He shed His blood as the only remedy for our gone-wrongness;

The High Priest in the context of our relationship with God, where His role as the Infinite-finite interceder grants us continual access to the Holy of Holies;

God the Holy Spirit, who serves as:

The Spirit of Truth in the context of our spiritual education;

The Advocate in the context of fulfilling the great commission;

The Sanctifier in the context of our authentic self-actualization, through which we acquire the desires, fruits, gifts, and capacities of the Spirit;

The Supracontextual Enlightener who grants us the Spirit's outlook.

God's narrative of finitude, though it hinges partly on us, is also embedded in creation itself. He reveals Himself through the created world, while actively engaging with it. By understanding His involvement in creation, we deepen our knowledge of Him. Throughout this journey, we will

Pause to reflect on these trinitarian insights and consider how they might shape your prayer practices.

explore God's role and His self-disclosure in this overall narrative, especially in His various forms of relationship with humanity, such as Father, Teacher, Loving One, Grace-Giver, Redeemer, Guide, Advocate, and more. Consequently, our growing awareness of our Creator helps us better understand ourselves and the world He made. Further, by following this narrative, we will examine the revelations of God's triune interactions within His entire creation. For instance, we will look at the Father as our Abba and Father of Lights from whom every perfect gift comes, the Son as our Firstborn Brother and Liberating King, and the Spirit as our Inner

Guide and Empowerer. Ultimately, this journey is profoundly essential for every believer seeking to grow closer and more personal in their relationship with God.

As our understanding of Yahweh's Triune Personhood deepens, we also discover the roles we are meant to play within the larger story of mortality and in our relationship with God. We believe our inner relationship with Him will develop and mature as we grow in intimate knowledge of the Triune God. While we navigate this overarching story on the Sea of Revelation, we will observe how each divine interaction with creation reflects triune relationships. Much like explorers chart every new plant, animal, and natural wonder in a new continent, documenting and understanding these triune revelations along our journey will deepen our grasp of our Creator's fundamentally triune nature in a way that resonates with our individual stories.

Only by exploring God's self-revelation can we truly understand and uphold the concept of Christian Trinitarian Monotheism, especially one grounded in Scripture. Before starting this journey, we must accept that our understanding of the Trinity cannot be entirely articulated from the beginning but must be confirmed through faith. Just as we cannot truly understand someone's nature without considering their life story, since this context reveals how their personality is shaped by their experiences, we should avoid judging based solely on isolated events or a collection of facts. Instead, we need to listen attentively to the unfolding story of their existence to develop a genuine understanding of who they are and how they became that way.

> *Are you on a journey to explore divine mysteries with a sincere desire to deepen your relationship with God and influence your future life story?*

Our pursuit to know God can be understood similarly. While God's personhood remains unchanged – meaning His personality is not shaped historically – He reveals Himself through a subjective, contextual narrative that shows His active role and influence in creation. Therefore, our journey is like an expedition along the timeline of existence, where we discover God's triune nature through His diverse interactions with the fabric of time and space in the world He created. By exploring this experience, reflecting His self-revelations from the beginning of time and space as we perceive them, we can seek a deep understanding of God's triune nature, ultimately affirming Christian Trinitarian Monotheism.

This journey allows us to fully utilize what is available in our spiritual connections with the 'Triune I AM'. We will learn to intentionally interact with the Father (as Abba, the attentive observer of our lives and the one we pray to), the Son (as Redeemer, High Priest, King, and Rabbi), and the Holy Spirit (as Guide, Empowerer, and Inspirer). Developing a deeper understanding of these three distinct aspects of our God-relationship will improve our ability to communicate and engage with our Creator. However, we must remember that God's triunity involves the threefold nature of one divine being. We should never mistake the Three Persons of God for three separate beings, each with their own qualities, agendas, or "personalities" – similar to dissociative identity disorder. God's three natures are always united, in harmony, and focused on us through His eternal love.

> *Consider dedicating a week to journaling, where each day you reflect on your life through the lens of God's triune identity – Father, Son, and Spirit.*

In conclusion, our upcoming journeys on the Sea of Revelation will focus on developing existential understanding and strengthening relationships. Our goal is to create opportunities for each person to inwardly seek the Holy Spirit for practical, relevant insights about our Creator's self-revelations. This will deepen our theological insights and improve our view of God, ultimately reinforcing our relationship with Him. The journey will not only prepare us to be finitely contextualized temples of His transcendent presence but also expand our engagement and awareness of the essential triune nature of this relationship. Instead of approaching this as an academic or mental exercise, we model our quest after the narrative-based way we deepen our understanding of each other. This approach is both the most humbly relevant to us as humans and divinely designed to reveal the intimate nature of a God who is both Creator and Participant, in Whose image we were fashioned.

The relationship with God highlights the unique bond that the Creator maintains with each of us. As we begin this journey, we deepen our understanding of His role in this relationship, especially how it reflects a triune participation, which is essential to His nature as the 'Triune I AM'. The more we understand Him and His mysteries, the closer we become to Him. As our relationship deepens, so does our role in His purpose: to serve as a dwelling place and intermediary for His self-disclosing presence. Thus, we need to commit to living in harmony with His triuneness as part of our effort to know and love Yahweh more fully.

The Way of Theology Befitting a Prophetic Priestly Calling

Let us now reflect on our existence as beings created to understand the Creator's self-revelation. Not all creatures can do so. How do these divine revelations reach us as insights beyond our usual context, even though they originate from a realm beyond our understanding? First, we should approach theology from the "mountain top" while seeking guidance for life in the "valley."

Since we are inherently subjective, we must trust that these revelations are meaningful to our limited, everyday lives. Our method involves prayer and worship, which connect heaven and earth, bringing the Divine's presence into our lives. We ask the Maker to "step into our world" and guide us from His perspective – the only objective view. He is the Source of everything that has been, is, or will be. His language is the true tongue of Creation, and we must learn to interpret it – one that surpasses any earthly language rooted in human thoughts. His transcendent perspective does not negate His immanent presence; He exists both in Eternity and with us in every moment of temporality. As finite beings, we cannot escape our created nature. The Infinite belongs solely to God, so our interactions with Him must be tailored to our reality. Therefore, we must always recognize our limitations as we seek faith, knowing we can never fully comprehend God as He does Himself.

True theology only happens in God's temple. We access this realm of Revelation through our inner Holy of Holies. All who enter are called to embody in the world as we proceed to walk with Him in life, as a living, walking, and talking Temple. Only by recognizing ourselves as living temples can we genuinely engage in theology. This calling requires fresh baptisms of the Holy Spirit, immersing us into the Spirit of Revelation. Theology based solely on worldly perspectives is flawed. It distorts the divine to fit human imagination, desires, and ideas. To avoid such pagan theology, we must let God elevate our spirits into the spiritual realm to avoid distorted views of divinity. We "drink" from the Living Waters of Divinity while consciously meditating in the divine presence. Consequently, we must not let ourselves become spiritually dry in the barren desert of a-theistic humanism.

> *Have you put into practice any lessons you have learned from this book?*

The altar of the human heart can never sit empty. Ultimately, we all follow are become a temple of either evil spirits or the Holy Spirit – there is no other choice. God created every individual as a spiritual being meant to be a temple. The question is not if we will follow a spirit, but which spirit defines our existential core. Are we engaged in a theology influenced by demons and celebrated by rebellious world-systems? Or do we engage in a theology freshly inspired by God, mediated by angels, and transmitted through the Spirit of Revelation and the Living Word?

An often overlooked but vital aspect of true theology is that only prophets or those gifted with prophecy can fully embrace participate in it. Unfortunately, many who claim to ascribe to the Christian "religion" often overlook the following *commandment* in our Guide:

> *Do you regularly heed the command to exercise the gift of prophecy?*
>
> *If not, how could you?*

"Pursue love and be eager for the spiritual gifts, especially that you may prophesy... For you can all prophesy one after another, so all can learn and be encouraged... If anyone considers himself a prophet or spiritual person, he should acknowledge that what I write to you is the Lord's command. If someone does not recognize this, he is not recognized. So then, brothers and sisters, be eager to prophesy, and do not forbid anyone from speaking in tongues."

(1 Cor 14: 1, 31, 37-39)

All genuine theological Wayfinding must submit to this command. To deny the universal gift of prophecy is to deny Christ and the Holy Spirit. It is to profane the Holy Spirit, since it disregards the meaning and value of this ministry of Spirit to the upbuilding of believers. It is to profane the blood of Christ that tore the veil so all might become priests of living God not just anointed by the Spirit of God like the prophets of old but baptized in the Spirit. For Paul, divine education among believers develops properly when priests exercise their prophetic calling through the Spirit of Revelation. Viewing our spiritual journey merely as a religious ritual without participating in the collective act of priests prophesying in turn hampers a congregation's ability to obey this commandment. Yet, this does not mean that to follow the Way we have to become like a solitary monk or an ascetic prophet like Jeremiah or John the Baptist. Instead, our Guide states that prophecy is accessible to everyone filled with the Spirit of God: "'And in the last days it will be,' God says, 'that I will pour out My Spirit on all people, and your sons and your daughters will prophesy" (Acts 2:17; Joel 2). As we pursue our spiritual journey, we must accept our divine calling to follow the example of the prophets. We must embrace our true potential as priests of the Living God, serving as His hands, feet, and voice in whatever unique life contexts He has called us to serve Him within.

We must never forget that we serve a living God who communicates with us. Idols, which divert our attention from this Living God, remain silent. A worship service led primarily by human words resembles idolatry. A theology that lacks the lively speech of the One who is "present" and interactively "engaged" with humanity risks descending into pagan idolatry. It should not surpise us that despite their knowledge of prophetic Scriptures and strict law observance, the religious leaders of Jesus' time acted like

> *Can you truly look in a mirror and say, "I have the mind of Christ"?*
>
> *If not, how can you make life changes to confidently affirm this statement?*

pagan homewreckers. When confronted with the Living God among them, they sought to eliminate Him, disrespecting Him and accusing Him of being demon-possessed. Even today, some dismiss the prophetic gifts and speaking in tongues as demonic manifestations.

Idolatry and pagan practices persist even in many "Christian" churches today, much like they did in Jewish synagogues during Jesus' era. Many spiritual leaders who met Jesus condemned His teachings as heresy and accused Him of blasphemy, as their godless views led them to see Him as a blasphemer. Likewise, those who display the gifts of the Spirit often face mockery from religious leaders who consider their manifestations of divine presence incompatible with their theology. As "heretics" in this humanist age, the metaphysical knowledge we seek along the "Way" will strongly influence our worldview, guide our lives, and alter our destiny—especially within the context of a genuine relationship with God and a prophetic calling as living temples of the Divine. Therefore, we must be prepared to leave behind even religious leaders and systems, as we abandon Babylon, wherever it exists, and set out in pursuit of our divine destiny on the Sea of Revelation.

> *Can you truly look in a mirror and say, "I have the mind of Christ"?*
>
> *If not, how can you make life changes to confidently affirm this statement?*

To remain faithful to our divine calling, we must live in and embody Truth, not just acknowledge it or claiming we "believe." We see Truth as God's core: "Jesus replied, 'I am the way, and the truth, and the life'" (John 14:6). But do we truly believe this? Have our educational experiences caused us to depersonalize Truth and disconnect information from the reality around us? Hundreds of millions worldwide claim to be Christian because they claim to believe in Jesus, yet how many genuinely follow the Way? How many sincerely wish to view the world through the "eyes," "heart," and "mind" of the Creator? Will we choose to overcome the all-too-common humanistic worldview – common today in the developed world – that excludes the spiritual dimension of our existence? Such a worldview diminishes and distorts the Voice of Creation, hiding its divine self-revelation. Therefore, we must become re-educated. Further, we must become rehabituated by regularly engaging in transformative theology as our Maker

> *Would you describe your theology as shaping your worldview, life perspective, and ambitions?*
>
> *Should it?*
>
> *Do you think you need spiritual re-education?*

intended. Through Christ from whom all revealed truths unfolds within our finite world, we can embody Truth. In the God-relationships is where our identity resides. After all, "The Word was with God in the beginning. He created all things, and apart from Him not one thing was made. In Him was life, and that life was the light of mankind" (John 1:2-4). As the Incarnate Word, the Uncreated entered His Creation to know us personally and phenomenologically. Consequently, those who see themselves as knowing God must recognize how our human perspective influences how we understand the Divine. We should foster a personal relationship with the Living Word and invite the Holy Spirit to fill us daily.

Conclusion

We are now about to conclude our current foray into the mysteries of the human situation. Let us take this moment to reflect on the deepest expression of Yahweh's homemaking within His creation, which happens in our innermost selves. God desires to connect with us, His most beloved creation, on this level, beyond the physical, mental, or emotional realms. Additionally, since the homemaking and tabernacling of our Creator unfold as a narrative, the Scriptures offer us a glimpse into the complexities of the divine-human relationship story. We learn and embody core truths about our existence and purpose through these revelations. We were created to be a finite dwelling for the Infinite, crafted by the Creator to serve as a bridge between the Infinite and the finite, the Uncreated and the created, and the spiritual and material. Taking up this priestly calling requires following the example of our pioneer, forebearer, and elder brother Christ, the second Adam in whom divinity and humanity were and still are united (1 Cor 15:21-22; Heb 2:10, 12:2). Within the God-Story, we discover our true essence, find genuine rest, and attain perfect harmony with Creation and find our way Home.

The story of homemaking between the Triune Creator and humanity, made in His image, provides insights into the fundamental truths surrounding a key passage in our navigation chart. This passage highlights how our relationship with God should mirror the dynamics within a household. Consider how God is depicted as our Father and we as His children in the following passage:

> "We are the temple of the living God, just as God said, 'I will live in them and will walk among them, and I will be their God, and they will be My people.' Therefore 'come out from their midst, and be separate,' says the Lord, 'and touch no unclean thing, and I will welcome you [Home], and I will be a Father to you, and you will be My sons and daughters.'"
>
> (2 Cor 6:16-18)

Out on the Sea of Revelation, we aim to uncover revealed truths about the Creator's history of self-disclosure within Finitude. These mysteries will reveal how God designed creation to be a suitable finite sanctuary for the Divine. We hope that by contemplating God's self-revealing splendor in this Temple of Creation, we will increasingly find ourselves at home within the Temple of God. This sacred world-dwelling transforms us into living stones and pillars of the Temple, as we were created not only to inhabit, but to be inhabited by the Architect of the Universe (1 Pet 2:5; Rev 3:12). As His self-disclosures uniquely shape our distinct experiences of world-dwelling, our lives are shaped and fashioned by His image, transforming us into co-managers of the homemaking and home-managing qualities of *agape*-love, *phos*-light, and *pneuma*-spirit (1 Cor 3:9-14, 8:1). Rather than this being an assimilation into Himself, where we forfeit our individualities, our divine purpose is closely linked to our self-actualization. Rather than an obstacle to be overcome, attaining genuine fulfillment in our individual lives can only be achieved through His inhabiting presence. Our foundational role as stewards of Finitude reflects the cornerstone of Eternity, stemming from the divine power flowing through us (1 Pet 2:4-9; Eph 2:18-22). This indwelling enables communion with God, and the divine nature within us to manifest our heavenly calling.

> Have you "come out from their midst" in the context of your life situation?
>
> What do you think this could mean for you?

As truth-seekers, we commit ourselves to dedication, investment, and surrender. Think of a ship's navigator observing every new development at sea – from the wind and cloud positions to the stars, bird flight paths, and even the water's movement and temperature (as ancient Polynesian navigators did)- all are vital for

[*Do you share this "one thing" desire?*] their journey. Similarly, we must view any account of the Maker's triune relationships with Finitude as essential "news" that holds deep importance for our lives. We humbly recognize that apart from God's opening our eyes through revelation, we remain blind to eternal truths. After all, we engage with the Gospel, not just earthly knowledge. With this mindset, we aim to foster unity within our community and our relationship with God, supporting each other on this fundamentally relational journey.

Additionally, we seek to weave our theology into our daily lives, worldview, and personal growth. Our goal is for theology to be a lived experience. Theology ought to guide us on our path. Authentic Christianity, after all, was and still should be called the "Way" rather than a religion, creed, or confession (Acts 9:2, 19:9, 23, 22:4, 24:14, 22). We navigate this journey – the Way – ultimately to achieve self-actualization, harmony within a spiritual community, and eternal union with God. We respond actively to the revealed good news, knowing that following the Way is the only path to discovering our destined, eternal place in the universe.

Authenticity as a child of God depends on our grace-filled acceptance of our theological identities as priests, temples of God, as well as students, manifesters, and lovers of His presence. God respects our free will; after all, He offered Adam and Eve the choice to obey or disobey. He could have forced obedience or never given them the choice at all. As C.S. Lewis stated, "though free will makes evil possible, it is also the only thing that makes possible any love or goodness or joy worth having" (Mere Christianity, 1996, pp.52-53). For this reason, we are to respond freely and keep choosing His call if we want to fulfill our divine destinies. Like the Psalmist, our theology should be shaped by our unwavering love for our "First Love," expressed in this desire: "I have asked the Lord for one thing—this is what I desire! I want to live in the Lord's house all the days of my life, so I can gaze at the splendor of the Lord and contemplate in His temple" (Ps 27:4; Rev 2:4).

The challenge for seafarers dwelling in this world is understanding what it truly means to exist as vessels in the Sea of Revelation and embody that essence. What does it mean for the realm of Revelation to be where we find genuine supra-contextual worth, meaning, belonging, purpose, and rest? Essentially, it is through our close relationship with the Creator from which we discover our eternal calling. We realize this calling and all it entails when we manifest His self-disclosures in our lives (Ps 27:4, 84:1-5). By knowing our Creator and acting as vessels of His supernatural power, we gain the right perspective to engage with the finite world, revealed to us by its Architect (Eph 1:17-23, 4:13; Col 1:27-29, 3:16-17). Do we not read the revelation, "We have the mind of Christ," and so when we remain in Him, anything we ask for is granted through His power (John 14:12-14, 15:7; Eph 1:17-18; 1 Cor 2:9-16). However, this invitation to ask God should not be mistaken for the freedom to treat Him like a genie. Viewing God merely to gain physical wealth reflects a flawed worldview – one not genuinely renewed or transformed by Him and our Guide. As Jesus commanded His genuine followers, "Do not accumulate for yourselves treasures on earth, where moth and devouring insect destroy and where thieves break in and steal. But accumulate for yourselves treasures in heaven… For where your treasure is, there your heart will be also" (Matt 6:19-21). As Jesus pointed out, to follow the proper Way of world-dwelling, we must follow the proper Way of world-viewing. "The eye is the lamp of the body. If then your eye is healthy, your whole body will be full of light. But if your eye is diseased, your whole body will be full of darkness. If then the light in you is darkness, how great is the darkness! No one can serve two masters" (Matt 6:22-24). Therefore, we must escape the darkness of trying to fit into Babylonian world contexts and walk in the Light of Eternity.

In what ways has this book influenced your perspective on the world and your place in it?

Epilogue:
Departing the Sinking Island of Transience

"I am coming soon. Hold on to what you have so that no one can take away your crown. The one who conquers I will make a pillar in the temple of my God, and he will never depart from it. I will write on him the name of My God and the name of the city of My God (the new Jerusalem that comes down out of heaven from my God), and My new name as well....

Listen! I am standing at the door and knocking! If anyone hears My voice and opens the door I will come into his home and share a meal with him, and he with Me. I will grant the one who conquers permission to sit with Me on My throne, just as I, too, conquered and sat down with My Father on His throne. The one who has an ear had better hear what the Spirit says to the churches.'"

(Rev 3:11-12, 20-22)

"Enter through the narrow gate because the gate is wide and the way is spacious that leads to destruction, and there are many who enter through it. How narrow is the gate and difficult the way that leads to life, and there are few who find it!"

(Matt 7:13-14)

Having reached the end of this volume, let us gaze back on the narrative we have unveiled; the story of us all whose lives unfold upon the stage of Finitude.

Imagine an island in the middle of a vast, turbulent ocean. It is a large island with many cities and cultures, though tiny when compared to the great waters that surround it. Picture yourself as a land-dweller and resident of this place, living your entire life there without ever setting foot beyond. It has everything you might need to survive and to feel secure and comfortable…and yet, for some reason, it is not enough. Often, when not occupied by the cares of your daily life, your mind wanders and questions whether this island is all there is. When the pleasures and pastimes available no longer distract you, you begin to feel trapped. Now, imagine that sometimes, during sleepless nights that rob you of the comfort and rest of your bed, you decide to take a walk beyond the cities toward the shoreline – a place few people visit.

There, you squint into the distance, futilely trying to see what lies beyond the chaotic waves crashing against the rough, jagged shoreline. All you can see, however, is an all-consuming void. It is a darkness so profound and total that it seems impossible to believe anything can exist beyond it. In fact, you realize that you and every other land-dweller had taken for granted that your island, which once seemed so vast, was the only inhabitable land. The true weight of this thought now presses down on you as you stare into the menacing black abyss, its cold logic piercing your soul with a hopeless emptiness.

{ *Have you ever experienced despair and hopelessness?*

How did these experiences shape your outlook on life and your future? }

To make matters worse, the longer you stare, the more you notice that this darkness, rather than staying in place, creeps closer to the land. You finally begin to understand the horrifying truth: the island will not last forever. With no way out, all you and every other land-dweller can do is wait in fear as the tumultuous ocean gradually erodes the small island, an inescapable fate like the tragedy of Atlantis. Any hope for escape from this looming disaster quickly fades. Even if someone managed to navigate the turbulent waves threatening to smash them against the rocky shore, where then would they go? A safe refuge might not exist beyond the horizon. Leaving these shores in search of another home might not be just a pointless but life-ending endeavor, condemning any brave "wayfinder" to a short-lived escapade of sailing a dark, unforgiving ocean.

What effect would such reflections have on a person? Confronting the true existential reality of their transient situation changes everything. Even if you rush back screaming to the cities of the island, nothing will satisfy you anymore. Anything you do – whether enjoying all the pleasures the island offers, reaching your full potential in the cities, or building a legacy – will be futile in the face of the coming flood. They are merely temporary pretenses of divinity, like a child believing that building the biggest sandcastle on the beach will secure their legacy. It will become increasingly clear to those stranded on the island that they cannot satisfy their inner longings born from homesickness and restlessness. They will carry the weight of an unfulfilled desire for "something more," like an itch that cannot be scratched or a thirst that can never be quenched. Therefore, if this is the unavoidable human condition, we might tell those we meet along the shores: "Deliverance is far from us, and salvation does not reach us. We wait for light, but see only darkness; we wait for a bright light, but live in deep darkness." (Isa 59:9).

What adds to this tragic scene is the truth that deep down, we all long for "another place," a distant homeland away from the dark, sinking island we inhabit. Many of us only catch fleeting glimpses of this desired homeland in dreams, through hidden currents in our shared stories, or in moments of longing stirred by encounters with beauty. Recall how the fictional character Luke gazed at the twin sunset on Tatooine, longing for adventure in Star Wars, or how Holden Caulfield watches his sister Phoebe on the carousel, moved to tears in *The Catcher in the Rye*. Consider Caspar David Friedrich's renowned paintings, *Wanderer Above the Sea of Fog* and *Monk by the Sea*, which evoke this sense of yearning with profound feeling.

Deep within all of us, feelings of homelessness sometimes surface, like the moments between waking and dreaming or during our imaginative "what if" scenarios that occasionally run through our minds, especially on a restless night. In those times, our subconscious longs for a home we have never truly experienced with our conscious mind. When our desires drift toward this unknown land of peaceful joy, we become lost in thought, often sinking into sadness over our apparent inability to reach such a place, if it even exists. These thoughts constantly haunt us with a harsh truth, leading us to believe, "I can never go home." Our repeated visits to the shore feel like a fiancé whose loved one has gone to war and whose ship will never return. She keeps returning to the shoreline, but each time, something inside her is lost forever. Whenever we pull away from the distractions of the island and peer into the abyss of our mortality, we lose another piece of ourselves. With a painful sigh that offers no relief, we turn away again and again, trying to see homelessness as an illusion of home. We bitterly regret the fleeting mirages of our dreams and the ecstatic moments that have slipped away. What folly.

> *When was the last time you felt a sense of homelessness?*
>
> *Why? How did you handle it?*

As we head back toward the "inland cities," some of us may clutch our fists against our chests, clinging to the illusion that we might someday escape and return "home." Faced with such a stark reality, some might resort to self-deception, trying to suppress their present sense of homelessness until this conscious denial becomes a self-fulfilling prophecy. Others may attempt to find peace with their situation, a resignation born from the decision to essentially abandon any hope that there is something more. No matter how we respond, this ongoing torment of shattered dreams stifles our innate childlike longing for paradise, reducing it to fading memories. Over time, our visions of a "castle in the clouds" fade into distant, half-remembered dreams, stirring feelings without creating anything vivid in our minds. The weight of this life grows heavier as the approaching tides signal the end of our mortal lives. Without an everlasting and fulfilling destination to aim for, we remain forever homeless, unable to hope for a return to the eternal refuge that we, as castaways, have never truly experienced with our waking eyes.

Such is our human situation... but then something happens. Imagine a woman who has come to the shore of that sinking island for perhaps the hundredth time. She is nearing total despair, with no amount of longing able to ease her sorrow. She begins to turn away when she spots a ray of light in the distance cutting through the darkness. With eyes wide in wonder, she questions whether what she sees is real, unsure if it is genuine or just an illusion. Then, she feels a whisper resonate deep within her soul, one that comes from both inside her and outside of her. And it speaks words that change everything: there *is* something beyond the horizon. Somewhere free from the darkness and despair that threaten the island. Somewhere we were all meant to be... and can still

> *Have your dreams of what should or could have been been inspired by the Maker's dreams?*

possibly reach. Against all the despair she has been conditioned to from years of hopeless longing... she believes the whisper. Overjoyed, she dances and sings like never before, unconcerned about injury or embarassment. Although she gazes into the unknown, her imagination now soars high above the clouds of despair, buoyed by the thought of freedom from the island and the certainty that there is more.

The truth is, our Creator, despite all seeming evidence to the contrary, has not abandoned us to the bleak outcome of our existential rebellion. In fact, He has taken every measure to remove the barriers that prevent us from reaching our true destiny and everlasting home. To bring salvation to the inhabitants of the island, our Creator has returned to fill this void with the sanctifying, all-encompassing presence of the Spirit of the Sea. As our nautical charts reveal, "Yahweh, our Savior, desires everyone to be saved and to know the truth" (1 Tim 2:3-4). This truth remains unwavering, firmly opposing the misleading notions of humanistic philosophy and theology, which are tainted by pagan concepts of a-theism, fate, and nihilism.

As you may remember from the start of this book, we who have chosen to embark on this journey are no longer confined to this island of temporality. Hope has pierced through the fleeting nature of our present world as we stand on the deck of the ship *Faith Seeking Understanding*. Braving the waves, we have broken through the seemingly endless dark clouds to discover that the sea is not dark and unforgiving, but alive, colorful, beautiful, and full of mysteries to discover along our journey home. This Path of Salvation, also known as the "Way of Holiness," allows those lost to escape the confines of homelessness. Much like the Israelites crossing the Red Sea in Exodus, we can now navigate through the turbulent waters of time that will ultimately overwhelm this world. "Those [of us] whom the Lord has ransomed return that way," leading us to one day "enter Zion with a joyful shout. Unending joy will crown [us]; happiness and joy will overcome [us]; sorrow and suffering will vanish" (Isa 35:8-10). This divine light, the same one that pierced through the darkness on the shore, penetrates the darkness of our souls and fills the empty spaces within us. The source of this illuminating ray does not arise from a void, emptiness, or temporality, but from the the Light of Eternity (John 1; 1 John 1:5).

Where is the destination we sail toward? What destiny beckons beyond the horizon of temporality?

Our eternal purpose in this life is to live as a "Wayfinder" out on the Sea of Revelation and to become a vessel of it ourselves (John 1:18, 17:3, 24-26; Eph. 2:19-22; 1 John 4:13). Just as we interact with the world around us and reflect our spiritual identity through our physical bodies, the Divine Creator desires to do the same through us as the Body of Christ. He calls us to be a finite yet eternal dwelling for the "Triune I AM," through which Yahweh engages with the world, just as He does through Jesus, the Incarnation of God (John 14:22-23; 1 John 2:2, 3:24). Only when this happens

{ *How has this book influenced your views on the Christian "Way of Salvation" and the Gospel?* }

do we truly "come home." Only here can we discover our existence can be shaped by the divine life of the Trinity. To this end, the "nautical charts" of Scripture guide us into the profound depths of the Sea of Revelation, where we can experientially uncover and experience the originally intended design of our true place of belonging.

Our adventure begins whenever we truly answer the Call of Eternity. On our return journey aboard our metaphorical "ship," exploring the depths of the Sea of Revelation, we discover our true home and our authentic theocentric selves. As seafarers, our home

IS the sea, through which we find our purpose and who we truly can and should become. Think about stories where people go on quests and eventually achieve destinies far greater than anything they were before. These stories fill the Scriptures, featuring figures like Jacob (a deceiver who became the patriarch of a nation), Moses (a stammerer turned prophet), Gideon (a cautious man who rose as a hero of Israel), and Paul (a former persecutor who grew into one of Christianity's leading apostles).

Only the humble, meek, and repentant can find the narrow, navigable path through the stifling darkness surrounding the dark island of temporality. Only those with "eyes to see" can perceive the omnipresent, sanctifying wind of the Spirit of Truth and His illumination upon the Sea of Revelation (Matt 13:16). Only those who believe the hope of resurrection, like that woman who first saw the light beyond the horizon, will run to the shore to see for themselves how they can find the Way. The rich, powerful, and worldly, who have managed to secure comfort and a mirage of satisfaction on the island, will be skeptical. But the humble? The desperate? The broken? The restless? The repentant? They are the ones who can respond to that call, take the steps to listen to the whisper, and find the Way to escape the island.

We must not take the Call of Eternity lightly. It asks much of us, not least of which is to leave the island, our old way of life, and our old worldview. Only by abandoning the land can we truly live as we are meant to: out on the sea, living an endless adventure. We can step into a life filled with uncertainty, joy, and fulfillment by giving up the certainty of comfort and fittingness in this world. And what is uncertainty but an invitation to faith? How can we live by faith in a world where all is certain, routine, and comfortable?

Our Guide provides us with the following declaration of sacrifice we must make to answer Eternity's Call:

> "I have been crucified with Christ, and it is no longer I who live, but Christ lives in me. Therefore, the life I now live in the body, I live because of the faithfulness of the Son of God, who loved me and gave Himself for me."
>
> (Gal 2:20)

Being crucified with Christ – "dying" to the present world system – is not an optional choice for genuine wayfinding seafarers. In fact, it is essential for everyone who claims to follow Christ. It is a fatal error to mistake this requirement and required only for "heroes" of faith, canonized saints, or "ordained" spiritual leaders. According to our Wayfinding Guide, all members of the priesthood of believers are all called to live as saints. All of us are called to leave the island and seek our destiny out upon the waters. To truly follow Christ, therefore, one must embody His self-giving spirit and follow Him even in this. This is the Narrow Way.

> "Dear friends, I urge you as foreigners and exiles to keep away from fleshly desires that do battle against the soul… Since Christ suffered in the flesh, you should also arm yourselves with the same attitude, because the one who has suffered in the flesh has finished with sin, spending the rest of his [or her] time on earth focused on the will of God and not human desires."
>
> (1 Pet 2:112:, 4:1-2)

Following the Narrow Way of Salvation requires a steadfast commitment to follow God's will and repent when needed. Importantly, this commitment continues even after we leave a religious service. It must be accompanied by the transformation of our mindset, attitude, and way of life as we seek to be changed by

> *How has this book shaped your view of your calling to be a priest and pilgrim?*

the Spirit, ultimately becoming a Temple of God here on earth. The truths we learned in this volume are ones we need to keep in mind and consistently adhere to throughout our journey. After all, those who tire of journeying on the sea can still, if they so desire, return to the island and the "safety" of dry land. As Jesus warning, "Remember Lot's wife! Whoever tries to keep his life will lose it, but whoever loses his life will preserve it" (Luke 17:32-33). Though it may seem strange to us to imagine anyone willingly going back to that dark, damned place, the sad truth is that it is indeed a strong and ever-present temptation.

We follow the Pioneer of our faith by seeking our authentic, self-actualizing identity. We can only find true contentment with ourselves and our surroundings by becoming co-members, co-dwellers, and co-abiders in the Divine Household of the Triune I AM (John 15:1-7, 17:26; 1 Cor 6:15; Eph 2:19-22, 3:6, 5:30; 1 John 1:7, 2:24). Essentially, to accept our "citizenship" in Heaven, we need to relinquish our "citizenship" on Earth (Phil 3:20). Our genuine identity, fundamentally, *is* a theological self that thrives through the Triune I AM. Figuratively, this signifies being a living stone within His temple and a member of His "holy priesthood," empowering us to live as His children who "offer spiritual sacrifices acceptable to God through Jesus Christ" (1 Pet 2:4-10). As we learned in this book, a sanctified life on Earth corresponds with the *oikonomia* intended for "a people of [God's] own, so that [we] may proclaim the virtues of the One who called [us] out of darkness into His marvelous light" (1 Pet 2:9). Motivated by profound devotion and firm belief in our eternal future, we must distinguish ourselves as "foreigners and exiles" in this fallen world, consciously choosing to embrace the freedom of living within the parameters of the Creator's original intentions (1 Pet 2:11, 16).

Like pilgrims departing for a new land, we undertake a journey to discover our celestial purpose, as those who have "returned to the Shepherd and Guardian of [our] soul" (1 Pet 2:25). Our spirit and soul traverse the Sea of Revelation, guided by the emblem representing our true allegiance to our genuine Home.

"Therefore, we do not despair, but even if our physical body is wearing away, our inner person is being renewed day by day. For our momentary, light suffering is producing for us an eternal weight of glory far beyond all comparison because we are not looking at what can be seen but at what cannot be seen. For what can be seen is temporary, but what cannot be seen is eternal."

(2 Cor 4:16-18)

Throughout our journey, Yahweh determines our commitment to the divine priestly calling He offers each of us (2 Chr 32:31; Exod 20:20). He "tests to see if we [truly] will love Him with all our mind and being," for such genuine love requires obedience shown by "following Him," "serving Him," and staying "loyal to Him" (Deut 13:3-4). Will we hold onto our initial faith in Him to guide us toward our eternal identity and fulfill our eternal purpose? Will we consistently place our trust in Him by surrendering to Christ's reconciling work? Will we commit ourselves to rebuilding God's house, the Body of Christ, according to eternal principles? A captain from the Age of Sail would not enlist sailors who he knew would spend their days yearning for land during a voyage around the world. Similarly, the Creator desires dedicated co-workers who embody their faith in daily life rather than lukewarm pew-sitters who appear religious on Sundays

> *Consider making it a habit to stand before the mirror and say, "Today, I will live by the Spirit, so help me, God."*

and indifferent to the Call of Eternity throughout the week. Hence, remaining on the sacred Path of Discipleship requires our dedication to the "first and greatest commandment": "Love the Lord your God with all your heart, with all your soul, and with all your mind" (Deut 6:5; Matt 22:37-38).

Our Guide offers practical instructions for embracing the Way of a homeward-bound pilgrim:

> "Continue in the things you have learned... from infancy you have known the holy writings, which are able to give you wisdom for salvation through faith in Christ Jesus.... It is useful for teaching, reproof, correction, and for training in righteousness that the person dedicated to God may be capable and equipped for every good work."
>
> (2 Tim 3:14-17)

This priestly calling is not limited to a select few. Many false calls to Eternity happen in our world, leading many down the broad road of destruction. These calls aim to keep people "settled" in this world or lead them to chase a distorted sense of "eternal" security. To fulfill our genuine eternal roles, we must dedicate ourselves to living as a priest and a temple of God. Only through this journey can we each humble ourselves in humble submission and gentle reliance on Yahweh's purifying Spirit in our priestly duties.

Like Scripture, which contextualizes the Divine through language, literature, and narrative, Heaven summons us to finitely express the Living Word of God (1 Pet 2:9, 4:10-11). The destiny of Scripture mirrors our own. Unfortunately, "religious" people have more often than not cherished Scripture more than a single human life, preferring to let a person suffer rather than let harm come to a physical translation of it. They react with horror if the text is dropped or a church building is damaged, but all the while they readily belittle a fellow image of God nearby. This reflects a worldview that fails to see human life from an eternal perspective. Christ's sacrifice was for the redemption of humanity, not for a book or building,

> *Have you encountered a religion or religious group that prioritizes Scripture or sacred texts over human beings created in God's image?*

no matter how divinely inspired or beautifully constructed. A true child of God serves as a finite "tabernacle" and "dwelling place" for God (1 Cor 6:19; Eph 2:22; Rev 13:6). Accordingly, God desires to reside within every single human existence, no matter how "lowly" or "unworthy"! Marvelous indeed! The path ahead involves tracing the self-revelation of the Infinite One who longs to inhabit finite beings like us (Isa 61:6; 1 Pet 2:5, 9; Rev 1:6).

We are called by Scripture to "show the same eagerness for the fulfillment of our hope until the end, so that we may not be sluggish, but instead emulate those who, through faith and perseverance, inherit the [everlasting] promises" (Heb 6:11-12). The Scriptures further encourage us saying:

> "[Let us] pay close attention to ourselves, so that we are not found in some sin... Each one [should] examine his own work. Then he can take pride in himself and not compare himself with someone else... Do not be deceived... For a person will reap what he sows, because the person who sows to his own flesh will reap corruption from the flesh, but the one who sows to the Spirit will reap eternal life from the Spirit. So, we must not grow weary in doing good, for in due time we will reap if we do not give up."
>
> (Gal 6:1-9)

We sail the ship *Faith Seeking Understanding*, recognizing our eternal destiny as we strive to enhance our spiritual ability to manage the priestly resources granted to us. These resources align with the identity and influence assigned to us through the Spirit's work of sanctification. While we anticipate our eternal legacy, we dedicate ourselves to the Spirit, who leads and empowers us to uphold and apply the principles of other-worldly living. We uphold these principles with the authority and power given to us (Rev 5:10). However, this divine authority and power can only be rightly exercised under the guidance of His Spirit (Rom 8:14; 2 Cor 13:4, 10). As God's children, our reliance on the Holy Spirit is essential for fulfilling our Divine mission into Eternity. The Spirit alone reveals the intent of our Creator, allowing us to manage His creation with truth. Therefore, we must remain learners of the Spirit of Truth, as the Spirit will be our eternal instructor in the mysteries of Creation and its divine purposes.

Every crew member on this journey must be fully committed in their minds, hearts, and spirits to a life guided by the revealed truths of Scripture. We must sincerely accept the Scripture's claims about our existential transformation and spiritual relocation. Following Christ goes beyond simply completing a list of religious rituals. It is much more than an intellectual pursuit or a journey of enlightenment. It involves transforming our self-view, way of life, and very core through our surrender to Him and His guidance. We can only navigate these waters we have chosen to make our home by truly dedicating ourselves to living as pilgrims heading for eternity, set apart from the fallen world-systems from which we have departed.

{ *What steps can you take to maintain perseverance along the Narrow Way of Salvation?* }

The existential importance of our journey home revolves around the notion that we can only achieve true self-fulfillment along this "seaway of sanctification." Through the storms and waves surrounding our island of transience, this route is largely outlined for us by the nautical charts found in Scripture. As we travel together on our voyage home, we are reminded that "everything that was written in former times was written for our instruction, so that through endurance and the encouragement of the Scriptures we may have hope" (Rom 15:4). Additionally, we hold the prophetic word as an entirely trustworthy guide [for our journey]. It is wise to heed this as we would a light guiding us through darkness, until the day breaks and the morning star rises in our hearts" (2 Pet 1:19).

Let us often remember that our present life serves as a kind of examination or evaluation for our eternal vocation. As Jesus' parables illustrate, if we neglect to serve well in His household during this temporal sojourn, we will be found among the unfaithful servants who will not be allowed to enter His eternal domain (Matt 24:45-51; Luke 12:41-48; Col 1:12-14). Elsewhere, the inauguration of Eternity begins with the following declaration:

> "And the one seated on the throne said: 'Look! I am making all things new!' Then He said to me, 'It is done! I am the Alpha and the Omega, the beginning and the end. To the one who is thirsty, I will give water free of charge from the spring of the water of life. The one who conquers will inherit these things, and I will be his God and he will be My son [child]... Night will be no more, and they will not need the light of a lamp or the light of the sun because the Lord God will shine on them, and they will reign forever and ever."
>
> (Rev 21:5-7, 22:5).

The Way of Eternity – the only true escape from the sinking island – lies in proactively submitting to our Creator and following the ways of the Spirit of God, illuminated by His sanctifying presence. By navigating the Sea of Revelation guided by the Spirit's light, we can walk, live, and experience existence within the nurturing embrace of Infinity. His indwelling presence not only guides us but also empowers our life of surrender. When we submit to Him, withdraw from the godless patterns of this world, and commit to becoming His tabernacles in creation, the door to eternal existential possibilities swings open. To tap into this eternal potential, we must consciously make our relationship with the Maker our foundation. Thus, we, the crew aboard the *Faith Seeking Understanding*, sail under the flag of Trinitarian Orthodoxy, as we undertake our divine calling. On the other hand, our refusal to embark on this journey home will ultimately result in a permanent separation from God's glory. Those who take this destructive path have chosen to remain on the sinking land of temporality rather than answer Eternity's Call. They have essentially decided to sever their relationship with God and be exiled from their eternal purpose, due to casting their lot in with a world fated to become submerged by the waves of desolation.

> *As long as you draw breath in this world, whether you are on the island's shore or have departed, you have a choice to sail the Sea of Revelation, seeking your true home and identity.*
>
> *What will yours be?*

Please visit www.TheologicalAcademy.org or download the Mobile App "Theological Academy." Here you can continue the journey online and have fellow-ship with other possible crewmembers, as we together explore the Sea of Revelation.

[i] It is important to establish a notion of God distinct from the many misconceptions people may hold about Him. An Infinite, transcendent Being is not simply an "All-Powerful Spirit," like an ancient Greek god with the utmost degree of goodness and power. A truly Infinite Being, as theology has characterized God, is more closely related to Existence or Reality itself than to anything within it. The Book of Acts describes God as someone *in* whom "we live and move and have our being" (Acts 17:28). He is not just someone with "the highest possible amount of goodness," but is Goodness itself. He is a Being for whom essence and existence are one and the same. Despite His ultimate transcendence, He is also deeply and intensely personal – desiring to relate to us and for us to relate to Him. This book addresses how we are to orient ourselves in response to such a Being. We explore these truths more deeply in the *Before the Beginning* series.

[ii] Religious studies differ from theology in that the former focuses on the academic examination of religious systems, organizations, beliefs, or practices. It is an inquiry from outside the realm of faith and belief, adopting a more detached anthropological or cultural perspective.

The latter, meanwhile, is an exploration from within these realms, beginning with the foundation of belief and concentrating on the nature of the divine and – most importantly for us – how the revelations we encounter should shape the way we live, think, and worship.

[iii] Though both involve learning and discovery, a journey of enlightenment typically affects the internal world of the individual undertaking it, rather than just the mind. For instance, consider how such journeys are portrayed in media such as television, movies, or novels. They usually involve a process that transforms the protagonist entirely, compelling them to confront various truths that challenge their lives along the way. Eastern religions like Buddhism view the journey towards enlightenment as influencing one's life, actions, thoughts, motives, and spirit rather than merely affecting their minds (where one only comes to realizations without applying them beyond the intellect). Although theology, particularly in Western Christianity (as opposed to, for example, Eastern Orthodoxy), has become associated with academia, we must never disregard this fundamental aspect of our pursuit of God – lest it devolve into just another "field of study" that enriches the mind while leaving the spirit and life unchanged. God calls us not merely to obtain degrees or write books, but to have our lives fundamentally transformed by Him as we seek Him and His truths.

[iv] The use of "dimensions" serves as a useful illustration to help us understand the difficulty of perceiving a "higher realm". According to mathematics and theoretical physics, we experience the world in three dimensions (length, width, and height). Conversely, to view the world in two dimensions means to see only length and width – like a flat drawing on a piece of paper or the flat worlds of old cartoons and video games. To "see the fourth dimension," however, entails perceiving in a realm beyond our own – one for which we have no point of reference. The novella "Flatland" by Edwin Abbott explores this concept in a fascinating way.

In the novella, we follow the life of a "Square" who lives in Flatland, a two-dimensional realm where all beings exist as flat lines or shapes. One day, he encounters a Sphere traveling through Flatland. However, unable to perceive the true nature of the Sphere in his perfectly flat world, he sees it merely as a circle appearing out of nowhere, growing larger, and then shrinking before inexplicably disappearing and reappearing elsewhere (as the Sphere levitates up and down through Flatland). It is very difficult for the Square and the other Flatlanders to understand how this is possible, as they cannot conceive of a realm above their own that they cannot see. Try imagining what a world in four dimensions looks like. If such a world indeed existed, it would be so far above our own that we could only perceive things of that dimension as manifestations in 3D rather than in true 4D. As 3D beings, we, like the Square, cannot truly understand or "see" a realm higher than our own.

The impossibility of truly grasping such a world should give us an idea of how impossible it is for finite beings to understand and comprehend the infinite realities of God.

[v] As opposed to uncreated reality, the province of God alone. Everything else created by Him (thus, everything having an origin – including fundamental concepts of the universe like space, time, and matter) belongs to "Finitude" or the "created realm". Throughout this book, we will make use of the former term to describe these things.

[vi] At this juncture, it's important to assert a disclaimer. The notion of God revealing Himself through the tangible realities we encounter should not imply that any insights or truths derived can take precedence over Scripture and established doctrines, which are also revelations through finite experiences.

In contrast to the concept of continuous revelation, as advocated by Latter-Day Saints- where new doctrines or Scriptures can be introduced even today- our statement conveys that the foundational truths of God can be communicated to us throughout our lives and journeys in various ways that God chooses. His plans and purposes for us are evident in the contexts we inhabit.

Most importantly, we must remember that any authentic personal revelation of God, experienced in our daily lives and relationship with Him, will not contradict His established Word. Such revelations should not exist in isolation; they need to be examined, evaluated, and prayed over. We do not endorse a complete democracy of truth or doctrine; rather, we emphasize the biblical concept that God reveals Himself and His plans for us through His creation, both in a general sense and specifically within our unique situations in creation.

[vii] A prominent example of this is Thomas Aquinas's effective use of Aristotelian philosophy, a thought originating from a non-Christian source, to elucidate and express Christian theology during the Middle Ages. His writings also draw from various non-Christian philosophies, including those of Plato, Avicenna, Averroes, and Maimonides.

As long as these philosophies are carefully analyzed to distinguish valuable insights from misleading concepts- thereby avoiding conclusions that contradict essential truths and teachings, such as God's existence or Jesus' divinity- any philosophical framework can significantly aid in bringing about the Kingdom of God in the world.

[viii] Consider this perspective: the concept of a job appears quite peculiar given our current practices. We willingly rise earlier than desired to travel to a prearranged

location, where we engage in tasks that may not seem inherently valuable or logical- like an office worker creating spreadsheets without grasping their significance to the large corporation they serve. We perform these tasks for a predetermined number of hours dictated by a clock on the wall, after which we receive an agreed- upon amount of currency- either paper or electronic- that society collectively recognizes as having a specific value for trading essential goods or otherwise. When viewed this way, it becomes clear just how intricate and abundant our surrounding contexts are. We also come to understand that life does not inherently have to conform to this structure.

Reflect on these alternative ways humans have lived: During the Middle Ages, individuals did not structure their labor around artificially imposed hours, a practice that gained traction only during the Industrial Revolution. Most people did not work for corporations or for "society" but typically for themselves, their families, or their local lords. Furthermore, the concept of a "workplace" was not strictly defined until the same revolution.

In prehistoric times, money as a medium for exchange may not have existed; trade likely occurred through bartering actual goods. The societal consensus regarding the value of money, such as paper currency or gold, had to be established since neither possesses intrinsic value. Biologically speaking, we do not need these forms of currency for survival. These are merely contexts surrounding us, varying across individuals, societies, and historical periods.

Work, money, schedules, and the economy are not fundamental absolutes of human existence. Rather, we exist in a society constructed around these contexts, which gain their importance from that structure, not because we would lose our humanity without them.

[ix] The Western Wall is a portion of the ancient retaining wall of the Temple Mount in the Old City of Jerusalem, left over from the time of the destruction of the Second Temple by the Romans in AD 70.

As current political and religious tensions forbid Jews from praying on the site of the Temple Mount itself (which is currently occupied by the Islamic Dome of the Rock), the wall is the holiest place in Judaism where Jews are still permitted to pray and make pilgrimage to.

It is even believed that the site of the Holy of Holies lay just behind the wall during the Second Temple period. Jews from around the world congregate there to pray (particularly for the restoration of the Temple), weep over the Temple's destruction, or insert prayer notes into cracks within the walls.

[x] Additionally, we should remember how Jesus, whose name is a form of Joshua, fulfills this prophecy as the King of Kings, who eternally occupies the priestly office of High Priest. With this eternal truth in mind, we can easily recognize how this royal priesthood fulfills the prophecy of an Anointed One who will permanently reign on a throne alongside a priest.

[xi] Even if we were to step back from this extreme scenario, the example of the Sibyl System from the Japanese anime Psycho-Pass offers an arguably even more chilling alternative. Unlike the earlier depiction, the world of Sibyl does

not resemble a hellscape fueled by eugenics. Instead, it resembles a utopia. Most inhabitants of the series live comfortably, prosperously, and securely under an AI that governs everything from policy to economic choices to the justice system. This last aspect is the show's main focus as it follows a group of police officers tasked with administering justice by aiming a weapon at a person and using psychological analysis and statistics to assess whether that individual might commit a crime or pose a future threat to society, similar to the film Minority Report.

Although the system accurately identifies these individuals, it bases its decisions on hard psychological data that is claimed to be beyond doubt. However, the show uncovers troubling exceptions to this supposedly infallible system. It reveals that medically psychopathic individuals do not exhibit the typical psychological cues that Sibyl relies on to dispense justice. As a result, these violent individuals are classified as "clean" by the AI. A police officer in the series faces the dilemma of rescuing a friend from such a person while the AI tool she usually depends on for justice is inoperative. Having relied almost religiously on the machine's judgement to discern right from wrong, she struggles to act independently to "judge" the psychopath and follow through based on that judgement, ultimately leading to her friend's death. Through Psycho-Pass, we confront another perilous potential of AI: the relinquishing of our own judgement and agency—whether in moral or political realms—to a machine that purports to understand better due to its "objectivity" and "rationality." Even more concerning, it illustrates a reality where divine oikonomia is supplanted by the law of the machine, compelling us to submit our wills not to a loving Heavenly Father, but to the cold logic of machines.

[xii] The beginning and peak of the Dune series exemplify the extremes of humanity's interaction with artificial intelligence. The former shows artificial intelligence taking humanity's place in the universe destructively, either threatening to wipe out humanity or, at the least, enslaving it under the machines' dominion. The latter illustrates humanity reaching its complete material and spiritual potential, nurturing true harmony between biological and artificial life forms, allowing them not only to coexist but to engage in a mutually beneficial partnership.

[xiii] Divine revelation encompasses more than knowledge gained from study and reflection. In fact, it is set apart from other knowledge forms by its method of being conveyed through experiences rather than mere enlightenment. While enlightenment often follows significant contemplation, revelation provides understanding from the outside, typically sparked by experiences that transform a person's heart or mind. The Abrahamic faiths- Judaism, Christianity, and Islam- are fundamentally defined by the concept of revelation. This differs from non-Abrahamic religions like Confucianism, Buddhism, and

Taoism, which emphasize enlightenment. For example, both Judaism and Islam assert that their sacred texts were revealed to prophets who received direct communication from God. In Christianity, God incarnated in human form to engage directly with people. In contrast, Buddhism emerged from the Buddha's personal journey, where he shared insights gained from his deep reflections on reality. Similarly, Confucianism originated with Confucius, who developed a belief system that combined traditional Chinese religious practices with ethical and philosophical elements. Many consider them to be more a tradition and way of life than a full religion. Regardless, it still serves our example by virtue of it being treated as an existential narrative of reality giving meaning and purpose for many people.

Made in United States
Troutdale, OR
07/17/2025